Understanding Scotland Musically

Scottish traditional music has been through a successful revival in the mid-twentieth century and has now entered a professionalised and public space. Devolution in the UK and the surge of political debate surrounding the independence referendum in Scotland in 2014 led to a greater scrutiny of regional and national identities within the UK, set within the wider context of cultural globalisation. This volume brings together a range of authors that sets out to explore the increasingly plural and complex notions of Scotland, as performed in and through traditional music. Traditional music has played an increasingly prominent role in the public life of Scotland, mirrored in other Anglo-American traditions. This collection principally explores this movement from historically text-bound musical authenticity towards more transient sonic identities that are blurring established musical genres and the meaning of what constitutes 'traditional' music today. The volume therefore provides a cohesive set of perspectives on how traditional music performs Scottishness at this crucial moment in the public life of an increasingly (dis)United Kingdom.

Simon McKerrell has interdisciplinary research interests focused upon the social impact of music and how this relates to policy. He is the author of *Focus: Scottish Traditional Music* (2015), and the co-editor of *Music as Multimodal Discourse: Media, Power and Protest* (2017). He is currently Associate Dean for Research & Innovation in the Faculty of Humanities and Social Sciences at Newcastle University. He has previously held positions at the Universities of Sheffield, Glasgow and the Royal Conservatoire of Scotland, and at the National Piping Centre in Glasgow.

Gary West holds a personal chair in Scottish Ethnology at the University of Edinburgh, where he also serves as Director of the European Ethnological Research Centre. His key teaching and research interests examine the ways in which we relate to the past from within the present, and he has published widely in the fields of folklore, tradition, heritage and traditional music. He is chair of Traditional Arts and Culture Scotland, a past board member of Creative Scotland, and he presents *Pipeline*, a weekly specialist music programme on BBC Radio Scotland. He is also an active musician, having toured widely in the UK, Europe and North America, and has performed on around 30 CDs.

Ashgate Popular and Folk Music Series
Series Editors:
*Stan Hawkins, Professor of Popular Musicology, University of Oslo and
Lori Burns, Professor, University of Ottawa, Canada*

Popular musicology embraces the field of musicological study that engages with popular forms of music, especially music associated with commerce, entertainment and leisure activities. The Ashgate Popular and Folk Music Series aims to present the best research in this field. Authors are concerned with criticism and analysis of the music itself, as well as locating musical practices, values and meanings in cultural context. The focus of the series is on popular music of the twentieth and twenty-first centuries, with a remit to encompass the entirety of the world's popular music.

Critical and analytical tools employed in the study of popular music are being continually developed and refined in the twenty-first century. Perspectives on the transcultural and intercultural uses of popular music have enriched understanding of social context, reception and subject position. Popular genres as distinct as reggae, township, bhangra, and flamenco are features of a shrinking, transnational world. The series recognizes and addresses the emergence of mixed genres and new global fusions, and utilizes a wide range of theoretical models drawn from anthropology, sociology, psychoanalysis, media studies, semiotics, postcolonial studies, feminism, gender studies and queer studies.

Other titles in the series:

The Songs of Joni Mitchell
Gender, Performance and Agency
Anne Karppinen

The Singer-Songwriter in Europe
Paradigms, Politics and Place
Edited by Isabelle Marc, Stuart Green

When Music Migrates
Crossing British and European Racial Faultlines, 1945–2010
Jon Stratton

Understanding Scotland Musically

Folk, Tradition and Policy

Edited by Simon McKerrell and Gary West

LONDON AND NEW YORK

First published 2018
by Routledge
2 Park Square, Milton Park, Abingdon, Oxon OX14 4RN

and by Routledge
711 Third Avenue, New York, NY 10017

Routledge is an imprint of the Taylor & Francis Group, an informa business

© 2018 selection and editorial matter, Simon McKerrell and Gary West; individual chapters, the contributors

The right of Simon McKerrell and Gary West to be identified as the authors of the editorial material, and of the authors for their individual chapters, has been asserted in accordance with sections 77 and 78 of the Copyright, Designs and Patents Act 1988.

All rights reserved. No part of this book may be reprinted or reproduced or utilised in any form or by any electronic, mechanical, or other means, now known or hereafter invented, including photocopying and recording, or in any information storage or retrieval system, without permission in writing from the publishers.

Trademark notice: Product or corporate names may be trademarks or registered trademarks, and are used only for identification and explanation without intent to infringe.

British Library Cataloguing-in-Publication Data
A catalogue record for this book is available from the British Library

Library of Congress Cataloging-in-Publication Data
A catalog record for this book has been requested

ISBN: 978-1-138-20522-2 (hbk)
ISBN: 978-1-315-46757-3 (ebk)

Typeset in Times New Roman
by Apex CoVantage, LLC

This book is dedicated to our most significant piping teachers who passed on their love for the instrument and the initial spark that began our lifelong love of Scottish music.

For Gary West: P/M Allan Cameron, P/M Ian Duncan, Gordon Duncan and Hamish Moore.

For Simon McKerrell: P/M Angus MacDonald; Kenny MacDonald; P/M Jimmy Pryde; Colin Pryde and Murray Henderson.

Contents

List of figures   x
List of tables   xii
List of musical examples   xiii
General editor's preface   xiv
Preface   xv
Acknowledgements   xvii
Notes on contributors   xviii

1 **Understanding Scotland musically**   1
 SIMON MCKERRELL AND GARY WEST

PART I
Policy and practice   15

2 **Traditional music and cultural sustainability in Scotland**   17
 SIMON MCKERRELL

3 **'A sense of who we are': the cultural value of community-based traditional music in Scotland**   30
 JOSEPHINE L. MILLER

4 **The emergence of the 'traditional arts' in Scottish cultural policy**   44
 DAVID FRANCIS

5 **'Eun Bheag Chanaidh' where the Gaelic arts and non-traditional theatre meet: a song discussion**   51
 FIONA J. MACKENZIE

6 **Referendum reflections: traditional music and the performance of politics in the campaign for Scottish independence**   60
 MAIRI MCFADYEN

PART II
Porosity, genres, hybridity   79

7   The changing nature of conceptualisation and authenticity among Scottish traditional musicians: traditional music, conservatoire education and the case for post-revivalism   81
JOSHUA DICKSON

8   Slaying the Tartan Monster: hybridisation in recent Scottish music   93
MEGHAN MCAVOY

9   'It happens in ballads': Scotland, utopia and traditional song in *The Strange Undoing of Prudencia Hart*   109
STEPHE HARROP

10   The problem with 'traditional'   122
DAVID MCGUINNESS

11   Salsa Celtica's Great Scottish Latin Adventure – an insider's view   139
PHIL ALEXANDER

PART III
Home and host   157

12   Distant voices, Scottish lives: on song and migration   159
M. J. GRANT

13   The globalization of Highland dancing   175
PATRICIA H. BALLANTYNE

PART IV
The past in the present   189

14   Locating identity in the aural aspects of Thomas Percy's *Reliques of Ancient English Poetry*: a bibliographic perspective   191
DANNI GLOVER

15   Routes, roles and folk on the edge: Scotland's instrumental music through the revival lens   201
STUART EYDMANN

16 **Links with the past in the present-day performance of Scottish fiddle music; or, the historicity of tradition** 217
RONNIE GIBSON

17 **Wynds, vennels and dual carriageways: the changing nature of Scottish music** 230
KAREN E. MCAULAY

18 **Understanding Scotland musically: reflections on place, war and nation** 240
GARY WEST

19 **Afterword** 252
SIMON FRITH

References 261
Index 283

Figures

3.1	Membership of GFW classes, % by instrument, 2012–2013	32
3.2	Map showing distribution of GFW membership in central Scotland, 2012–2013	33
3.3	Public funding awarded to GFW	35
3.4	GFW members, John Wheatley College, 2016	41
5.1	Margaret Fay Shaw 1935	52
5.2	Promenade walk on grassy track	58
6.1	TradYES banner at the March and Rally for Independence, Calton Hill, Edinburgh, September 2013	65
6.2	Innes Watson and Adam Sutherland, 'National Collective Presents. . . ' at the Edinburgh Festival Fringe, August 2014	67
6.3	TradYES at the March and Rally for Independence including the author, Calton Hill, Edinburgh, September 2013	74
7.1	Survey responses to the question 'How would you describe yourself in relation to Scottish traditional music?'	84
7.2	Survey responses to the question: 'To what would you ascribe professional, educational and artistic developments in Scottish traditional music?'	85
7.3	Top highest-rated areas of study deemed important or relevant to the learning and teaching of Scottish traditional music in a higher education conservatoire setting	86
7.4	Further comparison of areas of study deemed important or relevant to the learning and teaching of Scottish traditional music in a higher education conservatoire setting	86
7.5	Lowest proportion of 'strongly agree' responses in relation to areas of study deemed important or relevant to the learning and teaching of Scottish traditional music in a higher education conservatoire setting	86
11.1	Bars 31–40 of 'Ven, Guajira, Ven' (Shippey, Ainslie, Pompas). Conga and bongo parts omitted. (Discos Leon, 2014)	142
11.2	'Monstruous y Demonios, Angels and Lovers'	150
11.3	'The Great Scottish Latin Adventure'	151
11.4	'El Agua de la Vida' (Greentrax, 2003)	152

11.5	'El Camino' (Discos Leon, 2006)	153
11.6	'The Tall Islands' (Discos Leon, 2014)	154
15.1	Wachsmann model adapted by Eydmann	204
15.2	Tuckman model adapted by Eydmann	212
16.1	'Lady Charlotte Campbell's Strathspey'	222
16.2	The up-driven bow	223
16.3	'Duncan Swine's Wife'	225
16.4	Author's transcription of James Scott Skinner's 1910 performance of 'Tullochgorum'	227
16.5	'Three Drunken Fiddlers'	228
18.1	*The Battle of the Somme* (William Lawrie, author's setting)	243

Tables

15.1 The first phase of the clarsach revival in Scotland, 1890–1940   205
15.2 The first phase of the revival in Scottish bellows-blown
      bagpipes, 1975–2000   206
15.3 The revival of the concertina in Scotland, 1950–1980   207
15.4 The revival of the fiddle in Scotland, 1965–1985   208

Musical examples

10.1 Gow, N., [1800]. *Callar Herring* [. . .] (from the *Original Cry of the Newhaven Fish Wives, Selling their fresh Herrings in the Streets of Edinr.*) To which is added Three Favorite Tunes. Gow & Shepherd, Edinburgh.   126
10.2 'Mrs Duff (of Fetteresso's) Strathspey' from Morison, J., 1801. *A Collection of New Strathspey Reels.* Gow & Shepherd, Edinburgh.   136
12.1 Robert Burns, *Farewell to the Highlands*, text as published in James Johnson (ed.), *The Scots Musical Museum*, vol. 3 (Edinburgh: James Johnson, 1790)   160
12.2 The tune *Crochallan* as generally sung with *My Heart's in the Highlands*; transcription from memory by author   161

General editor's preface

Popular musicology embraces the field of musicological study that engages with popular forms of music, especially music associated with commerce, entertainment and leisure activities. The *Ashgate Popular and Folk Music Series* aims to present the best research in this field. Authors are concerned with criticism and analysis of the music itself, as well as locating musical practices, values and meanings in cultural context. The focus of the series is on popular music of the twentieth and twenty-first centuries, with a remit to encompass the entirety of the world's popular music.

Critical and analytical tools employed in the study of popular music are being continually developed and refined in the twenty-first century. Perspectives on the transcultural and intercultural uses of popular music have enriched understanding of social context, reception and subject position. Popular genres as distinct as reggae, township, bhangra, and flamenco are features of a shrinking, transnational world. The series recognises and addresses the emergence of mixed genres and new global fusions, and utilises a wide range of theoretical models drawn from anthropology, sociology, psychoanalysis, media studies, semiotics, postcolonial studies, feminism, gender studies and queer studies.

Stan Hawkins, Professor of Popular Musicology,
University of Oslo and
Lori Burns, Professor,
University of Ottawa, Canada

Preface

The book is a wide, and taken as a whole, deep examination of the question, how might we understand Scotland musically? It arose initially from a conference sponsored by the Arts and Humanities Research Council's grant to Dr Simon McKerrell (AH/L006502/1) at Newcastle University in October 2014. Many of the conference papers are included but not all, and we have added a key contribution from Mairi McFadyen who reflects on her understanding of Scotland, through the prism of the Scottish independence referendum in 2014. That year, was a seminal moment in Scottish culture standing alongside other key cultural turning points in the history of Scotland as significant as others such as 1999, 1979, and 1707. Scotland has changed both culturally and materially both for the people that reside there but also for anyone who engages in these globalising and deterritorialised times in attempting to answer our question wherever they might live. Looking back (whilst looking forward) there has been an emancipation of Scottish belonging; definitely not so much a reflowering of banal cultural nationalism, as an emergence of a more critical and internationalist set of voices attempting to understand the notion of Scotland and her musical culture(s). The year 2014 catalysed this process, but writing today in 2017 as we look forward to a continued debate on Scotland's place in the world and the cultural interior, we need more than ever critical voices willing to examine Scotland's music and culture within a robust scholarly framework. The cultural debate has flowered, and continues to grow, and this book is a remarkable collection of essays where all authors grapple with the changing notion of 'tradition', 'nationalism' and 'Scotland'. Concepts with meaty intellectual tethers which we hope infuse this work and connect us to a shared past, without immutably binding us to it.

The best work that this collection of essays can do is to bring forward some key scholarly voices and narratives grounded in the evidence of musical performance and scholarship that makes a positive, critical offering to a shared future. There is original research in this volume around various topics which we have chosen but which are grouped naturally into the following themes: policy and practice; porosity, genres, hybridity; home and host; and the past in the present.

This is a fair representation of the intellectual themes that emerged from the contributions to our conference and that have come to manifest themselves in the scholarship on Scottish music today. Perhaps the most contentious claim in this book is that in Chapter 1, where we suggest that Scottish traditional music is in today's world, the key musical genre in understanding the notion of 'Scotland' and 'Scottishness' musically. In Chapter 1, we set out the argument that suggests that in the Scottish context, there are strong reasons to suggest that traditional music is in fact the musical genre most closely intertwined with the national idea and that it has dwarfed the art music and popular music traditions in the construction of any notion of 'Scotland' or 'Scottishness'. This is not a binary, exclusionary argument. Many of the chapters in this collection deal with hybrid musics (see Alexander, Harrop, McAvoy and Dickson this volume) and there are valuable chapters dealing with the most personal complex reflections on Scottish music such as M.J. Grant's, Stuart Eydmann's and Simon Frith's contributions. It is therefore our view that attempting to answer the question of how we might understand Scotland musically, that the strongest cultural claim on that territory is from traditional music, that this necessarily demands an understanding of Scottishness in the fields of popular music and art music and wider cultural tropes that have continuously drawn upon the vast well of traditional tunes and texts of orally transmitted or developed Scottish traditional music. That being the case, we hope that readers of this volume will understand that as a whole it represents a plural view of what constitutes Scotland musically, but it is one that emphasises people, place and community where the national idea lives and breathes most vitally through its expression of universal hopes and emotions in the performance of the very local. To us, this is the short hand truth, *experientia docet vera*; Scotland is an idea, given life in our understanding of thousands of musical acts of performance grounded in place and time. The national finds its expression in the local expression of the universal. We hope you will find some useful ideas and scholarship within this volume and that it encourages further critically aware dialogue about the nature of music, Scotland and nationhood in the years to come.

Simon McKerrell and Gary West (May, 2017)

Acknowledgements

We would like to gratefully acknowledge the contribution of all the authors of this volume, and the delegates at the original conference at Newcastle University whose intellectual participation contributed greatly to the ideas and arguments developed in this book. To the music makers of Scotland, past and present, whose imagination and art have not only helped us to understand Scotland, but who have helped to shape it in the first place. To our colleagues at our respective institutions, especially Dr Adam Behr, Dr Ian Biddle, Dr Will Lamb, Dr Neill Martin, Dr Cathlin MacAulay, Dr Jamie Savan and Dr Desi Wilkinson.

Notes on contributors

Phil Alexander is a researcher on Glasgow University's 'Jewish Lives/Scottish Spaces' project. His PhD (completed 2016) focused on contemporary klezmer and Yiddish music in Berlin, in particular the relationship of the modern city to traditional musical forms and repertoires. He is also an active musician, leading several jazz and folk bands and performing regularly with a wide variety of UK and international musicians. www.philalexander.co.uk

Patricia H. Ballantyne is a dance scholar at the Elphinstone Institute, University of Aberdeen, researching traditional Scottish music and dance. Her PhD, completed in 2016, focuses on Scottish dancing masters and the influences that have contributed to the current state of traditional music and dance in Scotland. She has been dancing, teaching and playing in a cèilidh band for a number of years and has taught and performed in Scotland, Europe and in Cape Breton Island where she has learned from some of the best contemporary step dancers.

Joshua Dickson is Head of Traditional Music at the Royal Conservatoire of Scotland. He is the author of *When Piping Was Strong: Tradition, Change and the Bagpipe in South Uist* (John Donald, 2006) and the editor of *The Highland Bagpipe: Music, History, Tradition* (Ashgate, 2009). His more recent published work has brought to light the role of women in the inheritance and transmission of traditional Gaelic canntaireachd in Hebridean life via the journals *Scottish Studies* and *Review of Scottish Culture* (2013). He is currently concerned with leading ground-breaking curricular reform which has helped position Scotland's national conservatoire as distinctive in the UK and wider Europe in the field of tertiary-level traditional music education.

Stuart Eydmann researches and writes on Scottish popular and traditional music in the modern era, especially instrumental revivals, and has undertaken studies on the fiddle, the clarsach, the free-reed and percussion instruments, on the musical cultures of Ulster and on the collecting and archiving of recorded sound. He was a lecturer at the Royal Scottish Academy of Music and Drama and at the Open University and Post-Doctoral Research Fellow and Traditional Artist in Residence at the University of Edinburgh. He is a tutor at Edinburgh College of Art, curator of the archive raretunes.org and an active musician.

David Francis is Associate Director of TRACS (Traditional Arts and Culture Scotland) and Director of the Traditional Music Forum. He compiled a report into traditional music for the Scottish Arts Council in 1999 and chaired the Scottish Government's Working Group on Traditional Arts which reported in 2010. Away from the desk, he is a dance-caller and storyteller, and as a guitarist and songwriter was one half of The Cast (with Mairi Campbell), producing 6 albums. He co-produces *Distil*, a long-running, creative development project for traditional musicians and is currently completing a Masters in Ethnology and Folklore at Aberdeen University.

Simon Frith is Tovey Professor of Music at the University of Edinburgh and a Fellow of the British Academy. He is currently working on a three volume history of live music in Britain since 1950. The first volume, covering 1950–1967, was published by Ashgate in 2013.

Ronnie Gibson researches the history of Scottish fiddle music, and has particular interests in performance and reception in the long nineteenth century. He is also the author of the blog-site scottishfiddlemusic.com.

Danni Glover is a researcher at Ulster University. Her research interests include eighteenth-century print culture, textual afterlives of the ballads, the Gothic, and urban Romanticism. Her PhD on the textual construction of British identities in the anthologies of Bishop Percy is due to be completed in autumn 2017. She has recently published on the poetry of Mary Queen of Scots and themes of suicide in Scottish ballads. www.danniglover.com

M. J. Grant is a musicologist working primarily in the historical anthropology and sociology of music. Research focuses include the social functions of song, especially in the British Isles; the musicology of armed conflict and torture; and new and experimental art music since 1950. From 2008–2014 she led the research group 'Music, Conflict and the State' at the University of Göttingen. Publications include *Serial Music, Serial Aesthetics* (Cambridge University Press, 2002); a monograph on the cultural history of Auld Lang Syne is awaiting publication. She is currently writing a third monograph on the musicology of war. www.mjgrant.eu

Stephe Harrop is Lecturer in Drama at Liverpool Hope University, where her research and teaching largely centres upon performances and texts adapted from, or responding to, classical drama and epic. Stephe also works as a professional performance storyteller, a perspective which informs her explorations of contemporary theatre-makers' engagement with the traditional arts.

Karen E. McAulay is a Performing Arts Librarian at the Royal Conservatoire of Scotland, where she is also currently seconded part-time to the Research Department as a postdoctoral researcher. Her research interests are in 18th and nineteenth-century Scottish music, and historical British legal deposit music collections. She maintains a professional interest in music bibliography, and the pedagogical best practice of teaching library and research skills.

xx   *Notes on contributors*

Meghan McAvoy recently completed a PhD in Scottish Studies at Stirling University. Her research interests include vernacular literature and music, postcolonial theory and education. She is also an amateur fiddle player, singer and award-winning composer in the Scottish traditional idiom. Meghan has published work on writing from Glasgow, and is interested in how the politics of contemporary vernacular texts counter dominant critical narratives.

Mairi McFadyen is an ethnologist, ethnomusicologist and cultural activist with a particular in interest in local traditional arts. Her PhD (2012) was awarded the Michaelis-Jena Ratcliff Prize for ethnology and folklore, exploring the embodied aesthetic experience of narrative song and the ballad imagination. Mairi supports teaching in Scottish Culture and Heritage at the University of Edinburgh's Department of Celtic and Scottish Studies; she is also a research associate at Heriot-Watt's Intercultural Research Centre (IRC) where she is interested in developing a creative ethnological practice. Outwith academia, Mairi works with several arts organisations interested in the promotion of and engagement with arts and culture, including TRACS (Traditional Arts and Culture Scotland) and the Saltire Society. From 2012–2014 she was involved as an organiser for the creative cultural campaign for Scottish independence.

David McGuinness is the director of the group Concerto Caledonia, with whom he has recorded thirteen albums, mostly of historical Scottish repertoire. He is senior lecturer in music at the University of Glasgow. In 2007 he produced John Purser's 50-part series *Scotland's Music* for BBC Radio Scotland, and he has also been a composer for television and theatre, most notably for E4's teen drama series Skins.

Fiona J. Mackenzie is the National Trust for Scotland's Archivist for Canna House on the Isle of Canna, the home of the Campbell Collections of Song and Folklore. She is also a well known Gaelic singer and performance artist and works regularly with bodies such as the National Theatre for Scotland. The Campbell Collections form the research and performance focus of the creative work she undertakes on the mainland and also on the island, where she lives full time.

Simon McKerrell has interdisciplinary research interests focused upon the social impact of music and how this relates to policy. He is the author of Focus: Scottish Traditional Music (2015), and the Co-Editor of Music as Multimodal Discourse: Media, Power and Protest (2017). He is currently Associate Dean for Research & Innovation in the Faculty of Humanities and Social Sciences at Newcastle University. He has previously held positions at the Universities of Sheffield, Glasgow and the Royal Conservatoire of Scotland, and at the National Piping Centre in Glasgow.

Josephine L. Miller founded the BA (Scottish Music) degree at the Royal Conservatoire of Scotland in 1996, and has created resources to support traditional music in Scottish schools since 1988. She has worked with many community groups, and is currently developing mentoring for practitioners. Her PhD from the University of Sheffield was an ethnographic analysis of learning and participation at Glasgow Fiddle Workshop, and her research interests focus on the development of teaching and learning contexts for traditional music, the implications for pedagogy, policy, and the music itself.

Gary West holds a personal chair in Scottish Ethnology at the University of Edinburgh, where he also serves as Director of the European Ethnological Research Centre. His key teaching and research interests examine the ways in which we relate to the past from within the present, and he has published widely in the fields of folklore, tradition, heritage and traditional music. He is chair of Traditional Arts and Culture Scotland, a past board member of Creative Scotland, and he presents *Pipeline*, a weekly specialist music programme on BBC Radio Scotland. He is also an active musician, having toured widely in the UK, Europe and North America, and has performed on around 30 CDs.

1 Understanding Scotland musically

Simon McKerrell and Gary West

Introduction

This book is an attempt to address the question of how we might understand *Scotland* musically. In setting out this question we are deliberately focusing upon the object 'Scotland' and sometimes 'Scottishness' in and through music. This is because we believe that previous generations of scholars have (quite legitimately) attempted to answer a linked, yet quite different question: how we might understand Scottish *music*. Scottish music as the object of study has less appeal to today's scholars because most of the arts and humanities disciplines where we might meet and try to answer this question, have moved to a position that rests upon understanding the contingent, changing and plural nature of national culture(s). Today, modern Scotland is a country that has a long and often contested set of national traditions, with rich histories of both indigenous and new genres of music that have emerged and which support hybrid, modern identities. Polish-Scots, Irish-Scots and Indian-Scots (amongst others) have also brought their own musical cultures, and indigenous Scots have become more adventurous in their musical culture, resulting in a rich and diverse constellation of musical subcultures. There has been a great surge in the porosity between musical genres since the advent of greater access online to different musical communities of practice, and this has been mirrored by a growth and atomisation of the voices across Scottish culture who are willing and able to contribute to understanding what Scottish music might and could be today.

The scholarly response to this, as in other areas of cultural reflection, has been to shift our attention from culture as a static object towards understanding culture as a process that people engage in. The benefit of this shift is that we now have the ability to move scholarship beyond the temporal, geographical and ethnic concerns that previously lay at the core of attempts to understand national cultures, and to focus instead upon how *people* today understand culture and what it can mean and do in society. Unlike the sciences, our task as scholars of music and culture is not to answer pre-determined hypotheses or questions posed by nature, but to help all people critically understand culture and thus in a very Aristotelian way, to live a good life (Hesmondhalgh, 2013). This book is therefore concerned with understanding how people understand Scotland and Scottishness in and through musical culture because this can help us collectively to inform our approaches to musical education, cultural policy, musical aesthetics, and perhaps most importantly, our sense of belonging to Scotland, wherever we might live.

The theorisation of musical nationalism[1] has a long and intellectually plural history, across a number of disciplines including the central ones that support the aims of this book such as ethnology, ethnomusicology, popular music studies, ballad studies, education, historical musicology and cultural studies (amongst others). Historically, much of this history has depended upon key cultural figures in national and cultural traditions who have curated a sense of the 'national' in terms of cultural signifiers that have been mythologised and collocated with sonic traditions. This mythologisation therefore has depended historically upon both the standing of these cultural and intellectual figures as well as the sense of shared authenticity of the signifiers that they have drawn upon. Think of the constant and ongoing re-negotiation of the cultural authority and significance of figures such as Robert Burns, Sir Walter Scott, Hugh MacDiarmid or Hamish Henderson[2] – all of whom are key to the story of Scottish national culture. The well-worn (and critically aware) scholarship of nationalism from Anderson (2006), Gellner and Breuilly (2008) and Hobsbawm (2012) reminds us that the national idea is highly contingent, malleable and yet extremely powerful in our lives.

That is still true today, and perhaps even more so with the rise of online musical culture. In some senses, music has become more, not less, powerful in constructing a sense of nationhood because many can now access it instantly and wherever they are in the world. As Bohlman reminds us, when considering music and nationalism in Europe:

> Nationalism no longer enters music only from the top, that is, from state institutions and ideologies, but may build its path into music from just about any angle, as long as there are musicians and audiences willing to mobilize cultural movement from those angles.
>
> (Bohlman, 2011, 56)

This deterritorialisation of musical nationalism has seen the rise of the political significance in music across the late modern West. In the recent European past, music has been freshly implicated in nationalist and political movements (for good and ill) in ways that have not been seen for decades, from musically constructed nationalist discourses (Biddle and Knights, 2007; Bohlman, 2004; Boyes, 2010; Ceribašić, 2014) to shifting sonic nationalisms in post-communist Europe (Buchanan, 2002; Nercessian, 2000; Rice, 2002), to the recent musical re-emergence of the nationalist far right (Machin and Richardson, 2012; Spracklen, 2013). Musical nationalism is today on the rise, and as much as some commentators wish to divorce music from nationalism, music continues to be crucial (and popular) in the construction of national identity and belonging precisely because of its affective power. Bohlman predicates the European love-hate relationship between music and nationalism within the tensions that arise between (1) the modern rationalist's wish for music to be autonomous of culture and often problematic notions within nationalism; (2) that nationalist music trivialises and reduces the unique sonic markers of identity in music into more bland, universalist texts ultimately moving towards kitschness; and (3) that nationalist musics give voice to the destructive and intolerant in society (2011). Of course, the counterpoint to all of these is twofold in that national musics have immense power to construct a sense of collective belonging (witness the popularity of national anthems and key songs at sporting events), and second, that not all music that constructs nationalism is 'national music' by any means.

This book sets out to understand Scotland musically which is at once both a plural and contested position, but we contend that there are certain shared values that underpin the cultural notion of 'Scotland' and 'Scottishness' which are evident across the book. Clearly, no single musician, group or canon of music can make the claim to constructing Scotland, and the variety of issues and styles raised in this collection evidence this position. One can feel 'Scottish' or more usually, a sense of national belonging when listening to anything from piobaireachd to pop. It is, however, our position that because of the authenticity lent to it by the process of oral development and historical transmission that the 'traditional music'[3] of Scotland lies at the core of almost all claims to 'Scottishness' or nationalist constructions of Scotland across musical genres. We contend that the process of re-imagining and mythologising Scotland is, and has been, always overwhelmingly constructed via the traditional music of Scotland. Such that when the notion of 'Scottishness' or a 'Scottish' voice has been explored within classical, or popular traditions, it almost always relies at source upon the orally developed and transmitted traditional music for the sonic signification of 'Scotland'.

Scotland's case is intriguing; not since the 1960s anti-nuclear protests songs have Scottish traditional music and musicians been so politically engaged. Almost the entire community of practice came out in favour of Scottish independence during the 2014 referendum, and the musical contributions to the campaign were highly visible in public gigs and key lobby groups such as *TradYES*, the national collective for traditional musicians in favour of Scottish independence (McFadyen, 2013).

Social media during the referendum campaign not only provided a route for democratic access to political activism for all flavours of nationalists in Scotland, it also launched a more politically engaged civic debate in Scotland which saw key hegemonic actors such as Scottish Labour and the BBC challenged by a wide array of citizens now thrust into new collectivist and exciting action (Anonymous, 2014; see for example Ferguson, 2013). The use of social media cannot be underestimated in the new production of Scottish nationalism: there are numerous striking examples of Scottish cultural and civic nationalists building support for independence in and through traditional music throughout the two-year referendum campaign including: new songs composed in support of cultural and political independence (MacKenzie, 2014); Scottish Government collocation of traditional fiddling and piping with nationalism in their political videos and in tourism marketing (Sanderson, 2015), and; gigs and albums explicitly in support of Scottish independence (for example Brown, 2014). Traditional music emerged in a new online public discourse about the independence referendum in a striking example of cultural nationalists supporting a determinedly civic nationalist campaign by the Scottish National Party. Despite the relative lack of a culturally nationalist discourse, traditional music was presented during the first referendum campaign as a sonic signifier of a future, more progressive, culturally independent and confident Scottish nation. The almost wholesale political alignment of traditional music in very public social media, gives perhaps a false view of the total community of practice who more closely reflected the political opinions of the population as a whole (55% against independence to 45% in favour in the 2014 Scottish referendum) when it came to rejecting Scottish independence. In a purposive online survey conducted during the summer of 2014 with the community of practice in Scottish traditional music, 'only 53% of respondents reported that they supported independence, with 21% undecided and 15% firmly against' (McKerrell, 2016, 96). Nevertheless, the public debate that emerged in 2013 and 2014 leading up to the first referendum on Scottish independence on 18 September 2014, brought the relationship between traditional music as a marker of national cultural independence and political nationalism back into plain view, and has led to a more highly politicised online discourse within the community of practice that has not been seen since the mid-twentieth-century Scottish folk revival. This online use of fora and social media within and beyond the musical community of practice is new, and cannot be ignored in any discussion of musical nationalism in the future.

At the time of writing, Scotland's constitutional position is a matter of significant public debate, precipitated through the June 2016 UK referendum on leaving the EU in which Scotland decisively voted to remain in the EU. 'Indyref2' when it arrives promises to be of a different character given the unstoppable macro-political forces in the British Isles during 2017 and 2018, and perhaps this time there will be more of a focus on the part culture plays in a people's vision for its future. What is certain however, is that regardless of whether Scotland remains part of the United Kingdom when the dust settles in 2019 or indeed, part of the European Union and/or the UK, Scottish traditional music will be a crucial part of many individual's identity, both those living within and without Scotland itself. In that sense, the *Scottish* part of 'Scottish traditional music' does matter, and matters intensely to many performers, listeners and fans. But if one listens carefully to the music and the people, one can hear a sense of Scottishness and music that is plural, contested and healthier than it has ever been. Scottishness is manifested not in any claim to oldness or provenance in this musical nationalism, with the concomitant and inevitable exclusionary logic; it is manifested humanely, in the sense of belonging and shared endeavour through performance and discourse where each person has a unique personal sense of Scottishness and its musical manifestation. This book evidences that claim with several nuanced conceptions of a musical Scotland. It is our hope that this plural and tolerant form of Scottishness is retained in whatever political future lies ahead, that those who perform and craft identities in and through Scottish traditional music, remain committed to an open and plural notion of what that might mean, without letting the destructive binary polarities of historical nationalisms take root in the music-political debate leading up to the next referendum on Scottish independence.

Musical nationalisms and genre

The question of understanding a musical nationalism has most often been approached from a concern with the musicological past of the origins and provenance of musical 'objects'. Much of the European construction of musical nationalism has always rested upon the historical, racial and ethnic provenance of musical objects. These include both the first publications of key traditional songs and tunes, as well as often conflating the public status of key cultural commentators with their pronouncements on the origins of their nation's music. Sometimes, such as in the case of *Highland Cathedral* or *The Blaydon Races*, it has been the vernacular popularity of the tune or song that leads to its adoption as a signifier of identity despite clearly having been imported into the home culture from elsewhere (Gammon, n.d.; Korb and Roever, n.d.). Much of the musicological historiography of nationalism grew out of mythologisation of dead, male, white composers in the art tradition. Whilst musicology itself has now mostly moved on from these elitist and hegemonic positions, it is safe to say that the 'pale and male' lineages of composers of classical music still hold great signification in the public square (Khomami, 2015). Not least with those Tory politicians who have repeatedly sought to reinstate and aggrandise 'dead white Germans' within the English GCSE and A-Level music curricula (Garner, 2014). But in the sense of how the national culture has been constructed, and who has agency in this task, the mythologisation of music and nationalism used to rest fairly squarely on the European literate elite. For example, Jean-Jacques Rousseau, the Swiss theorist who was so instrumental in the continental European enlightenment and particularly for his work on *The Social Contract* (pub. 1762), was one of the key mythologisers of the musical nationalism. He is not only responsible for the egregious (and highly problematic) idea that Scottish and 'Chinese' traditional musics are somehow related via pentatonicism and scale-type, but also for much national mythologising on French and Italian music. In broader terms, he espoused a view whereby music was fundamentally about melody and human morality, and that harmony and complexity were degradations of music (a view still sometimes shared). But Rousseau in common with many other enlightenment thinkers of the late eighteenth century plucked simplicity and melodic purity as ideals that were metaphorically close to the rural, simplistic and authentic lifestyle of the eighteenth-century peasant-class thereby, through nothing more than mere homology really, linking aesthetic ideals on Italian (good) and French Opera (bad) to sonic traits. Today's scholars have rejected that sense of a monolithic nature metaphor to recognise that it is people that create musical and national cultures, and therefore complexity is the starting point for any theorisation of musical nationalism.

Another key writer to do this was the foundational thinker of the musical enlightenment, Johannes Gottfried Herder. Herder in the 1760s was really the first European intellectual to make explicit the collocation between racial or ethnic nationalism and traditional culture (subsequently, so relied upon by the Nazi party (Atkins, 2010)). Herder's language advocated both the racial 'purity' of oral tradition amongst the peasantry as a means of understanding his 'nationalbildung' (the 'spirit of the nation'), and also provided the motivation to the literate elite to collect the stories, songs and tunes of 'das Volk' in order to safeguard the authentic music of the people. In so doing, he set the tone for at least 150 years of antiquarian and subsequently, scholarly interest in establishing the romantic link between the orally transmitted songs and stories of (ideally) rural, illiterate peasantry and the core enlightenment ideal of 'the nation' across Europe. Scotland at that time was interestingly one of the most literate nations in Europe, and so had a more complex relationship between orality and literacy, which found perhaps its most elaborate expression in the Ossianic scandals instigated by James Macpherson around the same period in the 1760s (Gelbart, 2007; see Trevor-Roper, 2008). But by the turn of the nineteenth century, and certainly by the time Sir Walter Scott was able to publish his *Minstrelsey of the Scottish Border* in February 1802, the heavy-set romanticisation and collocation of nature, race and orally transmitted music was established, and much of the Scottish cultural history of the nineteenth century can be thought of as a highly classed invention of 'Scotland' and 'Scottishness' that has only really been debunked in the last twenty or thirty years through careful scholarship.

What is apparent when one is seeking to understand the social semiotics or cultural history of a nation's musical culture, is that first, music and nationalism live on, and are indeed thriving within increasing cultural globalisation (Biddle and Knights, 2007) and secondarily, that not all nations are musically constructed in the same way. If one suggests, as we do here, that Scottish traditional music lies at the heart of almost all claims to cultural 'Scottishness', then one has to be clear that other genres of music cannot lay claim to a distinctively 'Scottish' voice that is independent of that nation's orally developed motivic and melodic tradition. Scotland cannot claim to have had a strong independent art music 'voice' in the international sphere, not because of a lack of music, but partially probably because of the teaching lineages and aesthetics of Scottish art music composers, who have almost without exception drawn upon Scottish traditional music for their sonic markers of 'Scottishness'. The key melodies, motifs, and structures of orally developed and transmitted traditional tunes and songs have formed the backbone of the sonic 'Scottishness' that key figures in Scottish art music history have sought in their composition. The eighteenth century attempts to produce Scottish art music, naturally enough drew upon traditional tunes in James Oswald's and William MacGibbon's output. Nineteenth-century figures such as Alexander MacKenzie and Hamish MacCunn are remembered more for their contribution to education, or for their orchestral and chamber adaptations of traditional Scottish ballads and tunes. More recently, every serious Scottish art music composer (with the possible exception of Thea Musgrave) such as Peter Maxwell-Davies, James MacMillan, Eddie McGuire, Bill Sweeney, and the late Ronald Stevenson have all heavily relied upon the pre-existing content of traditional music when developing a Scottish aesthetic. There is no denigration in this, in fact, it is a validation of the health and aesthetic beauty of the vernacular, indigenous oral traditions that every Scottish art music composer looking to develop a 'Scottish' sound in their work from the Earl of Kelly to today, has drawn upon traditional Scottish music. It is perhaps not contentious therefore to suggest that the Scottish art music tradition never produced a central canon with its own distinctive *art music* voice, comparable to other European nations in terms of compositional lineages. And therefore, if one is to understand Scotland musically, it is centrally important to understand how that Scottish aesthetic is and has been developed in the indigenous, orally developed traditional music of Scotland.

When we look to the continent, and compare the national art music voice of Scotland with the European traditions, it is clear that Scotland cannot claim a distinctive art music voice in the way that other nations can: France had Debussy, Ravel, Roussel, Stravinsky, even in terms of instrumental styles, it is not uncommon in art music traditions to speak of the 'French school' of composition, violin, vocal performance styles or for instance of chamber music. There were also for instance, almost 1,000 music publishers in France between 1820 and 1914 (Lesure, n.d.). Germany similarly enjoyed a particular sense of a national school or voice in composition across many instrumental and vocal traditions. For many aesthetic and historiographical reasons (their musical output amongst them), Germany probably can lay claim to the strongest national voice in composition, performance style and public engagement with classical music. Giants such as Beethoven, Bach, Mendelssohn, and Wagner all contribute to our sense of a cohesive German national voice in the art music tradition. The geo-political area known as the Netherlands is perhaps more comparable to Scotland in terms of its place in relation to the central European classical traditions. Indeed, Andrew Blake points out that Oskar Schmitz's well known wartime accusation against Britain that it was 'Das lande ohne musik' ('the land without music') was not without a basis in fact: there was a great deal of music in Victorian and Edwardian Britain, but it was of the popular and vernacular forms, rather than the elite art music forms (Blake, 1997). He goes on to suggest that Schmitz's accusation perhaps came a generation too late given the rise of Elgar, Vaughan Williams, and subsequently Tippett and Britten. But really, as is so common throughout the 'British' cultural commentariat, he is using 'British' as a synonym for 'English'. The rejection of this constant (and culturally debilitating) synonym has been one of the really positive outcomes of the recent cultural renaissance and renewed confidence in Scotland. 'British' composers in the art music tradition, really means the 'great' 'English' composers, and the canon of art music works that are supposed to define 'Britishness' largely depend upon Southern English pastoral, ceremonial (and now possibly) modernist art musics. Even when these 'British' composers are seeking to capture the national spirit of 'Britishness', they rely, as in the case of Vaughan Williams most clearly, upon well-known English traditional melodies, these too largely collected in the late Victorian and Edwardian period from traditional English singers almost exclusively from the Home Counties around London. Indeed it is not contentious today to suggest that there is no 'British traditional music', because for various cultural and imperial reasons, the only musical tradition that could even tangentially fulfil this moniker is the bagpipe music that grew out of the British Army.

Mass mediated popular music too has perhaps a stronger claim to constructing 'Scotland' and 'Scottishness' in music, but we often hear only about surface signifiers such as accent or language. Mass mediated popular music is also the single musical genre most often overlooked in the consideration of nationalism in music (Bohlman, 2011, 56). We argue here that it is only really in and through Scottish traditional music that there has been and continues to be a strong and plural relationship between nationhood and music, and that this depends both upon deeper musical structures such as motivic content, melodic contour and other orally developed Scottish musical structures such as the reel, piobaireachd and Gaelic and Scots songs, as well as upon the socio-cultural experience of belonging which is manifested in the lyrical texts of traditional songs and paratextual aspects of the tradition. That is not to suggest of course, that popular, classical or other forms of music do not have any claim to constructing a sense of Scotland – they do, and they have. But it is our intention here to demonstrate through the collection that the idea of Scotland and Scottishness has been overwhelmingly constructed within traditional music and its wider reception and mythologisation. The key histories of Scottish popular and mass mediated vernacular musics extend back to the nineteenth century, incorporating artists who in part defined the modern understanding of popular music in sound and on screen. Artists such as Harry Lauder and Will Fyffe drew heavily on traditional songs and melodies in constructing wildly successful international careers. Later popular music performers from Scotland, or that are seen as 'Scottish' popular music have tended to rely on surface sonic signifiers set within the deeper structures and lyrical themes of Anglo-American popular music. There is arguably a Scottish school of popular music and musicians, but like the art music tradition, their musical habitus is located in an Anglo-American imaginary rather than any distinctly Scottish sound. The aesthetic markers of choice here delineate this argument neatly, drawing fine boundaries of seismic aesthetic importance between rock, pop, punk, hip hop, grunge, garage, house, indie and that most political of genres – 'Britpop'. The aesthetics of popular music *in* Scotland are the same aesthetic markers that conjoin together in any discussion of popular music in the UK, and at the meta-levels, throughout the Anglo-American world. Who thinks of AC/DC for instance as having a distinctively 'Scottish' voice? Yet Angus, Malcolm and George Young of AC/DC spent their two first decades in Scotland before the family emigrated to Australia. Similarly, later big bands such as Simple Minds, Hue and Cry and Texas are all hugely successful popular music bands that came directly out of Scotland, yet were working in a much broader Anglo-American musical imaginary that is far less interested in nationalism than their folk and traditional counterparts. Wood's informants at T in the Park demonstrate this sense of a broader Anglo-American popular imaginary (or as she terms it, a 'chart' music sound), when the only musical element they recognise as distinctly 'Scottish' at the festival is the Céilidh tent where traditional Scottish music is performed by dance bands (Wood, 2012, 202–203). Wood's (2012) research emphasising non-representational geographies in her approach to understanding 'Scottishness' in and through music, suggests that the national is constructed in two key ways today: (1) 'through a perceived bond between audience members and performers that was based on a shared national identity', and (2) through the audience reception of music as 'Scottish' (2012, 201). Her ethnographic research, and that of the editors (McKerrell, 2016; West, 2012a) supports one of the key arguments of this collection, which is that when it comes to considering the relationship between the 'national' and 'music', there is no other musical genre that relies more heavily on the national idea for its own particular production of authenticity than traditional music, and that because of this semiotic interdependency, the key musical signifiers of 'Scottishness' exist primarily within Scottish *traditional* music as socially shared sonic authenticities manifested through performance in musical structures, musical semiotics, instrumentation and language use. And this close construction of the national with traditional music is a common feature across Europe. Even a brief familiarity with the traditional musics across Europe demonstrates the key agency that nationalist narratives have had in the production of 'authentic' traditional musics.

The issue of 'folk' music is more complex again, and to some extent is addressed by McGuinness and Alexander (this volume) in their consideration of the porosity and utility of boundaries between traditional, folk and popular musics (see also Middleton, 1981). In this collection of essays, the editors draw a distinction between 'folk' music which today describes a particular sub-genre of popular music that is often mass-mediated and depends upon national traditions, sometimes newly composed and sometimes based upon oral traditions, and the quite distinct 'traditional music'. What 'folk' music does in Scotland then is provide a commodified and mass mediated aesthetic set of values for professional artists who perform their own stylised versions of orally developed or national musics for a broad, and often, international audience. Folk music in Scotland then becomes essentially a Scottish sub-genre of popular music, but like the weaker and less ubiquitous art music tradition, it effectively relies almost wholly upon Scottish traditional music for its source materials. Whether it's the ballad singing of traveller singer Sheila Stewart reinterpreted by Alasdair Roberts, or the reimagined and heavily syncopated traditional puirt-a-beul sung by Capercaillie's Karen Matheson, the genre of Scottish 'folk' music has emerged in recent years as distinct from Scottish traditional music. To be sure, in today's heavily commercialised Anglo-American society, there are boundaries between 'folk music' and 'traditional music' emerging, but it is clear that the same musicians and singers can flow between them and do so on a regular basis. The difference is grounded in the social relations and musical materials of the genre, where 'traditional' denotes orally passed on, or newly composed music using musical materials derived from oral tradition, and shared within a performing community and 'folk', which implies a subsequent commodification of this music, or representations of traditional music without necessarily using orally transmitted materials and also shifting also into the relational sphere of mass mediation (both Roberts and Matheson are very talented traditional singers, but have chosen to also play a leading role in the construction of folk music).

Importantly too, the publication of this collection of essays also marks a shift in the musicological, ethnological and wider cultural scholarship demonstrating how the academy has moved beyond fairly narrow scholarship of national culture aimed at a knowledgeable (but small) group of scholars and aficionados, to a more ambitious and outward-facing scholarship of internationalism that speaks to scholars of many nations who are interested in how musical and traditional arts continue to be at the forefront of people's sense of national belonging, local engagement, hybrid identities, artistic aesthetics and cultural policy. The scholarship dealing with Scotland as a cultural phenomenon was once confined to departments of literature and ethnology, yet today, this collection builds upon multidisciplinary research by scholars such as Symon (1997), Henderson (2004), Trevor-Roper (2008), West (2012a) and Wood (2012) amongst many others, demonstrating just how far the growth of intellectual engagement with Scottish music and culture has come. This collection includes current research from scholars from those disciplines as well as musicology, ethnomusicology, popular music studies, heritage, history, policy, education, drama, linguistics, dance and performance studies. The key aspect in this scholarly narrative has been the awakening both to how malleable and contingent the notion of 'Scotland' is, and also a new recognition of the critical importance of Scottish traditional culture has been, and continues to be, in re-making Scotland anew in every generation.

Structure and content

The book has been divided into four thematic sections, each containing reflections, analyses or case studies which speak, in their own particular ways, to the overall concerns of this volume. We make no claims of unanimity of agreement amongst the contributors regarding the finer points of how to understand Scotland musically, nor indeed are we suggesting that what follows is in any way comprehensive in its presentation of the possible ways of achieving such an understanding. Rather, the volume is the product of the coming together of a community of scholars who share an interest in exploring such possibilities, and who have exchanged ideas and research findings through a process of mutual reflection and response.

The first section, 'Policy and Practice', brings together five chapters which explore the contemporary legislative, political or economic contexts of music making in Scotland. Looming large within these are issues of identity relating to constitutional arrangements – 1990s devolution, and the independence referendum principally – but they also consider changes in funding mechanisms and priorities, the creative economy, international policy frameworks such as those relating to Intangible Cultural Heritage (ICH), 'minority' language promotion, and the gathering momentum of 'the traditional arts' as a meaningful and recognised sub-sector within the contemporary cultural landscape of Scotland.

Simon McKerrell opens this section by discussing the changing role of both commercial and institutional influences in his chapter, 'Traditional Music and Cultural Sustainability in Scotland'. Through an examination of recent shifts towards professionalised and commodified traditional Scottish music production and reception, and situating these both within the policy environment and international models of ICH, he points towards the need for models of sustainability to embrace the commercial alongside the communal value in traditional music. In doing so, he takes us to the heart of a debate which remains contentious amongst performers and audience alike – should 'tradition' be bought and sold? Similar questions arise from Jo Miller's case study of the Glasgow Fiddle Workshop, a long-standing 'grassroots' teaching and learning project which has enjoyed a very strong participation rate, but which is highly exposed to the vagaries of funding decisions. Should finite state funding resources be channeled towards the excellence of the few, or the participation of the many? Indeed, are these two priorities really mutually exclusive? Read as a pair, these opening two essays frame such questions implicitly, and encourage us to re-think the relationships between core and periphery in relation to decision-makers and the communities they serve.

Indeed, one man whose own work has served many traditional arts communities contributes the next chapter in this section which deals with the issue of policy head on. David Francis, himself a key player in the development and promotion of traditional arts practice, here reflects on the gradual change in official attitudes to, and support for, these arts across Scotland. A groundswell of action and advocacy by a range of individuals and organisations over several decades, he argues, succeeded in redressing the history of neglect of the traditional arts in formal support structures, with the result that traditional music (alongside dance and storytelling) now enjoys a recognized place in cultural policy, backed by some financial support and a move towards a degree of parity of esteem.

The final two chapters in this section relate to a range of recent projects which have reached out across varying art forms but which each represent creative responses to contemporary issues of cultural or constitutional identities. Fiona J. MacKenzie presents a reflexive account of her role in creating a devised theatre production in Gaelic celebrating the life and work of the folklore collector, Margaret Fay Shaw, and in doing so highlights the potential for more new collaborations to emerge which continue to break down barriers of both language and genre in the presentation of the past within the present. It is interesting that neither MacKenzie nor Miller explicitly emphasise 'the national' in their case studies: as West argues later in the book, many other (sometimes competing) identities shape the nation today, and recognition of this fact takes us some way towards 'understanding Scotland'. That said, many artists do of course meet the issue of national identity head on in their work, a point which Mairi McFadyen explores in the final chapter in this opening section of the book. Focusing on the creative cultural campaign for Scottish independence leading up to the referendum of September 2014, and drawing upon a series of interviews with active campaigners, she discusses the extent to which changing perceptions of traditional music played a part in both challenging and constituting emerging conceptions of 'Scottishness'. Music and politics came together in a complex web of mutual influence, she argues, with the 'collective emotion' of imagined communities proving a powerful and potent pairing.

The second grouping of five chapters come together under the heading, 'Porosity, Genres, Hybridity'. The concerns of the contributors here relate to the increasingly 'leaky' boundaries which distinguish traditional music from other artforms within the contemporary Scottish context, and to the educational and performance-centred responses this 'leaking' has inspired. Joshua Dickson's chapter can be viewed as the scene-setter for this general topic, written from the perspective of a key provider of higher education programmes relating to traditional music in Scotland. As Head of Traditional Music at the Royal Conservatoire of Scotland, he has been a prime mover in the shaping of new pedagogical approaches within this context. His essay here reflects critically on the task of marrying formal education with the 'folk' ethos, and on the hybrid relationships which have emerged between 'trad' students and their classical peers.

As Dickson recognises, the quest for 'authenticity' provides a constant sub-text to these issues of hybridity, a theme that is picked up by Meghan McAvoy in the following chapter. Taking the devolution campaigns of the 1970s and 1990s as her contextual backdrop, she argues that contemporary Scottish literature, folk song and folk-influenced instrumental fusion artists jointly constitute an 'edgy national subculture', where perceptions of authenticity are constantly challenged and in which creators and performers attempt to marry the concerns of the local and the global as well as the national. Stephe Harrop then provides a detailed study of what might be considered a case in point: David Greig's ballad-inspired and ceilidh-infused National Theatre of Scotland production, *The Strange Undoing of Prudencia Hart*. Locating her analysis within a Scottish theatrical tradition of deploying traditional music with political intent, Harrop contends that Greig's dramaturgy can be read as promoting a lively, popular and multi-vocal debate concerning changing Scottish identities.

David McGuinness next tackles head on a question which sits implicitly within many of the contributions to this book – what do we mean by 'tradition'? All music is made as part of living traditions of performance, function, style and repertoire, he points out, and so is there really something unique about what we call 'traditional music'? Is this the best label? What are the alternatives? Drawing examples from the history of Scottish fiddle music and from the present day, this chapter examines the meaning of 'traditional' when applied to musical content or genres, to musical processes, and to musical communities. It suggests that a more careful examination of the operation of musical transmission might lead us to more appropriate categorisations, and also allow us to develop a more nuanced language to describe our conscious or unconscious position with regard to our musical traditions. Indeed, one band which does defy categorisation forms the focus of the final essay in this section. Phil Alexander introduces a case study of Edinburgh's Salsa Celtica, a band which promotes a particularly resonant blend of Scottish cultural hybridity, a marriage of traditional and newly composed Scottish melodies set against Afro-Cuban rhythmic patterns. As a one-time member of the band himself, his reflexive account is that of an insider, and producer of what he terms 'musically embodied multi-culturalism' and celebration of contemporary internationalism.

That global focus serves as a neat bridge to the third grouping of chapters, 'Home and Host', which deals with the Scottish diaspora and the complexities of Scottish musical identity as constructed and practised from afar. In another highly reflexive contribution, M.J. Grant explores the relationship between migration and song from a Scottish perspective, drawing on her own experience as a sometime Scot abroad. Touching on issues of transmission, memory and performance, and recognising the plurality embedded in songs such as Arvo Pärt's settings of Robert Burns's material, to the Proclaimers via Neil Gunn and Billy Connolly, she shows how 'understanding Scotland' necessitates an awareness of the complexity of musical globalisation. Patricia Ballantyne's chapter poses a broadly similar set of questions regarding the internationalisation of national cultures, in her case through an examination of certain 'exported' highland dancing forms, and their associated music. Both standardisation and homogenisation are key themes in her analysis as she addresses the role of formal societies and associations in the process of transmission of these cultural forms through both time and space.

The final section comprises a set of chapters which collectively consider the influence of 'the Past in the Present'. Here, the authors present case studies which examine the flow of tradition through time – the 'Carrying Stream' as termed by Hamish Henderson. Issues of archiving, revivalism, transmission, 'pedigree' and innovation are explored, again framing the 'national' within a wider picture of the local and global. Danni Glover focuses on the literary construction of identities in the work of Thomas Percy's *Reliques of Ancient English Poetry* (1765), identifying the national, class and gendered relations of his collection and its influence on the Scottish song and ballad tradition through the works of both Burns and Scott. Stuart Eydmann's chapter moves us forward by two centuries, as he shines a rare light on a range of groups and individuals which he considers to have been essential to the modern folk revival in Scotland. In doing so, he suggests that there are fresh perspectives to be gained by focusing on the more peripheral areas of the field, including musicians and musics deemed 'outlier' by those of the core. Ronnie Gibson also takes the contemporary instrumental scene as his starting point, as he interrogates the 'historicity of tradition' by evaluating links with the past in the present-day performance of Scottish fiddle music. Using evidence drawn from a series of case studies, he explores the dialectic between tradition and the creative autonomy of individual musicians based on Henry Glassie's definition of tradition as 'the creation of the future out of the past.'

The book is rounded off with three chapters offering personal reflections on the key issues of the book by Karen McAulay, Gary West and Simon Frith. Each, in their own ways and from varying perspectives, offer 'summing up' analyses, not as specific conclusions on the other contributions, but as critical responses to the central aim of the book, 'Understanding Scotland Musically'.

We hope therefore that readers, performers, and interested aficionados of Scottish culture will find this volume useful, both in coming to a greater critical awareness of how Scotland and Scottishness are manifested in music, but also perhaps in some oblique way, in contributing to our ability to enhance the public debate around musical culture in Scotland, how it is supported, taught, transmitted, listened to and performed. We argue here for the centrality of traditional music to any holistic understanding of Scotland as a cultural object, not because this genre has an exclusive claim on the national idea, but because almost every musical narrative that has attempted to refashion or capture some sense of belonging to Scotland, has drawn upon its deep resources. These resources are key to the authenticity of our claim in that they rest upon the oral traditions developed throughout modernity and before, and we believe that they continue to form a bedrock of shared identity that can be found at the core of what it means to be Scottish, or to perform Scotland. These values consist in a fairly generic way, of deep sense of egalitarianism, unostentatiousness and indefatigability that are socially constructed anew in every generation. There is great excitement and energy in the music of Scotland, and the range of voices in Scottish traditional music is now more eclectic and plural than ever before, yet we sense a shared commitment still in this newly commercial age to those values and we hope that the reader finds something of them running throughout the work of the formidable array of authors in this collection.

Notes

1 We recognise that the words 'nationalism' and 'nationalist' are problematic, especially within current constitutional discourse relating to Scotland. However, we use it here (not capitalised) as the preferred term to relate to music 'of the nation' which may not necessarily have political implications in terms of the constitutional preferences of the composers or performers. Of course, wrestling with the question of what constitutes work which is 'of the nation' is one of the central themes of this book.
2 The fighting between these last two on the pages of the 1960s *Scotsman* newspaper aptly demonstrates some of the contestation of what is important to national culture in Scotland.
3 We define 'traditional music' as 'music that functions as a marker of identity for a particular cultural group and that has grown out of their oral tradition or that has been composed using musical characteristics derived from oral tradition'. This is McKerrell's definition of 'traditional music' developed during the course of research into Scottish traditional music (see McKerrell, 2014b).

Part I
Policy and practice

2 Traditional music and cultural sustainability in Scotland

Simon McKerrell[1]

There are myriad traditional arts organisations within Europe today delivering publicly funded initiatives and tuition that are not bound together in any network or actively engaged in dialogue about best practice or sustainability. In Scotland, there has been a vigorous renaissance of the traditional arts in Scottish cultural life (see Francis, Dickson and Miller, this volume) which has been driven by the post-revival commodification of Scottish traditional music and more broadly through the heritagisation of public spaces and political growth of Scottish nationalism symbolically aligned with traditional music. In this chapter I outline some of the key ideas from the ethnomusicology of sustainability elsewhere and how they might relate to musicians and collectives working in Scottish traditional music today.

Financial support for the arts (broadly defined) in the UK saw a remarkable growth from 1997 under New Labour, where the performing arts were broadly speaking collapsed into a political narrative that constructed and reformulated them as having economic and instrumental benefits (Lee et al., 2014; Alexander, 2007). This narrative was very powerful and not only led to the retheorisation and emergence of the 'cultural clusters', 'creative economy' and 'creative industries' (over the term 'cultural industries') and saw an expansion of the 'creative industries' to include sectors such as computer software, but also a consequent expansion of the economic case linking them to growth (Hesmondhalgh, 2012, 175). In policy terms there was a resultant surge in UK public funding for the arts, and this included the traditional arts in Scotland (McKerrell, 2014a). Since the financial crisis of 2008, public funding for the arts in the UK has significantly decreased, and the sector has both bemoaned this fact, and also sought out alternative funding models and means of sustaining their economic activity and consequently the health of the performing arts sector itself. Part of this shift in Scotland has been the entry of the traditional arts into mainstream public funding alongside the other artistic genres such as literature, visual art, dance, classical music and drama. The UK has not yet signed up to the UNESCO 2003 Convention for the Safeguarding of ICH, which means that there is no formal, state-recognised, rights-based approach for recognising the cultural value of the traditional arts in the UK, and much of the support and policy for traditional music in Scotland is delivered within the commercial context of a highly professional performing arts and media sectors which form the context for these developments. This recent growth and subsequent exploration of different models of sustainability for the traditional arts has led to continuing professionalisation, festivalisation and heritage performances at home and abroad. In policy terms it is uncertain whether the Brexit might support or encourage greater engagement with UNESCO in the UK in a post-EU context, or whether it might shift Scotland and Britain further beyond the international heritage community. What is certain however is that in the context of the growth of Scottish traditional music, that analysis of the socio-political, pedagogical and cultural structures that support traditional music and dance is urgently required, both to interrogate the relations between the discursive and musical construction of authenticity and the mobilisation of it to support cultural tourism and sustainable musical communities in Scotland.

In various contexts at the local and national levels and at the pan-European level through the policies of UNESCO, traditional music has emerged as a key cultural performance of both indigeneity *and* Otherness in contemporary Europe. Festivals, musical performance, tuition as well as the manufacturing of musical instruments, clothing, artefacts, heritage tourism and literature, all now have emerged as economically and culturally significant across the European traditional arts. Traditional music, as well as having a significant commercial, professionalised presence in the performing arts sector, has also now been mobilised as ICH for heritage tourism, intercultural understanding within Europe, greater visibility of historical identities and important ethnic minority communities and improved public policy for the living cultural heritage of Europe's past. ICH policy has not only formalised some of the specific practices and policy support structures such as Fado (Portuguese song genre) and Latvian celebrations of Baltic song and dance as safeguarded and formally listed ICH, it has also lent both political and cultural authority to the practitioners of these art forms, assisted in securing state and regional funding and amplified local antagonisms between organisations, ethnicities and practitioners on the ground. The practice of nominating, securing and disseminating very discrete musical practices on the UNESCO representative list of ICH appears to be useful in the policy arena but less effective in terms of securing or sustaining these musical practices as living heritage. And in countries that have not signed the UNESCO convention such as the UK, Canada and the United States of America, there is a significant gap in our understanding of how the ICH agenda has been driven by proxy through the mediation and control of government quangos and the media. In these countries, commissioning editors, arts council officers, museum boards and broadcasters have in many ways acted as the tacit ICH policy makers. This may have had the advantage of allowing traditional arts in Scotland to flourish in some fairly strong experimental and creative ways, leading to commercially successful hybridisation in performances from bands such as Shooglenifty, Lau, Capercaillie and The Peatbog Fairies. However, in my view, Scotland has struggled to find state funded support for non-commercial ICH access, archiving and support, but in recent years, some has been provided via the organisation *Traditional Arts and Cultures Scotland* (TRACS) and partially via Museums, Galleries, Scotland.[2] The result of this has been that archival recordings, collection and non-commercial practice has struggled to find support in the public square, where professional bands, festivals and international touring has modestly flourished as part of the wider professional arts scene in Scotland.

Sustainability and authenticity

The sustainability or otherwise of a performing tradition that relies upon oral tradition, or is at least derived from oral traditions, necessitates that there is an intergenerational community of practice that feels strongly about that performing tradition, and wishes to perform and pass it on. The problem with the ethnomusicological literature in this area is however that it posits commerce in a binary opposition with sustainability. Indeed, much of ethnomusicological literature on sustainability is rooted in a tacit belief that indigenous, community-based practice of musical traditions are the ideal for sustainable, real-world traditions. This is placed in opposition to commercial spaces and commodification as though the two are mutually exclusive and usually justified because of the imagined gap in authenticity that emerges in commercial and/or heritage spaces. I believe that in certain late modern Western states such as Scotland, where there are healthy performing communities and rich traditional arts practices, this dyadic relationship is outdated and too simplistic. The ecological model does not yet account for the economic models that are so necessary to supporting the grassroots communities, and often disparage attempts to capitalise financially upon traditional arts. Sustainability does require collectivisation and active participation, but we need to consider it as it is often experienced in the real world where musicians and artists can be performing on one day in front of a large crowd of paying tourists or a concert audience and the next day engaged in entirely social music making at their local pub amongst genuine friends. Performers have multiple identities which they switch between, code switching too in terms of language, sartorial style and musical performance, but they can remain authentic in different ways, to different audiences.

Jeff Todd Titon's position on sustainability in music makes the argument for a cultural policy that is modelled upon ecological models with four key principles including, diversity, limits to growth, connectedness and stewardship (Titon, 2009). Problematically however, Titon's objection to economic models of sustainability, and in particular the use of ICH and cultural heritage paradigms, rests upon an objection to what he calls 'staged authenticity' which emerges out of managed performances in heritage tourism. This tacitly assumes that there is in fact a true authenticity, or a natural authenticity in traditional and folk musics that somehow exists in social music making where there is an absence of financial exchange. He refers to these spaces where financial exchange is mediated between the performing community and a paying audience as 'heritage spaces' and includes 'festivals, heritage trails, interpretive centers, and living history museums' (2009, 120). In his words, 'these spaces embody a paradox: what is presented there as authentic cannot possibly be so, because it is staged' (2009, 121).

What his, and other ecological viewpoints on musical sustainability raise for me, is the tacit assumptions and underlying values that ethnomusicologists and heritage professionals hold about the kinds of music cultures that are worth sustaining. There is a disdain of professional, commodified and commercial contexts for music in much of the writing on music sustainability which pits these forms of music making against social, participatory and grassroots performance. There are a number of problems with this conception of musical sustainability which include (1) a tacit binarism that assumes that growth of commercial contexts for traditional music degrade and deplete participatory social traditional music making; (2) a failure to recognise the mixed and portfolio profiles of professional traditional musicians who themselves move between intimate and public contexts in their music making throughout their careers; and (3) longer term problems for the disciplines of ethnomusicology, if it fails to embrace traditional arts practices that are embedded into late capitalist forms of society as well as more communitarian groups.

There are of course a number of different models operating as sustainable businesses and charities within the domain of ICH. Many of these individuals and organisations operate on a part-time basis, but since the success of the mid-twentieth-century folk revival, there has been a noticeable growth in the numbers and activity of professional traditional musicians operating in Scotland and throughout the world. In Scotland today, there are numerous local communities of practice for traditional music, some of which are sustainable in that they have been around for a very long time such as *The Clarsach Society* (established 1931) and The Shotts and Dykehead Pipe Band, which was formed in 1910, and who won the 2015 World Pipe Band Championships in Glasgow. If cultural sustainability is to maintain a useful conceptual presence in music studies, heritage, ethnology and related disciplines, not to mention serve a greater use beyond the academy, then it must encompass the tricky debates around representation, authenticity and globalisation, as well as the key consideration of financial and policy sustainability within the broader socio-economic and political landscapes. In considering these aspects, I begin from a position different to some ethnomusicologists which is that economic exchange and the heritagisation of intangible cultural heritage for profit is often a useful and positive development in the public sphere, and which if imaginatively configured, can not only support orally developed indigenous cultures, but also help them to grow and serve the communities in which they thrive. Profit is therefore not mutually exclusive with authentic social practice. Indeed, the commodification and commercialisation of ICH in Scotland has been always present throughout modernity, and the current acceleration of commodification and professionalisation of traditional arts are part of a longer socio-cultural narrative that stretches back to the entrepreneurial musicians, poets and artists of the eighteenth century such as Niel Gow and Robert Burns, who felt no serious conflict between their aesthetic and financial pursuits. However, today, because of the relatively recent emergence of traditional arts and the ICH agenda into UK public policy (see Francis, 1999, 2010; McKerrell, 2014a) and the continuing convergence of capitalism with culture (Banet-Weiser, 2012; Taylor, 2012), it is worth considering alternative, non-profit and more sophisticated models of sustainability within ICH that might support one of its key aspects, which is the support for the living performance of oral traditions in the communities in which they are practised. To that end, there are a number of key models of financial and professional practice in ICH, and some that offer the potential to policy makers for supporting this increasingly financially significant area of cultural activity. Current established commercial models in Scottish traditional music include:

- Sole trader musician or artist (most often involving production, performance, teaching and distribution of music, dance, drama, crafts and oral heritage, across a variety of public contexts domestically and internationally, either on a semi-professional or fully professional basis).
- The small-scale organisation, festival or band, educating, promoting, producing and distributing their own traditional music, dance, drama or crafts.
- The large-scale national and international businesses, festivals, lobby groups and organisations that exist to promote and further traditional arts in Scotland and abroad.
- Mass mediated commercial production and distribution of ICH via radio, television and online.

These models of sustainable practice have emerged only in recent decades, in the Scottish context only properly since the early 1980s from the first consideration of traditional music for arts policy in Scotland (Scottish Arts Council, 1984). In order for the scholarship of sustainability to have any real impact, it is essential for us to understand how these actually operate today for real world artists in a context in the twenty-first century quite radically different socially, culturally *and* politically from the closing decades of the twentieth century. My own fieldwork with various artists and musicians offers some generalisable narrative examples of how the financial models currently operate in traditional Scottish music. Interviews for this fieldwork were conducted in 2015 and have been partially anonymised in order to facilitate a frank and open exchange as well as protect musicians' personal and financial identities. The following vignettes offer some case studies from real world examples of the continuum of financial and musical exchange in Scottish traditional music today:

The sole trader

This musician's job involves performing traditional music with a number of bands, both self-started and for other projects, compositional commissions and teaching, and she has an established national, and an international reputation amongst the Scottish traditional music community of practice. She resides in Scotland yet performs all over the UK, occasionally in Europe and in North America and regards her role as a highly fulfilling one, embedded within a strong social group of other musicians and friends and family that support her work. In terms of income, this musician has been performing professionally for more than fifteen years, and has gradually built up performing and teaching opportunities which provide the vast bulk of her income throughout the year. Financially, her accounts for the last financial year show around £40,000 of total income, around half of which goes out immediately to other subcontracted musicians with whom she plays. Her personal income from all activity is usually in the range £12,000 to £18,000 per annum. Of this gross income, she claims around £9,000 of personal expenses, including equipment, travel, and the fractional expenses around place of business (home), broadband, clothing, per diems etc. currently permissible under the tax and revenue arrangements in the UK.

What is perhaps most interesting when considering this traditional musician's professional and financial approach is what she is now *not* doing:

> The thing is I'm saying 'no' to certain things that I don't think are worth it. It might be a community project, or a band featuring musicians that I totally love to play with and would have a great fulfilling rehearsal with, but I just know it's not marketable, it's not going to go anywhere, it's just a garage band. I can't do things like that now. Also, I used to do a lot of folk music sessions certainly one a week, and then one a fortnight, I just can't do those now because it cuts away a whole day. And because I'm not doing those now I've focused on things that are more important like promoting my own band [name removed] which has made a lot of money.
> (fieldwork interview, 24.08.2015)

This quote is representative of a considerable swathe of professional traditional musicians now working in Scotland. They have access to a successful career as a professional musician, which is a fulfilling profession, and *is* financially and culturally sustainable now and into the long term future. There is a genuine audience and market and a professional network both domestically and abroad. However, as shown in the figures above, the earnings for this full-time professional traditional musician are low, and also there is very little state support either in policy or tax status. This trend is fairly widespread as the Creative Scotland Music Sector review demonstrates:

> The music sector is characterized by high levels of self employment, freelance and part time working. 36% of the UK music workforce is self employed (30% in Scotland), and a third of employees (33%) work on a part-time basis (45% in Scotland) .... Average earnings in music are low. In the UK, 39% of people involved in the sector earn less than £10,000 per annum, with 5% earning more than £41,000. 84% of part-time workers earn less than £10,000 per annum, and there is a high incidence of second jobs within the industry.
> ('Music Sector Review: Final Report for Creative Scotland', 2013, 11–12)

Although the earnings for this musician, and many like her, are low within UK society, it does show that there is now a potential sustainable career for outstanding young traditional musicians in Scotland. This was not the case pre-revival, and has been largely the result of the success of the folk revival in Scotland in the 1950s–1970s. There is a new problem however, apparent from fieldwork which is that this gradual professionalisation of traditional music in Scotland has led to a stratification between the professional performing community and amateur communities of practice. Almost all the state support for individuals goes directly to the elite professional classes of musicians, often emphasising innovative and hybrid musical styles. This means that the forms of traditional music as community living heritage are underrepresented in the policy discourse where state support often depends on having professional administrative and fundraising staff, within a stable Scottish arts network (see Miller, this volume). To be sure, there has been some sizeable grants from Creative Scotland to organisations and individual musicians working directly in Scottish traditional music, and non-profit funding has recently been channelled through commissions distributed by TRACS. However, much of this is a conversation between professional musicians and organisations, and the arena of local, community groups is harder to reach and less visible in the media which makes amateur music making less prominent in the national cultural policy discourse whereas it is often one of the key areas at local authority level and for ordinary members of the public.

The online teacher

A relatively new and innovative pattern has emerged in the last decade of traditional (and other musicians) beginning to derive significant income from passing on the tradition online making use of the full range of digital technologies now available. One such is Jori Chisholm, a full-time bagpipe player and teacher, based in Seattle in the US, who performs at the highest levels of competitive performance and has developed the most established online bagpipe teaching business since the early noughties.[3] He has developed an online business model allowing him to teach pipers in the traditional style across the world. He has a range of online communicative strategies for his business which include: approximately forty students that he takes for live online lessons via Skype once a fortnight; pre-recorded 'tune-lesson' downloads of which there are currently seventy-four available, and in addition to this; he has developed a subscription-only innovative online 'studio' where he has hundreds of lessons and features on all aspects of bagpipe performing including teaching blogs, videos and sound files for his students. He has also begun bringing in other leading players to provide content to the online studio with an appropriate cut of the subscription fees. Jori's Skype students are spread across the United States, Canada, Europe, South Africa, New Zealand and Australia and in Scotland; a genuinely global reach for twenty-first-century oral tradition. In some senses too the online learning Jori has developed offers advantages to face-to-face transmission of oral traditions in the bagpipe tradition in that he can initially provide a 'canned' lesson on a tune for a student, and they can improve their playing so that the lesson time via Skype is spent on really improving their skills at the edge of their ability, essentially offering a flipped classroom model of teaching. He sees technological developments as key to the growth of his business:

> The first webcam lesson was in 2003. The technology keeps getting better and better, and now almost everybody has access to a webcam on their phone, iPad, or computer and most of us have access to broadband . . . I think it is a wonderful and natural use of the technology because of our specialized art form or craft that's spread out around the world. I receive emails almost every day from someone who has found me through my website, google search, or social media and they're interested. Online learning is becoming part of the general consciousness. It's quickly becoming just a standard thing.
> (Jori Chisholm, fieldwork interview, 21.08.2015)

This model is not now an outlier or unusual practice. Many traditional musicians are now transmitting their oral heritage online, and some institutions also offer Skype lessons and pre-recorded online tutorials. This now provides a deterritorialised reach for commercially sustainable tuition of music, and also has created a newly stratified market place for performers and teachers to compete both on the basis of their perceived authenticity, and their commitment to passing it on. This is embodied in the discourses used by these musicians online, with teachers of Scottish traditional music appealing to the heritagised authenticity of their personal performing experience with testimonials, teaching lineage and awards. Here are just three examples from people who offer online tuition in Scottish traditional music which show how this is typically achieved in some of the following ways:

> his music lives mainly in a world of oral tradition and memorisation rather than written scores, and of solo unaccompanied presentation rather than ensemble performance[4]

> . . . is a singer of Gaelic & Scots song from Neilston, a small town near to Glasgow. Drawn to Gaelic song through the Fèisean movement as a child, she went on to study the language and moved to Uist for several years to deepen her knowledge learning from local tradition bearers. Now living back in the Central Belt, she is involved in many musical projects has a great interest in exploring the links between the Scots & Gaelic song traditions. Her wide knowledge of both traditions means that she is much in demand as workshop leader and class tutor, and she offers song lessons both online and in person.[5]

> . . . a U.S. National Scottish Fiddling Champion, is a frequent and popular performer throughout the United States and beyond. Always drawing a crowd, she has been heard at everything from highland games and Celtic festivals to a Hard Rock Café and Esterházy Palace in Austria. She has also had the honor of performing for the 37th Lord Lyon King of Arms of Scotland, David Sellar. . . . Melinda has won numerous awards for her solo playing and her original compositions at regional and national Scottish F.I.R.E. competitions. She achieved fiddling titles such as the Allegheny Mountain Fiddling

Champion and the Potomac Valley Fiddling Champion several times prior to winning the 2003 U.S. National Scottish Fiddling Championship and becoming a sanctioned Scottish F.I.R.E. competition judge. She was a finalist for the 2008 Niel Gow International Scottish Fiddle Composition Competition held in Pitlochry, Scotland.[6]

These discourses focus around the personal authenticity of traditional musicians both in terms of their relational musical heritage, awards and experience. Competitions in fiddle and piping often provide clear badges of authenticity, and these musician-teachers often use recorded music invariably from a commercial album or sometimes with videos from live music events and testimonials from satisfied online students. These are innovative and essential ways in which traditional musicians are now making sustainable incomes online, and the quality and availability of these online portals across a range of different instrumental and vocal genres is proliferating and improving every year.

The institutional context

Many different institutions both physical, or simply symbolic, have come and gone in Scottish traditional music. Those that have survived have been those that have thought about their own long-term sustainability. One such example is *The National Piping Centre* in Glasgow. This is the premiere bagpiping institution in the world and arguably, the most sustainable and successful traditional music commercial heritage organisation in Scotland or its diaspora. The mission is stated simply: 'The National Piping Centre exists to promote the study of the music and history of the Highland Bagpipe'.[7] Having been established in 1996, the centre has grown substantially from its beginnings as an institution that provided fairly local traditional-style tuition in bagpiping, to an institution that has a global reach with tuition, summer schools both at home and abroad, a library, a national museum of bagpipes, online tuition, a major international festival (Piping Live!) every summer and that delivers elements of a degree in Scottish Music – Piping in partnership with the national conservatoire, The Royal Conservatoire of Scotland. From inception however, the institution also developed a commercial arm, which hosts a restaurant, bar, hotel and caters for weddings throughout the year and is crucial to its model of sustainability. The institution has grown substantially over the years and has an annual turnover well in excess of a million pounds per annum, and has developed a model of best practice in the arts, splitting its non-profit and commercial operations into two separate companies. The commercial arm channels all profits back into the educational charity business and this, alongside the city centre location and staff are key aspects of its sustainable success. Often, other large organisations or arts businesses do not properly conceive of the financial sustainability of their organisations, or rely fundamentally on state-support or grants from various third sector sources in order to stay afloat. The National Piping Centre has in many ways proven its sustainability over the past twenty years or so precisely because of its approach to long-term financial independence from the state or other third sectors (notwithstanding short term occasional grants from *Creative Scotland* to the institution). The National Piping Centre is therefore one of the only sustainable large-scale traditional arts organisations in Scotland, and has remained where others such as Balnain House, The Glasgow Folk and Traditional Arts Trust, various Folk Festivals and many others indirectly involved with traditional arts such as 7.84 Theatre have come and gone. What marks out this organisation as sustainable financially and musically, is its breadth of activity and the underlying structural model for sustainable support of its piping activities that relies on its commercial activities.

These three snapshot case studies of the individual, the digital and the collective, indicate approaches to sustainability both in an economic and in a socio-cultural sense and they are not outliers, but demonstrate some of the new economic and discursive strategies that have emerged in the last two decades. Traditional models of sustainability in ethnomusicology do not quite capture the essence of how sustainability works in these case studies. Whether the theorisation of 'endangerment' or the UNESCO 'rights-based' approaches, or simply as in the United States, where the use of public funding is directly used to support artists and community groups. It is clear from fieldwork, that in each of these Scottish examples, various approaches to sustainability both in an economic and in a socio-cultural sense are largely based upon commercial success building on heritagised authenticity. This is important for the largely Anglo-American world that has not, and is unlikely to, sign up to the UNESCO convention on intangible cultural heritage. Therefore in national contexts like Scotland and the wider UK, that are not signatories to the convention, commerce is fundamental to sustainability, and the scholarship and policy-making for a sustainable traditional arts must recognise this, and somehow develop a means for the non-commercial and amateur aspects of ICH to be recognised and flourish in the absence of a rights- or endangerment-based approach grounded in law.

The future in Scottish policy and practice

Cultural policy itself should recognise complexity in artists' lives, and also, that making money at one end of the continuum of practice does not preclude individuals from being engaged at the other. That commerce is not mutually exclusive with sustainable ICH. The policy context that supports traditional music as ICH in other European nations is of course slightly irrelevant in the UK context as the UK government has not formally signed the UNESCO convention. However, a quasi form of a rights and access based approach to traditional music as ICH has been partially implemented by proxy in Scotland and elsewhere, via key cultural gatekeepers such as the Arts Councils, television and radio executives and producers, local authorities, education departments, commercial tour operators and national tourism agencies. This agenda rests upon the views of the powerful cultural gatekeepers, with substantial cultural and economic capital lending them the authority to take financial decisions that directly affect the communities of practice. The current socio-political context therefore in Scotland means that the only state support for the traditional arts comes via the national arts funding body

Creative Scotland, where as of 2015, traditional arts have no ringfenced funding on the grounds of intrinsic national cultural value, but are provided with the opportunity to apply in competition with all other art forms. Therefore in Scotland today, the arms length arts funding body exists in a policy context where support for the traditional arts generally flows to professionalised organisations such as TRACS, Folk Festivals, The National Piping Centre, Feisan nan Gaidheal, Feis Rois, amongst others, and it remains the case in the Scottish context that most professional activity in traditional music rests upon market competition from audiences, broadcasters, educationalists, administrators and tourists. Of course, some of those organisations such as TRACS and the Feisan in particular are involved in provisioning music tuition for local and amateur groups (including school children), but mostly this is achieved through paying for professional musicians to teach small groups under the aegis of those organisations.

The problem with this approach is that professionals trained in media, tourism, education, cultural policy and civic administration have been taking decisions about what aspects of traditional music are worth focusing on, broadcasting, supporting through educational initiatives or advertising to tourists or in festivals and so forth. We are in the odd position in Europe where there is currently no meaningful role in Scotland for non-profit-driven approaches to ICH. The academy in Scotland and the UK has no real influence over how the national cultural heritage is supported, accessed, or valued in education and the public discourse. The most significant non-commercial resource for traditional music in Scotland in recent decades is the *Tobar an Dualchais* digital archival project, ironically funded by the UK Heritage Lottery Fund which by its nature made it a finite five-year project. There is no national archive for traditional arts, the national school curricula have fared slightly better in recent years, but music syllabi in schools, teacher training and even the national arts funding is still dominated wholesale by the art music tradition (which is ironically less popular with the Scottish public than popular or traditional musics).[8] Clearly, the implementation of the 2003 UNESCO Convention on ICH in the UK would help to alter this situation (despite its failings elsewhere), primarily, the benefit would arise from the implementation of a legal and state-supported route for the non-profit support and development of national cultural heritage. In a contemporary social context of increasing marketisation and a relentless focus on profit, that is why those of us in the applied-leaning disciplines must be lobbying for some form of state-recognition of the cultural and intrinsic value of traditional arts more broadly to our society.

One of the obstacles to this approach is the UNESCO 2003 Convention itself. Labadi (2012) analyses the policy discourse surrounding the 2003 Convention on ICH and makes the point that because the 'authenticity' of ICH traditions was not considered in the 2003 convention, the decision on whether to include a particular tradition rests upon its position with the communities of practice (2012, 132). Furthermore, because article 15 assumes that the state is the principal arbiter of representation of communities, this effectively filters the possible representations of ICH through the European states, and provides no formal route for oppressed or underrepresented minority communities to access the legal safeguards of the

UNESCO convention. In the Scottish context therefore, unless and until the Westminster UK government ratifies the convention in its current form there it is difficult to see how any non-profit driven approach to ICH could be supported through the state. An alternative of course would be for UNESCO to alter the convention to allow non-state actors to represent their interests directly, or perhaps via a network of scholars of the traditional arts. This would provide both non-professional communities of practice, and oppressed minorities with support from the academy, the ability to find legal recognition at the European level for their own (sometimes contested) cultural heritage.

Conclusion

In Scotland today, one of the reasons that this wider, relational view of policy is so necessary is the structural inequity in current Scottish cultural policy. Fewer than a quarter of Scottish state schools provide bagpipe lessons (Peterkin, 2016), this musical genre bias in favour of classical musical instruments is totally at odds with the statistical evidence from the Scottish Household Survey which typically shows that four to five times more Scots attend live popular or traditional music than attend classical music or opera performances, and these figures have been maintained across a number of surveys (Scottish Government, 2013a, 2014). Furthermore, the 2003 UNESCO convention explicitly defines 'safeguarding' as: 'measures aimed at ensuring the viability of the ICH, including the identification, documentation, research, preservation, protection, promotion, enhancement, transmission, particularly through formal and non-formal education, as well as the revitalisation of the various aspects of such heritage' (UNESCO, 2003, 3). Little of this access and archival work has been carried out in relation to traditional music with the one exception of the precariously funded *Tobar an Dualchais* archive at the University of Edinburgh. Most media and digitalised access for traditional music is driven via market forces through the commercial ends of various record companies and private individuals or the BBC which has no real archiving policy for its programmes on traditional music. The British Library's focus necessarily provides London-centred support for sound preservation, where there is little incentive or money to properly sustain the traditional music of Scotland. Today, Scotland has recently set up a National Sound Archive, *Scotland's Sounds*, however, rather predictably there is no funding for a physical headquarters, or fieldwork and the project is essentially a means to corral pre-existing recorded music and sound archives into an online portal. Neither is there any ring fenced arts funding for traditional music from *Creative Scotland* that is not subject to the political whims of quangos or politicians. These sort of disjunctures between educational and cultural policy landscape and the community of practice mean that there is urgent work to be done in securing the place of Scottish traditional music in relation to the wider policy landscape. We have not recognised traditional music as an issue of national cultural heritage for its intrinsic value, but have made some developments towards a professional and commercially sustainable industry both at home and abroad. This has largely been done independently of any heritage or arts state policy, but has meant that the focus for any financial support or policy recognition has almost exclusively gone to professional musicians working in a variety of contexts. By shifting the policy debate away from the UNESCO rights-based or any endangerment-based approaches to ICH, and considering instead the balance of various exchange values for traditional music, we might be able to offer a more meaningful policy framework for supporting both commercial and non-commercial traditional music as sustainable intangible cultural heritage. This framework would enable the economic exchange value of traditional music to be considered alongside the social, cultural and heritage exchange values of traditional music to produce a more balanced understanding of the sustainable heritage threshold in cultural policy within the UK. Whilst the hard left might criticise this view of musical value, it is clear that the extreme relativism in the ethnomusicological literature and even the grey literature within the UK has itself had little to say about the financial aspects of any sustainable approaches to traditional culture. To continue in this manner will ensure the irrelevancy of the academy to public (and private) debates about traditional music and dance into the future. However, understanding that making traditional music in a late modern, capitalist society is itself always already an activity requiring special dedication, often at odds with the legal, tax and even arts policy structures in Scotland and the UK, requires the academy and policy makers working in the arts, cultural and heritage fields to recognise these realities in their approach to traditional arts. Especially in the Anglo-American world where 'rights-based' discourses in the arts are under sustained attack, and in any event, difficult to defend in an increasingly unequal world.

Notes

1 I would like to gratefully acknowledge the support of the AHRC (grant number AH/L006502/1) and Newcastle University in both the production of this research and the support for the conference in October 2014 at Newcastle University.
2 See www.museumsgalleriesscotland.org.uk/projects/intangible-cultural-heritage/ and www.tracscotland.org/.
3 See www.bagpipelessons.com.
4 www.simonchadwick.net/harp/about.html [accessed: 29.03.2016].
5 www.naomiharveymusic.com/biog/ [accessed: 29.03.2016].
6 www.melindacrawford.com/biography.html [accessed: 29.03.2016].
7 www.thepipingcentre.co.uk.
8 See for instance the Scottish Household survey results and (McKerrell, 2014a).

3 'A sense of who we are'
The cultural value of community-based traditional music in Scotland

Josephine L. Miller

How are musical cultures sustained? Arguably, traditional music in Scotland does not depend on cultural agencies to flourish, having historically fostered a dynamic tradition. However, the means of transmission has been a major concern of both post-revival organisations and of arts policy, often under headings such as 'education' and 'participation'. How should such work be evaluated? The concept of 'cultural value' has been employed in many ways in policy discourse, largely in terms of economic and social impact. But a broader approach and better integration of methodologies, encompassing qualitative approaches such as ethnography and perspectives from different stakeholders, would provide a more holistic picture of experience of the arts. Furthermore, research must take account not only of professional and publicly funded arts, but also the wider landscape of amateur and community-based activity and personal experience.[1] Community is of course a contested term, and the focus not of uniformity but of wrestling with many aspects of identity and belonging. Here, I use 'community-based' to indicate a specific location which provides a frame of reference for activity, and which may or may not be incorporated into an organisation's name.[2] I also refer to the concept of 'community of musical practice' (Kenny, 2016), derived from the 'communities of practice' model (Lave and Wenger, 1991, Wenger, 1998).

In this chapter, I argue that the community-based learning of traditional music in Scotland deserves the attention of the traditional music community as a whole and the informed participation of policy makers and funders because of widespread engagement in such activities. They also have a role as training grounds for music leaders, and provide rich data on music learning in general at a time of growing interest in the practices of traditional and other popular music genres as a resource for music education. By way of illustration, I draw on a case study of Glasgow Fiddle Workshop, a traditional music group which I established in 1990, but had no involvement with after 1993.[3] Between 2012 and 2014 the organisation allowed me to access its archives, observe classes and events, and undertake fieldwork for a large ethnographic study which aimed to elucidate some of the processes through which music makers direct and sustain their practice (Miller, 2016). Glasgow Fiddle Workshop (hereinafter 'GFW') has encouraged participation in traditional music since its beginnings, and public funding has played a role in its evolution. There are similar groups of varying sizes elsewhere in Scotland, but little research on the actual learning and teaching in these environments, and its relationship to the musical lives of individuals and the wider community.[4] Such groups are a repository of experience and potential for music learners of all ages and abilities, but also sites of social and musical participation and performance, and in my view, an under-used cultural resource for building and maintaining communities. The paucity of research on organisations like GFW confirms their 'under the radar' status both in scholarship and in public dialogue.

David Francis has charted the growing recognition of the state's responsibility to the traditional arts since the 1980s, via a catalogue of working parties, steering groups, audits and reports (see for instance 2010, 2015). McKerrell (2011) has also shown that the 1970s and '80s established a commercial traditional music for performers in Scotland and elsewhere. However this is only part of the picture: the 1990s saw a rapid growth in opportunities not only to spectate, but also to participate in the traditional arts, as policy-makers and funders responded to the Scottish Arts Council's 'Charter for the Arts' (SAC, 1993) and other cultural reviews. McKerrell (2014) argues that the commodification of the genre is a good thing, and calls for the traditional arts to put a stronger case for state funding, based on both their intrinsic and instrumental value. Currently, the latter is better served than the former regarding research into learning and teaching traditional music. Consider the *Fèis* movement of Gaelic arts festivals. Research largely assesses the impact of *fèisean* in terms of social (Matarasso, 1996) economic (Westbrook et al., 2010) or attitudinal (Broad and France, 2006) factors, or derives from the organisation itself (Martin, 2006).[5] Musical impact appears to be measured largely through motivation and the potential to earn a living from music. For example, those who come through *fèisean* often go on to be tutors in the same organisation (Westbrook et al., 2010, 32). Data gathered for 2015–2016 from over 60 organisations shows that at least 23,239 people participate in learning traditional music in community settings, and that most of this takes place in groups.[6] However, with the exception of the 'music' reports from Creative Scotland (formerly the Scottish Arts Council), the only substantial evidence on the value of community-based traditional music projects in Scotland is the literature on *fèisean*.[7] There are no comparable studies for the many other groups doing similar work, and the hegemonic status of *fèisean* is exemplified by their consistent receipt of substantial regular public funding.

Glasgow fiddle workshop

As I have shown in my full study of GFW (Miller, 2016), the musical aesthetic there privileges participation, and the skills and repertoire required for participatory rather than presentational performance, though there are some examples of the latter.[8] The aims of the organisation are set out thus:

1 To promote an understanding and appreciation of Scottish traditional music.
2 To provide opportunities for learning to play and sing Scottish traditional music, with an emphasis on learning to play by ear.

32 *Josephine L. Miller*

3   To create a community of people with a common interest in Scottish traditional music.
4   To forge links with other organisations who have similar interests. (GFW, 2013, 3).

In session 2012–2013 GFW had 463 members, of whom 40% were either employed or retired. 415 (89%) members were adults, of whom the majority were aged over 40, and 48 (11%) were juniors. Fiddle was the most popular instrument, followed by ukulele (Figure 3.1). That session, GFW ran 40 classes over three evenings each week and employed around 30 tutors (GFW, 2013, 11–13).

Members came not just from the Glasgow area, but travelled substantial distances from other districts such as Argyll, Ayrshire, Stirlingshire and Lanarkshire, as shown in Figure 3.2.

The roots of GFW go back to 1990, when Glasgow was European City of Culture and large urban authorities were leading the development of arts policy in the UK. I was then employed at Glasgow Arts Centre with a remit to develop traditional music, and started a fiddle workshop which I led for three years. Eight members decided to continue, recruiting Iain Fraser as tutor, and in 1994–1995 GFW was formally constituted, set about publicising its activities, and received its first Scottish Arts Council grant of £750. In that year alone GFW made significant progress: a second fiddle tutor was appointed, audio cassettes of tunes were produced as learning aids, public concerts by Natalie McMaster

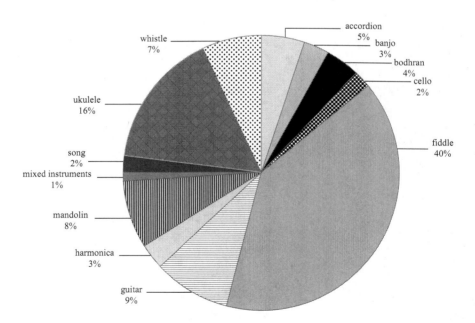

Figure 3.1 Membership of GFW classes, % by instrument, 2012–2013

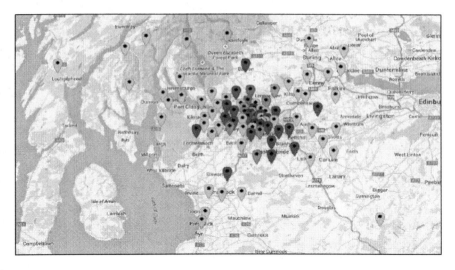

Figure 3.2 Map showing distribution of GFW membership in central Scotland, 2012–2013

and Alasdair Fraser were promoted, step dance and children's classes were introduced, a trust was set up to purchase instruments, newsletters were published, members attended 'Fiddle Force' winter school on Skye and organised a trip to Balnain House, Inverness.[9] The first administrator recalled the excitement of being part of these growing opportunities, and her awareness of broader cultural developments:

JM: How do you look back on that period?

O4[10]: I just think it was – amazing! [laughter] . . . when you look at these publications, I mean, I've got – you realise how much was going on . . . there was a lot of drive to get Scottish traditional music song and dance recognized . . . for example here [interviewee lifts up paper copies of reports to which she is referring] I've got – the 'National Cultural Strategy' paper, 'Creating our Future, Minding our Past', the first report produced by the Scottish Executive Education Department. 'A Soundtrack for Scotland', 'Common Cause – A Music Strategy for the City of Edinburgh'.

She also commented on the commitment to establishing a social network:

I felt it was my *responsibility* to know about all these things that were going on, being part of them if I could, to go along. Because again I was thinking of promoting the fiddle workshop, because you could see how it was just taking off, it was snowballing, it was just fantastic. And you thought 'this is an important resource', not just for people learning an instrument, but for so many other aspects, about enhancing people's lives in a way, and introducing a social aspect of it as well. We did a lot of concerts and ceilidhs and all that kind of thing to get people together.

This intensification of activity at GFW during the mid-1990s mirrored the growth of funding for the traditional arts in the years leading up to and following the re-establishment of the Scottish parliament in 1999, with many arts organisations benefiting from the new political and financial attention (McKerrell, 2014). In 2002 a move to a new venue, Stow College of Further Education, added to the number of extra-mural students at that institution in return for the extensive accommodation now required for growing classes. This partnership raised the possibility of a more formal teaching curriculum. Senior tutors were appointed, and attempts made to develop a fiddle syllabus. Progression through classes (particularly fiddle) emerges as a topic of perpetual debate during the life of GFW, including deliberations on technique versus repertoire, aural/oral versus notational learning, and tutor/participant responsibility for choice of class. At one point tutors were encouraged to keep a record of work, in case it was required by Her Majesty's Inspectorate.

JM: So it was because people were being enrolled at Stow that you had to provide something more structured?
O1: It was the enrolment. Yeah. But it wasn't too heavy at that point . . . it was a bit of a no-brainer; you didn't *need* to do it. There was no onus to do it, it just gave people a path to go if they wanted to. So in a whole year they would achieve something if they wanted to. You know, if in improving beginners [class] you're going to kind of learn the basis of a strathspey before you can go up to intermediate and whatever, and play in x keys.

It is worth reflecting that as the quote above suggests, such a development may not have suited all participants. It may also have altered the character of the organisation, influencing relationships there towards the pedagogical rather than the participatory. In 2003–2004 a grant from Glasgow City Council was used to extend children's classes and outreach work, and in 2006 a Development Officer was appointed to help enhance existing partnerships and nurture new ones, promote GFW and its activities, and identify new funding for specific activities. By 2008 the organisation had become a limited company, and in 2009 Youth Music Initiative funding enabled GFW to provide workshops at play-schemes and youth clubs.[11] By 2010, classes included accordion, mandolin and ukulele, and GFW were leading slow sessions and hosting 'Come and Try' workshops at the *Fiddle* festival in Edinburgh and *Celtic Connections* in Glasgow. The 2000s were, then, a decade of expansion and experimentation for GFW, developing links with other bodies increasingly involved in the provision of traditional music. Figure 3.3 illustrates the consistent and significant funding awards received by GFW during this period, enabling the growth in classes and the flourishing of new projects.

Year	Funding awarded to GFW
1990–1994	£0
1994–1995	£750 (SAC)
1995–1996	£2,500 (SAC)
1996–1997	£4,000 (SAC)
1997–1998	£9,000 (SAC)
1998–1999	n/a
1999–2000	n/a
2000–2001	n/a (SAC) £477 (Arts Council, England)
2001–2002	n/a
2002–2003	£12,000 (SAC)
2003–2004	£25,000 (SAC)
2004–2005	£25,000 (SAC)
2005–2006	£25,000 (SAC)
2006–2007	£25,000 (SAC) + £5,000 (Stow College)
2007–2008	£25,000 (SAC)
2008–2009	£25,000 (SAC)
2009–2010	£25,000 (SAC) + £3645 (Youth Music Initiative)
2010–2011	£25,000 (Creative Scotland – Lottery)
2012–2013	£0

Figure 3.3 Public funding awarded to GFW

Source: GFW archives and Scottish Arts Council, Creative Scotland and Lottery websites accessed 12.12.15. www.scottisharts.org.uk/1/funding/pastgrantsawarded.aspx, www.gotlottery.uk/creative-scotland-glasgow-fiddle-workshop-9-366802 http://gotlottery.uk/arts-council-england-glasgow-fiddle-workshop-2-83973

GFW has faced new challenges since 2010, including changes to funding and the closure of Stow College.[12] Creative Scotland withdrew its grant in 2012, and GFW had to make savings through cutting administrator's hours, the training budget for staff, and an events budget, so they could no longer subsidise events and special workshops. At present, GFW delivers its core programme of classes with the income generated from members, and there is a compelling argument that where participants can afford to pay, these should not be subsidised by the public purse. However, I would submit that there are other ways in which the group's experience, commitment and skills could be mobilised to better sustain and grow music makers and their communities, and where funding could help.

In constructing a case for this, I want to refer to two sub-groups at GFW. The first is volunteers, who make a substantial contribution in a changing environment. One tutor said:

> I think GFW has always run kind of by the skin of its teeth, on the basis of the driving passion of one or two people with a lot of energy. And those people get tired, or their lives take them in another direction or, you know, it's no longer for them, and someone else picks up and the character of it changes.
>
> (T1)

Simply running a large organisation such as GFW also takes significant time and energy, as a former administrator notes when comparing the current GFW to that of its early years:

> I'm not seeing them doing as much as we did in those early days, as far as networking and expanding and publicising . . . they're struggling getting the funding . . . We seem to be *fighting*, you know, instead of concentrating on the important things . . . And trying to cut back, reduce the size, or unable to fund people to run it properly. In the early days it was all voluntary – a lot of goodwill.
>
> (O4)

There is still a great deal of voluntary input, but nonetheless amateur, community-based groups like GFW can struggle to build long-term relationships across the public and private sectors because of the fluctuation of personnel and resources, and in my view this is partly why they may not be conspicuous in debates. The necessarily loose structure of such groups makes them vulnerable and often invisible to the professionalised arts policy community.

Tutors are the second group whose work with community-based organisations is worth particular consideration in the context of this chapter. It has been observed that teaching provides a significant 'part of the portfolio of work' for many young aspiring professional musicians and graduates of new degree courses (Francis, 2010).[13] They not only gain experience leading the music – 'it's shaped how I teach' (T15) – but also how organisations work. One former GFW tutor commented: 'every musician – particularly within our genre – needs a community' and described it as the 'backdrop' to her practice as a performer. She also felt a responsibility to contribute to sustaining employment opportunities:

> I do see a bit of a divide between people who . . . really grasp the idea that this infrastructure wasn't set up before we arrived and actually . . . you have to continue to contribute to it . . . there's a divide between the people who catch on to that quickly. . . [and those who] . . . just want to focus on the one single practice . . . and of course then *they* are kind of relying on the people who are contributing to the infrastructure to make sure that there's work for them.
>
> (O5)

Many tutors are professional performers who have at some point been employed in community settings, and probably could not support their performing careers without this work. They also play a significant role as bridge-builders spanning different communities. Organisations continue to provide an important context for developing music leading skills, but could better assist and retain tutors by remunerating them adequately for teaching, preparation, meetings, events, and professional development. All, perhaps, fostered by a more structured progression which recognises individuals' experience, supported by mentoring and other resources.

In a review of Scotland's music sector, the primary challenges facing future development of the sector were identified as funding and education.

> People and organisations in every area of the music sector, whatever their core purpose, have embraced education (in a broad and inclusive definition) as a natural part of their remit. There are few festivals, arts centres, promoters or performing companies that do not run education programmes . . . The music sector is now a full part of the informal education sector.
>
> (EKOS, 2013, [revised 2014], 90)

To my mind this suggests a view of 'education' or, as they are now more often termed 'learning and participation' programmes, organised largely as an adjunct to professional events.[14] Also, the term 'informal' has attracted significant debate: it is widely used of learning in general, and music learning in particular, especially the adoption by formal education of practices from popular music (see for example Folkestad, 2006 and Green, 2008). Here, however, 'informal' needs to be understood as a largely administrative term, rather than one which accurately reflects the processes of learning and teaching traditional music. For example, in 2012 *Fèis Rois* advertised a post entitled 'informal education portfolio manager'. The job description ran:

> You will *manage* a varied year-round *programme* of traditional music workshops for young people, including residential events; mentoring and *training* programmes; and developing online learning opportunities. You have responsibility for the *management* of all Fèis Rois projects taking place outwith school hours. The successful candidate will *source new funding* for both the continuation of these projects and the development of innovative new strands of work.
>
> (author's emphasis)[15]

The terms highlighted here illustrate a terminological minefield: a distinction must be drawn between the 'informal education' setting referred to here, involving managed, funded programmes outwith school, and the widely used meaning of 'informal' as a descriptor of an activity which (young) people organise and lead themselves, unsupervised.[16] It is noteworthy that none of GFW's aims quoted earlier in this chapter refer to teaching or educating, but emphasise nurturing environments and communities for learning and appreciation of traditional music. The music sector review, however, also says:

> The valuable and unique contributions of this large swathe of organisations are over dependent on short-term or vulnerable sources of financial support. Yet education projects provide considerable work opportunities for musicians and music organisers.
>
> (EKOS, 2013 [revised 2014], 91)

As this case study implies, the cultural value of engagement in programmes of traditional music such as those of GFW goes largely unvoiced in the Scottish arts policy literature. The value of the experience lies partly in encouraging an appreciation of individual and group autonomy: 'I think probably . . . the more people we have in front of us the more momentum we build and the safer we are. It's not really the economics of it, it's the bigger the gang of musicians we have, the more we have *a sense of who we are*' (T1) (author's emphasis). One GFW participant says 'it's the fact that you get to play a musical instrument wi' other people . . . everyone's an expert . . . Everyone appears at the same level. It's all pitched to your level' (P1), exemplifying features of the concept of 'communitas': equality of opportunity, the levelling of social roles, and a way of actively being together which functions to regenerate the group (Turner, 1969). Community music scholar Kari Veblen says: 'how do things get done in a large group? Often, it seems, one action sparks another, people join in, and energy wells up to satisfy an outcome. This dynamic deserves more study as a phenomenon of *community music*' (Veblen, 2005, 324). The cultural capital generated at GFW furnishes members and tutors alike with the means of participating in a more extensive scene, and this is fundamental to understanding how traditional music is valued, as suggested at the beginning of this chapter. Many participants have become aware of other musical networks locally, throughout Scotland and beyond: 'it's opened up a whole new world' (F20); 'it opens out the doors' (A1); 'the whole Scottish music scene is fantastic, there are so many different interconnections. You see the same people on different occasions' (M2). One tutor visiting Australia remarked:

> I did my research and I found a traditional music group in Melbourne . . . And I went along, and they lent me an accordion and I played wi' them that night! So there ye go, other side o' the world, playin' the same tunes as we were playin' in Glasgow, an' it was great!
>
> (T17)

Some groups happily operate locally or regionally, some nationally, but many paths between are possible, and those like GFW function as a gateway to further opportunities. One member of the original fiddle group, for instance, became its first administrator, went on to work for a record company, learned to repair fiddle bows, returned to GFW as a cello student, and is now a partner in a Glasgow music shop, welcoming regular customers from the Fiddle Workshop. These are what we might term 'horizontal' connections, made at a local level, and reinforced by regular personal interaction. An international comparison is illuminating here. A community project in Maine was started by fiddler Don Roy after funding and institutional support for public projects dried up. 'Fiddle-icious' contributes to maintaining the heritage of the Franco-American culture, and has, like Glasgow Fiddle Workshop, expanded beyond the bounds of the organised weekly gatherings. Roy says:

> I love what I'm seeing now, with people busting off, forming their own groups, going off to do things on their own. Good friendships have been

made. That's really what I want . . . to get people doing things on their own. And getting the better players to teach the others. Now some of the more advanced players – who came here a few years ago for lessons, and would NEVER have gotten up in front of a crowd to play – now they're playing and teaching all over the place. They've started a group up in Freeport. And they are getting together for potluck suppers. That's what's in it for me.

(Faux, 2009, 46)

Faux observes 'an intimacy that is cultivated by the face-to-face transmission; a looking into the eyes, an attention to body language, a sense of sharing' (48). GFW class members and tutors have similarly conveyed the importance for them of this physical proximity and shared space.

Returning to our case study, some GFW participants get involved because they have missed the opportunity earlier in life, and would have liked to encounter traditional music in their formal education, indeed they may view it as an obligation on the education system:

> F3: [traditional music is] part of our cultural heritage. I think it's really important that people are *encouraged* to become more aware of it. I think it's a big gap in Scottish schools, that minimum attention is paid to it. I mean, I had absolutely *nothing* at school about Scottish traditional music . . . it's not because I'm a nationalist or anything like that but I just think it's important for people to be aware of their culture.
>
> I mean I've always loved ceilidhs – I did always do ceilidhs, as a youngster. . . [My friend had a flatmate] – he was a kind of folksinger. So we would go to the pub and hear him singing and go along to kind of folk-style, folk-type events . . . I like the environment; I think it's very sociable, but I know there are huge gaps in my education.

It is salient that this fiddler differentiated between her previous social experience as a dancer, singer and audience member, and the lack of validation accorded it by her formal education. The GFW member quoted above is aged sixty, but younger musicians tell similar stories. A former GFW tutor (aged 32) who attended school in the 1990s said:

> where I grew up there wasn't . . . really any traditional music present in the schools. I had violin lessons in school and out with school, and I was part of all the regional groups – orchestras and string ensembles, choirs as well for a bit. But there was no real, I'm not going to say support, but there was no facilitation of traditional music within formal education.
>
> (O6)

This comment implies that the individual experienced acceptance or even encouragement for traditional music at school, but not practical assistance in developing this further. GFW is meeting a need for both learners and tutors by providing a context where the music can be valued, enjoyed and shared.

We know that participation in the arts brings many benefits, and traditional music has much to offer here. While the sonic and structural properties of Scottish traditional music are not the focus of this chapter, it is worth noting briefly aspects such as the short, repetitive forms associated with much participatory music making (Turino, 2008, p36–48) which particularly lend themselves to aural-based and group learning. But for some, taking part remains less accessible, and we need a much more nuanced understanding of the learning, teaching and performing of the genre so it can be best supported and developed. Intergenerational learning and music making, for example, offers considerable potential, yet the music sector review cited above largely treats 'youth music' separately from 'amateur adults' and those engaged in so-called lifelong learning. In my opinion, these are restrictive categories. Music educationalist Roger Mantie is also critical of such labels, asking 'when does one stop learning and start *doing*?' (Mantie, 2012). An additional and perhaps contentious notion is that environments such as GFW are not only about traditional music, but about learning and celebrating music in general. I have found many participants equally enthusiastic about many other forms of music. The performing group 'Scratchy Noises' has grown out of GFW and retains links with it. They meet regularly to play together, and from time to time invite tutors to lead workshops for them, including sessions on classical and old time music. During my fieldwork, while repertoire in GFW classes was predominantly Scottish/Irish, it also included items such as 'Keep your eyes on the prize', a folk song from the American civil rights movement (ukulele group), Hungarian tune 'Yoska' (fiddle class), Swiss waltz 'Septante Neuf' (accordion class) and blues standard 'Key to the Highway' (guitar class).[17]

The predicament of organisations like GFW is, then, that they are grassroots, flexible, reactive communities of musical practice making and remaking themselves, and this does not always make for a good correspondence with policy and funding criteria. As we have seen, the influence of GFW extends far beyond the provision of weekly classes: it contributes to the local economy in Glasgow through its use of venues from college premises (see Figure 3.4) to pubs, via its participation in festivals, the attendance of individuals and groups at musical events and courses throughout Scotland, and the employment of professional and semi-professional tutors, for whom it is a key component of their income.

GFW facilitates a way of learning and making music together which is welcoming, adaptable, and empowering. It seems that classes at organisations like GFW may not, in fact, 'stand in place of personal teaching relationships or local musicians' (McKerrell, 2014, 2), but exist in dynamic relationship with these. Some GFW participants regularly seek lessons with individual teachers to complement group learning, and take their music beyond the organisation, becoming active performers in the community at large. The very endurance of GFW and similar organisations is a testament to their resourcefulness, and they deserve closer scrutiny as places of successful music learning in the face of waxing and waning public funding. Expertise from these groups is now in demand more widely: the Scots Music Group partners other bodies in Edinburgh to 'offer opportunities

Figure 3.4 GFW members, John Wheatley College, 2016
(photo: GFW)

for vulnerable people in the community to take part in Scots music, song and dance';[18] Scottish Culture and Traditions in Aberdeen has developed partnerships with Aberdeen International Youth Festival and Aberdeen University; *Fèis Rois*, a 'National Youth Music Making Organisation' funded by the Youth Music Initiative, delivers traditional music in schools throughout the country.[19] These, like GFW and others, are now embedded in Scottish culture, and have a collective voice through the 'Traditional Music Forum'.[20]

The task is to negotiate routes between these diverse fields. In this way GFW provides a case study for how and why giving traditional music a voice at a national level should not neglect the nuances and particularities of local circumstances. Fleming (2004) has shown how such tensions have arisen in the case of *Comhaltas Ceoltóirí Éireann* in Ireland, and while top-down initiatives can play a positive role, they 'run the risk of being undermined by a complex set of issues including a lack of grassroots understanding, resources, control, and ownership that typically characterises approaches developed and implemented at the community level' (Grant, 2013, 4). In the case of the Louisiana *bals de maison* dance scene, as Mark DeWitt points out, the very nature of such voluntary and sometime short-lived ventures, unconstrained by educational bureaucracy, makes them well placed to respond to local need, and they should be seen in terms of much larger social networks (DeWitt, 2009). Transmission processes, however, may benefit from targeted support such as the identification of mentors:

> Experience has shown that if decisions are left to 'the market' and the random results of internecine politics, 'lessons learned' can be unlearned with breathtaking rapidity. Social and cultural capital painstakingly amassed by one generation or cohort can be thrown away by the next.
>
> (DeWitt, 2009, 31)

My research has highlighted ways in which different forms of evidence can demonstrate the cultural value of GFW, both for participants and wider society. While the arts are a form of capital in their own right, 'crucial to the aesthetic being in common of the life-world' (Dowling, 2008, 190), so-called third sector organisations such as GFW extend their influence beyond this, and should be understood as part of a greater social and musical ecology. The case study discussed here illustrates that professional performers and teachers are part of the same community of musical practice as adult learners, young musicians, dancers, singers and those who organise and promote traditional arts events. To sustain and advance this community and its music, cultural policy has an obligation to recognise the totality of activity, from professional bands to tutors, from local clubs to national organisations, since they are all interdependent. National cultural policy needs to facilitate rather than intervene in local organisations. While mass media and the mobility of teaching musicians have created a pan-Scottish canon, there are still strong associations with local repertoires, and new music being composed which community-based groups help to disseminate. Digital technological innovation has meant that musicians of all ages and abilities are the agents of their own learning, while also seeking social music making, and proximity to tutors and professional performers as role models. Music education at all levels in Scotland must work with understanding learning and teaching in traditional music in terms of cultural value, and further research is needed on how resources are accessed and used in a range of formats from tutor-led classes to online participatory culture. This is time-consuming labour, but as I heard one GFW musician say while practising playing tunes in sets, 'it's the joiny bits that need work'.

Notes

1 There is a growing body of literature on cultural value. See for example O'Brien (2013), Behr et al. (2014) and Crossick and Kaszynska (2016). Dunphy (2015) suggests a holistic framework for evaluating engagement in the arts which encompasses six domains: cultural, personal wellbeing, economic, ecological, social and civic.
2 'Community-based' arts may also be termed 'grassroots' activities (Ramsden et al., 2011)
3 http://www.glasgowfiddle.org.uk/ [Accessed 22.11.17]. GFW was re-named 'Glasgow Folk Music Workshop' in 2017.

4. Comparable organisations are the 'Scots Music Group' in Edinburgh www.scotsmusic.org/ and 'Scottish Culture and Traditions' in Aberdeen www.scottishculture.org/. See also Miller (2007) for a general overview of the teaching and learning of traditional music in Scotland.
5. Broad and France (2006, p. 4) aimed 'to map out the story of people who have taken part in *Fèisean*, and to ascertain how their participation has influenced their life, their career, and crucially, their attitude to the Gaelic language'. Martin (2006) is 'a social account of the development of a network of community-based initiatives described by people who participated in this process' (p. 9).
6. Traditional Music Forum (2017).
7. But see Cope (1999, 2002) for studies of Blackford Fiddle Group.
8. See Turino (2008) for features of participatory and presentational performance.
9. An eighteenth-century building restored in 1993 as a music heritage centre, but which closed in 2001.
10. To preserve participants' anonymity, quotes are attributed according to roles: T = tutor, F = fiddler, O = other (such as administrators and former tutors), P = participant.
11. The Youth Music Initiative, set up in 2003, is the national funding and development programme for young people and music in Scotland.
12. Founded in 1934, Stow was the first college of further education in Glasgow. GFW committee minutes from 2010 note intimations of its closure, which finally took place in 2016.
13. Miller and Duesenberry (2007, 10–11) note the importance of teaching work for the careers of the first graduates of the BA (Scottish Music) degree.
14. Posts previously titled 'education officer', for instance, are now 'learning and participation manager', and a substantial programme has raised the profile of artists working in 'participatory settings'. www.creativescotland.co.uk/explore/projects/artworks-scotland.
15. www.traditionalmusicforum.org/feis-rois-job/ (accessed 6.5.12).
16. The terms formal, non-formal and informal are now employed in such varying ways in relation to both settings and learning processes for music that they may not offer the best approach to studying any context in which music is transmitted.
17. GFW says: 'Teaching centres on Scottish traditional music although our tutors do introduce students to other related styles and traditions, such as Irish, American, English, Shetland and Scandinavian. This places Scotland's music within a broader cultural context and helps learners to understand why musical traditions from across the country vary in style and history.' (GFW Annual Reports 2012–15).
18. www.inspirescotsmusic.org.uk//
19. http://feisrois.org.uk/index.php?lang=eng&location=traditional_music_in_schools_project (accessed 22.11.16).
20. The TMF now has 94 members ('News and Views', TMF Newsletter November 2016) http://us4.campaign-archive1.com/?u=746aa7b23f2326fb1f60f592a&id=d097a0c2b6 (accessed 22.11.16).

4 The emergence of the 'traditional arts' in Scottish cultural policy

David Francis

My focus in this account will be mainly on the historical emergence of a cultural policy framework for traditional music in Scotland. The progress in public policy terms of the other performative traditional arts, storytelling and dance, intersects with music at various points but each of those have had their own separate development paths. In this necessarily brief account I have not addressed other policy initiatives, for example Cultural Co-ordinators, the Youth Music Initiative or the Cultural Commission, which have had an impact on the arts in Scotland as a whole. Nor have I attended to the Culture Bill which was pending before the Labour administration lost office in 2007 and which contained some interesting ideas which were not picked up by the incoming SNP government.

I want to begin with two important contextual matters which affected attitudes towards the development of traditional music in public policy: the National Companies and the twin 'mythic constructs' (Craig, 1982) of the Kailyard and Tartanry.

The national companies – the RSNO, Scottish Opera, the Scottish Chamber Orchestra and Scottish Ballet all began to come to the forefront of the arts in Scotland in the '60s and '70s. The SNO (as it then was) began to develop an international profile under Alexander Gibson in the '60s, and the same Alexander Gibson founded Scottish Opera in 1962. A Bristol-based ballet company, Western Theatre Ballet, migrated to Scotland in 1969, changed its name to Scottish Theatre Ballet, and became Scottish Ballet in 1974, the same year that the Scottish Chamber Orchestra was founded.

Despite the Scottish epithet in these organisations' titles there was little Scottish content in their programmes. Their presence was less about a distinctive Scottish contribution to metropolitan and cosmopolitan cultural production and more about having that production on the doorstep, available to a Scottish middle class audience that recoiled from indigenous Scottish expression, seeing in it the parochial taints of Tartanry and the Kailyard.

'Kailyard' was originally the description of a whole school of writing characterised by sentimentality, an idealisation of rural life and a certain kind of Scottish character. Despite the popularity of the authors associated with the school like J.M. Barrie and S.R. Crockett, their production was seen as describing a false picture which celebrated restricted horizons and limited ambition (Craig, 1982; McArthur, 1982; Weinberger, 2006). The kailyard was the cabbage patch: homely fare, plain yet sustaining, produced close to home, sufficient for modest needs and emphasising caricatured aspects of a Scottish character: dour, canny, shrewd and all the rest of it. It was mocked and attacked by writers such as Hugh MacDiarmid who excoriated its sentimentality and attacked it for its limited horizons.

The other distorting reflection in the hall of mirrors of Scottish identity was Tartanry, a cultural descendent of Walter Scott's romantic Highlander given shape through the likes of Harry Lauder, *Brigadoon* and other Hollywood idealisations, and the hugely popular mid-twentieth-century BBC television series, the *White Heather Club*.

Traditional music and song were lumped into these identity myths, any distinctions in origin, practice and reception lost in the un-nuanced world of the mass media. The world of letters was no better disposed. Hugh MacDiarmid wrote of the 'boring doggerel of analphabetic and ineducable farm-labourers, tinkers and the like' (Finlay, 1996), while Norman MacCaig asserted that it could be of no interest to him 'because I have read Homer' (Gibson, 2015). The national companies might have 'Scottish' in their titles, but association with the kailyard and tartanry was greatly to be feared and certainly to be avoided. Nothing was more likely to mark you out as unsophisticated and parochial in a world where London and America were the key reference points.

However, the folk revival was gathering strength even as the national companies were taking the stage. It was beginning to assert its interests, on behalf of a tradition perhaps, but certainly in its own interests as a developing constituency of 'folk' in its own right, following Alan Dundes's famous definition 'any group of people whatsoever who share at least one common factor' (Dundes, 1965). The common factor was an interest in researching, distributing, emulating, drawing on for artistic purposes, performing and, crucially, advocating for the music and song of those very same farm-labourers, sailors, tinkers, and industrial workers (male and female) belittled by those whom E. P. Thompson described in a letter to Hamish Henderson as 'the culture boys' (Finlay, 1996, 28).

The folk revival in Scotland from the '60s onwards was beginning to coalesce as a definable network within Scottish culture with an infrastructure of performance platforms of clubs and festivals, record labels, publications and in 1966 its first fully fledged membership organisation in the Traditional Music and Song Association (TMSA) (Munro, 1996).

Despite the growing systematisation of this community of interest it enjoyed minimal recognition or support from the Scottish Arts Council, which kept its focus on classical music (and that music's line of succession), literature, drama, dance and contemporary visual art, with the national companies taking the lion's share of its resources. By the late '70s there was a recognition, however, that not everything fitted into the canonical categories, due to a changing cultural awareness, inspired perhaps by the changing political awareness prompted by the frustrations of the 1979 Assembly referendum. There was a growing community arts movement, there were ethnic arts,[1] and there was cross art-form experimentation. In order to deal with these new developments the SAC had set up a 'Mixed Programme Committee'. This committee had also turned its attention to the question of 'heritage', noting an upsurge in interest in building conservation, local history, crafts and customs (Scottish Arts Council, 1984). Support for this field lay outwith SAC's responsibilities. However, the case was made that the *intangible* aspects of heritage were SAC's responsibility, as acknowledged by the limited amount of support being given to the traditional arts at that time.[2]

Interestingly, one of the foundations of SAC's concern was with a growing re-assessment of Scottish identity and prevailing perceptions of 'Scottishness'; here the horror of Tartanry raised its head once again. An alternative to 'romantic Victorian notions and *cultural debasements* such as those manifested through Haggis and Tartan nights in tourist hotels and networked Hogmanay TV shows' was being sought (SAC, 1984, author's emphasis). If there was little of Scottish identity to be found in the work of the national companies and too much of a certain kind in popular entertainment there had to be some kind of expression of Scottish identity that could be supported without embarrassment.

SAC had to know what it was dealing with. This was unfamiliar territory and it had to be surveyed, so in 1981 a Working Party was set up principally 'to consider the current state of the traditional and folk arts of Scotland and to advise SAC on the most effective ways in which indigenous artistic activities can be fostered, developed and encouraged'. It was also charged with assessing opportunities for performing artists, the state of the archive, and the platforms, including mass media, from which the traditional arts could be made more accessible. The language question, a persistent and universal feature of cultural policy, was also considered, with Scotland's indigenous languages being seen as 'fundamental to the performance and development of the traditional arts' (SAC, 1984, 8).

The group, which included ethnologist Hamish Henderson, the musicians Eddie McGuire and Aly Bain and Gaelic poet Aonghas MacNeacail, reported in 1984. It took a broad view of its area of study, reaching beyond the folk revival to include Gaelic music, piping and country dancing. Its recommendations were not only directed at the Scottish Arts Council, but at the wider policy environment including secondary and tertiary education, media, minority languages, copyright, and infrastructure.

Within SAC, traditional music and dance came under the care of the Mixed Programme Committee's successor, the Combined Arts Department under its director John Murphy. Murphy had come to Scotland from the Arts Council of Northern Ireland, where attitudes towards traditional music were much less cagey. In order to take some of the Working Party's recommendations forward, he argued for a more professionalised role for the TMSA and released funds which enabled it to employ a salaried development worker for the first time. The attention the traditional arts were getting did not always go down well with colleagues in the late 1980s. Murphy recounts how he was confronted by the then head of the drama department, quivering with indignation and shouting 'What are you trying to do? Take us back to the kailyard?' (Murphy, 2015).

Again we see the Kailyard being invoked as an anti-modern synecdoche for a Scottish culture stranded outside the powerful currents of the canon and modernism. But the increasing confidence and scope of musicians working in the revival context in particular showed an understanding of Scotland's traditional culture that went beyond the dead-end romanticism of Tartanry and the limited ambition of the Kailyard. It could speak to a Scotland thrown into turmoil by deindustrialisation and increasing alienation from the UK's political centre. Musicians like the Battlefield Band, the Easy Club, Billy Jackson and Dick Gaughan were belying the pessimism of statements such as this from Cairns Craig: 'the problem that these mythic structures [i.e. Tartanry and the Kailyard] have left to twentieth-century Scottish art is that there are no tools which the artist can inherit from the past which are not tainted, warped, blunted by the uses to which they have been put' (Craig, 1982).

The effects of the SAC Working Party and the heightened profile it gave to the traditional arts within official discourse were noticeable in the publication of the next milestone in arts policy in Scotland, *The Charter for the Arts*. The Charter came at a time when there was a feeling that the arts were being taken seriously 'as an aspect of public policy and economic development, and a major responsibility of local government' (McMillan, 1993). Glasgow's programme for its role as European City of Culture in 1990 had cracked open the notion of what 'the arts' encompassed. Traditional music had taken its place alongside Frank Sinatra, the Bolshoi Ballet, comedy, Brecht and Shakespeare, rock bands and ceilidh dances. The Charter, which was intended as a guiding document for SAC, the Museums and Film Councils, and local authorities,[3] took this broad definition to heart and opened up Arts Council policy to hitherto excluded practices such as amateur drama and some aspects of traditional arts, such as traditional dance. 'Scotland's cultural heritage in *all its forms* should be preserved, augmented and made accessible to the public,' stated the Charter's principles (McMillan, 1993, 5).

A sharp wind of change had blown in the windows and was ruffling the velvet curtains and turning up the corners of the red carpet. The change is exemplified by the Charter's author, Joyce McMillan:

> There is a sense in which the distinctions between high and low culture are doubly discredited in Scotland, because of the role they have often played in disparaging and marginalising aspects of Scottish culture and language. It is difficult to defend conventional cultural categories in a nation which has experienced 300 years of hearing its own languages described either as a barbaric, primitive tongue (Gaelic) or as a degraded and incorrect form of English (Scots) [. . .]; difficult to justify an arts funding structure which gives so little support to Scotland's great inheritance of traditional music and dance [particularly when] we are in the middle of 'something of a renaissance' in Scottish traditional music, crafts, language and storytelling.
>
> (McMillan, 1993, 17)

The consultation process for the Charter brought up an often repeated proposal for, if not a separate 'Traditional Arts Council', at least a department within SAC, modelled on the lines of the Irish arts councils, dedicated to the sector. This idea was rejected in favour of an arrangement which promoted 'maximum cross-fertilisation between Scotland's traditional arts and other sectors' (McMillan, 1993, 34).

The Charter had effectively given the Scottish Arts Council the task of taking a more active role. The question of how best to support traditional music in particular was still moot, however. The then Music Director of SAC, Matthew Rooke (who as a Berklee-trained jazz and rock musician had been the first appointee to the post from outside the classical world) instigated a series of consultations on the feasibility of a development agency of some kind for traditional music (Cudmore, 1995). The proposal was strongly resisted by several influential figures within traditional music who argued that there were still questions of equal status and respect for traditional music to be answered, and that these were best answered by SAC continuing to assume responsibility for it.

The consultation had, however, pointed to three broad areas of concern, namely 'Education, Information and Advocacy' and how, in the absence of a separate development agency, these might best be approached not only by SAC but by the traditional music community itself.

The task of exploring this question fell to me, and a comprehensive conversation started that took me from Stranraer to Shetland, South Uist, Skye to the Scottish Borders and all points in between. I took the decision that the definition of traditional music should be the widest possible and brought in the institutions of the revival but also piping, dance bands, strathspey and reel societies, musicians who had worked in tartan entertainment. This is because for all the criticism and strictures against Tartanry it does have a grounding in traditional culture, and in the case of the much-maligned White Heather Club an ethos of conviviality and hospitality which surely lies at the heart of traditional culture.[4]

The report (Francis, 1999) was published in 1999 just months before the opening of the Scottish Parliament, about to be reconvened after a gap of some 300 years. It fed into the new Scottish government's first cultural strategy 'Creating our Future . . . Minding our Past' (2000) and released an additional £1.5m for traditional music over three years.

One of the recommendations of the report was that the work of existing organisations such as the TMSA, Fèisean nan Gàidheal, the Scots Music Group and others should have their support from SAC enhanced in order to allow them to carry out their work more effectively. Some of that £1.5m went in that direction and organisations were able to expand their activities and their staff. However, in 2008, after a period in which the original additional funds had become mainstreamed, SAC changed its funding schemes and several of the organisations which had benefited from enhanced support found themselves cut back or even cut out in some cases. The resulting clamour brought protests to the door of the Parliament itself, a Parliament now controlled by the Scottish National Party.

There had been a sense in which Scottish culture had been seen with a certain degree of wariness by the Labour Party in Scotland. The traditional arts in particular were seen as something of a 'nationalist shibboleth' to use a phrase coined by the inaugural First Minister, Donald Dewar. His successor Jack McConnell's St Andrews Day Speech in 2003 in which the arts were touted as 'our next great undertaking' was 'the first time that any senior politician in Scotland had even mentioned culture like they meant it, let alone expressed a political commitment to its value' (Bonnar, 2012). The arrival of the SNP in government brought a feeling that that commitment was about to change and that the traditional arts were going with the grain of official thinking.

In response to the lobbying occasioned by the SAC cuts – and, of broader strategic importance, the imminent creation of the new cultural development and funding body Creative Scotland – the Culture Secretary Linda Fabiani announced the formation of a Ministerial Working Group on Traditional Arts. Its remit was to consider future support requirements for the field. The group reported in 2010 (Scottish Government, 2010), the year of Creative Scotland's foundation. By that time the government was on its third Culture Secretary in little over a year. The door to that office had been something of a revolving one since 1999, but Fiona Hyslop, the Secretary who considered the report, is still the incumbent (at the time of writing). Her tenure has been notable for a series of speeches in recent times which not only advocate for the intrinsic value of artistic practice and expression, but for the embedding of cultural policy in every other aspect of government policy.

The Minister's response to the Working Group Report (2010) was positive and detailed, with much of the responsibility for carrying out the recommendations given to the newly fledged Creative Scotland. This was a reversal of the process which followed the 1999 report, commissioned as it was by an arm's length public body which then took some of its recommendations to government and advocated action on them. But here we had government commissioning an investigation (it also had concurrent working groups on literature and Scots language) and requiring Creative Scotland, the 'non-departmental public body', to implement its recommendations and to report back to the Minister on progress.

As with all three of the reports some recommendations have been acted on fairly quickly while others lie under the mountain, like King Arthur's sleeping knights, waiting for the right time or the right champion to animate them. With regard to the 1999 report, commentators such as folklorist Ian A. Olson (2007) noted that little seemed to have come of it, particularly on the advocacy side of things. One is reminded of Chou En Lai's celebrated crack when asked about the effects of the French Revolution. 'Too early to say' was his answer. In fact, around the time that Olson was writing his review of contemporary developments in the traditional arts, a group which had been convened informally by the Scottish Arts Council in order to advise it in the aftermath of the 1999 report was on its way to becoming formally constituted.

Largely as a result of this new momentum, *The Traditional Music Forum*[5] went from being an advisory group to a network of around ninety traditional music organisations across Scotland from academic institutions to community music groups, clubs, festivals, labels and venues. It provides an information flow from, to and within the network, serves as a point of contact for traditional music in Scotland, and contributes to the policy environment in fields such as cultural policy, formal and non-formal education, cultural tourism, intangible cultural heritage and social enterprise.

One of the recommendations of the 2010 report was that consideration should be given to the creation of a broader traditional arts network, bringing together music with dance and storytelling. Work on this has been progressing since 2012 with the result that the music forum has been joined by a recently constituted *Traditional Dance Forum* and the existing *Scottish Storytelling Forum* to make *TRACS (Traditional Arts and Culture Scotland)* which advocates for all the traditional arts and brings them together in practical expression through a programme of courses and workshops and two festivals, Tradfest Edinburgh and the Scottish International Storytelling Festival.

TRACS is funded by Creative Scotland, which through its Traditional Arts Advisory Group is still monitoring the obligations put on it as a result of the Working Group. In the meantime the national companies, joined now by a fifth one in the National Theatre of Scotland, have come under the direct control of the Scottish Government. Whether they might be joined by a sixth dedicated to the traditional arts of Scotland is a question for further debate.

Notes

1 Around this time SAC published a report into minority ethnic arts (Harding, 1982).
2 In the year prior to the Working Group's report, SAC granted a total of £92,220 to projects that could be broadly defined as 'traditional arts', with further guarantees against loss of £10,789. However, £85,345 of the grant total was awarded to publishing and literary projects. £6075 was awarded to music, of which £5850 went to the National Mòd. The bulk of the guarantees against loss were for folk festivals, and one-off folk club concerts. (Scottish Arts Council, 1984: 23).
3 It is notable that central government is absent from this list. The Scottish Arts Council was at this time an autonomous body within the Arts Council of Great Britain and as such at 'arm's length' from government.
4 That broad approach has continued to be upheld by the producers of the annual Scots Trad Music Awards and is reflected in its categories.
5 The Traditional Music Forum began in 2004 as an ad hoc advisory group for the Scottish Arts Council. It was a closed group comprising many of the leading figures in traditional music at that time. The Forum changed to a constituted membership organisation in 2009.

5 'Eun Bheag Chanaidh' where the Gaelic arts and non-traditional theatre meet
A song discussion

Fiona J. Mackenzie

O mo dhùthaich

O mo dhùthaich, 's tu th'air m' aire,
Uibhist chùbhraidh, ùr nan gallan
Far am faicte na daoin' uaisle
'S far bu dual do Mhac 'ic Ailein
(Oh my land, you're always in my thoughts
Fresh, fragrant Uist, home of heroes
Where the noble people live
Hereditary territory of Clanranald).

'O Mo Dhùthaich' ('Oh My Land') is the first song in the unique collection of Hebridean folklore, *Folksongs and Folklore of South Uist*, compiled by American folklorist Margaret Fay Shaw (1955). The song describes the feelings of a South Uist man who had emigrated to Canada and it is probably the most well-known of all those she collected during her seven years spent in the Outer Hebrides from 1929. That this child of a wealthy merchant from Pittsburgh, USA, should make it her life's work to compile such a collection is fascinating in itself, but more important than her motivation is the question of its legacy and its relevance to our appreciation and understanding of the folklore, music and song of the Gaels, and of the cultural contexts which nurtured it. In this chapter I seek to address such questions by reflecting on the collecting work of Margaret Fay Shaw and her husband, John Lorne Campbell, as one example of how today's contemporary artistic processes can be affected and effected by past creativity. Specifically, I will discuss practical examples of creative work I have produced over recent years in Scotland inspired by the collections of the Campbells, and in particular a project undertaken in partnership with the National Theatre of Scotland (NTS). It is hoped that these ideas and principles of creativity which have drawn inspiration from the cultural legacy of the past could be transferred to any indigenous culture or country.

Margaret Fay Shaw was born in Pittsburgh, USA, of Scottish descent and following the death of both of her parents, was sent by her family to Scotland in 1919, as a 16-year-old, to attend St Bride's school in Helensburgh.

Figure 5.1 Margaret Fay Shaw 1935

There was little hint of the direction her life was to take until one night she was taken to a classical recital by the Scottish singer and folksong collector, Marjorie Kennedy Fraser, where she heard for the first time some of the Gaelic songs this formidable collector had arranged, albeit in a style far removed from their original form. Kennedy Fraser's approach to the musical arrangement and performance of the material she collected has been the subject of much contention, most Scottish commentators considering her use of standard Western classical musical 'clothing' in which to dress the songs as little short of a travesty. Those looking in from the outside, however, tended to be rather more positive, and her work attracted the attention of some of the key modernist cultural figures of the day. For Ezra Pound, for instance,

> These traditional melodies of the Gael are among the musical riches of all time, and one need use no comparatives and no tempered adjectives to express the matter. They have in them the wildness of the sea and of the wind and the shrillness of the sea-birds, and whether they will pass away utterly with the present industrious collector I am unable to say.
>
> (Pound and Schafer, 1978).

In contrast to that vote of confidence, on the other hand, is one modern day performer's assertion that 'most Gaelic-speakers . . . would argue that the obstinate refusal of their culture to "pass away utterly" owes little to the industry of Kennedy Fraser' (Gillies, 2007).

However, for all the criticisms and perceived failings of Kennedy Fraser, some recent revisionist considerations of her work have challenged the conventional dismissive view, arguing instead that she produced a good deal more of value than has hitherto been recognised. As Ahlander has asserted, 'Though still frequently maligned, her songs have been the subject of renewed interest in recent years, and have slowly begun to take their place among European art songs of the period' (Ahlander, 2008, 3). Whatever our personal stance on this debate, there can be no doubt that Kennedy Fraser was the catalyst which led Margaret Fay Shaw to her own musical mission, as she set about tracing these songs back to their traditional forms.

Her musical career from then on was wide and varied, taking her from her Pittsburgh home to the operatic scenes of Paris to the jazz circles of New York where she studied classical piano and learned notation, a vital skill for her future recording of the Gaelic songs of the Hebrides. When she finally returned to Britain in 1924, she spent a month on the island of Skye becoming increasingly intrigued by the sound of the Gaelic language and its songs. She returned to New York for two years but her determination to go to the Outer Hebrides did not diminish and so in 1926, she set off with a friend to cycle to the islands. Their initial journey took them through Barra, Eriskay, the Uists and Harris, ending up in Stornoway and from thence to further study in London, Paris and Ireland. After a bout of rheumatism which put paid to her plans of becoming a concert pianist, she returned to Glenshaw, Pittsburgh, where she announced that she was going to live in the Uists.

In 1929 her enthusiasm was further captured when she heard Peggy MacRae sing an old Gaelic song in Boisdale House and asked her to teach it to her (Shaw, 1955, 58). That song was 'O Mo Dhùthaich', the opening song above. From there she moved in with Peggy and her sister, Màiri, who lived in a tiny traditional croft house in North Glendale, South Uist, called Taigh Màiri Anndra.

She there spent the next seven years travelling through the Uists, Eriskay, Mingulay, Barra, the Aran Islands and St Kilda, just before it was finally evacuated by its residents in 1930. Manually transcribing the songs and stories she heard, her musical education, whilst being of huge help to her, also had to be largely ignored, laying aside basics such as major and minor scales and instead listening to modes which were unfamiliar and very strange to her. In her own words,

> I had to learn to listen outside of what I had ever heard before, because, even though I took down the tunes as accurately as I possibly could, I couldn't get certain half tones that were in it, and nobody can tell except the singer, and then she couldn't read the music!
>
> (Shaw, 1993, 81)

She also became one of the first female photographers to record a disappearing culture and lifestyle, with both black and white stills and even more revolutionary, with colour film. She undertook to learn to speak Gaelic, understanding that to accurately record the sounds she heard and the syllabic stresses on words, she needed to feel at home with the language and familiar with the rhythms of the verbal texts. Living in the remote glens of Uist was not an easy life and certainly not the lifestyle in which she had been brought up, but to Margaret this was the true and only method of learning about the lifestyle she was so determined to uncover and record. Unlike collectors before her, Margaret never undertook her work from an anthropological point of view – it was just for the pure enjoyment:

> I loved the songs. The tunes were heavenly. They appreciated the fact that I didn't want the songs that were well known. I wanted their own everyday songs, songs that they sang when they rocked the cradle or worked the spinning wheel.
>
> (1993, 81)

She transcribed the songs as accurately as she could, more so than most Scottish folklorists had done to date. Her initial transcriptions, before she learned the language, were understandably phonetic in character. For example, this song here, written as 'Se t-churam' eventually became 'Se Diuram'.

> Se Diuram, Se Diuram, Se Diuram ho ro
> Se Diuram Se Diuram Se Diuram ho e
> Se Diuram a hiu ree ree hu ro bha ho
> Se Diuram an t-Uasal Mac Ruaraidh nan airm.

She did at least recognise the importance of the final versions being completely accurate in content and style.

Her inherent awareness of how important the prosodic and hermeneutic value of the words and her unusual empathy with a strange language was what made her collected songs so unusual in their authenticity and still are to this day.

In 1934, Margaret met folklorist John Lorne Campbell of Argyll, Campbell of Inverneill, and they found a common bond in their passion for folklore. After their marriage, together they helped to rescue vast quantities of traditional poems and songs from oblivion over the coming years. They made their home at Northbay on the island of Barra in a small corrugated iron roofed house, with her Steinway grand piano, sent by steamer to Castlebay.

During their time on Barra, the strains of piano duets by Beethoven, Rossini and Mozart could often be heard wafting over the machair (1993, 139). It was this complete diversity of culture that inspired me to begin work on a creative piece of musical drama which would eventually become *Little Bird Blown Off Course*. The bulk of this work centred around research undertaken on the Isle of Canna which Margaret and John had bought in 1938 with the intention of establishing a profitable farm business and a centre of Culture and Gaelic.

Many other well-known and indeed world renowned musicians, composers, artists and writers were frequent visitors to Canna House, for Margaret loved to have art around her at all times, music at the centre of it but with an all-encompassing love of creativity surrounding her.

Scots Gaelic poet and writer, Angus Peter Campbell too, wrote of Margaret and her life's legacy to us:

Margaret Fay Shaw, a sparrow from Pennsylvania

Alighted in North Glendale and sang
A song that reached me, swinging in the making
Generations on; èisd ris a seo, mo ghràidh.
O ba o I, o mo leanabh
Ba o I, o mo ghaol
Caidil thusa shùgh mo chèille
Cuma slàn a dh'èireas tu.

(Chaimbeul, 2002: unpublished)

Margaret Fay Shaw died in 2004 at the age of 101 and her legacy to not only the Scots Gaelic folklore world but also the world's folklore in general is one of major stature and importance.

Gifted by the Campbells to the National Trust for Scotland (NTS) in 1981, Canna and its treasures have until recent times been relatively 'closed' to those outside of academia, and general knowledge of Margaret's collections has tended to have been restricted to those 109 songs and those photos included in *Folksongs and Folklore of South Uist*.

The Canna archives, until 2015 in the care of the dedicated and inspirational archivist Magda Sagarzazu, comprise one of the world's most astounding collections of Gaelic and Scottish folklore and historical artefacts as well as collections of other native folklore and in particular John Campbell's incredible collections of archive sound recordings. He was also acutely interested in the natural heritage of the island, especially butterflies and moths, building up one of the world's most complete and stunning collections of lepidoptera.

Margaret Fay Shaw Campbell described herself as 'a little bird blown off course' and that was my inspiration for what became a unique piece of Gaelic music theatre, developed as work in progress during 2013/14 by The NTS. As Gaelic Associate Artist for that organisation in 2012, I was invited to develop a piece based on a subject of my own choice. Given my lifelong fascination for Margaret's work, I had no hesitation in selecting her as my subject.

The production, with myself as lead artist, was the first of its kind in relation to the Canna archives and entailed working with a team of technical and production staff as well as an internationally known theatre dramaturg. Spending extended periods on Canna researching the archives, with the archivist's invaluable help, I made a contemporary video 'storyboard' of the island, its collection and of Margaret and John's life. The resources at our disposal on the island were rich indeed: we were able to make use of John's archived audio field recordings, Margaret's black and white stills and film, images of the original hand written transcriptions from the 1930s, as well as excerpts from her personal letters and notes. Using authentic period musical and 'film' props such as an original Edison recording machine (uncovered in a barn in Ardnamurchan) with the presence of a live band of some of Scotland's finest traditional musicians, the team created a musical and visually vibrant accessible storyboard telling of the importance of regeneration, and of the passing down of cultures and languages.

The aim was to create a high quality 'work in progress' show that would be easily accessible by non-Gaelic speakers, of all ages, as well as being of inherent interest to learners and native speakers of the language alike. We also wished to create a 'devised' piece of music theatre without the device of the traditional script. Our aim in this regard was to allow the music and the images to tell the story, rather than use the skills of a script writer who we feared might place a twist on the story which was not compatible with the aims of the NTS or which were at odds with my own or crucially, with those of the Campbells. I underwent a steep learning curve in the process of working with the dramaturg rather than with a producer and for the first time learned how to analyse and develop an idea from the base level of a raw artefact. The script was essentially a giant Excel spreadsheet, taking up a whole wall with the cells formatted from A4 sheets of paper. This became the focal point of my fascination with the 'collage' style of creative practice in which the focus of a project becomes part of a kaleidoscope effect, with edges of infinity blurred and intrinsic values and criteria, sharpened.

I also composed a new Gaelic song for the show as well as producing new arrangements of some of these ancient songs. The infrastructure of the NTS enabled me to work closely with some of Scotland's best musicians and producers to create a score of high quality and innovation. Input from set designers, wardrobe and lighting designers gave scope for providing stimulus for all of the senses of the audience and highlighting subtle points of meaning in the story.

Video art portrayed how songs are passed down through the generations in a process of vertical transmission and involved contributions from many singers, established and less well known, drawn from communities across the Highlands, and as well as international artists.

The overall message of 'Eun Bheag Chanaidh, (literally 'The Little Bird of Canna') was, 'Pass it on and keep it alive'.

The underlying message was that this should be applicable not only for Gaelic but for all indigenous cultures, all over the world. That if one petite, determined woman from Pennsylvania can learn our language, from source and leave an incredibly valuable and precious legacy of Scottish folklore to the world, then so too can anyone.

It is refreshing that a national creative arts company has the confidence and trust in artists to produce a piece of development work with no more to start with than a few black and white pictures and some scrappy song transcriptions. It is my opinion that for too long, Gaelic or traditional music and folklore has tended to be sidelined into the 'quaint or cute or folksy' arts category, when considered in the drama spotlight. The NTS has the creative foresight to understand that a story can be told in a contemporary, exciting and 'mainstream' manner whilst still being respectful of the subject matter and people – if our language and culture is to survive it needs to become more than an excuse for just 'another ceilidh or song about a drowning'.

The Theatre see 'no barriers'. The company had the confidence in me and my place in the Gaelic Arts, to develop a piece of work which had a direct message for audiences – a production which could be realised on different levels, as a piece of beautiful traditional music or as an exciting work with a powerful message of the need to regard our precious heritage as a living breathing entity, which can project a powerful message of identity and future worth as well as produce new work developed from the old. The show toured the eight Highland venues in 2013 including Canna and South Uist and played to two sell out audiences at the Tron Theatre in Glasgow as part of the international Celtic Connections Festival.

There were some very definite potential 'barriers' for this production including the vagaries of West Coast and Highland weather, ferry timetables, loading two tons of gear, manually down dangerous steps in the fishing port of Mallaig. Weather delayed flights in the Hebrides, and we performed in an island venue which had streams of water running through the electrics and a lack of accommodation for the team, on an island which had eleven residents.

But the NTS had a simple ethos – if it's appropriate, we'll make it happen. A story worth doing, is worth doing well. With the exception of the musicians, all of the team were non Gaelic speakers, but their enthusiasm, commitment and determination 'to make it work and work well', was compellingly refreshing. We need to examine how the Gaelic arts have evolved traditionally: 40 years ago the national arts were generally not interested in Gaelic, but with the evolution of BBC Alba and social media, interest has increased in the public arena.

Other examples

A body such as the NTS has shown its willingness to engage with the Gaelic world, but the Gaelic world may also need to be reminded that it should be really ready and willing to grasp the opportunity and engage in such opportunities from all perspectives.

May 2015 saw the NTS produce the online worldwide streaming for 24 hours of pieces of '5 Minute Theatre – the Yes No Don't Know Show' based on the theme of independence, whatever that means to the individual. Of the 180 pieces selected for broadcast, my own piece 'An Drochaid' based on the inspirational words of Gaelic poetess and political activist, Màiri Mhòr nan Oran, was the only Gaelic contribution.

Why should this be? This was not because the company did not want more Gaelic work, but because there was a distinct lack of Gaelic contribution. Opportunities such as this need to identified, absorbed and exploited by the Gaelic arts world.

In 2014 and 2015 I also developed a new self-composed piece and 'promenade music theatre', entitled 'An Sgàthan/The Mirror', based on my Master's degree

Figure 5.2 Promenade walk on grassy track

project. This work comprised the composition of a Gaelic song cycle, using seven of the songs collected by Margaret Fay Shaw as inspiration for the composition of seven 'mirror' songs, all based on the same subject matter or style as the traditional songs. These fourteen songs provided the framework for a 45-minute dramatic promenade performance held first in South Uist at Taigh Màiri Anndra (of the traditional songs) followed by a formal concert of the new material and then on the beach and in the arts centre on Canna itself. The walls of Taigh Màiri Anndra heard the traditional words for the first time in nearly eighty years. All of the songs were influenced by the environment in which they were originally composed: the same sounds, scenes, communities and animals were evoked. This project was a direct result of the confidence I gained during my formal experiences with the NTS.

Conclusion

Arts and heritage communities should remember that a story such as that of Margaret and John Campbell needs to be constantly considered and not taken for granted. These stories provide us with an insight to ourselves, to our communities and to our lives, in both historical and contemporary contexts. It provides us with a fascinating glimpse of an unusual life, of two remarkable people who shared a zest for, and understanding of, an adopted culture. The outcome is one which can inspire many of the national arts bodies of music, dance, film and drama to dig deeper and find stories to retell in adventurous ways to future audiences, to find identity for our future generations. They must be inspired to use that precious legacy of collection and develop new material for new audiences.

The curators of the Canna Collection, situated in Canna House, the National Trust for Scotland, are about to begin an intensive and far reaching programme of renovation and development work on the house and its treasures, to make the collections accessible to all, to academia and to the wider world. An ambitious and exciting interpretation programme will open up the sound archives, the butterflies, the maps, the incredible library of Celtic folklore, the Native American collection, the hundreds of songs and stories, and the flora and fauna of the island of Canna. All of these can provide a wealth of stimulus for new creative work if artists and funders are willing to consider new ways and techniques of using traditional material.

A poignant and telling comment was made by a senior audience member at the premiere of 'Little Bird', in St Peter's Hall in South Uist. When I was approached after the performance, she said 'Nis a 'chaileag, (Now lassie) I've got just one thing to say to you. Thank you for giving us back these songs. We had forgotten we had them'.

All photographs are the property of the author and the Canna Collection, the National Trust for Scotland.

6 Referendum reflections

Traditional music and the performance of politics in the campaign for Scottish independence

Mairi McFadyen

Introduction

September 2014 saw the culmination of a two-year referendum campaign for Scottish independence. Over three and a half million people expressed their views on the national question, 'Should Scotland be an independent country?' with the majority voting to remain part of the United Kingdom. Thousands of people were actively engaged in campaigning, mobilising the highest turnout of eligible voters for any political event in decades. Almost all commentators have agreed that the political spirit and activism that the national referendum awoke in Scotland was extremely positive, transforming the political and cultural landscape through a large-scale participatory and democratic process. Beyond the mainstream cross-party Yes Campaign – which was dominated by the Scottish National Party (SNP) – emergent groups such as National Collective (the 'non-party movement for artists and creatives who support Scottish independence'), the Radical Independence Campaign (RIC), Women for Independence and the Common Weal, to name a few, created alternative spaces for responding to the debate beyond the typical media focus. As well as standard activity such as canvassing and public meetings, the referendum provoked many other embodied and creative ways of engaging in the debate, both online via social media and in community contexts. Numerous grassroots events dedicated to exploring the issues around the referendum took place in village halls and communities all over the country. Many artists engaged with and creatively responded to the political context; music, spoken word, visual art, theatre and film were used as ways of celebrating and exploring the possibilities of taking the first steps to creating a more equal society – whether separate from, or as a part of, the United Kingdom. Bissell and Overend, in their reflections on the role of theatre in this process, argue that the referendum became the 'catalyst for a large-scale "relational aesthetic" to emerge' and that the 'performances' of the referendum had a particular value in creating autonomous relational spaces for participants to 'rehearse and formulate their individual politics' (2015, 250).

By 2014, almost all public political statements from traditional musicians advocated an independent Scotland, a trend which reflected the wider arts community in Scotland as whole. In one sense, the explicit political agenda of the referendum led to a very open acknowledgement of antagonisms and disagreement; in another, the heavily pro-independence voice of the arts community at large may have obscured the opinions of those within it who were less committed, or indeed, directly opposed. It could simply be that voices for the 'No' vote were reluctant to participate in such rigorous public debate. Whether or not the very public alignment of the traditional music community with support for independence in cultural and political discourse gives a skewed view of the opinions of the whole community, it is certainly true to say that not since the Scottish Folk Revival and anti-Polaris movement of the 1960s has this community been so politically active. At the time of writing, the conditions for the second referendum are emerging in the aftermath of Brexit; it is therefore a fitting time to reflect on this stage of the journey.

Drawing very much on my own experience as an activist and campaigner, this chapter offers a personal critical reflection on the role that traditional music and song played in the 'performance' of the 2014 referendum campaign. For my part, I am a supporter of Scottish independence, voted Yes and was heavily invested in the outcome. With broad support from key actors in the wider traditional arts community, I took a lead role in catalysing a campaigning group of 'traditional artists for independence' called *TradYES*, contributed written articles to the emerging cultural discourse and was actively involved as a national organiser for the campaign group National Collective. This chapter, then, reflects how vocal pro-independence members of the traditional arts community responded to this new and highly political context and highlights some of the various ways and contexts in and through which traditional music was used to galvanise support and encourage action in the months leading up to the vote. Using performance as a relational framework,[1] in the Schechnerian sense that 'any behaviour, event, action, or thing can be studied "as" performance' (2015, 32), I offer some observations on how traditional music was mobilised during this time as a social force for the performance of cultural politics, identities, shared vision, aspirations and values, transforming this community's sense of what politics is capable of, and of music's political agency within a political context.

An emerging vision

In May 2013, TRACS (Traditional Arts and Culture Scotland), a new cultural organisation supporting the traditional arts networks of storytelling, music and dance, hosted a discursive event called 'Open Fields'. This brought together members of the traditional arts community to explore the question, 'What now and what next for the traditional arts in Scotland?' The conversations that took place contributed to the thematic and theoretical underpinning of what is now recognised as an emerging traditional arts discourse. Ethnologist and musician Gary West presented the conference with a brief history of the traditional arts 'field' in the past, while also looking towards a future orientation, asserting the role of traditional arts not as shackles forever tethering us to an idealised past, but as roots continuously nourishing the culture of contemporary Scotland (West,

2012a, 265). A particular nod was given to the twentieth-century Folk Revival and the cultural politics of Hamish Henderson, inspired largely by cultural theorist and philosopher Antonio Gramsci.[2] Henderson's vision was to establish a 'new cultural field' (and a highly politicised one at that).[3] West invited the conference to reflect upon this Hendersonian vision, which could be said to embody the following characteristics: internationalist in nature; positive in mood; questioning in form; inclusive in attitude; decisive in action; challenging in tone; radical in outlook; rooted in place.[4] Given the looming contemporary political context, certain speakers were open about their political inclinations, with several participants voicing their support for an independent Scotland. Others chose to remain firmly equivocal. Irrespective of political leanings or a difference of opinion on the constitutional question, and very much intended in the spirit of inclusiveness, there was a strong and shared sense that, given its cultural and political heritage, the traditional arts community had a great deal, and a responsibility, to contribute to the national debate.

In a climate of rising political tension, public arts organisations and networks involved in the promotion and development of traditional music were careful to avoid taking any explicit position on the constitutional question. Contributions to the debate from the traditional arts community would need to come from artists and activists as individuals, and new independent networks, platforms or campaigning groups would need to be created. As a recent PhD graduate in ethnomusicology and ethnology and a freelance arts worker with experience of political activism, I decided – along with the help of others – to take a lead role in catalysing, articulating and organising an independent campaigning group of traditional artists in support of independence. This had broad support from key actors in the wider traditional arts community, both publicly and behind the scenes. In July 2013, we launched *TradYES*, the 'collective banner under which traditional artists can join together in support of Scottish independence', as part of the non-party creative cultural campaign National Collective. Drawing upon this emerging traditional arts discourse and cultural heritage, and reflecting the ethos of the wider Yes campaign, the tone was explicitly positive, inclusive and outward-looking:

> Our artists have a vital role to play in a national campaign for Scottish independence. We believe that the traditional arts have radical potential, both culturally and politically; community, mutual co-operation and conviviality are embedded in what we do. . .
>
> We believe that the traditional arts scene reflects the wider ethos of National Collective: it is inclusive, progressive and outward-looking. Showcasing and encouraging the diversity and creativity of Scotland's rich musical traditions makes a positive and crucial statement, helping build the confidence – in ourselves and in each other – to imagine possible futures and vote Yes in 2014.
>
> (McFadyen et al., 2013)

This online launch had had considerable impact, with an organic reach of over 12,000 people on Facebook in the first week. The campaign had public support from several well-known musicians and performers, several of whom offered short testimonials articulating and sharing personal reasons for voting Yes, in the three languages of English, Scots and Gaelic.[5] No claims were made to represent the traditional arts community as a whole. By empowering individuals and groups, welcoming diversity and creating a platform for artists to engage with the independence campaign, we aimed both to make visible and galvanise support for independence within this community of practice. Vital to this was the creation of a space for those who might feel uncomfortable with conventional party politics. Testimonials and images shared online created a critical mass within the community of practice inspiring confidence in others to speak out. In the first year, over 70 musicians contributed their reasons for voting yes, which were shared with the online community along with a photo or short video.[6] Lastly, using social media, we aimed to document campaign activity, making it highly visible through sharing on social networks such as Facebook and Twitter.

The distinction between 'civic' and 'ethnic' nationalism was central to the articulation of *TradYES*.[7] The mainstream pro-yes campaign was fought on a determinedly civic nationalist platform. This is not to say that ethnic nationalism was not present in any form in debate, but where it did exist, it was very much the minority voice and explicitly shunned by many. Certain campaigners, such as the pro-independence supporting Scottish Green Party, would not define themselves as 'nationalists' at all. This distinction is something that both the opposition in the No campaign and large sections of the mainstream media made sure to ignore or obscure. Instead of being seen as a movement that celebrated diversity and embraced internationalism, Yes activists were frequently portrayed as inward-looking ethnic nationalists, painted in Braveheart blue and wearing 'jimmy hats', or worse, accused of flirting with fascism.[8]

> Of course, it makes sense for proponents of the anti-independence campaign to paint Scottish culture in terms of those tacky souvenir shops, whose hackneyed pipe muzak and tartan themed paraphernalia blight so much of Edinburgh's old town. After all, if our cultural heritage comprises little more than a bad Mel Gibson movie and a 'see you jimmy' hat, we can't really be serious contenders for country status, can we?
>
> (Foster, 2013)

Much of Scotland's dynamic traditional culture is far removed from the version depicted by souvenir shops and is much greater than the export brand that is exploited by the tourism industry. Yet, for many, the traditional arts are often associated with the insidious 'cultural cringe' and written off as nostalgic, eccentric – or worse, as a product of dangerous nationalism. As a personal anecdote, a friend of mine, also an activist, commented, 'don't the traditional arts belong to the version of Scotland we are desperately trying to break free from?'[9] By raising awareness of the diversity of traditional music in the context of the mainstream cultural campaign and in wider culture, *TradYES* was also a self-conscious attempt to challenge many negative perceptions held about the traditional arts in

Scotland and their association with 'shortbread-tin nationalism' and the 'tartan monster' (McAvoy, this volume).

Historically, the essentialist relationship between traditional music and the nation has been close and problematic, especially in a European context (McKerrell and West, this volume).[10] In the twentieth century, scholarship on globalisation, post-colonialism and hybridity has, in varying ways, problematised social groups as bounded entities, revealing them to be fluid, negotiated, constructed, emergent, neither biologically or territorially given and shaped by relations of power. As such, people's national identities – their sense of belonging to the nation – are dynamic, and always in the process of production through an engagement with pre-existing discourses of national identity. In the context of the campaign, far from retreating to the binary polarity of historical and exclusionary nationalisms, traditional music was presented as open, welcoming and inclusive, literally as a 'welcome table' (MacKenzie, 2014), or as 'a sonic signifier of a future, more progressive, culturally independent and confident Scottish nation' (McKerrell and West, this volume). Commenting on the tone of *TradYES*, cultural geographer Fraser MacDonald (2013) observed:

> Anyone with a knowledge of Scotland's oral traditions might expect this to be a vehicle for an all too familiar brand of cultural nationalism. The carrying stream of Scottish 'folk', epitomised by the School of Scottish Studies, has long had something of a nationalist undercurrent. The stall [*TradYES*] lays out, however, is significantly different from these earlier movements. For one thing, it sees aspects of Scottish tradition within a much wider cultural frame. It also displaces 'the national' for 'the local' – an interesting move. What strikes me as most important is that *TradYES* is both generative and future-orientated. . .
>
> National Collective's campaign represents more a bringing-to-life than a saving-the-past. That distinction may prove significant. And the bid to foster an 'evolving sense of self' may resonate with a greater diversity of voices than could have been foreseen by Henderson and Maclean.[11]

TradYES had its first public outing at September's March and Rally on Calton Hill in 2013.[12] Over 50 musicians, singers and step-dancers travelled to Edinburgh, from the Borders in the south to the Highlands and Islands in the north and west to join the march and to perform on the stage as part of a programme of speakers and performers. There was a sense of humour about this; personal favourite placards included the slogans 'Bothy Yes – It started with a Kist' and 'Aye, Have a Dream'. Several generations of Scots and Gaelic traditional singers came together to sing Hamish Henderson's internationalist Scots language anthem 'Freedom Come Aa Ye', in both Scots and Gaelic, introduced by Steve Byrne.[13] This song describes a wind of change blowing through Scotland and the world at large, sweeping away exploitation and imperialism. It renounces the tradition of the Scottish soldier both as imperial cannon-fodder and colonial oppressor and ends with a vision of a future global society. The song, for many Scots, has come to symbolise 'a sort of socialist-egalitarian dream of international equality and tolerance' (McKerrell, 2016, 79). Robert Burns' 'A Man's A Man' was led by Sheena Wellington, who ceremoniously opened the devolved Scottish parliament in 1999 with this same song of egalitarian values and hope. Musician Rona Wilkie directed a cohort of talented musicians in a performance of well-known traditional session tunes with Scottish step-dancing from Sophie Stephenson,[14] and later led a session at the celebratory after party organised by online cultural magazine, *Bella Caledonia*.

> On this stage, *TradYES* contributed some of the best, and indeed most critically acclaimed, musicians in Scotland today. That is massively significant, not least because most of the crowd had probably never heard of them . . . Let's make no bones about it, this community is as important to the campaign as it is to Scotland, that is to say – crucial.
>
> (Foster, 2013)

In many ways, this was a public performance of a very familiar cultural politics. The politics of traditional music in Scotland has always been 'a mix of egalitarianism, outward-facing nationalism . . . and a small but significant history of communism and internationalism' (McKerrell, 2016, 70). Strands of such left-leaning ideology have run strongly throughout much of the history of traditional music since the eighteenth century; folk song in particular has always been an

Figure 6.1 TradYES banner at the March and Rally for Independence, Calton Hill, Edinburgh, September 2013

(Photo credit: Simon Baker Documenting Yes)

important vehicle for protest and carrier of political values, demonstrated by the Folk Revival of the 1960s.[15] Through the process of 'traditional referentiality' (Foley, 1990), the public performance of the March and Rally evoked a context larger than the event itself, bringing these voices of the past into the present. Yet while there were echoes of the earlier folk revival movement on the stage at the March and Rally, this new highly political and digitally mediated context was a stark departure from the fringe folk clubs of the past. Using the power of social media, these voices were able to reach new audiences in ways not possible in the cultural movements of the past. Newly enfranchised by the campaign, many citizens were discovering the cultural heritage of traditional music in Scotland – this Hendersonian vision – for the very first time. For many, this was the catalyst for an exciting journey of cultural discovery that was hugely significant to an emerging sense of identity and cultural possibility.

Creativity, dialogue and performance

As well as occasions for highly public mass participation such as the March and Rally, many small-scale, grassroots events took place in village halls, pubs and communities all over Scotland, organised by local 'Yes' branches and interest groups participating in the performance of the campaign. Many of these events had a similar format, with speakers, musicians, performances, films and discussion, generating creative and intellectual engagement with the debate. Participants came together to 'imagine a better nation' or speculate on how Scotland might achieve a more progressive politics. This kind of volunteer-led small-scale event was typical of the mobilisation of communities (and often women in communities) to encourage debate and conversation. Bissell and Overend suggest that the referendum in this sense 'acted as a catalyst for a new politics to emerge that is characterised by creativity, dialogue and performance' (2015, 243). Such alternative creative responses, they suggest, might be understood as a more community-based and democratic form of performance, creating a space beyond the reductive and divisive Yes/No question to explore a range of positions and arguments.

An example of this kind of alternative performative response that captured the imagination was the colourful *Yestival* that toured the country in the summer of 2014.[16] This was organised by the campaign group National Collective, crowd-funded and delivered on a shoestring budget. Over the 34 days, 1,786 miles, 6 ferry rides and with 16 tents and a silver Airstream caravan (fondly named Gloria Yestivan), Yestival visited town halls and back rooms of pubs from the Borders to Shetland. Joined along the way by over 200 acts, Yestival hosted free, open events featuring music, song, poetry, film, comedy, storytelling and the popular format 'Journey to Yes', where people were invited to share their own story of coming to support Scottish independence.[17] In contrast to the mainstream campaign, multi-coloured bunting and balloons were favoured over flags and saltires. Now remembered as the 'Summer of Independence', the festival atmosphere was heightened by what was a season of great summer weather and sunshine.

Figure 6.2 Innes Watson and Adam Sutherland, 'National Collective Presents . . .' at the Edinburgh Festival Fringe, August 2014

(Photo credit: Simon Baker Documenting Yes)

Given the mobile nature of traditional music as an art form, both traditional music and musicians were highly visible in this context. To give a flavour: in Haddington, piper Hamish Moore, singer Jack Badcock and fiddler Robbie Greig joined the bill alongside comedian and actress Elaine C. Smith and the infamous 'Lady Alba' (performed by Zara Gladman);[18] in Melrose, Dick Gaughan joined the bill along with a local choir who sang a new song for the campaign, 'Theme for the Early Days of a Better Nation' composed by Matt Seattle and lyrics by David Finnie;[19] in Ayr, Gaelic singer Anne Lorne Gillies joined a fine band of poets; in Edinburgh's Summerhall a huge ceilidh dance took place, with a house band, Gaelic singers Kathleen MacInnes, Brian O Headhra, Fiona Mackenzie and a Canadian Gaelic rapper, Steve Byrne and Mike Vass from folk band Malinky, stories from singer and actress Dolina MacLennan and fiddle and step dancing from Amy Geddes and Alison Carlyle. In Fort William's Shinty Club we were joined by left-handed fiddler of Lochaber Aonghas Grant (snr), Ingrid Henderson and Iain MacFarlane, Gaelic singer Dòl Eoin MacKinnon and Dick Gaughan; in North Uist we were joined by international students from the traditional music course in Benbecula; in Harris, playwright and performers Kieran Hurley and Julia Taudevin performed a piece from the contemporary ceilidh play *Rantin* in the same hall that theatre company 7:84 first performed the famous ceilidh play *The Cheviot the Stag and the Black, Black Oil* years before, followed by a singing session on Horgabost beach; in Ullapool, The Ceilidh Place welcomed musician and composer Mairearad Green who had travelled over from Achiltiebuie with her accordion and pipes, musicologist John Purser gave a stirring talk, George Gunn performed part of his new poetry and music piece 'A Walk in Strathnaver' and Rona Wilkie and Marit Fält performed music from the soundtrack to the new film 'Scotland Yet', evoking Davy Steele's original and much loved song of the same title. Inverness saw Gaelic song and *puirt-a-beul* from Mary-Ann Kennedy, a trapeze performance with the soundtrack of Martyn Bennett's album GRIT and contemporary singer and rap artist Eunice Olumide all on the same bill. Events followed in Orkney, Shetland, Lossiemouth, Aberdeen, Montrose, Arbroath, Dundee, Perth, St Andrews and Stirling, with Skye's independent Yestival performance bringing in local artists in Broadford. Later, during the Edinburgh Festival Fringe, National Collective hosted singer Bella Hardy, musicians Adam Sutherland and Innes Watson and English protest singer Billy Bragg, who sang 'Both Sides the Tweed', 'Take Down the Union Jack' and 'Keep Faith', with a powerful message of solidarity with friends in England.

Rather than a performance of overt Scottish nationalism, this was a celebration of grassroots democracy, and much more about the performance of local community and culture as it connected to the category of 'nation', rather than a celebration of the nation itself. Bissell and Overend (2015, 244) suggest that the spaces for dialogue and debate created by events such as *Yestival* are reminiscent of the 'democratic cultural expression' that Mikhail Bakhtin argues are engendered by carnivals and festivals, yet push beyond the boundaries of Bakhtin's democratic festivities which are all too easily managed and controlled by the State. In this sense, such events generated 'far more appropriate conditions for the democratic expression of a national debate' than mainstream campaign events such as the March and Rally, or indeed the televised TV debates on major terrestrial channels. The performance of the referendum at a grassroots level had particular value in this sense, as the 'cultural spaces where the flows of affect on display were less oriented towards measureable outcomes than towards the ongoing process of telling political stories, engaging in political debate and asking political questions' (Bissell and Overend, 2015, 249). Those who were unsure, or even those voting No, were welcome to participate (of course, when performance positions itself as 'political', it is often those who are already interested and engaged who will attend rather than those whose views might be challenged or reconsidered). Speaking from experience, these events were filled with delighted, enthusiastic and impassioned audiences spanning age ranges and backgrounds. The excitement, sense of community and possibility created, however temporary, was palpable: in those spaces and in those moments, what we experienced together was real, vital and transformative.

A relational aesthetic

Bissell and Overend, drawing on recent discourse on socially engaged art practices, suggest that the referendum created its own large-scale 'relational aesthetic' to emerge (2015, 250). In terms of understanding the role of art in the context of the campaign, it is useful to conceive of these shared transformative experiences as 'relational aesthetic experiences'. Relational art (sometimes called 'participatory', 'community' or 'activist' art) creates events in time and space that have tangible impact upon the audience.[20] Nicholas Bourriaud defines relational art as 'a set of artistic practices which take as their theoretical and practical point of departure the whole of human relations and their social context, rather than an independent and private space' (2002 [1998], 113). Bourriaud's theories are based on visual exhibition-based arts; he views both theatre and musical practice as limited relational artforms because they bring together 'small groups of people' and offer no opportunity for 'live discussion' during the event.[21] Beyond the visual and artefact-centrism that characterises such theories of art, music anthropologist Georgina Born (2011) makes the point that musical practice is always material practice enacted in – constituted by and constituting – networks of social relations, and that music 'materialises identities' through social mediation:

> Compared with the visual and literary arts, which we associate with a specific object, text or representation, music may therefore appear to be an extraordinarily diffuse kind of cultural object: an aggregation of sonic, social, corporeal, discursive, visual, technological and temporal mediations. Its multiple simultaneous forms of existence – as sonic trace, discursive exegesis, notated score, technological prosthesis, social and embodied performance – indicate the necessity of conceiving of the musical object as a 'constellation of mediations'.
> (Born, 2011, 377)

Music sociologist Tia DeNora, in her explorations of music's active role in the construction of personal and social life, reflects that 'just as music's meanings may be constructed in relation to things outside it, so, too, things outside music may be constructed in relation to music' (2000, 40). This challenges Bourriaud's position on the limits of certain forms of relational art. Evidence of the experience of the campaign demonstrates the potential for art forms such as music and theatre not only to respond in the moment to the political context of its performance, but also at the same time connect to a wider national dialogue and debate, offering a space for opposing ideas and values to co-exist through live discussion that was documented and shared online.

Campaign events were responding, in the macro sense, to a highly political social context; in the micro sense, each musical performance was always performed in relation to something else: alongside performance poets, rappers, comedians, writers, dancers, short films, political speakers, trapeze artists among others; and contextualised by talks and speeches – about politics, economics, welfare, forestry and architecture, among many other topics. Through a 'series of performances, conversations, art and music' audiences were encouraged to 'think about how we make decisions, where the human desire for independence comes from, and whether it even really matters' (Bissell and Overend, 2015, 247).

As musicologist Cook suggests, one of the most significant aspects of any relational analysis of music is that it shifts music from being the object of study to a social process that aims to 'create relationships between its spectators' (2012, 95). Bissell and Overend (2015, 247) suggest that the communal, convivial and participatory nature of campaign events such as those described above can be conceived of as artistically constructed and democratic 'relational spaces' which aimed to create relationships between spectators and 'give everyone their chance.' Bourriaud would conceptualise these relational spaces as 'micro-topias', which focus on the interrelations among artists and audience members (2002). In the context of traditional music, this idea is reminiscent of the kitchen-ceilidh or *taigh-ceilidh*.[22] In traditional communities, the ceilidh was the basic building block of community; it was the social context for social interaction in an evening of songs, stories, joke-telling and dancing for entertainment, dealing with issues and concern to those who staged it: 'To a village bard like the *Sgiobair*, who spent six nights a week in one of the [ceilidh houses], they are inseparably intertwined with community identity' (McKean, 1998). Reflecting on the inclusive potential of the ceilidh, Baz Kershaw notes:

> Given the right circumstances a kind of community can be created by a very disparate group of people in a relatively short time . . . tensions created and contained through people knowing each other fairly well . . . people moving closer out of social embarrassment . . . a community consolidating in order temporarily to incorporate others, [or all of these] at different points for different people.
>
> (1983, 154)

It is in this sense that the traditional arts have radical potential, both culturally and politically. The *taigh ceilidh* is itself a 'performative relational space' for the creation and performance of community. This 'spirit of the ceilidh' was present in many campaign events, particular at the small-scale *Yestival* evenings. Through creativity, dialogue and performance, a sense of community and shared identity was created, with people bound by shared values, aspirations and collective endeavours. As a campaigner and activist on the Yestival tour, witnessing this enthusiasm, excitement and connection night after night was particularly moving. For me, these events were some of the most profound and transformative experiences of the entire campaign.

In another cultural context, the 'creation of personal relationships' is the focus of Jocelyne Guilbault in her study of Trinidadian Soca music (2010, 17). Guilbault stresses the transformative capacities of music to produce what she calls 'public intimacies'. With this term she refers to the socialities and spatial proximities of performance as they unfold. She argues that these embodied and performative social interactions 'reiterate identities', while also enabling 'new points of connection [to be] developed (for example among artists and audience members of different ethnicities, nationalities and generations, and across musical genres)'. The socialities created also give rise to the establishment of what she calls 'affective alliances' through the sharing of feelings, expectations, values (2010, 21). Such performance socialities can therefore, she suggests, work either to reinforce or to reconfigure social norms. Other studies show how musical performance is not only entangled in wider social identity formations, but has the capacity to reconfigure or catalyse those formations (Bohlman, 2004; De Nora, 2000; Frith, 1996). In the context of the performance of the national identities, music has the capacity to presence imagined communities (Anderson, 2006), bringing its listeners together in socialities based on musical and cultural identifications. Edward Saïd (1991) writes that music is a 'mode of thinking through or with cultural practices; a way of ascertaining what is possible, attainable and knowable in the world'. This is significant as it suggests that music is a potential route to exploring identity: how identities are (re)produced, resisted and challenged (Wood, 2012).

Musical events that took place during the campaign for Scottish independence can be conceived of as relational aesthetic experiences through which the idea of 'nation' was performed, but also ways in and through which ideas of the nation were created, re-worked or redefined. Traditional music contributed a particular cultural politics in this context, rehearsing and performing many of the Hendersonian qualities and characteristics laid out by West: egalitarian relations, global connections, creative identities, an inclusive attitude, challenging in tone, positive in mood, a relation to the past, future oriented, radical in outlook, rooted in place (McFadyen, 2013b). This was much more than celebratory politics; these shared musical experiences were social moments of profound transformation through a performance of a shared discourse, vision and aspirations, transforming the traditional arts community's sense of what politics is capable of, and of music's political agency in such a context.

Songs for Scotland

During the campaign, ideas of the nation and shared vision were explicitly performed, created, re-worked and challenged through the medium of song. Song is an incredibly potent and affective form of embodied musical practice. The semantic power of words expands the awareness of possibilities ranging over past, present and future, while the sounds of voice and melody and their intonation focus the awareness in the present through a visceral, embodied experience (McFadyen, 2012). McKerrell contends that the power of political song 'provides a sort of relational empowerment where those who sing and those that listen bond to one another in the performance of shared values and aspirations' (2016, 84). As mentioned earlier in this chapter, there is a long history of protest song in Scotland. From the bothy ballads protesting the working conditions on the farms in the North East of the country, to industrial mining songs, to anti-Polaris songs in the campaign for nuclear disarmament to the apartheid struggles in South Africa, Scots have used traditional song as both a means for expressing and constructing political views and using musical practice as means to challenge larger structures of power.[23] Folk singer Dick Gaughan does not like the term 'protest song.' Protest, he argues, is easy: it is articulating an alternative that is difficult. Gaughan often alludes to a quote popularly attributed to dramatist Bertold Brecht: 'Art is not a mirror held up to reality but a hammer with which to shape it.'[24] In this sense, the 'socialities of musical performance and practice are potential vehicles for social experimentation or for the exercise of a musico-political imagination, in the sense that they may *enact alternatives* to or inversions of, and can be in contradiction with, wider forms of hierarchical and stratified social relations' (Born, 2011, 381, my emphasis).

During the campaign, many songs from folk tradition came to the fore, re-appropriated for a new context. These include the aforementioned 'Freedom Come Aa Ye', Robert Burns's 'A Man's a Man', Brian McNeill's 'No Gods and Precious Few Heroes', James Hogg's 'Both Sides the Tweed' made famous by Dick Gaughan, and Dougie Maclean's 'Caledonia', among many others. The referendum also inspired the composition of new songs. In the centuries-long tradition of writing 'new words to old tunes', Adam McNaughtan's 'Jeely Piece' song was re-worked as the 'Bedroom Tax Song: Ye Cannae Have A Spare Room in a Pokey Cooncil Flat';[25] similarly 'Iain Duncan Smith's a Ratbag' to the tune of 'The Battle Hymn of the Republic'; Burns's anti-war song was re-fashioned as 'Ye Unionists By Name' and Woody Guthrie's 'This Land is Your Land' spawned several new versions set in a Scottish political context.

Notable examples of entirely new compositions include Eilidh MacKenzie's 'The Welcome Table: A song for all the people of Scotland.' This song is a vision of an alternative future; it embodies an inclusive civic nationalism and self-consciously references the rich tradition of egalitarian song in Scotland.[26] The song was written in English, even though Mackenzie's output is more often in the Gaelic language. She reflects:

> I was conscious that I wanted to hark back to some of our landmark songs: the Proclaimers with their '500 miles' (and 500 more); of course Rabbie Burns and especially his 'A Man's a Man for A' That; and from the Gaelic tradition, I was keen to reference *MacMhaighstir Alasdair*. It was only when the song – the text and then the melody (a day apart) – was complete that I thought to include one of my favourite poems, an excerpt of the *Ruaraidh MacThòmais* poem *Eadar Samhradh is Foghar*.

Verse 2

Then listen to each single voice
Join in and sing our story
We folk of independent mind
Take Sense and Worth as glory
And weave a country's tapestry
In language, love and labour
As Man to Man the warld o'er
Feels welcome at our table.

Another example of a song that envisions an ideal future is Matt Seattle and David Finnie's 'Theme for the Early Days of a Better Nation.' This song, written in

Borders Scots, is inspired by the famous words of author and artist Alasdair Gray, quoting Canadian poet Dennis Leigh: 'Work as if you live in the early days of a better nation.' The lyric also uses two images from Scotland's natural heritage, drawing on a strand of rurality that has a long pedigree in Scotland (cf. Robert Burns):

> The wandering geese represent those who are welcomed as new Scots, and the shimmering salmon representing the struggle of all who swim against the current, as in the Peebles motto *contra nando incrementum*, which means 'against the stream they multiply.'
>
> (Seattle, 2014)

This song became a campaign favourite, later recorded by Lori Watson and McFall's chamber orchestra as part of the Distil project.[27]

Verse 1

> Skies whaur eagles are at thair ease
> Haud a walcome for wandrin geese;
> Hearts that open an hauns that feed
> Gie the weary warmth and shelter, gie the hungry broth and breid

Verse 2

> Simmer's hairst is aa gaithert in
> Skimmrin salmon lowp up the linn
> Teeming watters an fruitfu braes
> Sing a sang o peace, a common weal, the dawn o better days.[28]

An obvious example of the explicit use and performance of song during the campaign was the formation of the Independence Choir, led by Karen Dietz. During the campaign, this choir performed at many grassroots events across the country, with the aim of 'singing for a better, fairer nation'.[29] The choir, largely made up of members of the older generations, sought to contribute something 'uplifting and positive' to the debate. As stated on their Facebook page, 'We will be forward-looking towards an independent Scotland, and the songs will reflect and support this ethos.' New songs sung by this choir included 'This Land is a Song', and 'Say Yes' written by Ali Burns; the choir also sang choral arrangements of 'Both Sides the Tweed', 'Theme for the Early Days of a Better Nation' and 'A Man's a Man' among others.[30]

As well as the many small-scale grassroots events of the kind described in this chapter, towards the end of the campaign, several more explicit events took place in venues across the country. Two weeks before the vote, Canadian campaigner Kevin Brown, in partnership with online cultural magazine *Bella Caledonia*, produced the 'Songs for Scotland Festival' at the Oran Mor pub and venue in

Figure 6.3 TradYES at the March and Rally for Independence including the author, Calton Hill, Edinburgh, September 2013

(Photo credit: Simon Baker Documenting Yes)

Glasgow.[31] This was 'a national concert of Scottish singers singing their support for social justice and for Scottish independence', showcasing the rich tradition of folk song in Scots and Gaelic, as well as showcasing contemporary song in other genres such as hip-hop. Performers invited to take part included Dick Gaughan, The Proclaimers, Emily Smith, Ewan McLennan, Siobhan Miller, Paul McKenna, Kathleen MacInnes, Mary Ann Kennedy, Eilidh MacKenzie, Kaela Rowan, Allan MacDonald, Findlay Napier, Lady Alba, Adam Ross of Randolph's Leap, Loki with Rebecca Wallace, Will MC Gille-Goillidh, hip-hop artist Louie and DJ Dolphin Boy. A souvenir album was later produced which also included tracks from hip-hop artist, Stanley Odd and bands Shooglenifty and Capercaillie.[32] In the context of such a highly charged, emotional and exciting event, the collective emotion of an imagined community experienced through song proved a powerful and potent performance.[33]

Conclusion

The campaign for Scottish independence was a collective, relational and highly contextualised endeavour in which music and song played a key role. Traditional music was important not as the performance of a 'national music' with all its trappings, but in a relational, performative sense. Echoing the remark about *TradYes* being 'generative and future oriented' (MacDonald, 2013), resources of the past were used in this case not to construct an idealised present but to prefigure an achievable future. By empowering individuals and communities, welcoming diversity and creating a platform for artists to engage with the independence campaign, the campaign group *TradYES* made visible – and audible – many voices that were absent in the mainstream campaign. This group also created a critical mass and forum that gave others the confidence to speak out, inspiring citizens to participate in new and creative ways. The value of wider creative cultural campaign inspired by National Collective was the creation and activation of collaborative, open networks of campaigners, activists and artists. Individuals and groups were given a platform to voice their vision for a future Scotland and to articulate the role of traditional music and song in progressive, inclusive terms, alongside–and in relation to–other art forms such as poetry, theatre and visual art.

In the context of the campaign, musical events were more than celebratory politics; they were social moments of profound transformation and the creation of community. Local events such as *Yestival* created spaces for performance and dialogue, with music helping to create temporary socialities, 'affective alliances' and communities of shared values and aspirations. In this context, wider social relations, as well as the social imaginaries afforded by music, constituted a relational aesthetic experience for participants through which ideas of 'nation' were performed, challenged and redefined. In this sense, the grassroots events generated far more appropriate conditions for the democratic expression of a national debate than the mainstream campaign. In this context, we saw cultural nationalism re-performed as part of a civic nationalist, socially engaged political process, where music was promoted as a 'sonic signifier' of a culturally independent and confident Scottish nation. This was most powerfully embodied and performed in the case of song.

Many commentators consider the referendum process to have been a hugely progressive, creative, and formative period in Scottish politics. For some, the performance of the campaign was the beginning of a personal cultural discovery: a catalyst to search out the cultural heritage of traditional music, song and folk culture. This growing awareness, recognition and interest has left a legacy of growing cultural confidence, hugely important to an emerging sense of both cultural possibility and national identity. Since the events described, Scotland has seen more and more 'folk culture' made visible in mainstream culture, for example through the film *Hamish the Movie*, a biopic of Hamish Henderson, the performance of Martyn Bennett's GRIT on the stage at Edinburgh International Festival[34] and music festival Celtic Connections hitting the £1 million mark in ticket sales.[35]

The next #ScotRef, as it is emerging, promises to be of a very different character, given the unstoppable macro-political forces of Brexit across the UK. Perhaps this time there will be more of a focus on the part culture plays in a people's vision for its future. How we listen to and perform what we say about music contributes not only to our own sense of belonging and authenticity, but also how we project this on to others. It is my hope, whatever political future lies ahead, that the collective voice of Scotland is a confident and inclusive one and that those who perform and craft identities in and through Scottish traditional music remain committed to an open and plural notion of what that might mean.

Notes

1. McKerrell (2016, 88) has noted that the 'relational turn' in music analysis is useful because it offers an understanding of how people engage in community construction in and through music. To do this, we need to understand music as a process (Turino, 2008).
2. See Henderson (2004).
3. For an account of the cultural context of the Folk Revival see West (2012a); for an account of the wider international story see Munro (1996).
4. For conference report, see McFadyen (2013b).
5. See McFadyen (2013a).
6. For testimonials, see the TradYES Facebook page: www.facebook.com/TradYes2014/.
7. Civic nationalism is a political identity built around shared citizenship in a liberal-democratic state, united by a civic not an ethnic definition of belonging or shared citizenship. For definitions see Ignatieff (1993, 5–9).
8. A particularly striking example of this was when campaigners were described as 'Mussolini's Cheerleaders' by a prominent Unionist. See Campsie (2013).
9. Personal communication, 2013.
10. The relationship between music and national identity has been explored by scholars from a range of disciplinary backgrounds, including geography, musicology, sociology and psychology. See Wood (2012) for a review of the literature.
11. See MacDonald (2013).
12. See McFadyen (2014b).
13. To listen to Byrne's speech, visit https://vimeo.com/75263304.
14. To see a short clip of this event, visit https://youtu.be/EPZMxSf7WFw.
15. See 'Songs for Scotland' section later in this chapter for a discussion of protest song in Scotland.
16. See www.nationalcollective.com/yestival; for photos of each event during Yestival, see http://documentingyes.com/yestival.
17. A particularly powerful example of this format is this story from playwright and performer Julia Taudevin. See Taudevin (2014).
18. Lady Alba was a satiric character created by comedian Zara Gladman. See Sunday Post (2014).
19. For a discussion of this song, see the 'Songs for Scotland' section later in this chapter.
20. Relational art raises important questions about the meaning and purpose of art in society, about the role of the artist and the experience of the audience as participant.
21. Bourriaud's aesthetic model has been criticized by Bishop who argues that relational art often takes place within and the exclusions and antagonisms that are obscured by aspirations of 'link[ing] individuals and human groups together'. See Bishop (2004).
22. For a description of the taigh ceilidh, see Bennett (1998); McKean (1996).
23. For a discussion of Protest Song in Scotland, see McKerrell (2016) pp. 81–83.
24. This quote is attributed to Brecht in Leonard and McLaren (1993).
25. See www.youtube.com/watch?v=Bik9299kA0c.
26. See MacKenzie (2014).
27. Distil is a twice yearly gathering of musicians rooted in folk and traditional music, but who are interested in expanding their creative horizons into other areas of musical practice. See Hands Up For Trad (2017).
28. For the full lyrics, see Watson (2014).
29. This quote is from the Independence Choir Facebook page. See: https://en-gb.facebook.com/theindependencechoir/.

30 To listen to the Independence Choir, visit https://soundcloud.com/nationalcollective/sets/independence-choir.
31 See Bella Caledonia (2014) *Songs For Scotland*.
32 At the time of writing, inspired by the events of Brexit and the renewed interest in a second referendum, Kevin Brown and Bella Caledonia are currently working on Songs for Scotland 2.
33 For video footage of this event, see: www.youtube.com/watch?v=Bgodd7yYdt8 ; for photos see http://bellacaledonia.org.uk/2014/09/04/songs-for-scotland-a-night-at-oran-mor/.
34 For reflections on the cultural context of this performance, see McFadyen (2016).
35 See Ferguson (2014).

Part II
Porosity, genres, hybridity

7 The changing nature of conceptualisation and authenticity among Scottish traditional musicians

Traditional music, conservatoire education and the case for post-revivalism

Joshua Dickson

Introduction

The year 2016 marked the 20th anniversary of the founding of the Bachelor of Arts (Scottish Music) at what was then the Royal Scottish Academy of Music and Drama – the first of its kind in the United Kingdom. A great deal has been accomplished in that time; and a great deal of change has taken place. The pre-Higher Education (HE) landscape in traditional music has seen an increase in the breadth and depth of traditional Scottish music provision at secondary level, and a significant shift toward greater professionalisation, commercialisation and digitisation as folk or traditional music has increased in popular currency both at home and abroad.

This important milestone has therefore provided us with an unprecedented and timely opportunity to review candidly the role of traditional or folk music in an HE context to date – specifically in the context of a conservatoire; to question the balance between practice and context in the programme and the role of performance; and to take stock of the transformation in traditional music provision and opportunities in the pre-HE landscape over the past two decades, which in turn has had a tremendous impact on student expectations, aspirations, and baseline musicianship at the point of entry.

Essentialism, education and the alternate rurality

McKerrell (2016, 51) and Costello (2015, 54) have remarked on the influence of Johann Gottfried Herder on language, ethnicity, cultural purity and the role of 'the Folk' as contributing to the development of the concept of collective national culture, 'nationhood' and the 'national' character of music and literature as the nineteenth century progressed. This influenced notions of the 'noble savage' in Britain and Ireland, swept up in the search for Otherness – or exoticness – in the midst of the familiar. Such rules governing authenticity were based on a sense of purity or distinctiveness that required a pre-literate past, an exotic landscape and a never-ending cultural precariousness – an *alternate rurality*, as it were – not so much imagined by its acolytes as constructed for their own purposes (see for instance Sharp, 1907; Donaldson, 2008, 5–19; O Laoire, 2005; Dickson, 2009, 191–193; McKerrell, 2016, 51–56).

This pathway to identity and authenticity can be theorised as a school of nationalistic or linguistic essentialism. Costello, for instance, describes an essentialist school of *sean-nos* scholarship in Ireland in which the Irish language is regarded as the essence of Gaelic identity. The Gaeltacht, as the language's geographical locus, is equally regarded as the source of Gaelic identity. Because of its association with the Gaeltacht and the Irish language, *sean-nos* is regarded by essentialists as the source, or essence, of Irish traditional music (2015, 54).

In a similar vein, traditional or folk music education in Scotland at all levels has developed on the premise that the source, or essence, of Scottish traditional music is to be found by definition in the expression of language (Scots and Scottish Gaelic), and place (e.g. the Highlands, the Borders and Aberdeenshire). On these twin pillars, historically, rest the weight of identity and authenticity in our music, and indeed traditional music generally. Note that Scots and Scottish Gaelic are indigenous to Scotland, but also *other* – that is, not English – and that the geographical regions mentioned are also *other* – that is, not urban.

In Scotland, this essentialist school of thought found creative expression as the twentieth century neared through, for instance, the art music compositions of Hamish MacCunn in the 1880s (Oates, 2013; Dickson, 2013), a time concurrent with Highland land agitation and the recognition of crofters' rights. We can see this nationalistic essentialism feeding further into the intellectual, political and aesthetic foundations of the Scottish folk revival of the 1940s and 1950s (Henderson, 1992; Munro, 1996); Collinson's publication of *The Traditional and National Music of Scotland* (1966); and indeed the establishment of the BA (Scottish Music) at the Royal Scottish Academy of Music and Drama at the twentieth century's close (Miller and Duesenberry, 2007; Duffy et al., 2014, 49).

More recently, Costello has shown how *sean-nos* scholarship in Ireland has shifted somewhat from the essentialist perspective described above, with some scholars now criticising the essentialism of O Riada and O Canainn (Costello 2015, 54; O Laoire 2005). In Scotland, this essentialist school of thought – the finding of meaning in traditional music through the 'voicing' of language and land – has been both affirmed and questioned in recent scholarship in the context of the deterritorialisation of traditional music in modern times (West, 2004, 2012a; McKerrell, 2016, 11). We have also seen a shift away from such essentialism as regards performance in the years since the BA was founded, as cross-over developments and a growing eclecticism have given us such artists or ensembles as Treacherous Orchestra, Catriona McKay and Greg Lawson, and highly celebrated forums for composition, such as the Celtic Connections festival's New Voices commissions, which have led to 'beyond-tune' musical territory, as theorised by Watson (2012).

This chapter argues for a consequent need to effect a similar shift away from essentialism in the teaching and learning of traditional music in higher music education, if traditional music is to continue to flourish in that context. It argues that we have arrived at an impasse in the flowering of the *volksgeist* that fed traditional music scholarship and performance aesthetics in Scotland, if not the UK generally; an impasse in which the commodification, deterritorialism and mass mediation remarked upon by Tomlinson (2003, 273), Keegan-Phipps (2007, 96) and McKerrell (2016, 11) have prompted a shift away from the political and essentialist agendas of the twentieth-century folk revival movement and, consequently, a need to shift pedagogical thinking and practices in higher music education: in other words, a shift from the revivalist educational objectives of the twentieth century to what could be described as the post-revivalist educational objectives of the twenty-first.

Such objectives should include a shift in conceptual underpinning from essentialism to vocationalism; from the teaching of meaning in traditional music through the folkloric lens exclusively to the facilitating of meaning through the many lenses of a diverse world: social and cultural context; auto-ethnography; artistic research and the pursuit of innovation through both creativity and historically informed performance; and an engagement with the complexities of traditional music's performance practices and the communities borne of such practices: from the fireside to the concert hall to the recording studio to the chat room.

A review of Scottish music at the Royal Conservatoire of Scotland, 2014–2015

Research conducted between April 2014 and March 2015 suggests that the pre-HE landscape in traditional music in Scotland has evolved – pedagogically, commercially and professionally – since the BA was first established in 1996. Since then, we have seen an increase in the breadth and depth of traditional Scottish music provision at secondary education level in many Scottish council areas, including Plockton High School's Centre of Excellence in Traditional Music and Oban High School's School of Traditional Music; traditional music provision at Junior Conservatoire and the proliferation of Traditional Music Graded Exams, both innovations of the Royal Conservatoire of Scotland; the National Piping Centre; the National Youth Pipe Band of Scotland; and global visibility and credibility occasioned by festivals such as Celtic Connections, Blas, Piping Live in association with the World Pipe Band Championships; and festivals beyond Scotland such as Celtic Colours in Cape Breton and the Festival Interceltique de Lorient in France.

We have also seen developments in the way traditional music is learned, listened to, produced, engaged with and consumed in the context of digital communication and mediation in the modern world. Today one can find literally hundreds of recordings of piobaireachd on the Spotify streaming service; compare relatively modern renditions of the ballad 'True Thomas Lay on Huntly Bank', considered to have been first composed and performed 700 years earlier, on the Tobar an Dualchais/Kist o Riches online archive (www.tobarandualchais.

co.uk); and distribute a self-composed and recorded track through SoundCloud (www.soundcloud.com), to be downloaded and reviewed in online forums accessible through any smartphone or tablet in the world. Traditional music is far from unique in this respect of course, and the arguably democratising impact of such developments on the career prospects of the aspiring professional musician, folk or otherwise, have been and will continue to be debated. Whatever one's views, such developments, though relatively recent, have been noted (McKerrell, 2016, 10–12; Keegan-Phipps, 2016) as carrying significant implications toward the way traditional music is conceived of and indeed practised in our globalised world.

Research suggests that, either despite or because of these developments, folk or traditional music in a conservatoire context is undergoing significant pressures and challenges to its integrity and authenticity, if only in the sense that such concepts as *integrity* and *authenticity* are rapidly shifting in meaning from an older generation to a newer one; the expectations and aspirations of incoming students in 1996 were quite different from those of 2015.

Consider for example the results of survey research carried out from September to December 2014 as part of a review of the curriculum and key performance indicators in relation to the BA in Scottish Music (Dickson, 2015). Respondents (n = 63) included degree alumni and current students and staff, along with a wide range of otherwise unconnected professional and amateur musicians, teachers, academics, employers, publishers and professional organisation representatives in relation to Scottish folk or traditional music. The majority described themselves as professional singers and musicians (57%), teachers (60%) and students (44%).

Almost all (95%) agreed that Scottish traditional music has 'evolved' or 'changed' in the past 20 years professionally, educationally and artistically.

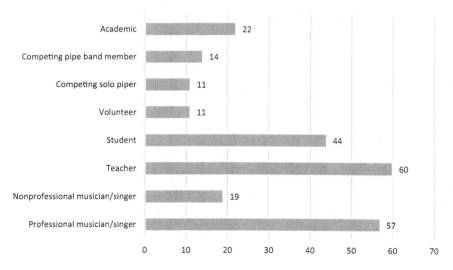

Figure 7.1 Survey responses to the question 'How would you describe yourself in relation to Scottish traditional music?'

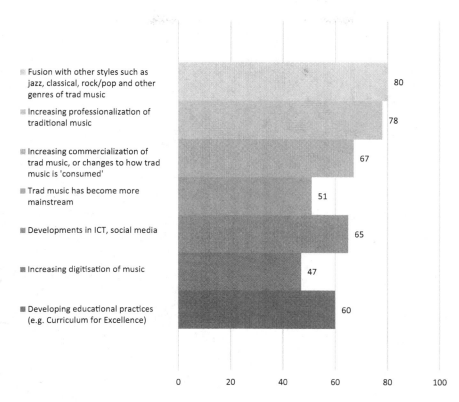

Figure 7.2 Survey responses to the question: 'To what would you ascribe professional, educational and artistic developments in Scottish traditional music?'

The top three factors believed to be responsible for such changes were noted as fusion with other styles, including jazz, classical, rock/pop and other genres of traditional or folk music (80%); increasing professionalisation of traditional music (78%); and increasing commercialisation of traditional music, or how traditional music is 'consumed' (67%).

Of the qualities, knowledge and skills a folk or traditional musician must possess for success today (success variously defined), 100% of respondents agreed or strongly agreed that performance standard was an important quality, followed by stagecraft and presentation skills (94%), versatility in terms of instrumental fluency and genre (90%) and a varied skill set, including academic, vocational, practical and business skills (83%). Nearly 98% of respondents would expect that degree-level study of traditional music and piping in a *conservatoire* setting (as opposed to a university setting) be structured with either a clear focus on performance practice or a notionally even split between practice and context. Of a wide range of knowledge and skills felt to be important or relevant to the learning and teaching of traditional Scottish music in tertiary conservatoire education, a majority of respondents 'strongly agreed' with the following:

86 *Joshua Dickson*

Subject	Strongly agree	Agree	Combined
Creativity in terms of composition and arrangement skills	53%	47%	100%
Performance skills in a soloist context	75%	23%	98%
Performance skills in an ensemble context	73%	23%	96%
Creativity in terms of artistic innovation and stretching boundaries	52%	40%	92%

Figure 7.3 Top highest-rated areas of study deemed important or relevant to the learning and teaching of Scottish traditional music in a higher education conservatoire setting

Similarly strong returns were seen in the following, with the proportion of respondents 'strongly agreeing' and 'agreeing' being more even:

Subject	Strongly agree	Agree	Combined
Music theory in a folk context	45%	52%	97%
Studio recording and production skills	44%	53%	97%
Entrepreneurialism and self-employment skills	38%	52%	90%
Collaboration with other forms of music practice (classical, jazz, other forms of folk)	42%	47%	89%
Digital literacy, promotion and distribution skills	38%	50%	88%
Cultural theory (conceptual issues/tools and how they can be applied in performance)	40%	47%	87%
Teaching skills and communicating with learners	45%	40%	85%

Figure 7.4 Further comparison of areas of study deemed important or relevant to the learning and teaching of Scottish traditional music in a higher education conservatoire setting

Feelings were strong but more muted for the study of languages, history and dance, which are traditionally the hallmarks of folk music studies in higher education in Scotland and elsewhere:

Subject	Strongly agree	Agree	Combined
Scottish History	25%	56%	81%
Scots language in and through performance	18%	63%	81%
Gaelic language in and through performance	18%	59%	76%
Scottish Country and Ceilidh dancing	13%	41%	54%
Scots language in terms of literacy and linguistic development	9%	44%	53%
Gaelic language in terms of literacy and conversation skills	7%	46%	53%
Solo step-dancing and its rhythmic link to repertoire and style	9%	41%	50%

Figure 7.5 Lowest proportion of 'strongly agree' responses in relation to areas of study deemed important or relevant to the learning and teaching of Scottish traditional music in a higher education conservatoire setting

The changing nature of conceptualisation 87

These findings support the impression that, whilst important, traditional or folk musicians in a conservatoire setting view the above knowledge and skills in and as context, and that performance practice is viewed as the chief prism through which they expect (and are expected by today's professional musicians, academics and educators) to learn.

The quantitative results of the survey complement and corroborate the qualitative findings of other avenues of research undertaken during the review of the Scottish Music programme in 2014–2015, including a range of focus groups involving potential applicants, current students, alumni, current renowned practitioners and representatives of a number of professional organisations (Dickson, 2015, 29–40). Across all sources consulted, a conviction emerges that:

1   The traditional music scene in Scotland has evolved significantly since the BA (Scottish Music), the UK's first Bachelor programme dedicated to traditional music performance, was first established.
2   The core focus of traditional music in the conservatoire learning experience, going forward, must reflect these developments and indeed must reflect the educational environment in which it and its students operate more fully.
3   Performance, creativity, artistic innovation, business skills and digital literacy are the main concerns of the emerging folk or traditional musician today.
4   The student's artistic path should be rooted in knowledge of what has been passed down, but should continually be interpreting anew according to new experiences and influences – in other words, constructing one's own artistic space in a traditional or folk context.
5   Heretofore entrenched subjects of study such as language, history and dance are important as context, but that performance practice should be the chief prism through which the student encounters and explores these subjects.
6   A degree designation of Bachelor of Music more accurately and appropriately reflects the above curricular priorities and learning outcomes than does Bachelor of Arts.

The above account supports the argument in favour of fresh approaches to pedagogy and curriculum if folk or traditional music education at the tertiary level, particularly in the conservatoire context, is to flourish.

Synthesis: an argument for post-revivalism

What do these findings signify? One way of interpreting the data is that this shift toward the mainstream has occasioned a confidence; a more external-facing eclecticism and fusion in contemporary Scottish traditional music, involving innovation and acculturation with jazz and orchestral western music as well as the traditional music of Ireland, Scandinavia, eastern Europe, Finland, Galicia and American bluegrass, to name a few. This gradual 'mainstreaming' of the traditional music of Scotland over the past generation has in turn led to a growing alignment between the conceptualisation of traditional music by aspiring folk musicians and the conceptualisation of classical and jazz music by their respective practitioners. Increasingly we find that musicians interchange between these performance and conceptual contexts to an extent that belies the sense of Otherness imbued on traditional and folk music up to and through the twentieth-century folk revival in the British Isles. We find, in fact, a cyclic nature to our understanding of and approach to music writ large.

In the eighteenth century, for instance, music was not divided artificially by labels such as 'classical', 'folk', 'traditional', and so forth; instead music was conceived and defined more by function and status, such as ecclesiastical music, courtly music, music for dancing, and of course what would eventually be termed 'national music'; it was this growing concept of music's relationship to nature, nationhood and a nation's people that was eventually to see a further demarcation by class – that is classical, or art music, and traditional, or folk music, in the nineteenth and twentieth centuries (Sharp, 1907; Collinson, 1966; Munro, 1996).

Enter the locus of 'the conservatoire', whose paradigm in terms of higher music education comprises the practical, intellectual and vocational training of future professional musicians (including robust tuition in technique and sound production, music theory and its ancillary applications in composition and arrangement, both soloist and collaborative). Students of traditional or folk music have often subverted this paradigm in a variety of ways: many assume a semi-professional status long before graduation, for instance, and historically at least have been less invested in technique and sound production; more so in cultural context, community engagement and the social value of participation: the very antithesis of the vertical, elite-amateur dynamic perpetuated by the conservatoire model in the popular mind (see for instance Keegan-Phipps, 2007; Hill, 2009; Duffy et al., 2014; Morton, 2014).

Today, further to the cyclic nature of our understanding in what may be dubbed the post-revival era with respect to Scottish traditional music, we find, in some important ways, a hybridity, or re-convergence, taking place. Creech et al. (2008) demonstrated both similarities and differences in attitudes to, and priorities of, learning between classical and non-classical (pop, jazz and Scottish traditional) music students in higher education based on questionnaire and focus group data conducted in 2007. Among differences, it was found that classical musicians on the whole prioritised technical expertise and notation skills, whereas non-classical musicians placed greater value on enjoyment, communality, memorising and listening. This latter would seem to support Sheridan and Byrne's view (2008) of the pedagogic value of traditional *ceilidh* culture to modern higher music education. But whilst underlying substantial differences in creative process, genesis, repertoire and style that distinguish classical from non-classical genre remain real and important, attitudes, priorities and motivations have become porous. At the Royal Conservatoire, it is common for an aspiring traditional musician today to expect a similar learning journey at conservatoire level to that expected by a classical musician, in the sense that technique, sound production, healthy practice and business skills have become at least as high a priority as cultural and functional context, and often more so; whilst increasing numbers of 'trad' students see parallels in their learning with, and aspire to benefit from, the harmonic landscapes and practices of jazz students – and vice versa.

In 1996, the Scottish Music degree's designers considered drawing upon elements of Western conservatoire classical music training for their students where they felt feasible and appropriate (Duffy and Duesenberry, 2014, 50), but did not in the end include explicit technical or music theory tuition for the students, in the western conventional sense, beyond the confines of the one-to-one dynamic between tutor and student. There were sound reasons for this at the time, taking into account the nature of folk music, the unvoiced synergy between practice and theory inherent therein and the designers' wish to avoid what Hill has referred to as the 'Westernisation' or 'artification' of traditional music in a conservatoire setting (2009, 208). What made traditional music *traditional*, in other words, was reflected in a focus on its social, cultural, linguistic, participatory and ethnomusicological foundations, and precisely a lack of focus on such explicit technical performance training as was considered so redolent (and therefore inappropriate) of the western art music paradigm. But in retrospect it can be argued that, once transposed into a conservatoire context, the lack of explicit technical training in some disciplines left students at risk of injury: traditional Scots singing staff struggle to teach students how to keep their vocal anatomy healthy, for instance; fiddlers struggle to avoid wrist problems over time. Students of today very much expect and desire such training, and are disillusioned when they do not encounter it.

Young musicians are no longer applying labels as a previous generation once did – there is a palpable sense of fluidity and mutual learning between genre in evidence that was not reckoned for in the mid-1990s. Young exponents are considered to be more diverse, more connected socially and more commercially savvy than in the past, driven primarily by the role of digital spaces and marketplaces in today's music production and consumption. Consequently, we must recalibrate this as the *starting point* of the student experience rather than its end.

This sense, or conceptualisation, can be described as the coalescing of one's notion of traditional music's authenticity more around performance practice – the act of music-making and the creative role of the individual as artist – and less around the cultural, political, historical and ethnological context that underpinned the revivalist generation's view (and the premise underpinning the Bachelor of Arts designation for Scottish Music in 1996). Though to be sure the latter is still thought of as inseparable from one's concept of traditional music: it remains by definition rooted in the concept of place, social and functional context and communality; it sees horizontally rather than vertically. Such concepts are simply no longer considered a barrier to innovation and personal development, if indeed they ever were.

Scottish traditional music exists and flourishes today in a vibrant and dynamic international context. Traditional or folk music *per se* remains, by its very nature, largely inseparable from the concept of place, or ethnic or cultural provenance. Hence most higher education institutions internationally which offer folk/traditional programmes or areas of study do so in a university setting wherein ethnomusicology and social anthropology are the chief intellectual parameters, and in the specific context of the institution's region or culture.

Some examples include the University of Limerick's BA Irish Traditional Music; the Dublin Institute of Technology (DIT) Conservatory's Irish Traditional Music studies; the University of the Highlands and Islands' BA Gaelic and Traditional Music; Telemark University College's one-semester programme specifically for foreign students in Norwegian Folk Music studies; and the Royal College of Music in Stockholm's Bachelor of Music Performance – Swedish Folk Music.

There are exceptions to the above. In the UK sector, Newcastle University offers a BA in Folk and Traditional Music, a title whose avoidance of regional or geographic specificity bespeaks the programme's broad intellectual and international outlook within which students' own specialist performance and academic interests can be developed. Outside the UK, the Sibelius Academy, part of University of the Arts, Helsinki, Finland, famously offers a degree simply titled 'Folk Music', but this title was chosen specifically to illustrate the programme designers' view that folk and traditional music around the world is ultimately 'one' in the context of the genre's improvisatory and oral-formulaic nature, and its aims and learning outcomes are chiefly focused on the composition of new work (Hill, 2009).

Where notions of authenticity and musical provenance are concerned, we find a different dynamic at play in Scotland, as evidenced by survey findings summarised above. The traditional music of Scotland has increased so markedly in its porosity and visibility in modern times that scholars and students alike have noted the impact this is having on how emerging folk or traditional musicians conceptualise the music they have inherited and the extent to which they are now innovating:

> I wouldn't call this course a Scottish music course; I would call it a traditional music course.
> (BASM student, 2007 in Morton, 2014, 192)

> Traditional music in Glasgow right now strikes me as the traditional music of Europe.
> (BASM student, 2014 in Dickson, 2015, 10)

> Increasingly, [traditional] musicians are performing deterritorialised and commodified music which is shifting attention away from musical provenance and authentic ideology towards more transient sonic identities and blurring established musical genres.
> (McKerrell, 2014b)

This shift toward the mainstream has occasioned a gradual shifting of attention and conceptualisation away from musical provenance in recent years, and more toward the creative role of the individual as artist, researcher and performer.

In the spectrum of extant pedagogical models in a folk context, one may think of those of Scandinavia, such as Stockholm and eastern Norway, as offering a firm foundation in the respective 'tradition', but allowing the student to construct their own parameters of authenticity over time; such personal authenticity may be more or less distant from 'the tradition', but the student arrives there via 'traditional' maps and landscapes, according to the head of the Folk Music Department at Stockholm's Royal College of Music (S. Rosenberg, 2014). Stockholm has struck the present writer as a particularly good example of a pedagogical approach at the tertiary level embodying balance between the affirmation of traditional parameters and continual exploration outward (or indeed inward). 'It forms a dynamic, developmental environment for folk music', according to its website, 'with room both for delving into tradition and for experimentation and renewal' (www.kmh.se/about-the-folk-music-department).

In a similar vein, a shift in title from 'Scottish Music' to 'Traditional Music', and indeed a more conceptually profound shift from a Bachelor of *Arts* to a Bachelor of *Music*, was contemplated on the basis of research conducted in 2014–2015, signalling the need for a curriculum that remains rooted in Scottish traditional music but allows ultimately for the construction of cultural space and meaning at the personal level, placing the onus on the students to construct their musical persona for themselves based on the tools Scottish folk and piping tradition offers them; a curriculum that is as vocational as it is intellectual and that supports student aspiration at two ends of a horizontal spectrum, as valid as they are disparate: on one end, the musicians whose outlook, musical identity, style and repertoire are rooted in the notion of place and provenance (specifically their own); and on the other, the musicians who approach folk and traditional music as a vehicle for their personal, eclectic and contemporary aspirations for professional performance.

Conclusion

The BA with Honours (Scottish Music) was established in 1996 with a focus on solo and collaborative performance, but the overall pedagogical context was that of the university paradigm within what was otherwise a very practical, proto-professional conservatoire environment. Its designers were very much the sons and daughters of the Scottish folksong revival movement of the 1950s, which of course carried (and still carries) significant political and cultural contexts and agendas. In relation to this, it has been remarked by one research informant highly placed in the political advocacy of Scottish traditional music that the degree seems to have been originally established not so much as a music or performance degree, but as a degree in Scottish ethnology, in which performance played a key role (Dickson, 2015, 36). I would argue that what is needed today in a conservatoire context is the reverse: a truly performance-based degree with ethnology (or, more appropriately, cultural, linguistic, artistic and historical context) playing a key role; a post-revivalist degree in other words, taking due account of the individual's role (and potential) as a creative artist in a wider folk or traditional context, and beyond.

As the culmination of the review undertaken in 2014–2015, the Royal Conservatoire of Scotland's Bachelor of Arts with Honours (Scottish Music) and (Scottish Music – Piping) was re-launched in the degree's 20th anniversary year as the Bachelor of Music with Honours (Traditional Music) and (Traditional Music – Piping).

The curriculum has been re-designed from the ground up to align with the Conservatoire's wider BMus framework, tailored to suit the expectations and aspirations of today's emerging folk or traditional musicians through performance studies focused specifically on (predominantly, but not exclusively) Scottish traditional repertoire, style, song, language and creative and collaborative folk musicianship. Alongside and feeding into this is an equally genre-specific contextual curriculum involving theoretical and practical skills, business and ancillary skills and a range of historical and artistic research methods. So performance practice in the new curriculum is offered as a significantly greater proportion of the student's notional effort across the year than what was previously the case.

Complementing the greater emphasis on performance practice is an impetus placed on creativity at every level of study, be it through arranging and composing skills, improvisatory practices and/or conceptual or artistic research methods and sources; an experiential, discursive and performed exploration of historical and socio-cultural contexts, embodying the development of the folk or traditional musician as a critical, creative and historically informed artist; the construction of personal and artistic authenticity and the communication of meaning in and through music; and the development of complementary and vocational skills such as sound recording and website design from the earliest stage of study, combined with the development of career and entrepreneurial skillsets in a digital context.

It is a curriculum that embodies a recognition that the porous and deterritorialised nature of Scottish traditional music today must be embraced; that the creative development of the individual is the surest guarantor of a flourishing traditional music scene from one generation to another (Hill, 2016, 121); that the student (or graduate) is ultimately the final and supreme arbiter of his or her own musicianship; that we are all trustees of tradition; and that as traditional musicians we bear a responsibility to interpret something at once deeply personal and much larger than ourselves.

In direct response to the continuing evolution in the role, breadth, depth and conception of Scottish traditional music, the way forward seems firmly post-revivalist: performance-oriented (in alignment with its conservatoire environment), contemporary, external-facing and eclectic; aligned with expectations, aspirations and forefront musical and vocational developments in the twenty-first century; but which continues nonetheless to be rooted in the musical cosmology of Scotland.

8 Slaying the Tartan Monster
Hybridisation in recent Scottish music

Meghan McAvoy

In an argument now familiar to Scottish Studies scholars, Cairns Craig has argued for the influence of cultural life to Scotland's political narratives, associating debate and innovation in Scottish cultural life with a frustrated desire for home rule (Craig, 1989). This chapter aims to trace these associated narratives of nationalism and innovation in Scottish folk song and the folk fusion practices of *Treacherous Orchestra*, demonstrating a dynamic and ambivalent relationship between popular nationalism and Scotland's music in the traditional idiom. This music is frequently associated with Tom Nairn's 'Tartan Monster': an image of an utterly debased and damaged Scottish popular culture, predicated on the tartanry and kitsch which has colluded with the prevention of an engaged Scottish nationalist political movement in the nineteenth century (Nairn, 1981). However, several examples of musical works and performances from the twentieth century demonstrate a backlash against such tartan monstrosity within folk music, aiming to establish a modern and politically engaged popular culture within Scotland, which is increasingly globalised in the practices of the 'folk fusion' sub-genre established in the twentieth century by artists including *Silly Wizard*, *Wolfstone* and – more recently – *Treacherous Orchestra*. Through musical performance artists informed by traditional music have demonstrated a dynamic and engaged response to the social and political institutions of nationhood – and to the kitsch, backwards paraphernalia of popular nationalism so derided by Nairn.

Out of the antagonisms between 'tartan monstrosity' and the folk performers who respond to it, a far more dynamic beast has emerged. This monster can also be described with reference to Nairn, as a 'Janus-faced' creature, which draws from the cultural resources of the national past in order to propel the nation into an era of global modernity (Nairn, 1981).

Recent Scottish traditional music has interacted with a wider dynamic in modernity, through which mediatisation has played a central role in the rupturing and transformation of traditional identities and structures (Appadurai, 1996). Such a rupture has resulted in interrogations of the nation-state on intellectual and cultural levels: an interrogation apparent in the lyrics of several celebrated twentieth-century songwriters. From Hamish Henderson and the anti-Polaris singers of the folk revival, to Brian McNeill and Dick Gaughan, there is a clear narrative in Scotland's political song in the traditional idiom which engages with, furthers and critiques the politics and traditions of the nation.

However, the mediatisation which has enabled twentieth century artists to bring traditional music to new and wider audiences, and establish its status as an integral part of a national popular culture, has also further integrated a countercultural musical tradition within global capitalism, furthering and transforming the role of marketing and commodification in the interaction between musicians, audiences and consumers of musical product. The repackaging of traditional music as a Scottish alternative to mainstream culture has drawn on commercially successful genres including rock, metal and art music, furthering the commodification and globalisation of Scottish traditional music.

Perspectives on Scottish music

For the purposes of this chapter, I am using 'folk music' and 'traditional music' interchangeably, eliding both terms to refer to orally transmitted Scottish culture. Simon McKerrell has explored the differences between these terms elsewhere, explaining the use of 'folk' as a marketing term describing a sub-genre of pop music, whereas he takes 'traditional music' to signify a genre with a claim to a historical authenticity of style and repertoire. However, the boundaries between these are increasingly porous, and many acts – including each of these discussed here – are able to easily switch between these musical identities for the purposes of marketing and performance context (McKerrell, 2016). My interchangeable use of these terms is in acknowledgement of the increasing porosity between these genres, and the ability of the artists discussed to utilise both.

Traditional music has frequently been associated with a working-class, 'low' culture. For celebrated revivalist collector and songwriter Hamish Henderson, Scotland's traditional music is part of an ulterior counter-culture, which he defines in opposition to intellectual, 'high' art:

> The truth is that the world of authentic traditional art – and particularly the world of folk-song and story – forms a kind of underground [. . .] It is a sort of 'anti-culture' and embodies ideas, predilections and values which are not those of learned culture [. . .]. Today such genuine folk culture as survives coexists uneasily with the majority 'art-culture' and it is quite possible to live right in the middle of it and never to apprehend its existence.
>
> (Henderson, 1992, 34)

For Niall MacKinnon, twentieth-century revivalism in folk music within Britain has sustained this tendency towards the privileging of 'low' culture, arguing that accessibility has remained a priority for musicians who have 'superimposed' traditional forms on new material, ensuring 'that the music can be performed by anyone and not only by highly trained individuals' (MacKinnon, 1994, 67). It is this accessibility which led to MacDiarmid's controversial rejection of Hamish Henderson's folk revival of the 1950s and '60s. MacDiarmid's hatred for a kitsch popular culture perceived as 'monstrous' and preventative of radical political engagement was manifest in his dislike of Kailyard, tartanry, Harry Lauder's music-hall (Goldie, 2006) and the use of the vernacular in work which did not fit his idea of high art (MacDiarmid, 1962). In an exchange of letters to *The Scotsman* newspaper between MacDiarmid, Hamish Henderson and David Craig, MacDiarmid made it clear that he viewed the folk tradition as archaic, nostalgic, and intellectually impoverished, associating the revival of folk song with 'nostalgia for an irrecoverable way of life, and one, I think, in every respect fortunately irrecoverable' (MacDiarmid, 1984, 821). Corey Gibson has ably critiqued exchanges between MacDiarmid and Henderson regarding the value of folk song, acknowledging 'the competing ideologies of MacDiarmid and Henderson's work; in the "high" and "low" arts, the popular and the elect, and the communal and the isolated' (Gibson, 2009, 57). Despite these apparent dualities, Gibson ascertains an artistic agenda common to both men. Both revivalist figures manifest rejection of kitsch and 'Celtic Twilight', antiquarian agendas, whilst utilising the resources of the past in order to engage with international modernity. Criticism of Scotland's tired and imperial traditions was also common to the major works of both men, demonstrating a shared desire to innovate and rupture institutionalised narratives of the nation.

The politics of folk

Recent research in the music of Scotland explores innovations in traditional music, problematising views which consider it to be a radical, grassroots, authentic culture, whilst equally interrogating accusations that traditional culture has become outmoded, amateurish and nostalgic. Where Henderson viewed folk as a vehicle for marginalised expression, the consensus amongst researchers is that the contemporary practice of traditional music in Scotland is a largely middle-class domain. For Marxist researcher Dave Harker, the bourgeois nature of traditional music and folk revivalism is rooted in the antiquarian practices of previous centuries, which have served to 'mystify workers' culture in the interests of bourgeois ideology and therefore of capitalism' (Harker, 1985, xii). Harker implicates nationalism in this process, since bourgeois 'support for "folk" culture is a small but significant part of their attempts to reinforce nationalism, and so fend off danger of the only power which can challenge them – international working-class solidarity' (Harker, 1985, xi). However, Scottish musicians since the mid-twentieth century have engaged with and combined both left-wing and nationalist politics, adapting and critiquing markers of Scottish identity in order to construct a left-wing, anti-imperialist, Scottish republican musical identity. This is manifest in the practice of the republican nationalist Anti-Polaris singers, and in the work of songwriters including Hamish Henderson, Dick Gaughan and Brian McNeill. Niall MacKinnon's study of revivalist folk club demographics demonstrates that the folk clubs of the twentieth century were mostly patronised by an emergent bourgeoisie, who wished to disassociate themselves from bourgeois values: 'the folk scene attracts those who have benefited materially from upward social mobility, but who have not chosen to identify with and refuse to aspire to the dominant competitive individualistic ethic' (Mackinnon, 1994, 130). MacKinnon's conclusions concur with ideas of Scottish traditional music as 'low' culture and as a site of nostalgia for lost origins, viewing folk culture as separate from and/or resistant to the bourgeois, capitalist values of consumerism. The work of these scholars reveals that, although folk music in Scotland continues to be associated with working class origins, tradition bearers and Scottish subcultures—such as Henderson's celebrated collection of source material from members of Scotland's rural and traveller communities – this is an idealised and outmoded view of folk music. Since the 1980s, folk is increasingly produced by highly trained professionals in commercial settings such as concert halls. The practice of folk 'fusion' explored in the final section of this chapter demonstrates processes of commercialisation in the genre, combining the idioms and forms of Scottish folk with techniques derived from commercially successful genres such as rock, metal and classical music. The use of the signifiers of a national tradition in music informs the process of 'hybridisation' enacted in the practice of bands including *Treacherous Orchestra*, whose performance and compositional practices transform Scottish dance forms into a more commercial, mediatised musical genre.

For MacKinnon, communalist solidarity continues to be manifest in the traditional modes of music practice which such hybridisation moves away from, rather than in the politics or class identifications of songs or performers. He argues that the communal performance of music resists processes of commodification and commercialisation:

> The folk scene seeks to celebrate continuity and participation, itself a protest against musical passivity, spectacle and commodity. [. . .] The emphasis upon vernacular musical creation is itself a powerful ideological and political statement, far more than the creation or singing of songs whose lyrics are overtly political.
>
> (Mackinnon, 1994, 135)

However, there are limits to the participation in the politics of resistance by folk musicians. Some twentieth-century musicians have engaged in more material, party politics in combination with the symbolic political resistances expressed in their lyrics. Where some musicians in Scotland demonstrated an anti-Thatcherist resistance through their lyrics and also through running for political office using the platforms of the Labour and Scottish National parties (Tranmer, 2016), resistance by prominent folk musicians on a grassroots, material level has been much more rare than symbolic, cultural resistance in the Scottish folk music scene. The Anti-Polaris singers discussed below—a group of protestors responding to the use of the Holy Loch at Dunoon for the storage of nuclear weaponry, provide a rare exception to this more general trend. More often, resistance among folk musicians is manifest through lyrics, fund-raising concerts and statements made during interviews (Tranmer, 2016). More recently, campaigns for Scottish independence have been used by musicians in Scotland as a platform for political action, in an attempt to bridge the gap between symbolic resistance and active grassroots engagement. This has been manifest symbolically through free-to-attend live performances and through a 'listening' bus tour of Scotland's artists, including prominent Scottish folk musicians (Brooks, 2014; see also McFadyen this volume). However, the ability of these initiatives to provide more than a symbolic engagement has been interrogated, most prominently by the rapper Darren 'Loki' McGarvey (Haggerty, 2015) and the journalist Alex Massie (Massie, 2015).

Throughout the latter half of the twentieth century Scottish folk music has become increasingly professionalised and commercialised, further alienating it from material resistance and political action driven by anti-capitalist agendas. Although folk sessions are still common throughout Scotland, folk music has long since moved into the sphere of concert halls and other mainstream music venues, and has increasingly adopted the performance norms of other genres. Where MacKinnon optimistically views recent developments towards the construction of a highly marketable hybrid genre as a rare example of 'small reversals which extend the vernacular domain over the commodified', the 'fusion' of musical production modes from more mainstream genres with folk has been crucial in the commercialisation and commodification of folk (Mackinnon, 1994, 137). Folk-fusion retains many of the musical qualities of the folk idiom. The use of conventional folk instruments such as fiddles, accordions, bagpipes, banjos, and so forth, formal structures derived from ceilidh dance forms such as marches, jigs, reels, strathspeys and hornpipes, trends in ornamentation, bowing (in the case of the fiddle) and phrasing, and the performance of long and carefully constructed 'sets' of music, are all retained by the genre (to a greater or lesser extent which varies between bands and between pieces). In light of these innovations – widespread in Scottish folk since the 1970s – professional folk practice can no longer be seen as a site of resistance to commodification. Rather, the practice of folk-fusion manifests a marketable subculture, designed to attract new generations of folk musicians and folk audiences, and to appeal to demographics who generally identify with other musical genres and subcultures. In contemporary folk practice there is less emphasis on the aural transmission of music with no known composer; rather, contemporary bands are performing and recording an increasing proportion of original material in the traditional idiom. For example, *Treacherous Orchestra's* debut album *Origins*, discussed below, consists almost exclusively of instrumental music in the traditional idiom composed by individual members of the band and their contemporaries. Only one tune recorded on the album, 'Sheepskins Beeswax', is 'traditional' in the sense that it is aurally transmitted with no known singular origin. Where for Simon McKerrell 'the commercialisation and commodification of traditional arts is wholly compatible with authentic creative practice and transmission', it cannot be denied that the communitarian, participatory qualities MacKinnon associates with folk can no longer be assumed as the norm in the genre, since: 'The distance between the audience and performer, once indivisible, has been growing steadily in the past 30 years' (McKerrell, 2014, 2). Where folk in Scotland continues to be popularly associated with socialist, egalitarian and left-wing ideology, the communal performance practices which MacKinnon posits as the primary site of these values are increasingly less prominent. The site of radicalism has shifted in the genre. Rather than a political, egalitarian and communal aesthetic embodied in the performance practice of amateur folk musicians, formal and aesthetic radical innovation is instead embodied through the fusion practices of professional musicians, collapsing into the sonic rather than any straightforwardly textual performance of protest. These practices are radical not in a political sense, but in the sense that they fundamentally change the nature of folk music, from a genre received as ancient, participatory, aurally transmitted, communal, led by amateur performers and resistant to commercialisation, to one which is contemporary, virtuosic, professional and commodified.

Scottish song and nationalism

This recent depoliticisation and aestheticisation embodies a considerable shift from the revivalist practices of the mid-twentieth century. Political and protest song in the folk idiom has been engaged in the questioning of government and state agendas from a Scottish nationalist perspective since the 1950s folk revival. In the 1960s, the Anti-Polaris singers, styling themselves the 'Glesca Eskimos' after a street song and a derisory comment from the police, protested the use of Dunoon as a base for nuclear submarines. The singing of political songs, with lyrics written especially for the purposes of anti-nuclear protest and Scottish republicanism, was central to this protest. For revivalist musician Ewan McVicar, the Eskimos' use of existing traditional melodies signposts a Scottish folk tradition associated with the working-class culture of the playground and the street (McVicar, 2010, 10). This engagement with a grassroots, 'low' culture based in Scotland's existing traditions and social practices constructed a left-nationalist, Scottish-republican musical identity, based in a shared experience of protest and a culture rooted in communal, public spaces. The tunes which the anti-Polaris singers used were less sophisticated than the airs, marches and other dance tuneforms associated with Scottish traditional music. Instead they plundered melodies from children's song, nursery rhymes, street song and sectarian songs. This is consistent with Ailie Munro's conception of a 'democratic muse' in Scottish traditional music, characterised by an 'all-embracing approach' to culture (Munro, 1996, 1). For Munro, Scottish folk is characterised by inclusiveness and identification with working-class culture. The anti-Polaris singers' use of tunes plundered from the street, the playground and the football ground conforms to both these criteria of folk as all-encompassing and as a site of 'low' culture. These songs embody a folk which is anarchic, irreverent, and left-wing. However, the singers also claimed parity and allegiance with both the literary traditions of medieval Scotland and Scottish literary Modernism, transgressing the boundaries between 'high' and 'low' culture through allegiance with both, demonstrating an example of the hybrid formations which characterise each of the Scottish musicians whose work is explored in this chapter. Extensive sleevenotes, most likely written by Hamish Henderson, Morris Blythman (alias 'Thurso Berwick') or a collaboration of the two, explained that the tradition of satire the Anti-Polaris Singers sought to embody was rooted in medieval literary flytings, via the MacDiarmid-led Modernist literary Renaissance and the international twentieth-century folk revival.

Henderson characterises the folk revival as one in which 'Everything was thrown in the pot', from army ballads, to Child ballads, to the work of collectors MacColl and Lomax, to Gaelic songs, to Glasgow street songs and the comic songs of Matt McGinn (Glasgow Song Guild, 1962). This is posited within a republican and left-nationalist context. The sleeve notes declare: 'The United Kingdom has never really been united', invoking 'the great flood of independent republican feeling that is rising throughout the "Untied Kingdom"':

> This is what the songs on this record are about. They are anti-monarchy anti-establishment and anti-Yankee. The American Polaris submarine, berthed in Scotland acted as a focal point, representing foreign political interference in Scotland at its most impertinent. This record has some pertinent impertinents to offer in return.
>
> (Glasgow Song Guild, 1962)

Examples of support for a Scottish state in folk song since *Ding Dong Dollar* are numerous, and include Davy Steele's 'Scotland Yet' (1998), which calls for national unity and self-determination; *Runrig's* Gaelic stadium anthem *Alba*, which references 'the empty house in Edinburgh/Without authority or voice' (1987);[1] and Dick Gaughan's popular 'Both Sides the Tweed' (1981). These songs were cultural carriers of frustrated nationalist sentiment after the failed Scottish Assembly referendum of 1979, constructing part of the wider cultural agitation towards the second referendum in 1997.

The songs recorded on *Ding Dong Dollar* set a precedent for folk songs engaging with Scottish home rule. For example, 'Coronation Coronach' reappropriated the Unionist, Orange anthem 'The Sash My Father Wore' to the cause of Scottish independence through the rewriting of its lyrics, juxtaposing a more comic, lighthearted register with evocations of historic Scottish seperateness and republicanism:

> Noo Scotland hasnae got a King,
> An it hasnae got a Queen;
> For ye cannae hae the second Liz
> When the first yin's never been.

Chorus:

> Nae Liz the Twa, nae Lillibet the Wan –
> Nae Liz will ever dae!
> For we'll mak oor land republican
> In a Scottish break-away.
>
> (Glasgow Song Guild, 1962)

However, despite the stated aims of the Anti-Polaris singers towards a Scottish republic and the creation of a Scottish state, several of the Anti-Polaris songs rallied against state decisions, criticising Scotland's representatives for collusion with these decisions:

> We've aa got rockets an missiles as well –
> Lets gie them tae Gaitskell, an send him tae hell!
> I wish some power the gift wad gie me
> Tae clap aa the Scottish M.P.s in Barlinnie.
> I doot but oor heids are made oot o wuid,
> Because we've never been had sae guid!
>
> (Glasgow Song Guild, 1962)

The cultural atmosphere dominant in many of the anti-Polaris singers is an anti-establishment culture of the street, which critiques and satirises parliamentary and party politics. Its rhetoric is swearing, sectarian songs, making fun of the police and demotic street language – characteristics all very far removed from official processes of elections and authoritative political discourse. However, historian Tom Devine relates crucial electoral breakthroughs for the Scottish National Party (SNP) to the Campaign for Nuclear Disarmament (CND) during this period, citing a significant overlap between the membership of both organisations (2006, 79). A popular desire for separatism amongst the politically radical groups making up the CND fed into an increased support for nationalist politics. The forces leading to the devolution referenda of 1979 and 1997 had their roots in these agitations of anti-nuclear, left-nationalist Scottish republicanism.

Hamish Henderson's celebrated 'internationalist' anthem, 'The Freedom Come All Ye', appeared on *Ding Dong Dollar* and continues to be performed both at protest contexts and at official, state-sponsored events – including the opening of Glasgow's Commonwealth Games in 2014. Its use of a rich literary Scots distinguishes it from the other songs on the recording, demonstrating clearly MacDiarmid's influence on Henderson. Henderson's affiliation to Scottish traditional music is apparent in use of the pipe march 'The Bloody Fields of Flanders' as the tune for the song, to which he sets new lyrics (Henderson, 2000, 44). Henderson's song embodies the anti-establishment values of the other songs on the anti-Polaris recording, since it rallies against decisions made by an imperial state, imagining a utopian Scotland led by outcasts, misfits, the working-class and immigrants. The lyrics yoke national song culture and socialism together in their stated affiliation with the republicanism of John MacLean, using the song tradition and a Scottish history of republican separatism to critique Scotland's role in British Imperialism. The 'Freedom Come All Ye' envisions a multicultural post-imperial Scotland, where 'Broken faimlies, in lands we herriet/Will curse Scotland the Brave nae mair, nae mair' (Glasgow Song Guild, 1962). This vision of an independent Scottish state, relieved of the baggage of imperialism, fed into an official, mainstream vision of Scottish independence embodied in the SNP policy of the time. Through the yoking together of 'high' literary Scots and a 'low' tradition of communally constructed folk song, Henderson's utilisation of the resources of the nation's past projected a vision of a future Scotland.

Slaying the Tartan Monster 101

In his lyrical practice, Dick Gaughan has engaged with the opposition between literary and song narratives embodied by Henderson and MacDiarmid. 'Come Gie's a Sang' sets poetry and song in opposition to each other, claiming the tradition of the 'makar' for song – despite that the title of 'makar' is often applied to Scots poets, particularly the medieval makars William Dunbar, Robert Henryson and Gavin Douglas. Gaughan's poet demands: 'What fame is there for one like me/Reciting poor folk's history?' (2006). This caricature of poetic elitism views traditional song as more rooted in the everyday lives of 'the people' than literature. However, in his critique of bourgeois literary values Gaughan echoes the sentiment of literary writers including James Kelman and Tom Leonard, who share his propensity to rail against elitism and self-interest in art and politics. Gaughan's song takes the long interaction between literary and traditional cultures in Scotland into the twenty-first century, continuing the construction of politicised folk song as a discursive space in which elite, bourgeois cultural values are critiqued and resisted. Corey Gibson has described this interaction as a 'dialogue' between 'different conceptions of authorship [. . .] one speaking from the singular to the many, and the other singing with the voice of countless anonymous "carriers"' (Gibson, 2013, 143). Despite the abundance of recent Scottish working-class literature, Gaughan's song espouses the view that traditional music is ostensibly closer to the working-classes than literature.

However, the argument engaged with earlier in this chapter, that folk is an increasingly upwardly mobile genre, undermines Gaughan's idealised view of folk song as the cultural embodiment of everyday working-class life. Elsewhere, Gaughan has engaged enthusiastically with the nation's past literary traditions. One of his best-known songs, 'Both Sides the Tweed', uses a tune of Gaughan's own composition, while adapting lyrics first published by James Hogg. Gaughan acknowledges the source of the lyrics in Hogg's *Jacobite Relics* on the sleevenotes of the album *Handful of Earth*, noting his own composition of a new tune as well as his desire to give the song 'more contemporary relevance' by changing some of the lyrics (Gaughan, 1981). He posits this as a response to the failed devolution referendum of 1979 (Gaughan n.d.). Gaughan's song embodies Nairn's 'Janus-faced' agenda described above, by using the resources of the national past to engage with contemporary political events, projecting a vision of a national future characterised by 'mutual respect and understanding' between Scotland and England. The lyrics echo the sentiments of the Anti-Polaris singers, sharing their values of nationalism, republicanism, solidarity and the moral virtue of the nation's poor: 'Let virtue distinguish the brave/Place riches in lowest degree' (Gaughan, 1981). According to Gaughan, 'The verses claim for the recognition of Scotland's right to sovereignty and the choruses argue against prejudice between our peoples' (Gaughan, n. d). For Ewan McVicar, the changes which Gaughan has made to the version of the song first published in Hogg's collection are crucial to the song's left-wing, republican aspect: 'Gaughan's alternation of the text from "our King's sacred rights" to "our land's sacred rights" shifts the song from right-wing to left-wing' (McVicar, 2010, 79). Where Hogg presents his own lyrics as a Jacobite song, the monarchist, regressive aims of Jacobitism are far removed from the civic nationalist republicanism associated with the songwriters discussed here. For Gaughan, this civic nationalism is the most crucial context for Hogg's verses, which he reads as 'an attack upon the Treaty of Union of 1707 which abolished the independent Scots and English Parliaments and set up the United Kingdom' (Gaughan, n.d.). The key feature of both Hogg's and Gaughan's versions of 'Both Sides the Tweed' is the song's invocation of the River Tweed, which in both works serves to signpost a political boundary and marker of the nation (Bohlman, 2011, 87). Gaughan's updating of 'Both Sides the Tweed' from a literary culture of song collecting and imitation embodies the ability of traditional song to comment on, and critique, the cultural practices of the past, and to modify these through envisioning a future for the nation which is morally and politically superior to the past.

Gaughan's collaborator and contemporary, Brian McNeill, shares this agenda to modify and critique past traditions. He is a songwriter, fiddle player and founder of The Battlefield Band: a traditional music collective who use the tagline 'Forward with Scotland's Past', demonstrating an agenda similar to Nairn's theorisation of a Janus-faced nationalism (Battlefield Band, 1988). Simon McKerrell has identified the Battlefield Band as pioneering in the professionalisation and commercialisation of Scotland's traditional music (McKerrell, 2011). Where this commercialisation is part of the embourgeoisment of folk music, the lyrical content of McNeill's song functions as a site of radical politics, evoking a working-class solidarity rooted in the past in order to counter bourgeois nationalist narratives.

'Forward with Scotland's Past' can be interpreted in two ways: as an imperative to continue national narratives of the past, and as a desire for a progressive Scotland borne out of the past. For Philip Bohlman, the simultaneous processes of identification with the past and innovation in the present are the basis for tradition, since 'Tradition is fashioned from both an authenticity that clings to the past and a process of change that continually reshapes the present' (Bohlman, 1988, 13). In several of his songs, McNeill critiques the manner in which Scottish history has been constructed and exploited by nationalist interests. The title of his best-known song, 'No Gods (and Precious Few Heroes)', invokes Hamish Henderson's poem 'Elegy for the Dead in Cyrenica: End of a Campaign', demonstrating the younger songwriter's allegiance to the revivalist agenda of the mid-twentieth century (Henderson, 2000, 52–53). For McNeill the nationalist rhetoric of being 'proud to be Scottish' obscures the class narrative which he wishes to emphasise (McNeill, 1991, 45). The song declares 'it's time now to sweep the future clear o'/ the lies of a past that we know was never real', asserting McNeill's desire to re-read the past in a manner that has contemporary relevance. The lyric 'there's plenty on the dole in the land o' the leal' makes reference to Scottish folk and literary traditions via the work of earlier revivalist songwriters and collectors Carolina Oliphant (Lady Nairne) and Robert Burns, signposting widely recognisable markers of Scottish national culture (Henderson, 1905, 86–87).[2] McNeill implicates the nineteenth century folksong revival's appropriation and romanticisation of Jacobite insurgency in his critique, arguing that these nostalgic attitudes serve a bourgeois nationalist agenda that detracts from more immediate, contemporary issues of class, poverty and social justice. His songs rally against sentimental Jacobitism with an invocation of the reality of the Clearances, which he connects to ongoing inequalities in Scotland: 'They cleared us off once and they'll do it again [. . .] There's nothing much to choose between the old laird and the new' (McNeill, 1991, 45). McNeill's critical commentary of the popular reception of the national past is a revisionist argument for alternative folk practices, which insists on the connection between the folk tradition and the nation's working poor.

In 'The Yew Tree' McNeill uses the imagery of medieval balladry in order to critically assess the border ballad tradition: a tradition central to revivalist collectors from Walter Scott to Francis Child to Alan Lomax, prioritised by Hamish Henderson as the foundations of Scottish folk song and its oral culture (Henderson, 1992, 23–27). McNeill's revisionist critique of the border skirmishes, central to the narratives of the ballads, eschews nationalism and advocates a class context as crucial to the ongoing, contemporary relevance of this period of the nation's history: 'when the poor hunt the poor across mountain an moor/The rich man can keep them in chains' (Battlefield Band, 1988, 85). Unlike other revivalist treatments of Scottish Border battles – Jean Elliot's 'Flowers of the Forest' is perhaps the best known–McNeill's lyrics are not elegiac but a call to arms, demanding a re-reading of Scotland's history in terms of class. In an uncharacteristically celebratory song, 'Lads O' the Fair', McNeill invokes an image of the nation as a community of the rural and urban working-poor, congregating at the market place (Battlefield Band, 1988, 91–92). The lyrics celebrate the history of working Scotland, insisting that even in the context of deindustrialisation, unemployment, and the redundancy of the rural culture the song celebrates, it is ostensibly the history of working-class and labouring identities that have created a national sense of community and continuity. As a body of work, McNeill's songwriting rejects the nationalist narratives which preserve bourgeois, monarchic narratives of Scotland's past, in order to reclaim that past – and the tradition of national song which carries it–for left-wing politics and working-class interests.

More mainstream than marginal: the new aestheticism in Scottish traditional music

In the contemporary folk scene, there is a significant tendency towards newly composed instrumental music, rather than the focus on traditional song and balladry which characterised Hamish Henderson's revival. In the twentieth century, bands such as *Silly Wizard, Wolfstone* and *Capercaillie* created a folk 'fusion' genre, which was rooted in traditional music. Folk fusion performers combine revivalist values with increasing professionalisation and commercialisation in the performance and marketing of Scottish folk music. Through the sonic characteristics of folk fusion, as well as the performance contexts and marketing strategies associated with the genre, the practice of recent performers such as *Treacherous Orchestra* fits easily within a context of neo-liberalism. Their work draws on the musical structures and playing styles of the Scottish folk tradition, combining these with sonic markers associated with other genres, including sampling, electronic instruments and an 'alternative', subcultural sartorial style. The resultant hybridised form constructs Scottish music as a subculture which reacts against mainstream musical norms, through a paradoxical engagement with more commercial genres, including rock, metal and electronica. This adaptation of elements of traditional music into a highly marketable hybridised genre is fully compatible with the logic of a globalised market capitalism, appealing to audiences of various age-groups and musical preferences. Where folk music is associated by some commentators with resistance to the logic of capitalism (see above), in folk fusion it is performed as compatible with market-driven agendas.

In Tamara E. Livingston's theorisation of the aims which drive folk music revivalism, she associates revivalist agendas with both antiquarian and counter-cultural agendas:

> I define music revivals as any social movement with the goal of restoring and preserving a musical tradition which is believed to be disappearing or completely relegated to the past. The purpose of the movement is twofold: (1) to serve as cultural opposition and as an alternative to main-stream culture, and (2) to improve existing culture through the values based on historical value and authenticity expressed by revivalists.
>
> (Livingston, 1999, 67)

Although several folk fusion performers identify with a national inheritance of traditional music, the values of authenticity and preservation associated with folk revivalism are superceded by their desire to modify musical form through innovative techniques. The desire to hybridise traditional music does not eschew its historical value, but instead desires to create a contemporary practice in traditional music which emphasises its 'alternative' qualities. For Corey Gibson, the Scottish folk tradition established by Henderson's Revival 'could naturally adapt to suit the modern age whilst also retaining something of its heritage' (Gibson, 2009, 54). This Janus-faced relationship between modernity and the national past can be seen to drive the work of each of the artists discussed here, and continues to be a central characteristic of a living folk tradition. In this sense, folk fusion continues a much older aspect of a national tradition in music, recasting the motifs of this tradition with the surface signifiers of more modern musical subcultures. In a press release for *Grind* (2015a), the band's second album, piper Ali Hutton discusses the band's aim to 'highlight the change in technology, the progressive nature of the world' within a recognisably national context:

> The whole album is a journey from past to present, highlighting good times, hard times, and looking to a brighter future. This reflects our current situation as a nation.
>
> The main goal with this album was to establish a very identifiably Scottish sound. For us to portray our national identity, and social and musical history through our music.
>
> (*Treacherous Orchestra*, 2015b)

Folk fusion elides a sense of past and present. Signposting the national past through the use of tune forms such as jigs, reels and marches, the genre embodies the nation's development from that past into globalised, commercialised, contemporary society. Mechanical means of sampling, electronic instruments and effects, amplification and mixing during live performances, and the dissemination of cultural product via CDs, broadcast performances, downloads and online videos are endemic to this hybridised construction. This utilisation of electronic media is part of a global hybridisation of cultural forms. Arjun Appadurai defends the resultant globalising effect of mediatisation on culture, interrogating socially constructed dichotomies between 'authenticity' and the cultural hybrids emergent in the age of mechanical reproduction, arguing that 'There is a great deal of evidence to show that indigenous traditions have always been plastic and pluriform' (1991, 473). He defends new, globalised and hybrid manifestations of folk culture against perceptions that they facilitate 'a degenerate and kitschy commercial world, to be contrasted with a folk world we have forever lost', positing hybridised forms as contemporary carriers of living folk culture, on equal footing with inherited, standardised and institutionalised forms (Appadurai, 1991, 473–474).

For Simon McKerrell, hybridised genres in folk music utilising mechanical innovations are 'effectively undermining essentialist readings of authenticity' (2011, 9). Changes in traditional music have relocated it from cultural nationalist contexts to a more commercialised, professionalised and commodified medium; from a site of 'authentic' national identity prior to and apart from industrial capitalism to an industry which manufactures 'musical product' for mass consumption. McKerrell associates this with 'a rejection of the earlier term "folk music" and its associations with socialist-nationalist identity of the 1950s and 60s revival', and a 'move towards more globalised manifestations of 'Scottish traditional music as an aesthetic construction rather than one that is geographically bounded' (2011, 9). This shift towards commercialism and aestheticism is also a shift in the location of the 'radical' associations of this music, which are no longer located in its accessible, participatory nature, since concert settings are now long established as the norm in the case of commercial folk bands. Where McNeill's work with the Battlefield Band has maintained an assertion of allegiance to radical political values through his lyrics, instrumental music by new traditional bands such as Treacherous Orchestra embody radicalism aesthetically rather than politically, through innovations in composition, musical arrangement and performance practices. In their work, there is a marked change in the nature, style, idioms and implications of the genre from those of the earlier folk revival. Through this shift, traditional music not only challenges assumptions based on authenticity, but eschews its utilitarian status as 'the music of the people' and concomitant, idealised views of traditional music as amateurish, left-wing and accessible. Their formal, ticketed, rehearsed concerts separate the audience from the performers, but also enable more complex harmony arrangements and the showcasing of performers' skill and musicianship. This trade-off between accessibility and aestheticism is a move that Lori Watson interprets as a desire to establish a more elitist view of traditional music:

> NTCs [New Traditional Composers] are eager for their work to be associated with 'high art', to gain recognition beyond that given to music for social function (not 'serious' music but 'fun' music), often itself undervalued, to 'ascend' beyond the realm of craft for function towards music for music's sake.
>
> (Watson, 2012, 230)

This desire to elevate a national culture to the status of high art would be familiar to MacDiarmid. Its modernist impetus marks a clear distinction between current trends in traditional music and the irreverent celebration of 'low' culture as counter-cultural protest by earlier twentieth century revivalists responding to the effects of globalisation – i.e. nuclear submarines berthed in Scotland as a result of international political alliances. However, in its catholicity of influence and adaptation of the sonic and sartorial characteristics of other musical genres, folk fusion can be seen to continue the Anti-Polaris singers' juxtaposition of a variety of influences and borrowings, from MacDiarmid's revival to street song.

Treacherous Orchestra self-style themselves 'Scotland's foremost group of anarchic tunesmiths', however, they are by no means the first band to adopt fusion as fundamental to their practice, citing artists including *Wolfstone, Shooglenifty*, Gordon Duncan and Martyn Bennett as precursors and influences (*Treacherous Orchestra*, n.d.). The band perform tune-forms associated with dance music in the Scottish idiom: reels, marches, airs and strathspeys form the vast majority of their repertoire, alongside modern forms such as a pipe piece in the irregular 7/8 time signature (Treacherous Orchestra, 2013). Their repertoire is drawn from composers within the band, as well as contemporary traditional composers including Brendan Ring and Gordon Duncan. They combine core traditional instruments – pipes, accordion, fiddles, flute, and banjo – with electric bass, electric guitars, full drum kit, and electronic sampling and effects. *Treacherous Orchestra* performances have more in common with concerts in the rock and metal genres than the communal pub session or the folk club. The band combine a high standard of technical musicianship, informed for most of the band members by years of degree level study through recently established, specialist courses in traditional music, with an energetic and anarchic atmosphere. The band's musical practice has attracted teenagers and young people in particular, creating a new youth counter-culture within Scotland which is paradoxically rooted in traditional practice. Their use of 'fusion' attracts fans and modes of audience interaction from other musical genres: *Treacherous Orchestra* audiences frequently engage in mosh-pits and engage in other activities more familiar to audiences of rock and metal (Shepherd, 2012). One of the ways in which the band encourage this behaviour is through their use of costumes, performing in black and white clothing which recalls goth and metal subcultures. Their performance of Scottish tune forms as extremely loud, very fast, and imbued with heavy bass riffs and atmospheric electronic effects derived from other genres, presents Scottish traditional music as an alternative subculture. Such performances bear no resemblance to the Tartan Monster imagery associated with the music hall, and could not be further from the popular, stereotypical associations bagpipes have as emblems of Scottish tourism or the Highland Regiments of the British army. However, they construct a different form of cultural monstrosity, one which has more in common with Frankenstein's monster than Nessie in its cyborg-like fusion of practices, techniques and genres. This is identity performed as subcultural spectacle. Instead of a stereotypical or kitsch version of Scottishness, *Treacherous Orchestra* manifest the national musical tradition as an alternative genre attuned to global subcultures and commercial musical influences. Accordionist and composer John Somerville has posited Scottish music as separate from 'mainstream' culture, particularly as a teenager:

> I felt at school I had to slightly hide from the mainstream [. . .] It wasn't trendy to be playing Scottish music. Now with the Feis workshops, there are people learning instruments because it's cool. I'm not saying it's changed everywhere but there is a greater awareness now and there's been a real renaissance.
> (Shepherd, 2012)

Through the use of sonic, sartorial and visual signifiers combined with traditional playing techniques, *Treacherous Orchestra* present an edgy, trendy face of Scottish culture, confronting audiences with traditional music's equivalent of Irvine Welsh's *Trainspotting*, characterised by something similar to the 'cool marginality' that Scott Hames observes in recent Scottish vernacular writing (Hames, 2013, 210).

However, despite this presentation of surface indicators of countercultural identity, *Treacherous Orchestra* can also be identified with a long-established aim within Scottish folk music: to recast the national in the context of modernity, using the motifs and signifiers of the tradition in order to continue the process of combining the indigenous with the modern, the local with the global, in a continually self-renewing process of tradition as 'carrying stream' (Henderson, 1992). The title of their debut album *Origins* (2012) indicates this strategy, as well as recalling the central characteristic of 'Janus-faced' nationalism, which utilises the cultural resources of the national past in order to project a modern, progressive vision of the nation:

> [I]t is through nationalism that societies try to propel themselves forward to certain kinds of goal (industrialization, prosperity, equality with other peoples, etc.) by a certain sort of regression – by looking inwards, drawing more deeply upon their indigenous resources, resurrecting past folk-heroes and myths about themselves and so on.
> (Nairn, 1979, 340)

The band describe their own 'origins', as individual band members and as a collective, at length on their website (*Treacherous Orchestra* n.d.). They frame their musical inheritance as a journey from rural, pre-industrial origins to cosmopolitan modernity. This provides an example of a 'national journey' in music, described by Philip Bohlman:

> National music [. . .] follows a journey that implicitly charts the landscape of the nation, beginning in the remotest core and reaching the end of the journey in the national metropolis. [. . .] When folk music follows the national journey, it undergoes a transition from representing the immanent quintessence of the nation to representing the nation itself. [. . .] In the course of its travels from the land to the nation, folk music becomes suddenly modern, and it is that transformation that makes it profoundly national.
>
> (Bohlman, 2011, 62–63)

This entry into modernity reterritorialises the global 'mainstream' culture which Somerville previously saw as in opposition to his own musical practice as a young traditional musician. The mechanical and stylistic innovations which have established the profoundly commercial, globalised and hybridised genre of folk fusion have reinforced and renewed our awareness of the contemporaneity of tradition and national culture. The genre manifests a Janus-faced nationalism which fuses the cultural resources of the national past with the contemporary, mechanical and mediatised resources available to traditional performers in the age of electronic media.

Notes

1 Lyrics performed in Gaelic are given here in a translation taken from sleevenotes: see Runrig (1987).
2 For an account of the contested authorship of this song's lyrics see McCue (1996), 46–48.

9 'It happens in ballads'
Scotland, utopia and traditional song in *The Strange Undoing of Prudencia Hart*

Stephe Harrop

In the National Theatre of Scotland's *The Strange Undoing of Prudencia Hart* (2011), the eponymous heroine is a collector of ballads, who views her role as the loving preservation of traditional artworks. However, Prudencia's perspective is challenged both by the jibes of academic rival Colin, who labels her scholarship 'sweet' – 'With a sort of old fashioned ethnographic notion of 'collecting'/ Or 'protecting'/Ballads' (Greig, 2011, 15) – and by her late-night encounter with the sinister Nick, whose own passion for collecting forces Prudencia to revise her sense of the ballad's nature, and potential functions. The ballad has long been a site of contention for debates about Scotland's musical traditions and national heritage, and David Pattie, in the 2016 article 'Dissolving into Scotland: National Identity in *Dunsinane* and *The Strange Undoing of Prudencia Hart*', argues that David Greig's play might be read as an index 'to the current state of Scottish identity', with the drama's characters (despite their apparently clear-cut, oppositional positions regarding the traditional ballad and its uses) becoming entangled in 'unending complexities' of narrative, location, and selfhood (Pattie, 2016, 30). The theatrical world of *The Strange Undoing of Prudencia Hart* is one in which received notions of tradition and authenticity are relentlessly contested and subverted, and in which apparently stable identities can be radically re-visioned. Becoming participants in the drama's ballad-fuelled dramaturgy, both Prudencia and Colin – and even the Devil himself – are changed, as 'all the main characters swing from order to misrule but at different times, in different versions, and in different directions' (2016, 29).[1] In Greig's drama, the ballad's protean form proves to be both infectious, and transformative.

This chapter argues that this process is not necessarily limited to the play's characters, highlighting the ways in which the ballad, in the course of the drama, becomes a catalyst for live, collective vocalisation. It contends that via processes of 'musicking' and 'presencing' the show's audience is also offered its own experience of ballad performance. Taking David Greig's evocation of an imaginatively transformative 'rough theatre' as stimulus, and informed by a new focus within ballad studies on the ways in which performers and audiences produce meaning together, the chapter then reflects upon the value of the traditional ballad for politically engaged theatre more broadly, utilising Jill Dolan's descriptions of a 'utopian performative' to consider how and why contemporary theatre artists might choose to borrow from of the sociable, participatory dynamics of the ceilidh. It concludes with the proposition that Greig's playful exploration of the ballad not only offers a stomping evening's entertainment, but can also be located within a wider project of promoting a lively, popular and multi-vocal debate concerning Scottish identity and destiny.

David Greig describes *The Strange Undoing of Prudencia Hart* as a play which 'is self-consciously in dialogue with the ballad form' (Wallace, 2013, 177).[2] Prudencia may regard the ballads she studies as heritage artworks to be collected, preserved and cherished, but her pieties are dismissed as 'middle class and reactionary' by Colin, who prefers to pursue 'working-class performativity', which:

> Isn't plainsong or ballad, it's all celebrity
> It's *X Factor*, it's flash mobs – it's being on YouTube – oh
> It's less Tam Lin and more like Su Bo.
>
> (Greig, 2011, 9)

When the two scholars are trapped in Kelso by heavy snowfall, this feud becomes central to the play's narrative and dramaturgy. As Prudencia treks alone through the midwinter midnight, she wanders from the world of the known into a realm of superstition and devilry, in which the haunting strains of 'Blackwaterside' indicate a shift into the dangerous territory of the ballad-become-real. Previously, Prudencia's musings on the snowy landscapes of the Borders have highlighted her sense of the ballad-as-Other, separate from her own contemporary experience:

> It was as if history had gone into reverse and the past returned like a tide over a beach wiping out our footprints so that all the mess and ugliness of modern life was smoothed away and the world was once more full of old pure things like sledges and rosy cheeks and a genuine need for warming soups.
>
> Thought Prudencia Hart.
> Tides and blankness
> As she drove south through a great bleezing blinding blowing blizzard
> South into the Borders
>
> This is exactly the sort of snow that if it were in a border ballad would poetically presage some kind of doom for an innocent heroine or an encounter on the moor with a sprite or villain or the losing of the heroine's selfhood in the great white emptiness of the night
>
> She thought.
> But this is not a ballad
> She thought.
> And so this is just snow.
>
> (2011, 5–6)

Practical Prudencia, proud of having fitted snow chains to her car and of carrying a head-torch in her handbag, perceives the numinous landscapes of the ballads she studies to be sealed off, both by their past-ness and by their fantastical tropes, from the modern world, although this passage's uneasy balance between prose and verse, and the ironical lilt of that repeated 'she thought', might begin to hint at some of the limitations of this point of view. Certainly by the time that Nick, the sinister proprietor of an unusual Kelso B&B, emerges out of the darkness (by this stage the performance-space is lit only by atmospheric candle-light, and the beams of that head-torch) we are firmly in the world of the supernatural ballad. For Nick's trade, as Prudencia realises just too late, is the entrapment of souls.

Finding herself imprisoned by her devilish companion, whose passion for 'collecting' ironically echoes her own academic pursuits, our heroine is forced to radically revise her sense of the ballad's nature and potentialities. Determined to escape Nick's clutches, and inspired by a quotation from her own thesis which argues that 'the topography of Hell is also the topography of unrequited love' (2011, 65), Prudencia begins to explore previously overlooked aspects of the traditional ballad, in so doing reversing some of her earlier assumptions. Prudencia's escape plan depends upon her realisation that the ballad form, with its rhythmic imperative and rich stock of romantic, fantastical tropes, offers a potentially liberating alternative to the prosaic tedium of their shared imprisonment. 'What would happen if we talked in rhyme?' (2011, 65) she asks:

> If you surrender your thought to metre
> You surrender yourself to the poem's beat, or
> Rhyme or formula or word or sound.
> The author is lost and creation found,
> The poem finds itself – its own *autonomia* –
> Where are you going with this Prudencia?
> – What happens if we let go of prose?
> We can't –
> – Why not? If we adopt a more poetic form, who knows
> What might happen?
>
> (2011, 65–66)[3]

The ballad, Prudencia now insists, represents a space where things can change, and where formerly rigid roles and relationships can be re-negotiated. Seducing Nick first into rhyme, then into intimacy, and finally into sleep, Prudencia is at last able to break free from her infernal captivity.

Nick pursues his quarry back into the mundane world, the chase provoking a dramatic denouement which is introduced to the audience under the knowing title 'the Ballad of Co Lin' (2011, 71), Greig's joke punning on the name of the traditional ballad 'Tam Lin'. This ballad (first collected in 1769, though referred to two centuries earlier in *The Complaynt of Scotland*) tells the tale of a kidnapped mortal knight, rescued from a hellish fate by the constancy of his lover, who clings to him as he undergoes a series of magical metamorphoses. In *The Strange Undoing of Prudencia Hart*, this traditional ballad tale is itself metamorphosed, as Nick and Colin (drunkenly emerging from a karaoke session) struggle for possession of Prudencia in a snowy Asda car park.

However, it is not only the play's protagonists who are lured into re-enacting a traditional ballad narrative. As the cast helpfully inform their assembled watchers (who have, in the course of the show, graduated from ripping up and throwing paper-napkin snowflakes to being co-opted into playing minor roles) this is a piece of ballad style storytelling which explicitly calls for the active participation of its audience (2011, 71). This is a significant moment for a play which has, throughout, operated upon the assumption that its audience does not belong to a living tradition of popular balladry and folk song.[4] Earlier in the play, Greig has been careful to introduce spectators to the style and content of a folk session (2011, 19), and none of the traditional songs which have been performed so far in the course of the play ('The Twa Corbies',[5] 'Blackwaterside') have called for any degree of audience participation.[6] But the 'Ballad of Co Lin' is different. Now the play's audience, like the play's protagonists, are about to get personally involved.

Of course, the refrain which Greig's audience are coaxed or coerced into singing is not a ballad in quite the traditional sense. Fittingly for the scholar who has infuriated Prudencia by getting 'actual grants/For the recording and analysis of football chants' (2011, 7), and whose conference paper is entitled 'The Pastoral Tradition as Expressed in Modern Terrace Culture, or "Sheep Shagging Bastards"' (2011, 64), Colin's mock-heroic entry into the fray is accompanied by a very contemporary instance of popular song, which is 'not exactly a ballad it's mair a/Football chant to the tune of 'Guantanamera'' (2011, 71). Still, the incongruous modernity of this chant does not stop it from functioning in some of the same ways as the refrain of a traditional ballad, using collective vocalisation to punctuate and structure an emerging narrative, allowing the co-present audience of a song to become (at least in part) its collective co-creators.

Now warmed up (and, in the performances I witnessed, possibly encouraged by the provision of free drams of whisky)[7] the audience need little invitation to throw themselves into the vocal landscape of Colin's combat with the devil, gleefully joining in the chanting that follows each successive phase of the enchantment, yelling out: 'But Colin held on' (2011, 76–77). Although many of the increasingly vocal crowd may not know it, this is a close structural echo of the traditional 'Tam Lin', where Tam's injunction to 'haud me fast, let me not pass' (or variations upon this theme) is repeated as the penultimate line of several stanzas (Scott, 1902: vol. 2; 399–400). The triumphal bawling of *The Strange Undoing of Prudencia Hart* is arguably not a million miles away from the kind of collective vocalisation invited by this repetitive phrasing.[8] And so as Prudencia and Colin collapse happily into the snow, the audience too find themselves in a changed relationship with the ballad tale being narrated among them, and with one another. The structures and subject-matter of a traditional ballad, no longer sealed in romantic archaism, have become the basis for a shared moment of immediate, rough and boisterous theatrical pleasure.

There is more going on here than Greig and his collaborators creating a self-consciously clever mash-up of ancient and modern balladry. In his 2007 essay 'rough theatre',[9] Greig envisions a theatrical event which might be:

> Poetic rather than prosaic.
> Irrational and intuitive.
> It would be childish and infantile.
> It would be transcendent and it would be about transcendence.
> It would take place in rough places.
> It would take over spaces and demand that they become theatres.
> It would be cheap.
> It would be written fast, rehearsed fast and performed fast.
> It would contain music and song.
> It would be enchanting
>
> (2007, 220)

In the same essay, Greig discusses his long-held desire to 'get away from theatre that proposed dialectical solutions in the old left-wing tradition and offer a theatre that tore at the fabric of reality and opened up the multiple possibilities of the imagination' (2007, 212). Distancing himself from the schematic, singular answers of didactic political theatre, the playwright instead advocates a mode of performance which might be both populist in style, and utopian in its imaginative scope. Above all, Greig's essay outlines an aspiration to create performances which would acknowledge and take advantage of the fact that 'theatre is all about people coming together in a local physical space – one of the few remaining public spaces – and experiencing something together.' (2007, 219). According to this argument, the potential radicalism of theatrical performance lies in its capacity to create temporary communities of artists and audiences, animated by a shared desire to encounter the transformative effects of collective imagining.

This emphasis upon the collective experience of performance aligns Greig with some important developments in the study of traditional ballads. Recent ballad scholarship has increasingly stressed the multimedia creation and transmission of traditional songs (Sorensen, 2007; Fumerton et al., 2010). In *The Anglo-Scottish Ballad and its Imaginary Contexts* David Atkinson emphasises the 'collaborative, social nature of text-making' within the ballad tradition, a process which (for any given song) may have included 'editors, printers, readers, actors, even censors' (2014, 21) as well as more classically 'oral' tradition bearers. Research in the field has also shifted from the analysis of ballad-texts as heritage artefacts (as exemplified by the perspectives of the pre-undone Prudencia) towards an understanding of the ballad as a complex nexus of text and music and collective imagining, re-activated in the unique context of each one-off performance, where a traditional song's meanings and effects are negotiated between co-present performers and audiences. Such scholarship presents a stimulating perspective from which to view *The Strange Undoing of Prudencia Hart*, and the discussion which follows borrows from the musicological concepts of 'musicking' and 'presencing' in order to reflect upon the experience of the play's vocalising audience in the later stages of the drama.[10]

In *Musicking: The Meaning of Performing and Listening* (1998), Christopher Small argues for the conceptual importance of the present participle, or gerund, of the verb 'to music' in discussing the experience of musical performance. He proposes that the act of 'musicking' is multiform, encompassing actions including:

> to take part, in any capacity, in a musical performance, whether by performing, by listening, by rehearsing or practicing; by providing material for performance (what is called composing), or by dancing [original italics].

He adds:

> We might at times even extend its meaning to what the person is doing who takes the tickets at the door or the hefty men who shift the piano and the drums or the roadies who set up the instruments and carry out the sound checks or the cleaners who clean up after everyone else has gone. They, too, are contributing to the nature of the event that is a musical performance.
> (1998, 9)

This wide-ranging conceptualisation of the nature of music-making re-focuses attention away from music as a product, towards an understanding of 'musicking' as collaborative, contingent and (crucially) processual. Small's arguments emphasise the contexts and relationships through which music is created and shared, stressing that: 'Music is not a thing at all but an activity, something people do' (1998, 2). Understanding a concert, gig or ceilidh as a process of 'musicking' also highlights the degree to which a performance is shaped by a range of participants. As Small observes, 'musicking' 'is an activity in which all those present are involved and for whose nature and quality, success or failure, everyone present bears some responsibility'. 'Whatever it is we are doing', he argues, 'we are all doing it together' (1998, 10). In terms of *The Strange Undoing of Prudencia Hart*, Small's insights help to identify the type of activity which is taking place when the play's audience gets charmed or coaxed into bawling out the refrain of the show's re-visioned 'Tam Lin'. The resulting cacophony may not be singing in any conventional sense, but this rowdy, multi-vocal reactivation of a ballad structure is definitely a form of 'musicking', for the satisfactorily joyous conclusion of which each member of the participating audience shares responsibility.

Such collaborative, processual re-negotiations of traditional tunes and lyrics are central to ballad performance. In his 2009 study of the changing contexts of traditional ballads, James Porter proposes that the interaction of singer and audience is critical to the creation of meaning in performance:

> the 'presence' of ballads is only meaningful when the singer or performer and audience are inter-responsive in a specific physical space that they share. We might even coin the neologism 'presencing' to express this active relationship.
> (2009, 7)

For Porter, the term 'presencing' represents the 'complete imaginative encounter' between song, singer or musician, and co-present audience (2009, 9), articulated in opposition to traditions of ballad scholarship which had focused principally upon the printed words of a song, in isolation from its music, performance context(s), and the influence of active listeners. Further, he argues that the impact of a ballad's 'presencing' might be dramatic, with both performers and listeners experiencing 'a departure from everyday norms into the unknown, unexpected, or transcendental territory of the imagination' effecting (following a return to normality) a 'community of feeling' between those who have shared in this process (2009, 189).

This idea shares some significant qualities with the kinds of 'rough theatre' envisaged by Greig in his 2007 essay, which celebrates theatre's ability to disrupt rationality, advocating the creation of theatrical work in which 'the fabric of "reality" will tear and we can experience transcendence' (2007, 220).[11] In relation to Greig's dramaturgy in *The Strange Undoing of Prudencia Hart*, ideas of 'presencing' and 'musicking' highlight the ways in which the drama's performers and spectators work collaboratively in order to generate a transformative, imaginative experience, potentially capable of stimulating in participants a new sense of community belonging, even once the immediate theatrical moment has passed. As Mairi McFadyen, in her chapter 'Together in *Sang*: The Embodied 'Ballad Experience' as Singularly Plural', which develops Porter's ideas of 'presence' in phenomenological terms, writes:

> the experience of folk song, both in production and reception, induces a sense of connectedness through the embodied experiencing of self and others as co-participants in a live, enacted and unfolding event.
>
> (2013, 161)

It might be fitting to compare the aftermath of Greig's 'Ballad of Co Lin', as Prudencia and Colin wake, dishevelled and befuddled, amid the snow of the car park. Neither quite remembers what happened last night (during the audience's collective voicing of the drama's new 'Tam Lin'), but both fervently agree that it was both embarrassing and, perhaps, tremendous (2011, 78–81). After the pair's unguarded re-performance of a ballad narrative, this is a moment in which, as they tentatively realise, new identities and relationships might have become possible.

These discussions of 'musicking', 'presencing' and 'rough theatre' all share a utopian quality; a sense that live performance might prove to be transformative in ways which potentially extend beyond the immediate moment of shared imaginative play. In *Utopia in Performance: Finding Hope at the Theatre* Jill Dolan explicitly argues that 'live performance provides a place where people come together, embodied and passionate, to share experiences of meaning making that can describe or capture fleeting intimations of a better world' (2005, 2). She develops the notion of 'utopian performatives':

> Utopian performatives describe small but profound moments in which performance calls the attention of the audience in a way that lifts everyone

slightly above the present, into a hopeful feeling of what the world might be like if every moment of our lives were as emotionally voluminous, generous, aesthetically striking, and intersubjectively intense.

(2005, 5)

Such 'utopian performatives', Dolan argues, can have the effect of heightening audience members' responsiveness not only to the narratives, images and characters appearing onstage, but also to one another. Utopian theatre, she proposes, 'offers a way to practice imagining new forms of social relationships', constructing performance situations in which audiences are invited to act in ways which might model 'civic engagement in participatory democracy' (2005, 61). According to Dolan's argument, utopian theatre provides a rehearsal space for real life, where performers and audiences can safely experiment with unfamiliar, unexpected ways of engaging with each other. This kind of utopian performance does not propose clear-cut solutions to particular social ills, or provide dogmatic, party-political programmes for making the world a better place. Rather, it opens a pleasurable, playful space within which new kinds of sociability and communication are revealed to be possible.[12] And, as in Greig's 'rough theatre', the 'something' experienced by each co-present audience depends upon the specific group gathered together in each unique space and place; an experience characterised by 'contingency', and (in consequence) offering a heightened awareness of the 'changeability of things' (Greig, 2007, 219).

The Strange Undoing of Prudencia Hart is not a directly political drama, although it is perhaps (in Dolan's terms) a utopian one. The play was conceived and created at a time when the question of Scottish independence was beginning to be debated with renewed vigour and a new sense of possibility, with the Scottish National Party presenting a draft referendum bill for public consultation in 2010, and gaining a majority of seats in the Scottish Parliament in 2011. Some scholars have proposed strong correlations between practices of ballad collection and historical relations between Scotland and England. For example, Valentina Bold, in her chapter 'Border Raids and Spoilt Songs: Collection as Colonization', explicitly links the practice of collecting traditional songs with histories of territorial annexation:

The colonization begins with the collector/colonizer's desire to conquer the territory, or intellectual property, of the native/performer who is, implicitly, incapable of managing it.

(2003, 353)

Bold was involved in the development of *The Strange Undoing of Prudencia Hart* as one of a group of scholars who collaborated with the play's production team in the work's early stages, and elements of the role of Prudencia may even have been modelled upon her; Greig thanks the scholar in his Author's Note to the play for having 'lent us the sparkle in her eyes' (2011: vi). However, Bold's direct alignment of ballad collecting with colonisation is not reproduced in Greig's play. The drama does show off its writer's awareness of ongoing scholarly debates about the historical appropriation of ballad-texts, not least in a critical nod to Walter Scott's project of shaping a civil, nostalgic, picturesque, and Act-of-Union-friendly Scottish identity founded upon his antiquarian gathering (and occasional authorship) of traditional songs from the Borders.[13] Colin characteristically infuriates Prudencia with his argument that Scott's plan was:

> To respond to the eighteenth-century popularity of *Ossian*
> By collecting Scots poems, laments and sagas
> To create a 'Scottish' identity 'every bit as artificial as Lady Gaga's.
> (2011, 12)

But Greig's own play eschews any such nation-building agenda. Indeed, a drama whose ballad hero, lurching sozzled from karaoke-singing to midnight derring-do clad in 'proud Calvin Kleins', his insides warmed by a mixture of 'Jack Daniels and Diet Coke', his (dubious) martial virtues causing him to be likened to 'Samuel L. Jackson', 'Jackie Chan' and 'a beer-bellied ninja' (2011, 74), clearly locates us within a contemporary Scotland which is both globalised, and culturally diverse. Instead of repeating the clichés of Scott-ish national sentiment, Greig develops a more playful and fluid sense of the utopian potential of the traditional ballad in contemporary performance.

In 'Dissolving into Scotland', Pattie argues that *The Strange Undoing of Prudencia Hart*, in common with many of Greig's earlier works, develops a sophisticated exploration of a complicated and unstable range of Scottish identities, within a country which is always 'shifting into a new, as yet unknown shape' (2016, 22). Pattie's analysis highlights how:

> What seems like a clear binary structure at the play's beginning has more or less disintegrated by the end of the performance; as this happens, the location of the narrative expands and the characters find themselves inhabiting somewhere which is infinitely extended and infinitely complex.
> (2016, 28)

For Pattie, the flexibility of the ballad is analogous to the many complex and changing notions of 'Scotland' which abound in Greig's works. As Dan Rebellato comments in his Introduction to Greig's *Plays 1*, 'David sees little merit in simplistic and narrow definitions of Scottish identity because it's the very slipperiness of Scottishness that is its prime virtue' (2002: xi). The traditional ballad is thus a fitting symbol for the radically unfixed nature of 'Scotland' in Greig's plays, which is frequently an 'absence given a shape and a location by the people who engage with it' (Pattie, 2013, 210). As David Atkinson states in *The Anglo-Scottish Ballad and its Imaginary Contexts*, 'the ballad cannot be located in a single place' due to its 'constant and multiple production' (2014, 19; 23). It is always as much 'imaginary conjecture' as fixed text or stable cultural artefact (2014, 22).

And the ballad tradition evoked by Greig's dramaturgy in *The Strange Undoing of Prudencia Hart* is not only protean – it is also participatory. As McFadyen writes, the 'inherent indeterminacy' of the form invites 'both ballad singer and audience to actively participate [. . .] to re-create and become co-creators themselves' (2012, 13). In performances of *The Strange Undoing of Prudencia Hart* the shape-shifting, popular orality of the ballad in live, collective performance opens a space for a raucous, inclusive and convivial exchange with and between members of the show's audience. Considered in the political context of 2011, the sociable dynamics of the traditional ceilidh, transposed into theatrical performance, might consequently be interpreted as exemplifying the kind of engaged, inclusive and potentially transformative citizenship that Greig has advocated for Scotland at large, both before and after the 2014 independence referendum. In a 2013 article Greig wrote:

> In the context of independence the parameters of politics suddenly turn out to be more malleable that we thought [. . .] nothing is a given any more, not even the idea of Scotland itself. Should Shetland be part of Scotland? Should Newcastle? This new malleability is married to a practicality that gives even ordinary political discourse an extra piquancy. Change is possible. Put simply, the Independence debate allows us to explore every aspect of our national life and ask ourselves the question – 'does it have to be like this?'
> (Greig, 2013)

The referendum, he argued, would be 'a one-off chance for everyone to question assumptions and imagine a different future', in a local and global conversation extending far beyond the binary 'yes/no' offered on the ballot's papers (Greig, 2013).[14] Although Greig was upfront about his own allegiances throughout the campaigns, his primary argument here is that a lively, multi-vocal debate concerning Scottish identity and destiny has the potential to play a positive role in re-defining and re-energising Scottish culture and identity, regardless of the ultimate outcome of the September 2014 vote. Considered in this context, the 'rough theatre' practices of *The Strange Undoing of Prudencia Hart*, the drama's knockabout deconstruction of the ballad's heritage status, and its endorsement of joyous, raucous, multivocal engagement with the traditional arts, can be interpreted as belonging to a parallel theatrical project. The play does not require that its vocalising audiences adopt any particular political position in relation to contemporary questions surrounding Scottish identity. As McFadyen points out, ballad experience 'is paradoxically both highly individual and simultaneously *always* a shared experience' (2013c, 159). Rather, the show's inclusive dramaturgy, which (at the play's dramatic crux) depends upon its audience being willing to risk the raising of their own voices in a potentially embarrassing (and potentially tremendous) re-activation of a traditional ballad narrative, can be understood as modelling the notion that Scotland itself, in a moment of transformative utopianism, might be radically re-shaped by the many voices raised within it.

Deploying traditional music with political intent is nothing new in Scottish theatre. As Trish Reid observes, the incorporation of 'popular modes', including 'music and song', has been a crucial constituent of an often radical tradition of 'folk populism' (2013, 47; 13).[15] In 1973 *The Cheviot, The Stag and The Black, Black Oil* (7:84 Scotland), described as 'a ceilidh play',[16] famously fused history, economics and folk-scored agitprop to critique capitalist exploitation of Scotland's natural resources. More recently, the popular success of *The Strange Undoing of Prudencia Hart* has made it the most prominent among a crop of works testifying to a revival of interest in traditional song among theatre-makers both in Scotland and England. Increasingly urgent issues of history, identity and nationhood have inspired works including *The Bloody Great Border Ballad Project* (Northern Stage at St. Stephen's, 2013) and *Rantin* (National Theatre of Scotland, 2013–2014), informed by a sense that Scotland and England's traditional songs might provide a valuable forum for re-visiting, revising and contesting individual and collective identities within a rapidly changing UK. Common to these projects is an emphasis on popular practices of collective singing, an awareness of the provisionality and potential flexibility of inherited narratives, and a desire to promote audiences' sense of their own vocal and imaginative agency.

In *Theatre & Scotland*, Trish Reid observes that 'The popular continues to be a vital medium through which the Scottish nation performs itself to itself'. She further asserts that *The Strange Undoing of Prudencia Hart* represents a 'celebratory, or even ecstatic' instance of the ways in which theatre drawing on popular performance traditions can promote public engagement with contentious issues of heritage, identity and nation (2013, 48–49). A similar set of aspirations can be seen informing *The Great Yes, No, Don't Know, Five Minute Theatre Show* which David Greig co-curated for the National Theatre of Scotland in the summer of 2014. Introducing the project, the playwright described it as:

> an extraordinary celebration of democratic and creative spirit in Scotland. Over one tremendous day in June we'll bring together hundreds of plays, sketches, songs, polemics and poems made by groups around the country [. . .] At this key moment in the nation's history it's a way for the Scotland to speak to itself – not in formal political tones – but in a relaxed, rambunctious, celebratory and personal way; and crucially, it's a chance for everyone to contribute, not just a political or artistic elite.
>
> (National Theatre of Scotland, 2014)

This advocacy of a relaxed, rambunctious and celebratory approach to performance-making, and to national discourses, represents the point of intersection between *The Strange Undoing of Prudencia Hart* and many of Greig's more explicitly political projects of recent years.[17] It is in the play's convivial, ballad-inspired dramaturgy that the drama most eloquently reveals its political affinities.

Disputing with a gloomy, prose-bound devil, Greig's Prudencia is adamant that embracing the poetic form of traditional balladry might prove liberating in unexpected ways. To Nick's assertion that 'We're in Hell./Love is impossible.' Prudencia replies 'It happens in ballads' (2011, 65), setting the stage for an uproarious shift into a 'utopian performative' mode in the play's second half. Seducing the audience into their own process of 'musicking' via the 'Ballad of Co Lin', and 'presencing' the old song through this tale's raucous, close-up comic immediacy,[18] *The Strange Undoing of Prudencia Hart* mischievously positions its audience as the co-creators of an imaginative world in which the boundaries between the mundane and the fantastic, what is and what might be, are revealed to be more permeable than we might have assumed.

In 'Radical Democratic Theatre', Tony Fisher argues that democratic theatre 'cannot "liberate" anyone but it can destabilise the matrices of a given political distribution', and thereby make possible 'forms of reciprocal action and empathetic identification on which new forms of sociability might be based' (2011, 15). Greig makes a similar point in the essay 'rough theatre', as he argues: 'Theatre cannot change the world, but it can allow us a moment of liberated space in which to change ourselves' (2007, 220). In *The Strange Undoing of Prudencia Hart*, it is the play's multiple re-makings of collective ballad singing which facilitate this temporary, collective space of utopian potential. The drama's sociable celebration of popular vocality, and the collective re-visioning of old songs and stories, holds up a mirror to the idealism and ebullience of the pre-referendum years, and to a utopian sense that nations as well as songs might be re-imagined through collaborative, creative interactions between the diverse voices raised within them. In his essay 'Music and Identity' (1996) Simon Frith famously argued that it is '*through* cultural activity' that people come to know themselves as members of communities (2007, 296). As this chapter has proposed, in *The Strange Undoing of Prudencia Hart* audiences are invited to rediscover the participatory performance traditions associated with the borders ballad as part of an ongoing, popular, inclusive (and potentially radical) discourse about the communities and nations we inhabit, and the utopian spaces we might collectively imagine.

Notes

1 I am grateful to David Pattie and Marilena Zaroulia for their support and advice in developing this chapter.
2 For details of the genesis of the drama see Wils Wilson in Wallace (2013: 227–30).
3 This scene is echoed in Greig's own account of writing the play's text: 'because I had to write in rhyme I couldn't control where it went' (Wallace, 2013: 175).
4 On the often unspoken rules concerning participation in English folk singing sessions see further Hield (2013).
5 The ballad 'The Twa Corbies', which opens *The Strange Undoing of Prudencia Hart*, is a fitting choice for a play which strategically de-stabilises our sense of traditional song's heritage status, since modern ballad scholars have posited Walter Scott's possible authorship (or at least invasive 'editing') of this supposedly 'traditional' song. Sorensen (2007: 23–24).
6 *The Cheviot, The Stag and The Black, Black Oil* similarly differentiates between English-language folk and protest songs, with which audiences are invited to sing along, and Gaelic lyrics sung by an unaccompanied female voice which, like Annie Grace's rendition of 'Blackwaterside' in *The Strange Undoing of Prudencia Hart*, are more often framed as set-piece solos.
7 My own encounters with *The Strange Undoing of Prudencia Hart* took place at the London Welsh Centre, and the CLF Café (Peckham) during the summer of 2013.
8 Compare, for example, McFadyen's account of singing the ballad 'Young Emslie' (2013c: 160). See also Hield (2013: 114).

'It happens in ballads' 121

9 Its title recalling that of Peter Brook's seminal 1968 essay, describing: 'the theatre that's not in a theatre, the theatre on carts, on wagons, on trestles, audiences standing, drinking sitting round tables, audiences joining in, answering back: theatre in back rooms, upstairs rooms, barns; the one-night stands, the torn sheet pinned up across the hall, the battered screen to conceal the quick changes' (1990: 73).
10 For a discussion of ways in which ballad 'experience' might be defined see McFadyen (2013: 155–157).
11 An image echoed in Greig (2011: 69).
12 Compare Zaroulia's account of the utopian pleasures of the Eurovision Song Contest (2013: 45–6).
13 See further Oliver (2005: 19–68), Dentith (2006: 20–47) and Stafford (2007). Bold's (2003) language choices echo Scott's own descriptions of his youthful practice of riding 'raids' into Liddesdale in search of 'songs and tunes' during the 1790s (1902: vol.1, xi).
14 On Greig's recurring subversion of 'yes/no' narratives see Pattie (2016).
15 On the historical conditions which encouraged the persistence of popular and traditional forms within Scottish theatre, see Reid (2013: 31–43).
16 A phrase which appears on the front cover of McGrath (1974).
17 See, for example, Pattie (194–210) in Wallace (2013).
18 Porter notes that '"presence" does not necessarily imply solemnity: tongue-in-cheek parodic or bawdy or humorous songs, for instance, can also elicit "presence".' (2009: 8).

10 The problem with 'traditional'

David McGuinness

The use of the term 'Scottish traditional music' to frame a debate carries some risks. The terms 'Scottish' and 'traditional' are both prone to misunderstandings, and have such a variety of meanings to different users, that they can obscure rather than clarify. What I propose here is a more nuanced description of musical traditions, to move the discussion away from the labelling of particular practices as 'traditional', a process which can ring-fence them into a revered canon, or alternatively into an isolated ghetto.

After a brief consideration of the 'Scottish' part of the designation, I will consider the word 'traditional' as it can be applied to genres, processes and communities, drawing examples from the present day and from the history of fiddle music in Scotland. After touching on the topics of canons (of practice rather than of repertoire), oral transmission, and the interaction of tradition, history and heritage, I will argue that a consideration of such interactions and co-dependencies is more useful than attempting to define the limits of the 'traditional'. Becoming tradition-conscious in all genres of creative work can lead to a fuller understanding of the ways in which traditions may operate.

Introduction: musical terminology

The difficulty with the term 'Scottish traditional music' lies not in the meaning of the words themselves. The Latin root of the word 'tradition' here (the verb *tradere*) implies a handing over, passing on, delivering, or even a surrendering of the action of music making, and a spirit of generosity in its cultural and social transactions. However, to use this 'tradition' as a defining characteristic of a particular form of musical practice, and then to base wider policy on the music so defined, is problematic even on the semantic level. To set boundaries upon music which is under the operation of tradition, is to deny the intrinsic freedom of the process of handing on and surrendering the material to its next bearer.

Since the mainstream categorisation of 1960s acoustic singer-songwriters as 'folk music', that term has been moved on from its nineteenth and early twentieth-century meaning, where it denoted music identified with a people (*Volk*): folk music had been seen as something set apart from art music, and also from popular music (Gelbart, 2007, 260–262). Accordingly, in the introduction to this volume, the editors use 'folk' to describe a commodified and mass-mediated version of the more authentic 'traditional' music. So what is now termed 'traditional' was previously, at least in part 'folk', and 'folk' has lost something of its cultural elite status by an association with the world of commerce.[1] Unfortunately this works against the derivation of both terms, as 'traditional' carries with it an implicit sense of evolution and change (whether commercial or not), and 'folk' one of personal and collective identification. As we shall see below, the continuing use of the term 'folk music' in its earlier sense by some writers adds to the potential for confusion; more recently, the etymological waters have been clouded further by a designation which has made itself at home at the highest levels of international cultural policy: 'heritage'.

What is 'Scottish music', anyway?

In an increasingly globalised world, geographical cultural designations undergo far-reaching changes. Music from Scotland is now played around the world, by people who may or may not personally identify with a Scottish heritage. As a result, the music's articulation of national identity in Scotland, and of wider cultural or ancestral identity in other parts of the world, can vary widely, from a generalised sense of Celtitude or Celticity, to intensely focused expressions of personal history.

One striking aspect of the campaign for Scotland's independence in 2014 was its careful avoidance of notions of nationality by origin. In the *Scotland's Future* white paper which set out the Scottish Government's proposals for independence, the phrase 'the people of Scotland' appeared 24 times, and 'the people who live here' twice, including on the very first page of content, before the phrase 'the Scottish people' finally made an appearance on page thirty-seven (Scottish Government, 2013, 37). Those behind the independence campaign clearly considered residency, or locality, to be much more relevant to the debate than place of birth or ethnicity: to borrow Matthew Gelbart's terminology for Scottish national culture in the eighteenth century, a citizen's function was counted more important than her origin (Gelbart, 2007, 14–39). The *Scotland's Future* document further contained the proposal that any 'British citizens *habitually resident* in Scotland on independence will be considered Scottish citizens' (271, emphasis in original): presence in Scotland was considered more relevant than Scottish descent to Scottish citizenship. This was with good reason, as any allegations that the Scottish National Party were engaging in 'blood and soil' nationalism had to be easily refutable.[2] While the far right is not currently a substantial force in Scottish politics, the espousal of English traditional music by some in the extremist British National Party around 2008, and the horrified reactions of the musicians, show that attempts to construct a national culture, particularly one which concerns itself with the origins of that cultural material, can easily be misconstrued (see Morra, 2013, 45–46).

In the context of music, the use of locality rather than origin to define 'Scottishness' can be expressed by the use of the phrase 'music in Scotland' rather than 'Scottish music'. 'Music *from* Scotland' can also be useful when dealing with music which takes place elsewhere but which contains Scottish elements: for example, to describe Cape Breton fiddle music simply as Scottish inevitably leads to confusion, despite its original basis in traditions from Scotland.[3] The growing Irish music scene in Japan similarly now has its own identity which is no longer confined by its original Irish (and Scottish) models (Oki, 2015). If such small differences in nomenclature seem trivial, then consider the difference between the phrases 'Northern Ireland' and 'the North of Ireland'. To an outsider they may seem identical, but the weight of meaning carried by each, and particularly the latter, is substantial and far-reaching.

The categorisation of 'Scottish music' by geographical origin rather than a consideration of 'music in or from Scotland' can also lead to some absurdities. In the search for a genuinely Scottish national musical instrument, a prime candidate is the dulcitone, a keyboard instrument designed in the 1880s whose mechanism strikes tuning forks on a resonating soundboard. It was only ever made in Glasgow by its inventor Thomas Machell and his sons who carried on his business successfully over several decades, so its intrinsic Scottishness is beyond doubt (Machell, 1888). This is in stark contrast to all of the usual candidates for Scotland's national instrument, such as fiddle, pipes, or accordion, which have long and distinguished histories elsewhere in the world, from before they acquired their additional Scottish citizenship.

I have to admit that this argument is somewhat absurd and not entirely serious: Machell was following in a French nineteenth-century tradition of celeste-like inventions. But it is similarly absurd that the Royal Conservatoire of Scotland's traditional music degree course was named 'Scottish music' until August 2015, despite it largely ignoring Scotland's contributions to other forms of music than those normally considered 'traditional'. The assumption that Scotland's most valued contributions to musical culture begin and end with the 'traditional' has been strong within some communities of traditional music practice in the late twentieth century, but not necessarily outside them.

Defining 'traditional music': try, give up, move on

The landmark definition of folk music given by Maud Karpeles from London's International Folk Music Council in 1952 is still worthy of repetition:

> Folk music is music that has been submitted to the process of oral transmission. It is the product of evolution and is dependent on the circumstances of continuity, variation and selection.
>
> (Karpeles, 1955, 6)

Its present rules, as the *International Council for Traditional Music*, state the following:

> The objective of the Council shall be to assist in the study, practice, documentation, preservation and dissemination of traditional music and dance, including folk, popular, classical, urban, and other genres, of all countries.[4]

Neither of these presents an attempt to define the characteristic musical materials of a genre. The first defines a process, and the second makes it explicitly clear that 'traditional' does not delineate a genre: in fact, it embraces a number of musical genres, including popular, classical and urban, each of which has been considered at some time to be entirely antithetical to 'folk'.

In his 'Folk Music' volume in OUP's series of Very Short Introductions, Mark Slobin attempts to come up with a definition of 'folk music' (again in its earlier usage) after first offering the proposal 'we know it when we hear it' (Slobin, 2011, 1).[5] Unfortunately for this proposition, we all hear things rather differently from one another, and the hearing of people from within a tradition will lead to quite different perceptions to the hearing of those outside it. However, Slobin's framework of practice describes how *aims* shape *strategies* for dealing with musical *resources* (2011, 3). This is a very elegant and useful scheme, but it can be applied successfully to any music whatsoever: it is not the definition of a particular subset of musical practice.

Tradition in content or in genre: examples from Nathaniel Gow

Whether consciously or unconsciously, traditions involve a relationship with the past. It may be the recent past or the distant past, but without the operation of time, no tradition can be established. Another, often more readily accepted mechanism or discipline for our engagement with the past is history, and historical materials can provide a useful commentary on the action of tradition. Field recordings from the twentieth century are good examples of this, and the consideration of such recordings now forms part of the practice of many musicians working within musical traditions. However, there are also plentiful materials from before the recording era: from 2012 to 2015, in the AHRC-funded research project 'Bass culture in Scottish musical traditions', I was involved in a study of printed sources for Scottish fiddle music from before 1850. In their expression of a tradition, these sources can only provide a very limited picture, mediated as they are through the technology and commerce of printing and publishing, but nonetheless they provided some unexpectedly provocative material.

Early in the study, we came across Nathaniel Gow's first collection of French Quadrilles 'as performed by Mr. Gow and his band' (Gow, 1817), and my initial reaction was 'Well, we don't need to bother with these'. The book presented what appeared to be newly imported self-consciously French dances in simple arrangements for the piano, and the choice of dances, if not all of the tunes, came from the first set of quadrilles by the London dancing master Edward Payne, although Gow substituted a tune which is most likely Hungarian or Polish for one of Payne's.[6] Quadrilles had arrived in Britain the previous year at the end of the Napoleonic wars, and the musical content of the volume appears at first sight to be unlike anything considered as Scottish fiddle music today.

However, what might seem to be a short-lived imported ripple in an otherwise continuing flow of tradition turns out to be anything but. James Scott Skinner was still teaching the dancing of French quadrilles from Payne's (or Paine's) books in Forres in the 1880s (Ballantyne, 2003), and the dancing of quadrilles still survives in South Uist. In my personal experience I had never danced a quadrille at a ceilidh, or heard a French quadrille played in a session in Scotland, so I was ready to deny part of Nathaniel Gow's repertoire its place in the traditions I was studying. Given that Gow's was the most successful Scottish dance band of its generation, this would have been a substantial mistake. In my defence, I can only plead that this particular musical genre just did not look or sound like what I knew as Scottish traditional music: this rather gives the lie to Slobin's 'we know it when we hear it'.

Performing these dance tunes with Concerto Caledonia at a commemorative ball 200 years to the day after their introduction, in the same ballroom in Edinburgh's Assembly Rooms, was a thought-provoking experience.[7] There was the challenge for the musicians of figuring out what to play from the published piano arrangements, which seem to be for domestic rather than public use, although the inclusion of harp in some dance bands of the time (including John Gow's) could have allowed for the music to be played as printed. Also, such a formal and lavish event did not have the usual social or musical characteristics of what we now think of as 'Scottish traditional music'. From a commercial point of view, Gow's annual ball was one of the most important events of his year, so while he may have been playing this repertoire as a cultural import to keep himself financially stable, it is also possible that the music was already in aural/oral circulation among musicians in Edinburgh. The eastern European tune for 'La Gertrude' may have been

Example 10.1 Gow, N., [1800]. *Callar Herring* [. . .] (from the *Original Cry of the Newhaven Fish Wives, Selling their fresh Herrings in the Streets of Edinr.*) To which is added Three Favorite Tunes. Gow & Shepherd, Edinburgh. By permission of University of Glasgow Library, Special Collections.

passed on by some of the Hungarian musicians active in the city since at least the arrival of the Reinagle family in the 1760s.[8]

Nathaniel Gow's most celebrated piece is *Callar Herring*, in which he took a street cry from Edinburgh's Newhaven fishwives, and fashioned it into a simple programmatic piece of piano music to be sold for a shilling and played by young ladies in the New Town (Gow, 1800). It later acquired words by Lady Nairne, and I can remember my grandmother playing a much-Romanticised version, which she most likely learnt in the 1940s or possibly earlier.

Gow was unusual in that his publications show him acting both as an insider to a tradition, publishing the tunes played by his band in order to further his career, and as a collector of other musicians' work with a view to building a sense of cultural awareness. Here he presents ethnographic fieldwork ('The Original Cry of the Fish Women') quite separately from his own adaptation of it (Example 10.1). His piano piece in time came under the operation of oral traditions, both as a popular song,[9] and eventually in its reworking back into a piano piece again, as played by my gran. Gow was careful to make his transformation of genre explicit in this instance, so can we consider which parts of Gow's publication are traditional? Is it only his fieldwork, given that his transformation of the material into another genre deliberately takes it out of its original context and mode of transmission, and fashions it into a fixed commercial product? If so, this commercial product came back within the action of tradition by means of the later variation upon it, so the separation of 'traditional' from other material through an analysis of its musical content can be seen to be an artificial and inconclusive process.

'Invented tradition' as process: handing on and bringing in

If setting the limits of traditional music by genre or content has its pitfalls, then what about thinking of traditional music as a process? The process of handing on is clearly built into the principle of tradition, and the sense of common, shared, or universal ownership that results underpins the notion of a song or a tune being 'Trad.' Scottish traditional music processes include social situations such as sessions and ceilidhs, playing for dancing, and learning material orally from other musicians, but there is also the identifier of playing on instruments which are generally considered to be traditional. For example, the particular character of the Highland bagpipe leads almost all music for it to be labelled as both 'Scottish' and 'traditional', just as music written for symphony orchestra attracts the label 'classical'. Similarly, it was Bob Dylan's use of the electric guitar in 1965 that finally provoked his dramatic expulsion from 'folk music' by its self-appointed guardians such as Ewan MacColl (Shelton, 2011).

One difficulty here is that these processes or identifying instruments, particularly when a 'Scottish' qualifier is added, can imply a closed system without outside influences: any intervention from outwith the usual practices might lead to an 'invented tradition', to use Eric Hobsbawm's phrase. In Adrian Scahill's discussion of the beginnings of the Irish ceilidh or céilí band, which was first constituted for social dance events in London around 1910, and later spread to Ireland itself and became popular through broadcasting, he noted that

> the ceilidh band can therefore be understood as an example of an 'invented tradition', according to Eric Hobsbawm's description of the phenomenon as something 'invented, constructed and formally instituted... [, being] a set of practices, normally governed by overtly or tacitly accepted rules... [which are] responses to novel situations which take the form of reference to old situations, or which establish their own past by quasi-obligatory repetition'.
> (Hobsbawm, 1983, 1–2, cited in Scahill, 2004, 244–245)

The 'novel situation' of the popularity of the pedal harp led to the re-invention of the clàrsach in the nineteenth century as a gut-strung instrument, quite separate from its 'traditional' (or should that be 'historical'?) wire-strung counterpart: it could be argued that calling the gut-strung instrument 'clàrsach' has led to an invented tradition of its own.[10] However, it would be entirely unreasonable to suggest that this harp tradition is of lesser value because it cannot be traced back for centuries unbroken. Invented traditions are not of themselves a bad thing, but they are an inevitable result of modernity, and societies which are mobile and ever-changing.

The placing of special value on unbroken traditions is evidence of a cultural conservatism, and an extreme example of this can be seen in Roger Scruton's fetishising of the Euroclassical tradition (the emphasis is in the original):

> It is precisely because the tradition of Western music still lives that we can gain access, through the music of previous generations, to states of mind that we no longer encounter in our daily experience. The unbroken tradition of polyphonic writing enables us to hear, in Victoria's great *Responsories for Tenebrae*, exactly *what it was like* to believe as Victoria believed, seeing the world in terms of the Christian drama.
> (Scruton, 1997, 449)[11]

The notion that hearing Victoria's music as performed today can enable listeners to adopt Victoria's sixteenth-century worldview unchanged confers a miraculous, mystical power on this tradition; to the non-believer (in the tradition, that is) or the critical observer, this is a huge overstatement of the music's effect. Less grandiose claims that a music's grounding in particular forms of tradition gives it a special power to express national characteristics are not really that far from Scruton's assigning of this magical property to the classical.

All traditions have to be invented at some point, and this very invention can involve the absorption into a pre-existing tradition of something which was previously considered to be outside it, borne along on what Hamish Henderson called 'the carrying stream'. In ceilidh bands, this included the introduction of the piano (also admitted to the Glasgow Caledonian Strathspey and Reel Society in 1912) (Lockhart, 1998, 75), and in the case of the clàrsach, a re-definition of the instrument according to contemporary models. The widespread use of acoustic guitars in present-day Scottish musical traditions can be traced to the influence of 'folk music' from the USA as recently as the 1950s. As a tradition by its nature will adapt and eventually include elements which are initially considered to be outside it, defining object-based markers for the 'traditional' will always be an incomplete task.

Oral transmission: time to get over it

Oral transmission has long been appealed to as a marker of tradition since it was identified as characteristic of 'folk music' in 1952. In the case of Scottish fiddle music, we run into a number of issues here, not least that most of its key figures such as the Gows, William Marshall, and James Scott Skinner were highly musically literate, and used staff notation as a key means of dissemination. In Scotland, fiddlers' manuscript notebooks survive from the early history of the instrument onwards, so it is clear that this particular tradition has long been literate as well as oral.

Stepping back from this particular case for a moment, we can see that the oral/literate binary is something of a red herring. Even in Euroclassical orchestral music, which is one of most literate and heavily notated forms, and which was the 1950s establishment norm against which the 'folk' definition was distinguished, only the repertoire is notated; the musical styles and practices are passed on orally, and the oral master-student relationship was (and largely still is) the foundation of the European conservatoire tradition. In any case, whatever the musical genre, people do not learn how to play the violin by reading a book.

The interaction between oral and literate practices can, however, cast interesting light on music in transmission. Robert Tannahill's enthusiasm for Irish music led him to collect tunes in notated form, and repeatedly to urge George Thomson in Edinburgh to publish them.[12] Nathaniel Gow tried to use notation to undermine another key aspect of the 1952 definition of 'folk music': that of variation. In *Part Second of the Complete Repository of Original Scots Tunes, Strathspeys, Jigs and Dances*, the dedication to the Duchess of Buccleuch includes the following manifesto:

> The ORIGINAL SCOTS STRATHSPEYS, REELS, and JIGS, of which this Collection Consist, are brought forward with a view, to serve as a STANDARD of those NATIONAL TUNES and DANCES; for, we Cannot avoid mentioning, that in every part of SCOTLAND where we have occasionally been, and from every observation we were able to make, have not ONCE met with TWO PROFESSIONAL MUSICIANS who play the SAME notes of ANY tune! This being the Cace [*sic*], the Standard now proposed, will we hope, appear abundantly apparent; and that a CONFORMITY in playing those tunes, may with great propriety be adopted. [. . .]
>
> In the hope, that our efforts to add to the Stock of NATIONAL MUSIC, will have a happy tendency, we send this Collection forth into the world; &

will deem ourselves highly gratified to hear, that it meets with approving reception.

We have the honour to be with profound respect, your Grace's most obedient, much obliged, and very humble Servants. Niel Gow & Sons.

(Gow and Sons, 1805)

By the time of the fourth book of the *Complete Repository* (c. 1817), the dedication speaks of the authors

expressing their satisfaction on their Original Aim being obtained, namely, that of conformity being observed throughout the Island, by Amateurs, as well as Professional People, playing the same notes of every tune, without the confusion which prevailed previous to the appearance of the Repository.

(Gow and Sons, 1817)

However, it is hard to imagine that the publication of an expensive book, even a series as successful as the *Complete Repository*, could really have had as wide an effect as Gow claimed. The variation evident even in other printed sources of the time certainly suggests otherwise: attempts to regulate a tradition are only likely to result in a small subset of 'regulated tradition', although this ethos of standardisation imposed by staff notation was also taking hold in the world of piping with more success (for better or worse) (Donaldson, 2008, 98). There is another potential anomaly here: can Nathaniel Gow's aim be seen as anti-traditional, in its insistence on conformity and faithfulness to a printed text? If so, a notion of tradition that excludes the son and musical heir of one of the founders of Scottish fiddling is one that requires some further interrogation.

Gow was acutely conscious of his musical inheritance and of its power as a marketing tool: the titlepage of the fourth book of the *Complete Repository* still carries his father's name, a decade after Niel's death. As the subscriber lists of Nathaniel's books attest, the inherited material wealth of others provided a considerable part of his income, so to present his family as a new musical dynasty built on inherited *cultural* wealth would have seemed quite natural. An uncritical acceptance of this principle as part of musical traditions in the present day may not be quite so easy: by virtue of its provenance alone, a song learnt by the performer from her mother has no more intrinsic value *to its audience* than a song learnt from a recording, even though it will in most cases have a much greater significance to the musician herself.

Socially constituted tradition as canon

Nathaniel Gow's attempts to standardise a national music with one eye on his paymasters (the dedicatees of the fourth book of the *Complete Repository* were 'the nobility and gentry of Scotland') is comparable, perhaps unexpectedly, with the setting up of the 'Jazz at Lincoln Center' programme in New York City in 2004. This institutionalisation of a musical practice necessitated a working definition of jazz, and, as with traditional music, the process of definition is a political issue hiding behind an aesthetic one. In Christopher Washburne's critique (Washburne, 2004, 138–139), he notes that by taking the 'canon' position rather than 'process', Wynton Marsalis and his associates unlocked access to large public funds, but also narrowed the definition of jazz in order to assume an ownership of the genre. The two 'definitorial' stances (borrowing terms from Jerome Harris) are:

> the 'canon position', where jazz is seen as a music defined by a specific African American originated genealogy and socially constituted guild, and the 'process position' where jazz is viewed as the result of certain African American originated processes and aesthetics manifested in the music.
> (Washburne, 2004, 138)

The canon is not a canon of repertoire, but of social belonging. Substitute 'traditional music' for 'jazz', and 'Scottish' for 'African American', and another way of describing these two positions might be a closed tradition, to which you can only belong if born into it (as Gow was) or invited, and an open one, in which the processes are freely available for all to take part and contribute, regardless of their Scottishness or their recognised place in 'the tradition'.[13] While the canon position can produce a form of officially sanctioned and well-funded traditional music, the 'unofficial' traditional music will carry on regardless (as has non-sanctioned jazz), albeit capitalised to a lesser extent.

Washburne continues:

> the canon position defines jazz as a sort of endangered species whereby limitations are placed on the constituent boundaries of the music, a high art status is affixed, and the music undergoes an open-ended process of sacrilization. When the jazz tradition is viewed more as an open-ended process, individual musicians are empowered to innovate through a much broader spectrum of media forces [. . .]. In reality, most musicians use both of these positions, and at specific times, locate themselves on whichever side of this binary that serves them best.
> (Washburne, 2004, 138)

Washburne's point about what musicians really do holds true in the case of Scottish traditional music: creative musicians take the processes and aesthetics forward in whatever way they see fit, and considerations of their relationship to a canon of tradition (whether or repertoire, practice or community) are usually a secondary concern. Defining a genre or a tradition in terms of a canon may work reasonably well when considering the practices of the past, but applying the same principles as restrictions to the present is to put strictures upon practice that creative artists will simply ignore; assuming that these canonic rules will also continue to apply in the future is clearly futile.

The present-day issue in Scotland parallel to 'Jazz at the Lincoln Center' is the question of whether 'Scottish traditional music' should be added to the list of privileged, or over-subsidised, musics: the main target here is orchestral music (including opera) with its 'national companies', whose state grants are given directly by government, rather than through the funding agency Creative Scotland. If to join this list of national institutions would mean the adoption of canonic and thus discriminatory definitions of practice, I would argue instead for the removal, or at the very least the reduction, of existing privileges, on the simple principle that two wrongs don't make a right. In 2000, Philip Tagg expressed the dangers of taking the canon position very eloquently, addressing himself in this case to scholars of popular music:

> Without [. . .] self-reflection and historical awareness, popular music scholars could end up like the rearguard of the old aesthetic canon, ethnocentrically claiming universal, absolute and other supra-socially transcendent values for one set of musical practices and ignoring the real conditions, functions, contexts and structural complexities of others.
>
> (Tagg, 2000, 167)

Tradition as community: what about those outside?

Is there value in identifying 'Scottish traditional music' within a community of practice? With fiddle music, there may be a case here, as in the late twentieth century the rise of sessions as a means of sharing tunes and cultivating a sense of belonging has meant that community is more important to Scottish fiddling than, say, Quebecois or Métis fiddling, where individual variation has led to the development of crooked tunes, a brazen individuality of which Nathaniel Gow would not have approved. Is inclusion as part of a musical community enough to define what Scottish traditional music is, with a *collective* sense of 'we know it when we hear it'?

In their turn, recording, broadcasting and the internet have made this picture rather more complicated, simply because Scottish traditional music is now widely practised outside Scotland. Owe Ronström has suggested that, as the Cape Breton fiddle style has now spread across the world, the style played in Cape Breton itself may in time become 'inauthentic' as the music develops further elsewhere (Ronström, 2010, 279). While it is unlikely that this will happen to musical traditions from Scotland for some time yet, a number of speakers at the 2015 North Atlantic Fiddle Convention found that geographical designations for traditions are becoming inadequate or obsolete, whether at the local level (North East fiddling, Shetland fiddling) or the national.[14]

Placing the authentication of tradition within a community will always suppress individuality to some extent, whether of performance style or of repertoire. I hope that singer and songwriter Alasdair Roberts is amused rather than perplexed by the categorisation of his work as mass-mediated 'folk music' in the introduction to this volume: his lack of qualification for admittance to the 'traditional' probably has more to do with his early background in indie rock and his outsider aesthetic, rather than any lack of tradition-consciousness on his part, whether in his performance of traditional ballads, in his own songwriting, or in his curation of historic field recordings.[15] He can even point to a cultural inheritance in that his father was the folk singer Alan Roberts,[16] but Alasdair's acceptance into that community of practice, or indeed by its audience, remains at time of writing unconsummated, an example of how traditions can sometimes be closed rather than welcoming to those from outside their orthopraxies.

There is the related possibility that there may be more than one community of 'Scottish traditional music'. In February 2014, the Scottish football team unveiled a new away strip in pink and yellow hoops, and the satirical website *The Daily Mash* ran a story headed 'New Scotland kit reflects country's tradition of twee indie music', which began 'Scotland's new away kit represents the country's history of producing delicate indie music for manchildren', and cited a selection of 1980s Glasgow bands including Camera Obscura and The Pastels, and the later inheritors of this musical tradition, Belle and Sebastian.[17] The presence of the words 'Scotland', 'tradition' and 'music' in the headline are very clear, but the post-Postcard Records Glasgow indie tradition it describes is not one under consideration in this book, even though it falls within Simon McKerrell's definition of 'traditional music' given in the book's introduction: it is a marker of identity for a particular cultural group, and the music grew from oral tradition. Indeed, it also satisfies definitions of Intangible Cultural Heritage by being passed from one generation to another. That this particular musical tradition expresses that 'Scotland has long been a global leader in wistful disappointment, thanks to our natural abundance of sexless, pasty-faced introverts' could be viewed as a stereotypical view from London ex-pats, but in the context of a discussion of Scottish traditional music, it demonstrates that Scotland's musical traditions are numerous and varied, that they have their own communities, and that they denote subtle aspects of 'Scottishness' when interrogated, whether this is for comic effect or not.

Popular music in Scotland is too diverse to be represented by a single community, or a single soundworld, but since the 1980s when commercially successful bands began to base their careers in Scotland as a matter of course, the fact of their Scottish residency has brought about something of a distinctive tradition of practice (this development is described in Harvey (2005)). In itself, this is a powerful expression of Scottish 'independence': an independence from the customary London-centric music business practices. On the final weekend before the referendum in September 2014, a high-profile Vote Yes rally in Edinburgh's Usher Hall, billed as 'A Night for Scotland' and attended by the SNP's leader and deputy, featured amongst others, Franz Ferdinand, Frightened Rabbit, and Mogwai: the lack of traditional music artists on the bill suggests that their role in the campaign can easily be overstated (Morrison, 2014; Brooks, 2014).

History, tradition and heritage

I have already noted the potential for the interaction between musical history and tradition in the use of field recordings and early notated musical sources, but another musical tradition has already undergone a well-documented encounter with history. In Euroclassical music, traditions of practice were challenged from the 1950s onwards by what became the historical performance movement, when musicians found that the performance traditions handed down to them for music of the past were not as artistically convincing as those which they constructed for themselves under the influence of historical material and evidence. This in turn has led to a diversity of practice (albeit a limited diversity) and a subsequent interaction between 'traditional' Euroclassical practice and so-called historically informed performance (HIP), which is in fact a distinct aural/oral tradition. It is just as ineffective to try to learn to play baroque violin from a book as it is modern violin, although the historical books may guide your practice in a particular direction.

John Haines has described the HIP movement in the broad context of folk music revivals and alongside the more recent rise of ethnomusicology (Haines, 2014), but of particular interest to this discussion is that historical knowledge brought about a greater awareness of the action of tradition, and a broadening of the realm of practice. Could historically informed tradition (HIT) have a similar effect,[18] infusing traditions with an awareness of cultural history, Scottish history, or indeed the history of Scottish music, about which we are still on the whole remarkably ignorant?

For example, to state that the sequence of March, Strathspey and Reel (MSR) is a long-standing tradition in the playing of the pipes and the fiddle in Scotland is to include it synchronically within the definition of the 'traditional'. Add to this some simple historical information about when this sequence came into being, and what influences brought it about (why it combines military and dance-based forms, for example), and that tradition is afforded a greater depth of meaning, and can be freed from ossification as an unchanging 'given' from the past: it becomes part of the process of history rather than simply a product of it.

Although it remains a contested term, heritage is not so much a way of looking at the past, as a means of dealing with its legacy. The clear distinction drawn by Owe Ronström between the operations of tradition and of heritage describes the move towards the latter as the result of globalisation, where 'local styles are uncoupled or disembedded from their former musical mindscapes, their specific places and pasts, and made available over large spaces' (Ronström, 2014, 54). Despite its backward-looking focus, 'heritage music' could in time become a more useful and specific term than 'traditional music', and certainly one more suited to the drawing up of lists of cultural practices which are considered worthy of preservation away from their original contexts. This domain of heritage could also become the best home for geographically defined musical styles, whose designations are already becoming less accurate as their music is made more widely available to develop away from its place of origin.

Interaction and borderlines

It would be nonsensical to argue here for an abandonment of the use of the word 'traditional'. As a broad signifier of genre, 'this is traditional music' (it conforms to generally received notions of traditional music) and 'this is folk music' (a more commodified version of the above, although given the term's history this is not a universally accepted meaning) are both generally effective. The self-identification by many in Scotland as 'trad' rather than 'traditional' musicians is not merely an abbreviation: the updating of the terminology denotes a subtle shift towards something less firmly rooted only in the past.[19]

If we return to Maud Karpeles in the 1950s, the final paragraph of her paper on the definition of 'folk music' already describes a move away from hard definitions:

> In any country in which art music and folk music exist side by side there is bound to be inter-action between the two types of music and there will always be a certain number of songs that are on the border-line [. . .]. In the same way that folk music may constitute the raw material of art music, so may art music constitute the raw material of folk music.
>
> (Karpeles, 1955, 7)

Karpeles only mentions two genres, but to these we could now add countless others including commercial music, pop music, avant-garde music, indie music, and even the music that plays in your head. While the 'raw material' metaphor has its limitations (which is raw and which is cooked?), the notion of interaction and borderlines is more fruitful, and indeed describes part of the action of tradition itself. In academic research, disciplinary purity has become an unfashionable pursuit, in favour of porous boundaries and interdisciplinarity: this could be described as a move away from thinking in terms of Aristotleian individuated substances towards something of the Buddhist philosophy of Pratītyasamutpāda, or 'dependent co-arising'. Fashion aside, it seems more realistic to look to constantly changing networks of co-dependencies and relationships for our knowledge of the world.[20]

As further evidence of how 'individuated substances' and hard definitions can be musically unhelpful, Example 10.2 shows a strathspey from John Morison's *A Collection of New Strathspey Reels* of 1801. Morison was far from being an individuated substance himself, as to earn his precarious living as a musician in Peterhead, he was a fiddler, organist, piano and organ tuner, a music copyist, and also traded as a ship's chandler. Despite this versatility, he was bankrupted at least once: Morison's professional life can be traced in the advertisements he placed in the *Aberdeen Journal*, collected by J. Murdoch Henderson in GB-En MS21708, ff.8r-23v, and his chandlery is mentioned by Alburger (1983, 89–90).

'Mrs Duff of Fetteresso's Strathspey' has no defining musical characteristics of strathspeys as they are now traditionally played, notated as it is almost entirely in equal quavers, like a reel. So, can this tune be defined as a strathspey?

The answer of course is 'I think you'll find it's a bit more complicated than that'. Even in 1801, strathspeys were still not entirely distinct from reels, as is hinted by the title of Morison's book. In the second half of the eighteenth century, many tunes appear in the sources in both forms, or in what now appear to be hybrid forms that combine aspects of the strathspey and the reel. While Morison's title may be an indication that he intends the tune to be played according to

Example 10.2 'Mrs Duff (of Fetteresso's) Strathspey' from Morison, J., 1801. *A Collection of New Strathspey Reels*. Gow & Shepherd, Edinburgh. By permission of University of Glasgow Library, Special Collections.

the conventions of a strathspey, his other strathspeys in the book have differing proportions of dotted and straight rhythms, and these are systematic rather than haphazard. Five of the 24 tunes labelled as strathspeys are notated in equal quavers, and a further three contain only a single instance of a dotted rhythm, so defining these tunes simply as strathspeys in the present day could be misleading: the notation makes clear that they were not conceived to be played in the manner of a twenty-first-century strathspey, and that the present-day understanding of what constitutes a strathspey is quite different from Morison's.

What might make more sense in modern terms would be to note their strathspey-like characteristics and their reel-like characteristics, and then explore how these might interact in the playing of the tune. At a rehearsal for the Gow quadrille bicentenary event mentioned above, dancing master Stuart Marsden turned to the band to ask 'This is a strathspey, isn't it?', and received the laughing response 'I really have no idea any more!', from a musician whose detailed understanding and experience of the defining musical elements of a strathspey had been challenged by playing from historical materials.

Becoming tradition-conscious

Taking this idea forward, the categorisation of an entire musical practice as 'traditional' is a similarly blunt instrument. When music is multi-layered and sophisticated (and it usually is), we need to be able to identify more closely which aspects of the music have come from which traditions, in order both to describe it and to study it.

For many musicians, a simple version of this principle is already a part of their working practice. Album sleeve notes now often give lists of sources, and in performance, the phrase 'I learnt this tune/song from' is now commonplace. The US-Canadian fiddler David Greenberg uses the abbreviations FTRO and FTPO in his own notes, to distinguish between 'from the repertoire of', where he has adopted a tune from another player, and 'from the playing of' where he has sourced a recording and the previous player's personal style has had some influence on the details of his own.[21]

Those engaged in the study of traditions can go further. For example, we might identify a fiddle player as being rooted in a particular style of playing, but what about the guitar player who is playing at the same time? In what traditions are her playing, or indeed her very presence as a guitar player with the fiddler in the first place? In my work with eighteenth- and nineteenth-century sources of Scottish music I was looking for evidence of how Scottish musical traditions became fixated largely on the top line of the musical texture: why have the songs and the tunes become considered more 'traditional' than all that goes on underneath? As a keyboard player, with no universally accepted traditional models to follow, I hoped to find (and indeed did find) a basis in the historical materials for a practice that could be defined by something other than my own musical habits and preferences: the patronising and demeaning term 'accompaniment' can be unhelpful here, as it defines a hierarchy of value within the musical texture. If, instead, we develop a fuller awareness of the many musical traditions that are now expressed alongside and simultaneous to the more obviously 'traditional', this will teach us a great deal about how the music has evolved and is evolving, and it may also offer us a vocabulary for dealing with hybrid material such as Gow's *Callar Herring*.

Conclusion

Tradition is simply one of many frameworks within which to describe musical activity. We can choose, if we wish, to describe the action of tradition within music, and 'tradition-conscious' describes the mindset required for this better than labelling the music itself as 'traditional'. Marking particular strands of music and musicmaking as 'traditional' is divisive, inaccurate, and ultimately of little use other than to build a protective wall around an area of narrow practice defined by those making the categorisation.

Current knowledge of the history of music in Scotland is generally at a very elementary level, but development of this historical awareness will lead to a richer understanding of the music's evolution, and to informed judgments of its nature as heritage. A broad, inclusive consciousness of the action of traditions and transmission in the past and the present can enable us to understand more fully the interactions, connections and serendipities that have shaped music in Scotland and elsewhere.

Notes

1. The term 'roots music' can be read as implying mass-mediation more clearly than 'folk', as the music is assumed to have grown from its roots, but it is rarely applied to music in Scotland.
2. When Alistair Darling, the leader of the No campaign, appeared to make such an allegation in an interview in June 2014, accusations flew for some time on both sides. BBC News – Scottish independence: Salmond in Darling interview apology call, 11 June 2014. URL www.bbc.co.uk/news/uk-scotland-scotland-politics-27793285 (accessed 1.11.15).
3. In his landmark radio series and book, John Purser's use of the inclusive term 'Scotland's Music' was deliberate (see also Purser, 2007). The same form of words had been used by Cedric Thorpe Davie in Davie (1980).
4. Taken from the present ICTM Rules at www.ictmusic.org/rules-ictm (accessed 1 November 2015).
5. I have suggested elsewhere that the volume should really have been entitled *Ethnomusicology: A Very Short Introduction*: see my review McGuinness (2012).
6. Thanks to Alena Shmakova for alerting me to the connection between Gow and Payne, and to Karen McAulay for exploring it further. Gow published further sets of tunes for the dance figures annually into the 1820s.
7. The event was arranged by Talitha MacKenzie, with dancing master Stuart Marsden.
8. Joseph Reinagle *senior* was appointed royal trumpeter in Scotland in 1762, but he may also have been in Edinburgh in the 1740s before moving to Portsmouth (McGrattan, 1997, 87).
9. Dugald Ramsay took such offence when The Glasgow Herald referred in passing to 'that vulgar tune, "Caller Herrin"' in 1871, that he published a spluttering 16-page pamphlet detailing its sophistication (Ramsay, 1871).
10. The gut-strung harp may have been played in the 16th century, but in the Scottish Lowlands. (Sanger, 1992, 45).
11. Thanks to John Butt for drawing this passage to my attention.
12. Elizabeth Ford notes that his biographer David Semple in 1874 ridiculed Tannahill for being 'a sedate Scotsman' attempting to write 'verses to suit the wild airs of Hibernia', tunes which Tannahill had collected from his friend James Clark, a bandsman in the Argyll Militia (Ford, 2016, 57–59).
13. Although the term 'heritage' can be as contentious as 'tradition', this framework corresponds quite closely to the distinction between 'tradition' (closed) and 'heritage' (open) given in Ronström (2014, 52–53).
14. Oki (2015); Emma Nixon's presentation on Scottish fiddling in Australia, and Ronnie Gibson's on regional Scottish fiddle traditions also demonstrated the limitations of geographical designations.
15. One of Roberts' recent albums was his selection of material from Alan Lomax's recordings from 1950s Scotland: *Whaur The Pig Gaed On The Spree: Scottish Recordings By Alan Lomax*, 1951–1957, 2011. Global Jukebox / Twos & Fews / Drag City.
16. Alan Roberts was also a key promoter of Scottish folk music in Germany in the 1970s and 1980s.
17. New Scotland kit reflects country's tradition of twee indie music, 2014. The Daily Mash. URL www.thedailymash.co.uk/sport/sport-headlines/new-scotland-kit-reflects-countrys-tradition-of-twee-indie-music-2014022784082. The journalist founders of *The Daily Mash*, Paul Stokes and Neil Rafferty, both had experience of writing for Scottish newspapers, and the site's material on Scottish cultural affairs can be unusually sharp.
18. Thanks to Bill Sweeney for pointing out that the additional designation 'Scottish' would be inappropriate in this case.
19. The OED places the origins of the abbreviation in the 'trad jazz' of the mid-1950s.
20. Thanks to Martin Parker Dixon for these observations (personal correspondence).
21. Personal correspondence.

11 Salsa Celtica's Great Scottish Latin Adventure – an insider's view

Phil Alexander

> It's amazing how that group of people, the majority of whom didn't grow up in the salsa world at all – the complete majority, almost 100 percent – ended up producing some salsa that people liked in Latin America and New York. And that's kind of an incredible thing. But it also existed in a really vibrant live scene in Scotland, which it couldn't have done without that, because it was a live band. And then that's sort of an interesting thing socially, it was popular in Scotland because it was kind of different and people were excited by that difference. If it was just a salsa band it wouldn't have been so interesting to Scottish people, even Scottish people who aren't massively into folk music.
>
> (Toby Shippey, Salsa Celtica)[1]

Introduction: la sonora de Escocia

Salsa Celtica is an Edinburgh-based band which has been energetically gigging for nearly twenty years. In that period, the group has become a significant presence on the world music stage, playing Womad, Cambridge Folk Festival, Denmark's Tønder festival, Womex Seville, Celtic Connections and Proms in the Park, as well as regular UK, European, North and South American tours. The band's third album 'El Agua de la Vida' made the Billboard Latin top 10 and the follow-up 'El Camino' narrowly missed out on four Radio 2 Folk Awards (mercilessly trumped by an up-and-coming Bellowhead). Salsa Celtica's 2015 Glastonbury gig was voted top live show of the year by the Latin UK Awards. Wary of the limits of record-bin categories, one might effectively describe the group's sound as exactly what its name suggests: a mix of Celtic[2] tunes and salsa rhythms, played out with style, wit, virtuosity and a lot of fun. Moving seamlessly from deep Latin grooves to driving reels, this is an aesthetics of shape-shifting and fluidity that never fully rests in one musical space or the other. Sonically, linguistically and performatively, Salsa Celtica embodies a philosophy poised at the semi-accidental meeting of traditions – one which is robust, flexible, fearless and inevitably prone to short-lived conflicts of artistic difference.

Part of my reason for writing what follows is that for six very happy years I was a central part of the band before moving away from Scotland. In that time we travelled to Germany, Algeria, New York, Israel, Malaysia, Benelux, Iceland,

Czech Republic, Ireland and more, winning converts along the way to this strange Cuban Scottish sound. I came to understand the group not just as a great bunch of talented musicians, but as a dynamic illustration of the possibilities of musical juxtaposition, creative *bricolage*[3] and cultural open-mindedness. Being neither Scottish nor Latino and possessing little prior experience in either tradition, I soon found that the Salsa Celtica admixture of organic inclusivity and self-conscious construction works to actively promote an appealingly liberal approach to musical thinking, enacted in the moment and heavily dependent upon the immediacy of performative style and energy. And as such, it is open to musicians well beyond its apparent genre borders. The band's collective ability to mostly glue together, and occasionally dissolve, taught me valuable lessons about ensemble dynamics. It also played repeatedly back into my own ideas about the unpredictable web of relationships spanning musical tradition, personal roots and artistic innovation. In what follows I outline a developing image of the band, an identity in which Scottish signifiers are always mediated (often via an avowedly non-purist salsa vernacular), consciously avoiding and subverting any suggestion of Scottish musical essentialism. I will explore how the band presents both salsa and Celtic elements as raw material continually available for recombination and recontextualisation, registers of belonging between which it migrates fluidly and creatively. I hope also to show a clear ideological coherence behind the musical excitement and dynamism – the transmission of Scottishness-in-music as fluid, contingent, dialogic, and deeply meaningful.

Kilts and suits, fiddles and congas, whisky and rum . . . the Salsa Celtica narrative, as expressed through song titles, album covers, and of course the music itself, is a case study in hybridity. But whilst it draws on multiple musical legacies, this is also a discourse that is highly personal and subjective, a playful musical world-in-process. The band's self-conscious subversion of musical authenticity and provenance ultimately points to a dynamic and motivating dialogue around Scottishness and cosmopolitanism, one which remains both deliberately ambiguous and firmly rooted in the musical here-and-now. Because most importantly, this is a live music band – a collective, breathing, unpredictable musical reality where unlikely cultural possibilities only fully come together in the act of their creation. That its particular Scottish-salsa balance is never static is always fully reliant upon the particular competence of its members, who have over the years established various versions of a distinctive 'Salsa Celtica' musical approach. Consequently, the band's oeuvre speaks to a modern, internationalised discourse of Scottish traditional music, whilst offering a particularly localised version of the now global language of salsa.

Tech spec

Salsa Celtica's line-up has varied greatly across its lifespan, and no band member has ever been present at absolutely all gigs, but a few key people have been constant across most of the group's existence – most importantly of all bandleader Toby Shippey. Shippey's role throughout has encompassed musical director, brass and percussion player, chief songwriter and arranger, media liaison, financial coordinator, personnel fixer and rehearsal planner – in short, the whole gamut necessary to the continued existence of a successful big band. As a proven commercial entity (existing almost completely without funded support) and an innovative and sociable group of musicians, Salsa Celtica has over the years also been able to attract and incorporate a wealth of Scottish-based musical talent. The band's alumni include musicians from Capercaillie, Shooglenifty, Treacherous Orchestra, Peatbog Faeries, Fiddler's Bid, Blazing Fiddles, Scottish National Jazz Orchestra and Mr McFall's Chamber.

Inevitably, the instrumental set-up has morphed slightly over time, but over the last ten years has settled pretty steadily on the following: piano, bass, lead vocal(s), fiddle, tenor banjo, pipes and whistle (also doubling bouzouki), some combination of trumpet, sax and trombone, congas, bongo bell and timbale. In addition to this, several band members sing backing *coros* and for the last few years fiddle player Megan Henderson or vocalist Maeve MacKinnon (Glasgow) have sung lead for three or four Scottish Gaelic language numbers. Onstage, the band is divided conventionally into instrumental sections. Stage right are horns and percussion, upstage left are bass and piano, singers stand front and centre. The folk unit sits and stands downstage left, although banjo player Eamonn Coyne performs a helpful linking role, his long lead allowing him to wander across to the horns for sax solos, head upstage for piano and banjo *montunos*, and sidle up to lead vocalists just for fun. This stage layout is more than practicality; it is also an embodiment of the synecdochical function of each grouping: the Latin percussion section acting as a shorthand for salsa; fiddle and pipes diagonally opposite representing (one version of) Scottish music. Performatively, then, the band makes explicit its musical direction, consciously combining fundamental sonic elements of salsa and traditional Scottish music yet maintaining them physically as separate, semi-independent and occasionally conflicting musical units.

Honed over many years writing, rehearsing, gigging and recording, the band's sound is a deft combination of salsa grooves, traditional or original Scottish and Irish folk tunes and mostly (but not exclusively) Latino lead vocal style, including plenty of *inspiracion* improvisation and *coro* backings. Folky breaks and salsa mambos have always played an important part as oppositional elements, and much early repertoire was structured around the rapid real-time juxtaposition of these two textures: layering *montunos*, horn and vocal backings to build tension behind folk tunes, for example, or dropping dramatically from heavy salsa percussion into an *a cappella* reel. In recent years, however, the band has shifted to a more integrated conception of the two musics, using Celtic material and instruments in traditionally brass mambo territory, heavy Afro-Cuban percussion over jigs, slip jigs and reels, and incorporating Gaelic song lyrics into *coro* roles. Harmonically, the group stays mostly within established *son* structures: I, II, V and VI chords predominate, although there is also greater emphasis placed on a more modal accompaniment basis – borrowed from folk music – than in conventional salsa. Unlike much conventional salsa, however, instrumental melodies

142   *Phil Alexander*

are given equal prominence to vocal parts, and are almost exclusively derived from the balanced linear phrases of Scottish and Irish music rather than salsa's more angular and percussive melodic structures, albeit with a greater degree of syncopation.

In line with onstage divisions, musical roles between melody instruments have in the past been clearly assigned: fiddle and pipes playing the 'heads' with horns providing backing and solos, although these boundaries have also blurred over time. A good example of the band's current sound-mix of Scottish and salsa material is the following excerpt from 2014's 'Ven, Guajira, Ven' (Figure 11.1). Here we can see bass and percussion parts built around standard salsa patterns, with piano *montuno* filling out the tune's implicit harmony whilst also providing a rhythmic counterpoint. With a couple of important melodic exceptions, Ross Ainslie's tune is built entirely from a D (Bmin) pentatonic scale, but its occasional syncopations are also a notable nod to salsa *clave* phrasing. Played in octaves by whistle, fiddle and banjo, it is answered by horns which hold a nice line between percussive stabs and longer harmony lines.

Figure 11.1 Bars 31–40 of 'Ven, Guajira, Ven' (Shippey, Ainslie, Pompas). Conga and bongo parts omitted. (Discos Leon, 2014)

Origin myths

The networked relationships of cultural production to ideas of nation, heritage, past and future are complex and open-ended, as many of the essays in this volume demonstrate. One of Salsa Celtica's strengths lies in its declared allegiance to several 'imagined communities' (Anderson, 2006) at one and the same time: the sophisticated urbanity of the capital city, an international world music network (musicians, festivals, recordings), and simultaneously a cosily parochial club of musical mates (as expressed through a city's local music scene). Through this balance, the group enacts a contemporary, rooted and pragmatic internationalism which nevertheless retains a familiarly local, insider feel. It is a double-viewpoint embodied through the group's sound, the unabashed joyfulness of its live performances and also its internal ethnic make-up, comprising as it does musicians from Scotland, Cuba, Ireland, Venezuela and England. But Salsa Celtica's easygoing fusion is not simply a reflection of the avowed (and genuine) musical multiculturalism of its participants, rather a direct outcome of the particular local conditions of the band's inception and development. Multilayered musical discourse is produced through ongoing lived experience, a point nicely made by Simon Frith:

> What I want to suggest, in other words, is not that social groups agree on values which are then expressed in their cultural activities (the assumption of the homology models) but that they only get to know themselves *as groups* (as a particular organization of individual and social interests, of sameness and difference) *through* cultural activity, through aesthetic judgement. Making music isn't a way of expressing ideas; it is a way of living them.
>
> (Frith, 1996, 111)

So on one level, the band *is* the musical pluralism of its members. But more importantly, a cultural space is created through musicking, a space which embodies and develops a musical language both constitutive of, and in continual dialogue with the multiple discourses of its surrounding urban context. To explore this, it is useful to look at the band's early development around the session scene of mid-'90s Edinburgh, as articulated by Toby Shippey in a 2009 BBC Alba interview with Julie Fowlis:

Toby Shippey: We started off playing nearly pure salsa, in the beginning, 1995–1996. And then that kind of Edinburgh scene, you know, it was all Shooglenifty, Martyn Bennett, and we were all playing together, we all used to play together in Edinburgh. Tunes started playing with the band.

Julie Fowlis: An experimental time, as well, for traditional music in Scotland.

TS: It was brilliant. Because people often ask, 'why did you do that combination?' And it wasn't really like an idea, it's just that's what everybody was doing. You know, we were all hanging about the same bars, playing the same gigs. Shooglenifty was doing African music with Scottish traditional, Martyn Bennett was doing drum and bass with Scottish traditional music, Peatbog Faeries were doing dub and reggae. So it wasn't – we started off doing that and then it just sort of came together like that because we would play sessions in Whistlebinkies and it just became that way.'[4]

Band origin myths notwithstanding, the initial impetus is understood simply and explicitly as an urge to play salsa. This is of course a statement of a certain sort of musical cosmopolitanism – Scotland's first salsa band. But Edinburgh is a city of varying musical environments, busy enough to develop creatively, small enough to overlap constantly. We might think of Jonathan Stock's formulation, in which '[an] urban ethnomusicology . . . will have to cope with the heterogeneity of the city, where multiple, overlapping musical communities are intermingled, and musical networks criss-cross one another temporally, socially, physically and electronically' (Stock, 2008, 201). These networks have a pervasive and unpredictable life of their own; the implication, and indeed the reality is that given the particular open-ended context of this early salsa band's genesis, a certain amount of 'folkiness' was perhaps inevitable. Especially in the freewheeling musical atmosphere of 1990s Edinburgh, where Shippey points to Shooglenifty and Martyn Bennett as fellow musical explorers, part of a fluid session scene which inevitably provoked a certain amount of crossover and mutual influence. Hybridity here, then, is a dialectic: the initial spark being a desire to connect cross-culturally (even to the point of recruiting a Venezuelan singer and persuading him to move from London to Edinburgh), the longer-term result an open-ended, iterative and contingent musical conversation.[5]

What began as an interesting and unexpected piece of urban culture clash has over time developed into a finely honed idiom, internationalising an idea of Scottishness but also localising the international language of salsa along the way. We can explore the band's development further in these terms. The chronology is less that of self-conscious artistic choice, and more a bunch of young musicians getting together to play salsa in a Scottish folk context (i.e. pub session), the tangible musical result of their particular environment being the ongoing influence of Celtic music. And through this lived experience of playing salsa and Celtic music, the band members have begun to understand themselves and their music as increasingly multi-textual, able to exist across several musical spaces at once. Frith again: 'identity is *mobile*, a process not a thing, a becoming not a being . . . our experience of music – of music making and music listening – is best understood as an experience of this *self-in-process*. Music, like identity, is both performance and story' (1996b, 109).

Musical practice, in other words, here creates a space for cultural effect, not the other way around. And this particular cultural space, in the form of a successful and much-liked working band, then feeds back into the musical life of its own city. The group is simultaneously an outcome of, and influence upon, its urban musical environment:

> When you set up a band which has gigs, it therefore exists. People need work, they end up in town, people gravitate towards it and this thing becomes real. And you try and hone it. It gathers energy, it becomes a heavier star and people come towards it. And you end up with this great bunch of musicians who've been through the band. But it is a bit of a quirk that it happened.
> (Toby Shippey, fieldwork interview, October 2015)

This musical lens roots the band simultaneously inside and outside an idea of Scottish music: a product of its social and historical environment, but also something of an anomaly. It speaks to an approach which begins not with the expressed aim of being either 'traditional' or 'different' (in either genre), but develops its point of view through its ongoing and inclusive social processes. As Toby Shippey's 'quirk' description points out, the continued existence and success of the band is also an implicit acceptance of a certain degree of unpredictability, given musical form and meaning through the urban: 'Everyday life may be the city's greatest invention ... a mutant, undisciplined creativity that is worked out through the properties of existence' (Amin and Thrift, 2002, 95).

Tradition?

Importantly, the group did not begin by stepping away from a 'traditional' musical aesthetic. In a band that began with an urge to play salsa, Scottish traditional music is in fact the radical element. And this tradition plays a substantive role, not mere semiotic gloss, initiating a trajectory which was eventually to take in collaboration with Julie Fowlis and a sustained ongoing Gaelic repertoire. This moves beyond the accidental urban encounter, towards a clearer, developmental narrative of a 'Salsa Celtica' sonic and cultural aesthetic. In the wider context of Scottish music, it points to a vital fluidity and flexibility, an ability to incorporate and adapt, to re-present and ultimately re-create. As simultaneous product and process ('performance and story'), Salsa Celtica are both influenced by this flow and a corresponding influence upon it.

Referring to musical cross-fertilisations such as these, Simon Frith, this time in *The Discourse of World Music*, suggests: 'What's involved here is less a sense of subjective instability than the negotiation of new cultural alliances' (Frith, 2000, 318). In other words, whilst many contemporary musicians undeniably feel drawn in several creative directions simultaneously, the forging of new networks also produces a discursive effect back upon the new musical map being drawn – in this case the connections between traditional music and salsa. We might think about these cultural alliances for a moment. Ironically, a more integrated incorporation of Scottish music simultaneously pushes the boundaries of the band's *salsa* foundations in newer and more radical directions. For Salsa Celtica, getting more traditionally

Scottish is tantamount to taking greater risks with salsa. This is reinforced by the band's regular appearances on both folk and salsa stages, suggesting – by and large – a listener perspective that is also happy to live with ambiguity.

The band, therefore, performs a neat balancing act, mediating an idea of Scottishness through salsa cosmopolitanism, whilst at the same time endowing salsa with a significant amount of Scottish directness and swagger (perhaps cutting through some sequins and red satin shimmys along the way). This localised internationalism skilfully incorporates contrasting musical signifiers to create a liminal zone within which its emic/etic position can be imaginatively manipulated. Through various albums and even within individual gigs, the constantly shifting balance will be at times more Celtica, at times more salsa, but never fully one nor the other. And of course, within the band itself the insider/outsider debate is fluid: the Salsa Celtica narrative voice (depending on who you listen to, and who is doing the listening) is that of Edinburgh, Scotland, Cuba, Ireland, Venezuela . . . and ultimately global. In this way, the band maintains the ability to drive its own musical discourse, relying on a certain sort of fleet-footed creativity in order to avoid the pitfalls of stagnation inherent in any 'invented' musical idea:

> The criteria by which the boundaries are erected and maintained are not always easy to see, and are capable of shifting quickly, enabling a core of insiders to redefine themselves . . . in the face of encroachment on the part of predatory outsiders.
>
> (Stokes, 1997, 20)

These boundaries are of course where Salsa Celtica most comfortably sits, and it is this which allows the group its proven flexibility with both idioms.[6] It is not always an easy equilibrium, however, and can trip up when the performance context sets up an expectation of only one side of the equation. Lead singer Ricardo Pompas comes to mind, bounding onstage resplendent in his gleaming white suit and white patent leather shoes in front of the grungy Flemish audience of 'Zeltic festival' (the next act on was Carlos Nuñez and thirty Galician pipers). Or certain flamboyant salsa instructors who will occasionally take over the entire dance floor audience for an impromptu class, only to stand around looking nonplussed when the reels kick in and the whole band begins jumping up and down on stage. In a sense, each audience decides for its own purposes whether the group is at any time a folk band or a salsa band, dependent upon context and performance space. And even within the band this argument is never fully settled. For new members with a particular stylistic bent, the clash of cultural narratives usually requires some adaptation. The presence of a musical Other in both worlds forces a creativity of musical material and a rethinking of performance approach.

Bricolage in practice, sound and structure as ideology

Nothing, therefore, is ever unambiguously 'Scottish' (or 'salsa') about Salsa Celtica. Signification is always mediated through a particular point of view, symbols and icons playfully juxtaposed, and identity bricolaged from a range of cross-cultural elements: language, dress, musical ways-of-being, instrumental embodiment. This Salsa Celtica liminal zone is also created textually through the band's song titles, many of which reference a consciously invented Scottish Latino vernacular. Certain elements offer themselves up as particularly plastic. These include place: 'El Sol de la Noche' is a salsa homage to Shetland, while 'El Portobello Malecon' evokes an imaginary Cuban-Edinburgh beachside promenade; musical practice: 'Seis, Ocho, Nueve', referencing the time signatures of a set of jigs and reels and 'Descarga Gaelica', a Gaelic/salsa jam session; and of course the cheerful overlap of cultural signifiers and social interaction: 'Whisky con Ron' and 'El Agua de la Vida' (*uisge beatha* in Spanish). The band's liminality is also embodied on stage, with a very loosely co-ordinated aesthetic that takes in smart suits, occasional kilts, oversize multi-coloured shirts, salsa steps, full-band pogoing, and multi-accented bilingual stage banter.

And of course, this restless crossover happens fundamentally through the music. From their first album, nineteen years ago, only one song remains in the band's repertoire, 'Guajira Sin Sol'. This tune has expanded across time to become a central part of the band's set, reappearing in different guises on two more albums and incorporating material from two subsequent recordings in the process. Toby Shippey refers to the development of this song as a formative point in the band's sound, a eureka moment where the sonic clash of the two idioms began to make sense. It is a simple, three-chord minor-key *guajira*, this simplicity allowing a great deal of flexibility. In its initial 1997 form, the song opened with a slow guitar *montuno*. Since then, however, the live performance of this tune begins with an extended border pipes or highland pipes solo, reinforcing the increasing centrality of the pipes sound to the band as a whole. From out of this solo, originally by Fraser Fifield and more recently by Ross Ainslie, a loping *guajira* groove kicks in, driven by piano and banjo. Melodically and texturally, the tune sets up a pleasingly deep, salsa-drenched expectation. But this is immediately subverted by the appearance of the opening descending mambo not on brass, but on pipes and fiddle, which in turn gives way to an extended pipes improvisation: salsa form here being played out through an ambiguously 'Celtic' sonority. The emergence of the chanted chorus roots the piece mostly back into the salsa world, whilst the lyrics – 'guajira, para mi *Escocia*' – remind us that this particular incarnation exists symbolically some way apart from Cuba or New York. A fiddle solo at the emotional highpoint two-thirds of the way through the tune further reinforces the musical mix, both in sound (a folk instrument replacing a more expected trumpet or sax), and in playing style (more akin to the linear structure of a folk tune than a spikier jazz-inflected horn solo), before a decrescendo-ing mambo reprise leads the tune out.

This piece on its own illustrates the continual back-and-forth travel of varying emphases between the two idioms. But in live performance this ambiguous tune is only the first part of a larger set. At the conclusion of the darkly mellow *guajira*, pipes, fiddle and banjo pick up the driving reel which heralds the start of 'El Agua de la Vida' – one of the band's full-on salsa/Celtic anthems, and a piece which powerfully stakes out the band's aesthetic territory and implicit musical ideology. The reel is on a loop throughout much of the tune, but it gains momentum in that each successive repetition is contrasted by constant change in the salsa backing – beginning with tight horn stabs, through energetic *coros*, leading to vocal *inspiracion*. A characteristic salsa break leaves an empty bar to foreground the reel's move from first-part (in A) up to a D-major second-part, structurally integrating the two styles further. The reel stops after its third time through to give way to a sax solo, vocals, and brass mambo. When it reappears, the folk melody does so unaccompanied and then backed only by group *coros*. With Lino Rocha as the band's vocalist, this song would also feature an extended ragga rap, rounded off by horn stabs laid over the reel's final appearance. Full of activity and verging on the showbiz, this finale nevertheless is not the end of the set – at the song's two-stab ending, banjo, fiddle and pipes launch *attaca* into the jig 'Cailleach 'sa Mhaistrim'. This plays once through before moving up to Am for the jig 'An Cailleach', at which point the folkies are joined by a backing of heavy Afro-Cuban 6/8 percussion and a vocal chant adapted from Fania All-Stars' classic 'Coro Miyare'. Once again, midway through the piece, the jig gives way to an open percussion/vocal breakdown, the texture of which suddenly turns the music darker and sparser. Re-emerging at the other side, the old woman ('An Cailleach') now finds herself at the head of a steam train of full Afro-Cuban-Celtic technicolour – surrounded by a joyful din of dense percussion cross-rhythms, full band *coros*, and brass and sax stratospherics.

Whilst descriptive text is an unsurprisingly inadequate means of conveying musical excitement, this rudimentary scheme is a useful way to break down the Salsa Celtica structural aesthetic. It is a music of constantly moving focus, utilising the contrasting ensemble sonorities to telegraph dynamic and dramatic shifts in the musical narrative. Where certain formal materials (pulse, tune, groove) are held steady in order to keep a coherent danceable flow, these are nevertheless continually moderated by the changes taking place around them. At the points where continuous elements (such as a reel) disappear from the mix, the dense web of activity behind them is suddenly revealed as a basis for exploration and improvisation. In this way, straightforward four-square musical material gains complexity, form and texture in its evolving combination and re-combination across the length of a set. The semi-accidental cultural hybridity of the band is explicitly foregrounded as a musical structuring device.

In its straddling of traditions, Salsa Celtica also raises questions around stylistic competency and expectation. My own background is in classical, jazz and klezmer music, and on arrival in Edinburgh in 2002 I had just the barest experience of playing salsa. However, I needed gigs, and with a lucky confluence of failing interband relationships and a few hastily developed connections I soon found myself lined up for some Salsa Celtica dates – Dundee and then a short Belgian tour. This was my initiation into the world of salsa piano – for a working musician the story of rapidly assimilating the basics of new style or repertoire is not an uncommon one. However, there are very few (if any) 'neutral' musics; competency carries with it a number of expectations, a point well made by Thomas Turino:

> Knowing and hence being able to perform appropriately in the style is itself a dicent index of belonging and social identity, because performance

competence is both a sign and simultaneously a product of shared musical knowledge and experience.

(Turino, 2008, 43)

How, then, to approach the minefield of belonging and social identity surrounding a Jewish Londoner playing salsa piano in Scotland? Arguably, the fact that the band exists at the margins and intersections of its particular traditions goes a long way to undermining this particular musical dilemma. For me, the multifaceted nature of Salsa Celtica's musical identity was like a huge cushion under the high-wire trapeze of learning to play salsa. The 'salsa police'[7] are surely on less secure territory with a Scottish folk/salsa group than they might be with a more conventional outfit – the rules and normative practices are already stretched and compromised, endowing the resulting style with a certain necessary elasticity. In other words, Salsa Celtica's inherent hybridity acts as a mitigating force on the pressures of learning to play 'in the style': the performance competence of which Turino speaks is already mediated by the explicit non-purism of the overall musical aesthetic. One might go further than this, to suggest that the band's particular musical mix has in fact created its own way of approaching its constituent parts: both the smoothness of more straightahead salsa and the lilt of more conventional tunes playing have to adapt to varying degrees in search of common ground. It has taken the percussion section in particular a long time (and not a few arguments) to learn how to listen to the folk musicians and to nuance their accompaniment accordingly. And equally, the folk musicians have had to reappraise their tune-based contributions in a wider, busier, more heterophonic context than they might usually find themselves. These adaptations point towards the development of a musical and performative style which admits the formative role of historical and geographical context:

> The dialogue went on between those two different energies, and there were probably some different feelings. Some of the aesthetics from Latin America wouldn't work so well, and some of the tunes we've done wouldn't work so well in Latin America. In general you get a sound which was basically honed for playing to audiences in Scotland, not Latin America. And often it was themes that were more European, melodies that were more Scottish, at times some jazz, that sort of sound.
>
> (Toby Shippey, fieldwork interview, October 2015)

Nevertheless, this sort of dialogue can produce surprising cross-cultural connections – where a local musical practice, formed around specific social requirements and conditions, unpredictably connects with structural expectations from afar:

Phil Alexander: Do you think the salsa bit is played differently [in Salsa Celtica]?
Toby Shippey: There's lots of ways the salsa is definitely played differently. If you're from Latin America, it's an incredibly precise, learned culture to play that well. And we were very new to it and playing with different swing. Funnily enough, one of the places

the band is most popular is Cali, in Colombia. They play salsa incredibly fast in Cali, and they love it fast. And that's where we've had the biggest hits. Because we also play fast! The idea of playing more sophisticated, suave-y salsa wouldn't appeal to somebody at minus 2 on New Year's Eve in Scotland, or in a village hall tanked up on whisky. Playing a very smooth, romantico salsa would just turn people off. So we have this very energetic, not aggressive, but high energy salsa. And Cali is where they dance like that. (fieldwork interview, October 2015)

Look and feel

As a final illustration of appealing cultural ambiguity, I want to look at how the band presents a shifting image of itself through its album covers. 1997's 'Monstruos y Demonios, Angels and Lovers' makes a bold but non-specific statement of place and intent. A single Highland cow's head confronts us, slightly comic but not self-mocking (Figure 11.2). The image has directness and weight as well as humour, the cow's not inconsiderable horns framing the band name, creating the juxtaposition which will characterise the band from now on. The cow's head has no implicit musical connection, and is severed from its body and its habitat. It asks us to make something of it; metonym for rural Scotland? Metaphor for roughness,

Figure 11.2 'Monstruous y Demonios, Angels and Lovers' (Eclectic Records, 1997)

solidity, traditional practice? It is perhaps a monster, a demon, or even a curious angel (though possibly not a lover). From the outset, with a single image, this is a band that is happy to leave meanings open, a perspective echoed by the four-part bilingual title itself.

With the second album, 'The Great Scottish Latin Adventure' of 2000, the cows have multiplied, been given some corporeal materiality, a landscape, and are joined by the band themselves (Figure 11.3). Multiple signifiers are at play here in a self-consciously lighthearted narrative of adventure, frontier-spirit and heterogeneous camaraderie. The colours are imagined, remembered, the montage-style dreamlike. Metaphors of place and history float and collide. The band's dress is individualistic, the instruments diverse. Gaucho hats, big skies and far-reaching gazes evoke the open plains of music to be explored, whilst the comic juxtaposition of visual elements reminds us that this is, ultimately, a bunch of Scottish lads (at this point) having fun. This openness of spirit finds a match in the music, which mines a fluidly experimental seam ranging from rootsy guitar and *tres* patterns, through reels and airs, to communal singing duties (at this point the group had no lead singer).

The posse of adventurers, mostly intact, is replaced in 2003's 'El Agua de la Vida' by a smart group of lads about town (Figure 11.4). The rural imaginary has given way to a shiny urbanity, the fantasy sepia of Scottish South America is now the hard clear lines and brightly contrasting human-made colours of Leith's

Figure 11.3 'The Great Scottish Latin Adventure' (Greentrax, 2000)

Figure 11.4 'El Agua de la Vida' (Greentrax, 2003)

Cameo Bar. Overt metaphor is noticeably lacking, replaced by a journalistic, snapshot metonymy of coherent urban solidarity. The contrapuntal dress-style has been supplanted by a uniform of smart suits, overcoats and leather jackets – it could be a band, it could be a football team, it could be a group of would-be entrepreneurs. What the image does not reference, in any way, is a group of people involved in traditional music, or salsa music for that matter. Conventional signifiers of history, tradition, the rural or the home are conspicuous by their absence, as are conventional (one might say clichéd) salsa signifiers of dancers, warm colours, parties and a star lead performer. This is a modern gang, declaring its togetherness through a shared sense of place, style and humour. They are also still having a lot of fun doing it. Musically, this shift is paralleled by a more streamlined, unified sound – a harder, more coherent and modernist approach. The open-ended explorations of Scottish Latin Adventure have been modified into a strong, straight ahead salsa of tight horns and vocals, matched by an equally powerful traditional Scottish contingent led by (at that time) rising stars Chris Stout and Fraser Fifield.

By 2006's 'El Camino', life on the road, el agua, and the monsters or demons seem to have taken their toll. The gang of urban lads has fragmented into a shifting group of disconnected souls, apparently lost in the same urban space that brought them all together in the first place. Seen in transit, cropped and blurred, the band have become passers-by at their own movie (Figure 11.5). Rather than a place of adventure or dynamic teamwork, the city here is dystopic, offering neither individualism nor togetherness. Signifiers of tradition, coherence and Scottishness are gone, even as semiotic playthings. Curiously, this more 'anarchistic' synchronicity (to paraphrase Steven Feld)[8] was to yield the greatest musical integration of the two idioms so far: *montunos* switch to banjo and accordion, folk tunes to piano and saxophone. With the exception of one number, all the Scottish material is originally composed, suggesting a further integration of tunes into the musical concept – functionally and musically occupying a significant and more important space than that of Celtic 'breaks'. Equally, folk melodies have become more plastic – mambos, *montunos* and tunes built out of the same musical material. And finally, for the first time a traditional British folk song receives a Salsa Celtica treatment, in the form of Eliza Carthy's haunting version of The Grey Cock, reframed as 'Grey Gallito'.

This last was to herald a new musical approach, as Julie Fowlis and Kathleen MacInnes were drafted in to join the band for a high-profile Celtic Connections gig one year later. With the inclusion of Gaelic material, a completely new vocal resource opened up and for the first time the band has become lyrically bilingual. And visually, with 2014's 'The Tall Islands' we have come full circle to an open signifier of place – only this time the semiotic material is a sun-bleached door or boardwalk, more Cuba than the Highlands. Ironically, where this album represents

Figure 11.5 'El Camino' (Discos Leon, 2006)

Figure 11.6 'The Tall Islands' (Discos Leon, 2014)

the band's most substantial inclusion of traditional Scottish material, its strongest visual reference is to an idea of Otherness, of elsewhere (in relation to conventional representations of Scotland). In the weathered look of this image, however, there also rests more than a nod to an idea of age, of seasoning, of natural materials, and of repose, of restlessness quieted – which is in fact pretty much where the band currently lies. Like the group itself, it is a signifier that skirts the linked concepts of tradition and history without explicitly naming them, and without expressing clear allegiance one way or the other.

Conclusion

My chapter has attempted to draw some conclusions about how Salsa Celtica interacts with, draws from, and furthers an idea of Scottishness-in-music. I have argued that for this particular band, traditional music is a fluid resource over and above a static element. It is not a found object to be used and discarded at will, but neither is it a sacred text promoting only limited narrative strategies. Both inside and outside an idea of tradition, or better traditions, Salsa Celtica attests to both the elasticity and robustness of Scottish musical material. And equally, the band's own musical journey evinces the pervasiveness and centrality of that resource, moving as it has from incidental idea to fundamental musical building-block. In a wider sense, the discourse from which the band draws (and contributes to) opens up notions of Scottishness itself as equally fluid and adaptable, available for playful and ambiguous recombination: a sense of collective Scottishness as fantasy adventure, as urban gang, as disconnected wanderers and ultimately as participants in an international dialogue around 'tradition' and its meanings. The sonic and semiotic result is a loose yet richly multivalent version of a certain form of contemporary authenticity.

Toby Shippey occasionally refers to his background as an architecture student as a key influence on his musical guiding principles, a creative ability to select and recombine as much as to begin from scratch which is at the heart of the band's continued appeal. And ultimately, because the group's multi-culturalist discourse is rooted in an organic urban narrative of encounter and *bricolage*, it lacks any self-congratulatory polemic. Recognising fully the unpredictable role of circumstance and context (as well as the commercial realities of musical hybridity), Shippey is also nicely self-deprecating about both the band's evolving adventure and the ultimate impossibility of second-guessing its trajectory: 'when we started, we were completely a salsa band, and we were invited to play loads and loads of Celtic festivals. Now, we play loads and loads of Celtic music, and all we ever get is salsa gigs'.[9]

I will end with an opening. This chapter has looked at what the discourse of Salsa Celtica might bring to an idea of Scottish identity. It has not touched upon any corresponding emotional and cultural resonances for immigrant South American, Cuban and Spanish audiences and musicians in Scotland. The ability of diasporic musics to re-connect cross-culturally to ideas of homeland, exile, migration and new beginnings deserves at least a passing mention before we finish, if only to explicitly recognise that musical identity is always many-headed. As a coda, then, here are a few lines from the 2006 tune 'Esperanza', written by long-time vocalist Lino Rocha (originally from Venezuela). Romantic and open-ended, they remind us that one musician's departure is another's journey home.

Me fui de la tierra santa	*I left the sacred land*
En busca de nuevos caminos	*To search for new paths*
Dejando atrás mis amores	*Leaving behind my loves*
Pero tengo que seguir con mi destino	*For I have to follow my destiny*

Notes

1 Fieldwork interview, October 2015.
2 At this early point, it is worth noting that the band uses 'Celtic' in a fairly generic way. The non-salsa traditional musical material is primarily Scottish but also occasionally Irish. By his own admission (interview, 2015), bandleader Toby Shippey picked the term 'Celtic' for branding reasons (i.e. as a sub-category of 'world music'), and precisely because of the lack of specificity that the term allows. Timothy Taylor (2014, 171) suggests: ' "World music" is a brand warehouse that contains other brands such as "Gypsy" or "Celtic" music', whilst Malcolm Chapman (1997, 42) pithily observes: 'The "Celts" in the British context, simply form the largest regiment in the phantom army of "folk" who are the notional makers of "folk-music".'

3 This is a term originally theorised by anthropologist Claude Levi-Strauss (1968). Although it has now gained widespread use, I am sticking fairly closely to the original formulation, which describes a process of patching-together from what is available rather than starting with the 'correct' tools for the job. John Clarke (1976) notes: "when [an] object is placed within a different total ensemble, a new discourse is constituted."
4 'Salsa Celtica', *Cuirm @ Celtic* (BBC Alba, 2009). Last broadcast 22 September, 2013.
5 Tajbakhsh (2001, 83) suggests that the 'promise of the city' lies in 'the freedom to glimpse our own hybridity, our own contingency'.
6 Bohlman (1988, 57): 'In settings where cultural contact is pervasive the assertion of cultural boundaries is often a matter of choice, making them flexible'.
7 Like the jazz police and folk police, the salsa police are more metaphorical than real: a symbol of (heavy-handed) correct practice usually invoked as a rear-guard warning against the pitfalls of blind musical obedience, perhaps to frame one's own perceived iconoclasm.
8 In his work on Kaluli *dulugu ganalan*, Feld discusses: 'relations that are simultaneously in-synchrony while out-of-phase. By "in-synchrony" I mean that the overall feeling is of togetherness, of consistently cohesive part coordination in sonic motion and participatory experience. Yet the parts are also "out-of-phase", that is, at distinctly different and shifting points of the same cycle or phase structure at any moment' (Feld, 1988, 82).
9 Fieldwork interview, October 2015.

Part III
Home and host

12 Distant voices, Scottish lives
On song and migration

M. J. Grant

My heart's in the highlands, my heart is not here

This is a chapter about migration, and how it makes us. In the year 2000, the Estonian composer Arvo Pärt created a setting for countertenor and organ of Robert Burns's song *My Heart's in the Highlands* (or *Farewell to the Highlands* as Burns named it; Example 12.1).[1] Pärt came to international prominence in the late 1980s after leaving the then Soviet Estonia under duress with his family.[2] After a brief stay in Vienna, they settled in Berlin, around the same time that a series of recordings by the record label ECM propelled the composer to fame of a level highly unusual for living composers.

Pärt's setting of Burns's song is typical of much of his output in its reduced yet extremely effective use of the simplest musical elements. This is most apparent in the vocal line: in each of the first three verses a single pitch is used; over the course of these verses, these pitches trace an extenuated, upwards arpeggio of the chord of F minor. In the fourth verse, this progression is reversed and condensed, with the first three lines being on C, A♭ and F respectively, resting on F for the final line. The process is gently offset by the equally simple and repetitive organ, in particular by a voice at organ stop II Oboe 8'; this intercedes a total of twelve times, in phrases extending from two to six notes, sometimes seeming to comment on the vocal line, at other times gently dissonant with it.[3]

Under the still surface of Pärt's music, the interweaving of the different parts, as simple as each of them are individually, reveals them to be models of careful crafting. But it is the monotony – in the most literal sense – of the vocal line that is the most striking aspect of Pärt's setting, especially for anyone familiar with the wide-ranging contours of many Scottish tunes. Commentators on Pärt's music have noted that his works on English texts often tend towards a style 'similar to chant techniques of liturgical recitation' (Hillier, 1997, 184). Here, this tendency is taken to extremes, and for reasons that chime well with the verse's sentiment. When we are upset, or afraid, our spoken voices tend both to monotony, and to heightening of pitch: Pärt's setting captures these moments of longing, and of anguish, as well as of despondency and resignation; it is this, perhaps, that led to the composition's integration at two points in the film *La Grande Bellezza* (dir. Paolo Sorrentino, 2013), which is very much about the nostalgia of lost youth.[4]

My heart's in the Highlands, my heart is not here;
My heart's in the Highlands a chasing the deer;
A chasing the wild deer, and following the roe,
My heart's in the Highlands, wherever I go.

Farewell to the Highlands, farewell to the north,
The birth place of Valour, the country of Worth,
Wherever I wander, wherever I rove,
The hills of the Highlands forever I love.

Farewell to the mountains high cover'd with snow;
Farewell to the straths and green vallies below:
Farewell to the forests and wild hanging woods;
Farewell to the torrents and loud pouring floods.

My heart's in the Highlands, my heart is not here;
My heart's in the Highlands a chasing the deer;
A chasing the wild deer, and following the roe,
My heart's in the Highlands, wherever I go.

Example 12.1 Robert Burns, *Farewell to the Highlands*, text as published in James Johnson (ed.), *The Scots Musical Museum*, vol. 3 (Edinburgh: James Johnson, 1790)

Thus, Burns's song is out in the world again, in a form that could hardly be further from its musical beginnings. The tune to which it was originally set, an air known as *Fàilte na miosg* (*The Musket Salute*), has a range of almost two octaves and is classed by Kirsteen McCue and Marjorie Rycroft as 'virtually unsingable' (McCue and Rycroft, 2014, 287): Burns probably encountered it in one of James Oswald's tunebooks. The song is now generally known to a different tune, *Crochallan*, introduced to it at some point in the nineteenth century (see Example 12.2).[5] The name 'Crochallan', known to Burns scholars from the eighteenth-century drinking club called the Crochallan Fencibles referenced in *Rattlin, Roarin Willie*, is actually an anglicisation of *Crodh Chailean* (*Colin's Cattle*), a Gaelic song said to be a favourite of Daunie Douglas, landlord of the Edinburgh tavern where the club met (Irvine, 2013, 342). The Gaelic song, too, is a lament, the song of a woman magicked away by fairies not long after her wedding to Colin, and allowed to return only one day a year to milk his cows.[6]

In many ways the beautiful tune *Crochallan* makes up for the lyrics, which can hardly be classed amongst Burns's best. Carol McGuirk may rightly describe it as 'this most iconic of Burns's Highland songs' (McGuirk, 2014, 109), but for contemporary Scots this is as close as it gets in Burns to a 'shortbread and heather' version of Scottish culture, a version that speaks not so much of exile but of third- and fourth-generation descendants on a mission to discover their clan heritage. But where did the song itself come from? The scholarly literature has long argued that the first verse is from *The Strong Walls of Derry*, reputed to be a personal favourite of Walter Scott, who even sang it on occasion;[7] there is at least one extant chapbook source for this ballad, published in Glasgow in 1793.[8] The related song *Portmore*, published by Peter Buchan in 1828 and attributed by him

Example 12.2 The tune *Crochallan* as generally sung with *My Heart's in the Highlands*; transcription from memory by author

to Donald Cameron, shares four of the verses, including the one used by Burns, and the chorus (Buchan, 1828, 158, 324; Shoolbraid, 2010, 290). There is also a well-known Irish song, *Bonny Portmore*, which as it is known now shares two lines with these songs, and which is generally understood to be about the felling of oak woods in Antrim in the seventeenth century.[9] *Bonny Portmore* must have been known in Britain in the early eighteenth century since it is named as the tune for an unrelated song published in London in 1716.[10]

The verses of *The Strong Walls of Derry* move effortlessly and not entirely logically between the Highlands of Scotland and the north of Ireland, in a way that does indeed suggest incorporation of elements from different, older songs. It begins as a lament for a lost love: the moment he arrives 'on Irish ground', the protagonist learns that she has married another. Is this girl the reason for his move to Ireland? In the second verse, however, his description of the attire he wore in the Highlands, including a blue bonnet, suggests he may have come to Ireland to fight the Stuart cause: this interpretation is favoured by McGuirk and others, who regard *The Strong Walls of Derry* as a Jacobite song.[11] The third verse is again a lament for the lost 'lilly' [*sic*] of Portmore (this verse may derive from *Bonny Portmore*) while the fourth opens with someone calling on Donaldie and asking him where he has been (this is the first verse in Buchan's version).[12] Then comes what is now known, in very slightly altered form, as the first verse of *My Heart's in the Highlands*.

O, Bonny Portmore thou shines where thou stands,
The more I look to thee, the more my heart warms,
But when I look from thee, my heart is full sore,
When I think on the lilly [*sic*] I lost at Portmore,
Let us drink and go home, &c.

O Donald O Donald, O! where have you been,
Ahawking and hunting; gar make my bed clean,
Go make my bed clean and stir up the straw,

> My heart is in the Highlands wherever I go,
> Let us drink and go home, &c.
>
> My heart's in the Highlands, my heart is not here,
> My heart's in the Highlands a chasing the deer,
> A chasing the deer, and following the doe,
> My heart's in the Highlands wherever I go,
> Let us drink and go home, &c.

The sixth and final verse turns to folk wisdom, with the narrator concluding that 'I speak by experience, my mind serves me so, But my heart's in the Highlands wherever I go'.

The twists and turns taken in the extant chapbook version of the song make some sort of sense if we imagine this to be the song of an older man fitfully remembering things past. Alternatively, and bearing in mind that the song's chorus of '*Let us drink and go hame*' classes it as drinking song, we might imagine this to be the work of many singers, adding their contributions (from various sources) round the table. In either case the end result leaves us thinking: why did the protagonist stay in Ireland after his love, or his cause, was lost? If his heart's in the Highlands, why not return there? Burns's version of the song, on the other hand, is as vague and impersonal as it is moving and compact. We know the protagonist is bidding farewell to the Highlands, but that is all. Perhaps it is this generality which has helped the song become so well-known and so easily reused. McGuirk suggests that *Farewell to the Highlands* played a key role in the establishment of a (relatively) positive, Romantic view of the Highlands in the wake of the region's previous portrayal as a hotbed of savagery and rebellion; she adds that 'Imagery of this region as a place of astonishing beauty and noble resistance certainly did not begin with Burns, but he sent such imagery around the world through the ultra-portable (today we might call it viral) medium of songs' (McGuirk, 2014, 110). The idea that songs also migrate has been a mainstay of folklore studies for over a century. Sometimes lyric and air become separated in transit, sometimes individual verses make a bid for freedom, too. It is easier for songs to travel if they have a name like Burns stamped on their passports, but sometimes songs travel without papers as well, bits of them turning up like flotsam and jetsam in very different contexts, and seemingly unbidden. '*You don't look for songs, they find you*' commented my singing teacher, a German who runs a Gaelic language school in Bonn.

Baby, Please Don't Go

In 1995, I left Scotland first for London, then onwards to Berlin, to pursue research into contemporary art music. My undergraduate studies in Glasgow had prepared me for that task, and whetted an appetite that Scotland could not satisfy. And thus I left, as so many do.

Though the reality was somewhat more complex. It took about a year for me to convince myself to follow the advice I'd got: that if I was serious about the direction I wanted my research to take, I needed to be in a place where I could actually hear the relevant music performed on a regular basis. In Scotland, such concerts were a rarety outside of the Edinburgh Festival or the specialist Musica Nova festival organised by the then Scottish National Orchestra. It was at the last ever Musica Nova in 1990 that I encountered the music of German composer Wolfgang Rihm, which subsequently became the subject of my Master's thesis in London. At that point, there was hardly any writing on Rihm in English and not that much more in German, which of course left a young graduate student with a certain amount of freedom of interpretation. That suited me: I wanted to find a language appropriate to *this* music, this new music I loved; I wanted a language that captured what the music *was* rather than what it wasn't. And I found this language in the work of a Scottish author, Neil Gunn, whose book *The Atom of Delight* provided the title for my master's thesis and, through the following quotation, its epigraph:

> The moment of happiness in life which comes not to order but unexpectedly. But is happiness quite the word, or even delight? Sometimes the moment seems one of insight from which the emotional tone or colour comes away. Think of a note of music struck in absolute silence and of the ear listening to the overtones. Now 'insight' is not enough. No word is ever quite enough, not in this kind of hunt. For instance, the sudden note of music does something to the silence of which one had become unaware; it arrests the silence, brings awareness of it, and by so doing defines it for the listening ear. It is an insight into the silence. It cleanses the moment, and through the clarity one's listening ascends with the overtones, while one's being remains at the centre of the experience, in that tranced condition not yet capable of saying, 'My God, that was wonderful!' So the insight is into something more than the silence, it is an apprehension of other factors, even of that other kind of silence into which the ascending overtones finally vanish. Yet this whole complex, unanalysable because inexhaustible, is a moment of simple experience that happens to everyone. If so many words seem to obscure so simple an affair, blame the words, but hang on to the happening.
> Hang on to the happening, however elusive the quarry may be.
>
> (Gunn, 1989[1956], 6)

In the final year before I left for London, my sister and myself became regulars at two of Glasgow's most famous pubs, the Scotia Bar and the Clutha Vaults, which sit less than two minutes' walk apart between Argyle Street and the River Clyde. Both bars had been legendary venues for formal and informal music-making for decades. In the preface to a collection of winning entries to the Scotia's first competition for writers, Billy Connolly described his own formative experiences of the Scotia thus:

> Some of the most wonderful and funny moments of my life were experienced there as bluegrass banjo mingled with Irish air, as raucous Border-ballad

shared a room with poems about blackberry picking in rural Ireland. Political debate raged alongside Beachboys [*sic*] melody. 'Sinky', the great joke-teller from the fish-market, regaled us with endless jokes as old Paul, the Jewish furrier and ex-boxer, told us of the great nights he had spent listening to mandolin orchestras in a Gorbals long since disappeared. Paul, incidentally, was able to give us impromptu proof of his illustrious boxing past when he flattened a rather loud-mouthed and bigoted man half his age with a real haymaker of a right hook before our startled and rather amazed gaze.

(Billy Connolly in McLaughlin, 1990, 10–11)

On Sunday afternoons in the mid-1990s, the Scotia would be full – heaving, as locals would put it – with people listening to regular band The Blues Poets. On Sunday evenings, which sometimes seemed the logical progression (especially after a few drinks), the remainder of the crowd would relocate to the Clutha to hear another band, Dr. Cook and the Boners. My real memories, though, are of The Blues Poets, particularly their renditions of Bob Dylan's *North Country Fair*, and my favourite of all their numbers, the blues song *Baby Please Don't Go*, which in their version ended with a thumping coda consisting of a repeated, ascending minor scale. Both were among the songs recorded by the band in an accompanying CD to James Kelman's play *One, Two, Hey* in which lead singer, the late George Gallacher, played the lead role.[13] But the recorded version of *Baby Please Don't Go* doesn't have that ascending minor scale, nor of course the atmosphere of the live performance, crammed in under low-beamed ceilings among pictures of shipyards and tenements. Glasgow sings the blues: for years afterwards, that kind of music would always make me think of home.

The Water Is Wide, I Cannot Get Over

Home: there's no place like it; it's where the heart is; 'home is the place where, when you have to go there, they have to let you in'.[14] Few concepts are so romanticised: Henry Bishop's *Home, Sweet Home*, from which Dorothy quoted in Oz, was possibly the most commercially successful English-language song of the nineteenth century. But it is a song that is oddly shallow in the sentiments it expresses, reflecting neither the pain of loss, nor the complexity of the reasons why people leave; nor the depths of hardship often experienced both by those who do leave and those who don't, or can't.

Since its publication in William Thomson and Allan Ramsay's pivotal collections in the early eighteenth century, *O waly waly* has been one of the most well-known of Scottish songs, at least among historians and folklorists. It is the song of a woman left in the lurch by her lover at a time when the choice Scottish society gave her was between public shame if she revealed the pregnancy, public hanging if she didn't and was found out.[15] Walter Scott, who was only too aware of the darker sides of the Scottish legal system, used the song as the chapter epigraph to the commencement proper of his tale of Effie Deans in *The Heart of*

Midlothian; possibly the song was also Scott's inspiration for setting much of the action around Arthur's seat, referenced in several early versions of the song.[16] But many people nowadays, when they hear the phrase *O Waly Waly*, think of a slightly different song, and a different tune. Also known as *The Water Is Wide*, this modern song, as Jürgen Kloss describes in a painstaking reconstruction of over two centuries of transmission and redaction, is the descendant of elements from several different songs. In terms of the lyrics, these included one called *The Unfortunate Swain*, and an Irish song known from its chorus as *I'm Often Drunk*;[17] an early version of the tune appeared in the sixth volume of *The Scots Musical Museum* with a song entitled *In Yon Garden* that 100 years later was collected by Cecil Sharp in a version known as *Down in the Meadows*. The modern song is largely due to Sharp's efforts as a collector but also his editorial decisions: the song as he published it, Kloss argues, is a compilation from several recordings he made in Somerset in the early twentieth century. Recognising the relationship of some elements to *O Waly Waly*, Sharp was also responsible for thus naming this modern song, even though the tune is different from the one known by that name in eighteenth century sources, and though the actual phrase never appears.[18] Pete Seeger, who called the song *The Water Is Wide*, helped seal its fate by recording and performing it from the 1950s; since then it has been sung by countless others, including one of my sisters, who used to sing it to me when I was wee.

Scotland, Ireland and England had therefore all contributed to this song before it crossed the sea again to America and back. Before Seeger's version became famous, Benjamin Britten had created his own rendering in volume 3 of his *Folksong Arrangements* (1948). Britten's arrangement, sung by Peter Pears, accompanies the closing scene of Terence Davies's film *Distant Voices, Still Lives*, the story of a working-class family in Liverpool in the 1940s and '50s. Davies's film is a remembrance of things past that stops far short of sentimentality. The father's brutality towards his wife and family is portrayed in straightforward and unflinching terms; after his death, the violence continues through other men in the marriages of one of the daughters and her friend. In his commentary to the film, Davies described *O Waly Waly* as an 'eighteenth century English folksong', and said that the final scene was scripted to it because the song is 'about the nature of love, its mystery, and the fact that it can go'; the choice of the song as such preceded Davies's choice of this particular recording, picked on the strength of Pears's interpretation.[19] It is only one of several pieces of recorded music that act as interludes and framing devices in the film, which is constructed as a series of snapshots tracing this ordinary family's history through various lifecycle events – marriages, births and baptisms, deaths. Focusing as it does on family gatherings in pubs and houses, this structure opens up the space for another and highly significant use of music in the narrative: the film is a constant series of sing-songs, and it's almost always the women who sing.

Sing-songs: until I left Scotland I took them for granted (see Grant, 2008). Once, at a friend's birthday party in Berlin, a guest who was of German and English stock and performed regularly in Irish pubs, produced a guitar and announced that his gift to the birthday girl was to sing her a song. One led to another; you know the kind of songs I mean, but no one there did except me and him. Others listened intently but did not join in at the chorus. That's when the penny dropped; and I realised that this is what I'd been missing at all the other parties I'd ever been to in Berlin.

> The folk were arranged in semi circle round the fireplace. [. . .] A man of about 40 years of age was singing a country and western song. This was Rab's Uncle Gus. He sat on a wooden dining chair, his eyelids were closed and he was holding his head raised, his face almost parallel to the ceiling; and his adam's apple was very prominent, jutting backwards and forwards as he sang. [. . .]
> The song ended and a little round of applause greeted it. Rab's maw was saying: That was smashing Gus smashing.
> What about an encore? asked an elderly woman who was sitting on an armchair close to the corner of the fire.
> Uncle Gus shook his head. We'll spin the bottle missis, everybody's to get a shot.
>
> (Kelman, 1987[1985], 111)

Here are some of the songs that stick in my mind from the sing-songs of my own childhood: *Bachelor Boy* and *Summer Holiday; Sally Free and Easy; The Boxer* (with sound effects in the chorus); *The Wild Rover; Saltcoats at the Fair; Wild Mountain Thyme; The Jeely Piece Song*. Most of them were linked to particular family members who sang them. On my mother's side, the *pièce de resistance* was a communal rendition of *Two Little Boys*. On my father's side, no event was complete without various generations of men singing *On Ilkley Moor Baht' At* in harmony. Ask other generations and other family members, and they would provide other songs: *She Mov'd Through the Fair*, I learnt recently, was the song my father and uncles associated with a particular great-aunt. In my own memories, I find myself drawing a distinction between songs that were sung at the parties of my childhood, and those that came after (*Space Oddity*; *Caledonia*). We all differ in what we regard as being the 'old' songs, the songs that most deeply express our sense of origins and belonging; this has more to do with our own age when we encountered these songs than the age of the songs themselves.

Looked at through the frame of my life in Berlin, then, the sing-song, like the sessions in the Scotia and the Clutha, thus became part of my Scottish experience and identity, though the repertoires concerned were only partly 'Scottish'. But is even this experience 'Scottish'? The family in *Distant Voices, Still Lives* is English, but they were a working-class Catholic family just like mine and the families of friends in Glasgow who lead the singing at our own parties (*The Water Is Wide* is part of their repertoire, too). Is it a class thing? An Irish thing? A British thing? An urban thing? Or just an old-fashioned thing? If I had not moved to Germany, if I had not experienced that distance and displacement,

I probably would never have thought of this as a central part of my culture, or started to ask, as the Germans put it, *Wer bin ich, und wenn ja, wie viel*? Who am I, and if so, how much?

Your Scotland's story is worth just the same

Ultimately, we are faced here with questions about how we categorise, classify but in so doing also rank musical practices. And as a result, what seems like an individual reflection on identity and belonging turns out to be about much more: class history, migration history, privilege, power. In his short story 'A Song for Glasgow', published in the aforementioned Scotia collection (Munro, 1990), Michael Munro tells the tale of Tam, a folk musician from Glasgow, poised to return home after several years touring and living elsewhere. His departure is in part a rebellion against the immigrant identity endowed on him by his family:

> It was always a home full of music. The old boy's fiddle and his mother's singing; the supporting cast of musical relatives and neighbours coming about the house for the regular 'nights'. All the children could play something, but only Tam had stuck with it [. . .] It was the Irishness that sat uneasily on him [. . .] Tam grew to feel oppressed by the cloying green-hued cycle of Irish music, John McCormack on the record player, chapel and holy pictures, the girls at the step-dance in dresses embroidered to out-fantasise the Book of Kells, the boys off to Parkhead in the green.
>
> (Munro, 1990, 161–162)

Tam's years of touring Europe are thus in part his attempt to define himself as Glaswegian and Scottish. En route, and ironically, he falls in love with an Irish singer in West Berlin; she eventually leaves him, but not before making many a comment on Tam's long-stated aim of writing a song for and about Glasgow, a song that

> was to say what the city meant to him, to his Irish forebears and other incomers, to all its citizens past and living in the last twenty years of its greatest century. She would laugh and say it was a suite he was planning, an opera, with all he wanted to get in: the politics, Red heroes and fierce women, the shipmakers, the working life, the idylls of green parks and doon the water, the humour and strength, despair and degradation, the triumph of humanity over the perversion of the human spirit.
>
> (Munro, 1990, 164)

Though he remains emotionally committed to performing this service to his city, Tam, too, ultimately concedes that this song of songs is just too big to be written. At the end of the day, as the story implies but never states, the song isn't the thing, it's just what brings the other, really important things together.

The sheer number of songs about parting and homecoming, and the prominent position they hold in Scottish repertories, point to the centrality of these events in our experience and collective memory. The Scots, some historians suggest, have long had an interesting propensity for migration to other shores (see Grosjean and Murdoch, 2005); an island nation with a long-standing seafaring culture could hardly be any different. Indeed, it makes a big difference to understanding Scotland, musically or otherwise, if we redraw the world map in terms not of land masses but sea routes that link us, beyond the British Isles, to France, to the Iberian peninsula, and to northern and western Africa on the one hand; and to northern continental Europe, to the Baltic countries, to Scandinavia on the other. And the traffic, of course, goes both ways.

The original bias of folklore studies towards viewing cultures as hermetically sealed biotopes, has now been recognised and rejected, as has the relationship of such discourses to xenophobic nationalism and racism, to *Blut und Boden*. The interest of folklorists in emigrant communities comes in part from these communities' tendency to self-containment, self-consciousness, and the ensuing slower rate of development of traditions compared to the homeland. Useful as such approaches are for our understanding of the musical past, the more problematic legacies of the discipline can only really be shaken off by looking at the impacts of immigration as well as emigration.

A tendency in national historiography to flag up some groups of immigrants at the expense of others was captured well by Charlie and Craig Reid, better known as The Proclaimers, in the lyrics of *Scotland's Story*.[20] The problem with this story, as they describe it, is its antiquity and whiteness, the focus on '*the Gael and the Pict, the Angle and Dane*', while Indian, Italian, Jewish, Ukrainian, and Chinese names are largely missing; even the Irish names are limited to those from the distant part. Recent migration to our shores, particularly where driven by poverty, war and persecution, is somehow extraneous to the 'real' story of our nation. We may eat Italian and Indian food every week, but the idea that Italian and Indian musical traditions may not just have deeply influenced Scottish music, but now themselves be forms of Scottish music, seems more difficult to swallow. Where imports, borrowings and transformations become so established that they seem self-explanatory, and especially when they have the label of national identity thrust upon them – the bagpipe is a case in point – folk can get very resistant to suggestions that they are not exclusively ours, after all. In history however, migration and cultural exchange is the rule, not the exception. Globalisation and technological advances may have accelerated this process, but as Douglas Adams pointed out with his usual wit and mirth, such technologies tend to be successful precisely when they allow us to do things we would be inclined to do anyway (such as interact) (Adams, 1999). The whole world, potentially, has a place in the history of Scotland's music just as Scotland's place in the history of the musical world is not limited to what we might think of as essentially 'Scottish', which at best is a celebration of cultural pluralism, at worst however a reduction of musical identity to the Scotch snap and the badly imitated bagpipe drone, markers of musical Scottishness which hardly predate the later seventeenth century. As Matthew

Gelbart has shown, the problem with the construction of musical nationalism in the eighteenth and nineteenth centuries is its relationship to a 'centre and periphery' model of music history which was intertwined with a growing dichotomisation between 'art' and 'folk' music (Gelbart, 2007). Within Britain, this had its own correlate in the way that Scottish music and Scottish culture generally was portrayed, satirised, and exploited for an array of political and especially military ends. Whether the associated sentiments were fascination or revulsion, whether the context was British imperialism or European romanticism, whether the intentions good, bad or indifferent: to be Scottish meant to be other, to be on the edge of civilisation and not necessarily on the right side of that divide (a fate we share with other 'others': descriptions of Turkish music from around 1800 seem oddly familiar from the early historiography of Scottish music).

Understanding the ideological backdrop to the question of what 'Scottish' is, musically, does not mean rescinding the idea that there is such as thing as Scottish traditions, or arguing for a kind of cultural relativism. It does however invite us to be critically aware of the stories we are told about their and our origins, about who we are and are not. It cautions against defining Scottish traditions in opposition to the rest of the world, rather than as particular instances of global flows of peoples and ideas (and the idea of 'flow' seems particularly relevant for Scotland, given that so much of this exchange came via the sea). And with specific regard to what, not only in Europe, is the ideologically dominant tradition of art music, it invites us to look more critically at how, but particularly why, Scotland was viewed as peripheral at best. One of the most important musical manuscripts to have survived from the European Middle Ages is now held in the famous library of Wolfenbüttel in Germany, and generally known by the acronym W_1. But it is also known as the St. Andrews Manuscript, after the Scottish city where it was created, probably on the initiative of Guillaume Mauvoisin, the French Bishop of St. Andrews from 1202–1239.[21] As well as organum from the Parisian masters Leoninus and Perotinus, the manuscript also contains music written in Scotland following this Parisian tradition. In conventional music histories, Notre Dame polyphony of this period is widely represented as the true beginning of Western art music; we may challenge that representation and the limited view of music history it presents, but no longer deny that scribes in Scotland are in great part responsible for the material evidence on which that history is based.

And now I'm going home

'Home', then, makes little sense without the related concept of movement and travel. In a society where most people are settled, home is the start of every other journey we will ever make, and even nomadic and traveller communities will generally have fixed points to which they return at periodic intervals. 'Home' is synonymous with security, with safety, and it's this which makes being unsafe in one's home, either as a victim of domestic violence or of war, particularly traumatic: *thy wee bit housie, too, in ruin*. It's also what makes the idea not just of a home, but a homeland, so politically significant and volatile, particularly when we forget that almost nowhere on earth was our original home, that we all have ancestors who made treacherous journeys across sea and land in search of safety.

The song *Caledonia* was written by Dougie Maclean in 1977 while he was touring mainland Europe with the Irish musician Alan Roberts. It first appeared on an album they released in 1979, also entitled *Caledonia* (this might explain why a German friend of mine learned it as an *Irish* song). A new recording by Maclean concluded his first solo album, *Craigie Dhu* (Dunkeld Records, 1983). But it was a version recorded by the Glaswegian rock singer Frankie Miller in 1991 that made the song famous. Subsequently released as a single, this recording started life as the soundtrack to a TV advertisement for Tennent's lager. The advert shows a young man commuting to work in a packed, anonymous and unsmiling commuter London; suddenly, he ditches his briefcase and office security pass, and at the crucial word in the song, 'home', the backdrop changes to Edinburgh Castle and Princes Street.

'*Caledonia, you're calling me/And now I'm going home*'. The Tennent's advert was directed to people in Scotland, but more recently the song was also used as the official anthem for the Scottish government's Homecoming Scotland initiative in 2009. Using the 250th anniversary of the birth of Burns as the pretext, Homecoming Scotland was a tourism campaign aimed at people of Scottish descent throughout the world, and since repeated in 2014. The official television and cinema advert for the 2009 campaign saw the first verse and chorus of Maclean's song being sung or recited by a series of Scottish celebrities from film, music, and sport, against a backdrop of Scottish landscapes and landmarks.[22]

Caledonia demonstrates how specific media events and personalities can propel songs into public consciousness, setting them on a very different trajectory than they might otherwise have travelled. Although MacLean is now fêted as the song's composer, and performs it widely at major events – including the closing ceremony for the 2014 Commonwealth Games – *Caledonia* became known through Frankie Miller's version, a rendition that took the song from its 'folk' background into the soft rock genre very popular at the time. The harmonic structure of the song undoubtedly made this transition easier: a song that can tick so many boxes in terms of taste, genre and context has an easier passage to renown than most. Not infrequently suggested as one of several contenders for a future Scottish national anthem, the song thus clearly has something to tell us about contemporary Scottish identities. But for all its contemporaneity, *Caledonia* also speaks of much older themes. As a song about the emigrant's journey home, it is linked thematically, for example, to the most famous of all Scottish songs, Burns's version of *Auld Lang Syne*, one of only several eighteenth-century songs on that sentiment and about emigration and return.[23] But where *Auld Lang Syne* focuses on the ties that bind us to the people we leave behind, *Caledonia* is a love song to Scotland itself – whatever that may be. There is no reference in it to the Scottish landscape; no extolling of the virtues of Scottish folk; no praising of Scottish values. The song is at once vague in its love and yet specific in recognising the inevitability of the pull: *Caledonia's been everything I've ever had*. Perhaps this is why the song is so popular, including among people who have never lived anywhere else *but* Scotland. And perhaps, as well, this is no bad way to define a nation. Languages change; landscapes change; yesterday's heroes and battles are rarely the struggles we face today. When nationalism does not recognise this, it becomes dangerous, imposing the history of a few on the futures of us all. This is why it is so important to keep singing songs that tell a different story, making present those distant voices that have made these journeys before.

I walked from Garve to Ullapool

A song found me in Bonn, a Gaelic song about North Uist that convinced me it must be the most beautiful place on earth, at least for the person who wrote it. A year later, I took the song back there, or it took me, and I wasn't disappointed. I sat overlooking the beach at Illeray, close to an abandoned cottage, and sang the song with the bleating of new lambs looking for their mothers as counterpoint; *hó ró Iolaraigh, Iolaraigh, Iolaraigh*. I scoured my Ordnance Survey map for the other places referenced, and walked to most of them. The real map, of course, was the song.

It had been a song in the English language that set me to learning Gaelic song in the first place: Dick Gaughan's *Why Old Men Cry*, originally released on his album *Redwood Cathedral*. Gaughan's control of the vocal line, the inflexions that are not so much *around* it as *are* it, the effortless ease with which his voice holds a whole world in each moment of its span, even the song's semi through-composed structure suggest immediately that its musical heritage is Gaelic. In fact, Gaughan's mother, a Highlander from Lochaber, won prizes for her singing at the Mód, and Gaughan has spoken about the influence both of this tradition and the music of his paternal, Irish grandparents on his own work.[24] His maternal grandfather is the starting point for this song, however, which by its end has journeyed through three generations and a century of social and political change. The song commences with a walk from Ypres to Passchendaele retracing the steps of the grandfather, who died of gas poisoning in the First World War. The second part of the song takes us from Leith, whence Gaughan hails, to the former mining village of Newtongrange in Midlothian, where his own father struggled to make a living for his family. In the concluding and shortest part of the song the focus shifts to the present, as Gaughan walks '*from Garve to Ullapool*', reflecting on the beauty of the land that bore him, and on what lies ahead for the people who live there.

It is tempting to divide the song's temporal span across three dates – 1914, 1984, 2014. While these don't correspond to the actual timing of the events described, they stand as markers for three experiences that thematically underpin the song, historic turning points that Gaughan describes by giving voice to his own family's experience. The first, 1914, marks the beginning of the Great War; the second, 1984, the beginning of the year-long Miner's Strike that was the culmination of the struggle of mining communities, but also precipitated dramatic changes in the relationship between working people and the state in Britain more generally.

The third date is more imaginative, not least because the song was written not in 2014, 'Scotland's year of living dangerously' as Lesley Riddoch put it (Riddoch, 2014, 315), but in 1998, on the cusp of the reconvening of the Scottish Parliament one year later. But the close of the song predicts well the reconfiguring of Scottish political identities which gained real momentum during the referendum campaign, though it was part of a longer process of people questioning the narratives they've been given and starting to create their own, of people gaining confidence in the fact that their voices, too, each and every one of them, are as good as any others, always have been, always will be.

> And I looked into the future [sings Gaughan],
> Saw a people proud and free
> As I looked across Loch Broom
> Out to the sea.[25]

Author's note

This chapter is dedicated to the memory of my cousin Kathleen Mary Blair Lynch, née Logan, born Motherwell, Scotland, 1971; died Brisbane, Australia, 2015.

Notes

1 In this section, I use the word 'song' in the additional, old sense of a lyric to be sung.
2 For a moving account from the composer's wife Nora Pärt of the family's forced emigration, (see Enzo Rastagno, 'Mit Arvo Pärt in Gespräch', in Rastagno et al., 2010: 53–55).
3 Pärt's use of this stop may or may not be a nod to the long-standing tradition of mimicking the sound of the bagpipes using oboes, though otherwise there is no resemblance to such portrayals. The oboe is also Pärt's own instrument.
4 I am grateful to Vivien Estelle Williams for drawing my attention to this. The other non-original music in the film includes compositions by Henryk Górecki and John Tavener, often grouped with Pärt in the early 1990s.
5 McCue and Rycroft (2014), state that this transition to the new tune was completed by around 1840.
6 A version of *Crodh Chailean* with English translation can be found at https://scotsgaelicsong.wordpress.com/2014/03/18/scots-gaelic-song-crodh-chailein/ (accessed 3.11.15). Alan Lomax recorded Kate Nicholson of South Uist singing the song as a milking song in the 1950s: the tune is almost identical with that now used for *My Heart's in the Highlands*; http://research.culturalequity.org/get-audio-detailed-recording.do?recordingId=3038 (accessed 3.11.15). A different version can be heard on a 1968 recording of Donald Sinclair, Tiree, in the archives of the School of Scottish Studies, available at www.tobarandualchais.co.uk/en/fullrecord/57427/1 (accessed 3.11.15). His tune is related to that collected by Elisabeth Ross in the early nineteenth century: *The Elisabeth Ross Manuscript: Original Highland Airs Collected at Raasay in 1812 by Elisabeth Jane Ross*, edited by Peter Cooke, Morag MacLeod and Colm Ó Baoill. Available at the time of writing (accessed 3.11.15) at: www.ed.ac.uk/files/imports/fileManager/RossMS.pdf, a performer's edition is also published by Musica Scotica. Sinclair's version, however, makes clearer a relationship to the tune *Lochaber*

No More (in the first and final phrases of the chorus), which may help explain why this tune and Burns's song came together.
7   Stenhouse's annotated edition of James Johnson's *The Scots Musical Museum* gives Charles Kilpatrick Sharpe as the source for this theory (Stenhouse, 1853: part 3, 313–4). James Dick's edition also cites Kirkpatrick Sharpe on this issue (Dick, 1903, 453–454). McGuirk's discussion (op. cit., 112) erroneously implies that *The Strong Walls of Derry* was published in the original fourth volume of the *Scots Musical Museum*, rather than in Stenhouse's much later commentary on volume 3, as a note to *Farewell to the Highlands*.
8   The Greenwich Lady: to which is added, The Strong Walls of Derry. The Gunner's Lamentation. Brave Admiral Russell ([Glasgow]: n. p., 1793). NLS shelfmark Ry III e. 16 (18).
9   *Bonny Portmore*'s opening two lines are related to the first two lines of the penultimate verse of Buchan's version and the fourth verse of *The Strong Walls of Derry*. The 'strong walls' mentioned in the latter song – 'lang woods' in Buchan's version – seem to derive from this. In Buchan's *Portmore*, the final line of this verse is 'When I mind upon Valiantny, and on Portmore', while in *The Strong Walls of Derry* it is 'Adieu to valendery and bonny Port-more' [*sic*]; the original reference may therefore have been to Ballinderry, a town close to Portmore Lough.
10 The true Scot's-man's lammentation [*sic*] with an acrostick, to the tune of, Bonny Portmore (London?: n.p., 1716?).
11 It is possible that the references to Derry (*doire* = oak wood) were understood in some quarters as references to Jacobitism, since the oak was an important Jacobite symbol. A thread on the traditional music website mudcatcafe.org refers to a 1746 chapbook version of *You Jacobites By Name* followed by a song that, from the description, could well be *The Strong Walls of Derry*. http://mudcat.org/detail_pf.cfm?messages__ Message_ID=16969, posted by Bruce O. on 1 December 1997 (accessed 14.11.15). According to the English Short Title Catalogue, the relevant song is published under the title *The Valiant Soldier*.
12 The 'lilly', too, could be a political reference if we see a connection to the unrelated song *Lillibullero*.
13 Gallacher and Blues Poets bassist Fraser Watson were members of the 1960s rock band The Poets.
14 Robert Frost, "'The Death of the Hired Man"'.
15 The logic of the latter was that a woman who concealed the pregnancy must be intending to kill the baby at birth. The death penalty for concealment of pregnancy was an attempt to reduce very high rates of infanticide, which however only came down when the practice of publicly shaming women was abandoned by the church.
16 Including one in circulation around 1701 that had *Arthur's seat shall be my bed* as its title; Jürgen Kloss, '"The Water Is Wide": 'The History of a "Folksong"', www.justan othertune.com/html/wateriswide.html; a broadsheet featuring the song is at http://digital. nls.uk/broadsides/broadside.cfm/id/14523 (both accessed 12.11.15).
17 As Kloss, op. cit. notes, the phrase 'I'm often drunk, but seldom sober', crops up in a variety of different songs, including two which he doesn't mention, *I'm a rover* (recorded amongst others by The Dubliners and the Corries) and *Carrickfergus*, which also includes the phrase '*But the sea is wide and I cannot swim over*'.
18 Kloss, op. cit.
19 Terence Davies, director's commentary, on the British Film Institute DVD edition of *Distant Voices, Still Lives*, BVIVD733, at 1:15:40.
20 On the album *Persevere* (Persevere Records, 2001).
21 The suggestion that Mauvoisin rather than his successor David Burnham was responsible was first argued by Everist (1990). The article also summarises the main stages in the debate on the provenance of the manuscript.

22 Specifically, singer-songwriter Amy MacDonald, champion cyclist Chris Hoy, actor Brian Cox, golfer Sam Torrance, singer-songwriter Eddi Reader, rugby stars Thom Evans and Kelly Brown, singer-songwriter Sandi Thom, actor Sean Connery (the only one to recite rather than sing his line), and the singer Lulu. See www.youtube.com/watch?v=ENq8CLKEnJo (accessed 22.10.15); documentation of the campaign, including distribution and viewing statistics for this advert, can be found at www.visitscotland.org/pdf/homecoming_scotland_2009_-_the_story.pdf (accessed 22.10.2015).
23 For a full discussion, see M.J. Grant, *Auld Lang Syne: A Song and Its Culture*, forthcoming, Chapter 3.
24 'Biography', at http://dickgaughan.co.uk/biography/index.html (accessed 13.11.15).
25 Lyrics copyright Grian Music, 1998. Permission pending.

13 The globalization of Highland dancing

Patricia H. Ballantyne

Introduction

Contemporary Highland dancing, with its associated images of Highland Games, tartan, bagpipes and ancient customs is considered to be an emblem of Scottish culture. Highland dancing competitions attract international entrants which some commentators believe is exactly as it should be. As one noted, 'No longer is it possible to label a competitor as Australian, South African, Canadian or American because of the steps used or differences in technical approach' (SOBHD, 1993, u.p.). How might Highland dancing have become a globalized and standardized form of dance?

There appear to be two main contributing factors behind the globalization of Highland dancing. The first is that it is run according to strictly defined rules, every aspect of which is specifically set out so that anyone in the world will practise and perform this dance form in the same way. It should not be possible to tell a dancer's country of origin by watching that dancer perform. This is in marked contrast to the situation in the eighteenth century when improvisation appears to have been encouraged, and in the nineteenth and early twentieth centuries when many versions of dances and styles of performance were common. The second contributing factor is that links between this dance form and Scottish Highland culture have been systematically removed or diluted since Highland dance steps were first noted down by the eighteenth century Aberdeen dancing master, Francis Peacock. This removal or dilution of the cultural links with particular respect to Peacock's observations, continued throughout the nineteenth and twentieth centuries and the result is the uniformity of the competition dances of today.

This chapter traces the story of the standardization and globalization of Highland dance from the early nineteenth century to the mid-twentieth century, through a consideration of how the regulatory dance societies were formed in response to a demand from the dancing profession, a demand which was to increase in intensity during the 1890s and 1900s. This narrative includes contributions from dancing masters and evaluates the effect that professionalization had on dancing as a social practice.

The eighteenth-century background

In 1805 the Aberdeen dancing master, Francis Peacock (c. 1723–1807) published a manual of 'hints for teachers' of dance (*Sketches* 1805). It contains fifteen chapters which Peacock referred to as 'Sketches'. Other than the fifth, these chapters have largely not been analyzed by commentators on Scottish dance. *Sketches* provides significant information towards the body of knowledge of eighteenth century dance in North East Scotland and demonstrates Peacock's interest in education, philosophy, dance and people and also provides evidence of his keen observational skills.

Sketches is important on a number of levels. Not only does it tell us what and how Peacock taught, it also provides an insight into his influences and into what shaped his philosophical thinking. It illustrates his own theories and observations on topics such as choreography, posture, music and dance. The fifth sketch in the book deals specifically with the dancing of Scottish Highlanders, and describes ten reel steps that Peacock had observed Highlanders dancing.

The contribution of these descriptions of Highland dance steps to the history of Scottish dance should not be overlooked, for they provide evidence, not only of the type of reel step that was performed in some parts of the Highlands during the eighteenth century, but also a starting point from which to assess the subsequent development of Highland dancing. An analysis of the steps and comparison with subsequent dance step descriptions shows how the steps Peacock described developed from travelling and setting steps used for reels, and were incorporated into certain dances that became known as Highland Dances (Ballantyne, 2016). As such, Peacock's descriptions are an important part of the history of Highland dancing in particular, and of Scottish dancing in general.

In the eighteenth century Highland dancing was not confined to Scotland. In the 1780s for example, reels were popular stage dances in the Drury Lane theatres in London (Milhous, 2003). Peacock noted that in the eighteenth century, London dancing masters would travel to Edinburgh specifically to learn Highland dance steps. 'It is no uncommon thing, at Edinburgh, to see men of our profession who come there with no other view, but to acquire a knowledge of the proper steps made use of in that dance [Scotch Reels]' (Peacock, 1805, 87). By the beginning of the nineteenth century, London based dancing masters such as Thomas Wilson were offering tuition in choreographed dances such as the *Highland Fling* and *Shantruse* [sic], the latter better known today as the *Sean Triubhas* (Wilson, 1808). George Jenkins, a dancing master who was also based in London, had composed the melody *The Marquis of Huntly's Highland Fling* in 1793 (Gore, The Scottish Music Index, [date accessed 2012]) and the dance appears to have taken its name from the melody.

It may have been in an attempt to ensure that the dancers from the Highlands achieved proper recognition as the originators and best performers of Scotch reel steps that Francis Peacock decided to record his direct observations of some of these steps in his manual. He provided Gaelic names for the steps, possibly through his acquaintance with Ewan MacLachlan who was the librarian at King's

College, Aberdeen, and who had translated Homer's *Iliad* into Gaelic (Thomson, 1983). Peacock explained that he was:

> Prompted by gratitude to acknowledge my obligations to a literary friend, (well versed in the Gaelic language) who has obligingly favoured me with the etymology of the terms, or adopted names, of the steps I am about to describe. These terms may be of use to the [dancing] master, as they serve to distinguish the different steps from one another, and may induce a degree of speculation in the philologist.
>
> (Peacock, 1805, 88–89)

Peacock stressed that the dancing master should know and understand the music being danced to and how the dance and its music – the reels and strathspeys – fitted together. He provided clear explanations of how the dancing master should interpret the music, and observed that the steps could be improvised upon in response to the music. In a statement that is of some significance, particularly given how Highland dancing was to develop, he stated:

> You have it in your power to change, divide, add to, or invert, the different steps described, in whatever way you think best adapted to the tune, or most pleasing to yourself.
>
> (Peacock, 1805, 98)

This improvisatory and responsive aspect of dance teaching appears to have waned in importance as the nineteenth century progressed. Even whilst Peacock was writing his text, a number of versions of named dances had developed, each with specific steps that were to be performed in a certain order. As noted, these dances were often danced to the accompaniment of certain named melodies, such as *The Marquis of Huntly's Highland Fling* or *Ghillie Callum*, perhaps because this encouraged audience familiarity.

Nineteenth century developments

During the nineteenth century the number of dancing masters practising in Scotland and in particular, itinerant dancing masters teaching in cities, increased. This reflected the population increase in urban areas as people moved from the countryside to the towns to find work in factories and industries (Tyson, 1988, 19–36). In 1801, Aberdeen, for example, had a population of around 27,000 (Tyson, 1988). By 1881, this population had grown to around 105,000 (Tyson, 1988). Many advertisements appeared in Aberdeen newspapers which demonstrates both the interest in dancing and the number of dancing masters practising in the area in the nineteenth and early twentieth centuries (Mitchell, 1932a, 1932b). Travelling dancing masters would spend periods of between six and twelve weeks in a particular location, providing a complete series of dance classes for local people during that time. Many of those active in the north of Scotland taught what came to be known as Highland dances as well as popular ballroom dances, quadrilles and cotillions.

At the end of each teaching period the dancing master would hold an 'Assembly' which might be reviewed in the local newspaper, although the review may have been provided by the dancing master himself. End of term assemblies were a useful marketing device as they allowed the dancing master to demonstrate what he had taught that term and to encourage new pupils to attend the next course of lessons. This was important, because the dancing master may not have been the only such teacher to visit the area.

Developments in Highland dancing can be traced through considering what dances were performed during these closing assemblies. 'Professor' William Scott taught in various locations in the North-East of Scotland from the 1840s until 1897. It was not until 1849, for example, that his pupils started to perform the occasional Highland dance 'in character' – or in costume (Mitchell, 1932d). This suggests that the concept of the uniformed or kilted dancer may not always have been the case. That Highland dancing was popular in the North-East of Scotland is clear from an examination of Scott's closing assembly programmes (Mitchell, 1932d). In a closing assembly held in Peterhead in the summer of 1855, the second half of the long programme was entirely devoted to Highland dances. Again, the programme demonstrates what dances were popular at the time. The first half comprised an eclectic mix of thirty items which began with:

> Processional Entrée of the Pupils – music by D'Albert, and from 'Roberto il Diavolo.'
> Reel o' Tulloch – All the Pupils.
> Quadrille – 48 Pupils – Little bo [*sic*] Peep-[music by] D'Albert.
> Favourite Dance – Little Set.
> Sets of Steps – Ladies (Mitchell, 1932d).'

and culminated with the quadrille 'Les Lanciers, which was performed by all the Pupils'.

The Highland dances in the second part of the programme included:

> Grand Highland March, &c., introducing Caledonian Ballet – Highland Fling – Ghillie Callum [Sword Dance] – Medley Dance – finishing with the Double Reel o' Tulloch, by all the Pupils.
>
> (Mitchell, 1932d)

The programme was followed by 'Fashionable Assembly Room Dancing', in which the audience was invited to participate (Mitchell, 1932d).

Mid-nineteenth-century Highland dancing appears to have contained a lively and varied genre of dances. Frederick Hill's manuscript 'Notebook of Dances', which he began to compile in 1841, describes over seventy dances that he had learned from various dancing masters in Aberdeenshire. This is a particularly significant source because it is one of the rare surviving instances of descriptions of dances and steps that were popular in the North-East of Scotland in the first half of the nineteenth century. Hill had been taught these dances by four different itinerant dancing masters who were active in the area and the Notebook includes variations, such as the two different versions of the *Marquis of Huntly's Highland Fling* that he learned from two dancing masters (MacFadyen and MacPherson, 2009).[1] Although there are strong similarities between the two versions, there are some differences in at least two of the steps. Furthermore, the versions appear to mirror each other as one describes the steps commencing by hopping on the right foot with the left foot as the working foot, whilst the other reverses this. This demonstrates that even within a relatively limited geographic area, versions of individual dances might vary according to how the dancing master had learned them and then passed them on. Whilst very few actual step descriptions survive from this period, the existence of such stylistic variations as these suggests that there was a lively and thriving body of dance material. It was with the intention of regulating this variety of styles and methods of performance that the twentieth century organisation, that the Scottish Official Board of Highland Dancing (SOBHD), was to be set up 100 years later.

In a booklet produced by the popular newspaper, *The People's Journal*, the fiddler and composer James Scott Skinner, who began teaching dance in the 1860s, described a *Highland Fling* danced by his elder brother, Sandy (1833–1880) (Skinner, 1905, 53). Sandy had also been a dancing master, as had their father William (Skinner, 1994) and Sandy may have learned some Highland dances and/or steps from William. Sandy Skinner's version of the *Marquis of Huntly's Highland Fling* had ten steps, unlike Hill's versions which each had eight steps. Whilst Skinner's dance demonstrates some similarities to both Peacock's and Hill's descriptions, it demonstrates that a variety of steps existed in the nineteenth and early twentieth centuries.

By the mid-to late-nineteenth century, a substantial number of dancing masters were operating in Scotland. As a result, it became increasingly important for the dancing master who wished to succeed in this busy market to adopt a business-like approach. One method adopted was to send reviews of end of term assemblies to the local press, which seems to have been a useful way to encourage prospective pupils to attend the next series of lessons in the area. James Scott Skinner was particularly adept at this form of marketing. Not only did he ensure that assembly reviews appeared in the local press in each of the areas he taught in but he also gathered these reviews together and republished them in his collections of music, such as the *Miller of Hirn* (1881) and *The Elgin Collection* (1884). Any opportunity to maximize potential income was of the utmost importance to professional dancing masters and such attention to marketing was to assume more importance as the nineteenth century progressed.

Competitive pricing and client testimonials were also popular marketing devices. It was common practice within the profession to offer half price lessons to the second and subsequent members of the same family. James Scott Skinner published long lists of influential clients on his advertising material. However, pricing and testimonials were not sufficient and it became common for the astute dancing master to differentiate himself from the competition by offering tuition in the latest fashionable dances from the London ballrooms. Offering the latest, fashionable dances demonstrates that Scottish dancing masters did not confine their teaching to Scottish dances alone. To make this even more appealing to potential clients, some dancing masters announced that they had learned these dances directly from the devisor (Mitchell, 1932b), which was not a new departure. Peacock for example, made some references in *Sketches* to his own visits to London, for example, his meeting with the dancer Sir Giovanni Gallini (Peacock, 1805, 114).

The career of Aberdeen dancing master A. Cosmo Mitchell (1860–1932) encompasses the establishment of the regulatory dance societies which were to encourage the standardization and homogenization of dances. Mitchell was closely involved with the establishment of one of these societies, the influential Imperial Society of Dance Teachers (ISDT). As a vice president of that organization for over ten years, from its inception in 1904, he held a position of some importance for a Scottish provincial dancing master.

Mitchell was a highly respected, successful and influential dancing master in Aberdeen from 1881 until he retired in 1924. In common with many members of his profession, he started his career as an itinerant dancing master. Born and brought up about forty miles north west of Aberdeen, in Kennethmont near Huntly, he held his first professional classes in Nairn in April 1881 and seven months later, commenced teaching in Aberdeen where he was eventually to be based full-time. He included Forres, Elgin, Inverness and Stonehaven in his circuit, but by 1892, he taught exclusively in Aberdeen. Mitchell was an astute businessman. In common with many dancing masters of the 1870s and 80s, his handbills demonstrate that he charged half fees for the second and subsequent members of the same family. He also used respectable members of the local establishment, in each area that he taught in, to provide testimonials. During his first years of teaching, Mitchell offered a series of twenty lessons over a twelve-week period. Other itinerant dancing masters who visited Aberdeen during the late nineteenth century such as the Brouneaus from Belfast (Mitchell, 1932b)[2] condensed their classes into a six-week period. Mitchell expanded his business reach by taking dance classes into schools. This proved to be so successful that by 1891 he had employed two assistants to help him to cope with the demand. By the early 1900s he was teaching in every one of Aberdeen Town Council's Board Schools (Mitchell, 1932a, 1932e, 1932f).

During this time he worked hard at marketing. He took every possible opportunity to promote his classes in the local press and became a well-known and respected member of local society. He gained a reputation as a popular master of ceremonies at official functions, arranged for his best pupils to perform at these functions and ensured that they were well reported in the national press. He also became known for providing new dances for balls and theatricals (Mitchell, 1932a). He promoted himself as an authority on dance teaching and from the 1890s took advantage of every possible opportunity to increase his knowledge and his authority, and made regular visits to London to acquire the latest dances.

Through a keen business interest and awareness, Mitchell had realised the importance of keeping abreast of the latest and most fashionable dances that were being taught and danced in London which Aberdeen dancers were keen to acquire. He used his London visits as exercises in continuing professional development and became acquainted with the most influential dancing masters in London. He attended numerous professional summer school courses offered by such establishments as Espinosa's British Normal School of Dancing, Miss Harding's Academy and R. M. Crompton's Academy of Dancing. Espinosa's school offered diplomas through a series of examinations for professionals in both dance performance and teaching in an effort to improve standards of dancing and teaching (Mitchell, 1932b).

He ensured that he learned new dances directly from their devisors. In 1890, Edward Scott, a well-known London-based dancing master, dance devisor and author of books on dance (Buckland, 2006) created *Chorolistha*, which its author described as a 'new round dance'. Scott taught the dance to Mitchell and provided him with a certificate which licensed him to teach it (Mitchell, 1932a). The issue of such a licence suggests that some members of the dance teaching profession, particularly those who devised new dances, were concerned that other members might be teaching those dances incorrectly. This in turn may have sparked the need to ensure that a certain professional standard of knowledge of a dance had been reached and that the dance would then be correctly taught. The issue of a certificate – the licence to teach correctly, foreshadows what the regulatory societies were formed to do. Licensing was already happening within the profession in London where the British Normal School of Dancing had been founded specifically 'for the training of teachers of dancing' (Mitchell, 1932b). Between 1891 and 1893, Robert Morris Crompton, an influential dancing master in London, published *Dancing*, the first journal aimed specifically at the profession.[3] From his very first editorial, Crompton was adamant that dancing masters should form an association to promote high standards of teaching (Mitchell, 1932c) and Mitchell appears to have agreed wholeheartedly with him, as his frequent contributions to *Dancing* attest.

Professional recognition through the attainment of examination certificates and diplomas, which Mitchell appears to have been keen to acquire, was increasingly viewed by some members of the profession as a suitable method of raising the status of the dancing master and therefore raising the status of the profession itself. Dance teachers appear to have identified a need for the establishment of a professional regulatory body or bodies, that would set out guidelines for 'correct' methods of instruction as well as guidelines for professional dance teacher training.

There was increasing recognition of the need for dancing masters to group together and create organizations that would protect both their business interests and their professional integrity and so the scene was set for the emergence of the regulatory dance societies that would regulate both teachers and what they taught. By the early 1890s, many teachers throughout the country were complaining about bad or poor quality teaching by ill-prepared teachers, who were collectively known as 'charlatans'. Even Peacock had complained about bad teaching in *Sketches* (Peacock, 1805, 74). As a letter from a Scottish dancing master describes, the dance teaching profession perceived charlatans as poor teachers who undercut the prices of established teachers and stole pupils from them (Service, 1891).

It was generally believed amongst the profession that charlatans were those dancing teachers who had merely taken a course of lessons and as a result, considered themselves good enough to teach, and who then undercut genuine teachers in their drive to acquire pupils. This was why members of the profession believed they were losing business through 'the slovenly teachings of the large number of self-styled professors' and why it was also felt that the public should be warned 'against these charlatans, who have already brought no little discredit upon our honourable calling' (Crompton, 1891).

Crompton's publication appears to have been intended as a vehicle to further his wish to form a national and influential society of dancing masters (Buckland, 2007). The following excerpt from a letter to the press, published in 1891, written by a Scottish dancing teacher summarizes why the profession wished to organize. It was written by John Service, a Scottish solicitor and dancing master, who held the position of Secretary of the Scottish Association of Teachers of Dancing.

> Sir, – I have read with much interest the correspondence in your columns of the 'Dancing Question.' Although in England no attempt seems till now to have been made to form an Association of Teachers, such an attempt was (and I think I may say, successfully made), in Scotland, in the year 1884, when the 'Scottish Association of Teachers of Dancing' was formed at Glasgow. This Institution is still in existence, and under the able presidentship of Mr J. F. Wallace, of the Glasgow Dancing Academy, is doing good work. [. . .] I may, perhaps, be allowed to give, in his own language, the views on the subject of a leading member of the Scottish Association. 'Previous', says he, to the formation of the Association we were teaching in our own particular way and style, according to our own ideas and tastes, and without any concert or unanimity, and any person taking a fancy to be a teacher had (as, unfortunately, he still has), the right to designate himself professor of Dancing. To give my own experience in a nice little suburban town where I have taught for over twenty years, and where there is only room for a single teacher, I have had to suffer from the competition of a *Stonemason* who, having taken into his head to teach dancing, has, by charging little more than half my own very moderate fees, deprived me of considerably more than half my pupils. Now, however, matters are much improved. The members of the Association do not encroach upon each others' preserves. Examinations are held by duly qualified and experienced teachers. Certificates are granted to the members after examination, which are, guarantees to the public that they will really get what they pay for; and last, but not least, something like uniformity of style has been secured. All now wanted is that the advantages of the Society should be more widely known, and that all qualified

teachers throughout the United Kingdom should co-operate in forming a strong Society.

(Service, 1891)

Service appears to have felt that there was only room for one teacher of dancing in his locality and that as a professional member of a regulatory organization, he was best qualified for that position. Perhaps the real crux of the matter was that professionalization, through the establishment of a regulatory body, was felt to be an important step forward, as it would rid the dance teaching profession of the competition that undercut the rates of the 'qualified' teachers.

This model of a regulatory body, which would provide economic stability to accredited teachers, was to become dominant. Mr Service's references to losing pupils and fees, suggests that a key driver for forming these associations and societies may have been to maximize income for professional tutors.

In 1892, the British Association of Teachers of Dance (BATD) was formed with this same intention, but it was slow to attract members and took ten years to really catch on, whereas the Imperial Society of Dance Teachers (ISTD) which had its inaugural meeting in 1904, was instantly successful. Cosmo Mitchell, with his wide network of London contacts, but particularly because of his association with Crompton who was the main instigator of the ISDT, was elected as one of the ISDT's first vice presidents, a position he was to hold for over ten years. A central aim of each professional society was to protect the interests of its members by creating a system of examinations which would licence these members to teach and therefore guarantee high standards of teaching. The societies regulated the dancing profession by adopting a specific method of theory and practice that each teacher and student within that association would adopt, with the result that all teachers who joined an association would teach the same dances in exactly the same way. The BATD, the United Kingdom Alliance (UKA) (1902), Scottish Dance Teachers Association (SDTA) (1934) and the Scottish Official Board of Highland Dancing (SOBHD) (1950) all followed the same model.

Twentieth century developments

During the first half of the twentieth century, Highland dancing evolved in two main directions. On one hand there was an increasing balletic influence, where the dancer 'turned out' the leg and pointed the foot. This was initiated by the MacLennan brothers in the late nineteenth century, influenced by their own ballet training. As ballet teaching spread – Cosmo Mitchell, for example, was offering ballet classes by the end of the nineteenth century (Mitchell, 1932g) – so did its influence on other forms of Scottish dance, such as Highland dancing (Ballantyne, 2016). By 1929, when G.D. Taylor's teaching manual of Highland dancing was published by the ISTD, the balletic influence had become more pronounced (Taylor, 1929). On the other hand, there was an increasing rise in regional variations of steps and methods of performance, perhaps on account of the number of dancing masters teaching in Scotland. By the early decades of the twentieth century,

Highland dancing had been taught by dancing teachers for well over 100 years. It was hardly surprising then that it should be a vibrant area of culture, with many regional variations of steps and execution.

In 1910, before the balletic influence had become widespread, the Stirling based dancing master Donald R. Mackenzie published a textbook of Highland dances which ran into a number of editions. In the *Illustrated Guide to the National Dances of Scotland*, he attempted to teach some Highland and country dances through the use of detailed drawings and dance step descriptions (Mackenzie, 1910). He suggested melodies that he considered suitable to accompany each dance and provided metronome speeds for these. This demonstrates that 100 years ago, the dances were performed significantly faster than they are today. For example, he suggested a speed of 152 beats per minute for the *Marquis of Huntly's Highland Fling* which is significantly faster than the present day's 'official' speed of around 112 beats per minute (SOBHD, 2015). Mackenzie also included an 'alphabet' of symbols which represented each of the foot positions he had identified as being used in these dances. His descriptions appear to have a masculine slant for not only did his illustrations depict a male dancer but the implication in the descriptions was that only the *Strathspey* and *Reels* were suitable for women to participate in. For these dances he provided some steps that he deemed suitable ladies' steps. The rest were specifically designated for gentlemen as was each step of the *Highland Fling*.

The following theatrical instruction which appears immediately before the final 'quick' step of the *Sword Dance*, demonstrates that Mackenzie wished to impart the suggestion that the dance was particularly unsuited to women:

> Without stopping, the piper still playing the same tune, the dancer claps his hands for tempo at 169 M.M., takes off his bonnet with right hand, holding up both arms, turning twice round by left side upon the sword blades.
> (Mackenzie, 1910, 46)

A woman would be unlikely to have been wearing a bonnet whilst dancing.[4]

Through his use of illustrated and detailed descriptions of dance steps, Mackenzie appears to have been attempting to perform a similar function with his manual as the technical committees of the ISDT and other dance regulatory societies attempted to do with their annual technical meetings which were held to shape exactly how particular dances would be taught and performed each year. When *National Dances* was published, there were many different styles of Highland dancing in existence and many different steps for each dance.[5] For example, James Scott Skinner described his brother's version of the Highland Fling or 'round the leg' step, where the dancer's working foot moves around the supporting leg, as 'round the knee' (Skinner, 1905, 53). The Aberdeen physical education teacher Isobel Murray included photographs in her training manual of that very movement (Murray, 1910, 133). Mackenzie meanwhile, stated that in Highland 'civilian' dancing, the (male) dancer should raise the foot 'no higher than 12 inches from the floor' (Mackenzie, 1910, 13). In suggesting that the Highland dances were mostly masculine, Mackenzie accords with the efforts of the regulatory dance societies to improve upon, reform and create uniform styles of dancing.

National Dances appears to have been the first Scottish manual of Highland dancing published after the formation of the Imperial Society of Dancing Teachers and Mackenzie's manual won the support of that society. As Mackenzie was a member, the organization appears to have been happy to promote his guide amongst its membership, which extended throughout Britain. A review in the *Dance Journal*, the publication for ISDT members, suggested that it would 'afford abundant food for study and reflection and is an ideal guide either for reference or for self-instruction' (ISDT, 1911). From this it could be argued that Mackenzie's manual was the first definitive set of instructions on the path towards the standardization of Highland Dancing.

In 1929, the ISTD published Pipe Major G. Douglas Taylor's manual *Some Traditional Scottish Dances*.[6] Taylor, originally from Aberdeen, taught piping and dancing in the London area (Balloch, 1939). This was the first monograph of Scottish dancing to be published by the ISTD which suggests that rather than a self-help guide for the general public, it was intended as a definitive guide for teachers who were members of the society. The manual includes instructions for the main Highland and some of the more popular Scottish country dances. Taylor acknowledged the help and advice of the ISTD's publisher Cyril Beaumont, who was a ballet expert, and Taylor's manual describes a style of dance that was significantly neater and more balletic than Mackenzie's. Taylor's was the first manual to stipulate that dancers should wear dancing pumps (Taylor, 1929, 17–18). These were heelless shoes, the use of which meant that dancers were less likely to injure themselves when performing the round the leg step and could therefore easily slide the foot around the leg instead of flinging it in the iconic *Highland Fling* step. Taylor does explain that the dancer should slide the working foot neatly round the supporting leg, keeping that foot 'pointed down, and close into the leg; the heel to be just under the knee of the supporting leg' (Taylor, 1929, 21). Taylor appears to have been the first commentator to make this suggestion, which suggests a dramatic alteration in the visual effect of the step from the high 'round the knee' movement described by James Scott Skinner and Isobel Murray amongst others, and its associated 'fling' of the foot round the leg. The 'round the leg' terminology used by Taylor was later to be used by the Highland dancing standardizing body, the Scottish Official Board of Highland Dancing (SOBHD).

In direct contrast to Mackenzie's male gendering of the dances, the drawings in Taylor's manual depict a female dancer. However, in common with Mackenzie, Taylor describes certain strathspey and reel steps as being suitable for 'Ladies' to perform and others as more suitable for 'Gentlemen'. As the book appears to have been intended to function as a manual for teachers who would understand the terminology used in the step descriptions it is likely that it had the effect of standardizing what ISTD members might teach. As was the case with Mackenzie's manual, it appears that Taylor was adapting steps to suit a particular agenda, namely standardizing the dances. In a significant departure from Mackenzie's manual, Taylor specifies 'Theoretical Principles' which include descriptions of foot, head and arm positions, and explanations of how the feet, legs and hands are used. He also describes 'Basic Movements' or descriptions of the principal steps.

In 1934, five years after the first edition of Taylor's manual, the Scottish Dance Teachers Alliance (SDTA) was formed as a breakaway group from the ISTD. This was because some Scottish teachers believed that the London-based society was somewhat remote both geographically and professionally (SDTA, 2015; SOBHD, 2010).[7] The SDTA became increasingly concerned about what its members felt were the difficulties of judging Highland dancing competitions owing to the wide variety of regional and individual styles of performance that prevailed at this time. Eventually it called a meeting of a number of other dance and piping societies as well as individual dance experts, in an attempt to establish an official board of control to regulate and standardize every aspect of the art of Highland dancing (SOBHD, 1993, u.p.). The inaugural meeting of the Scottish Official Board of Highland Dancing was held in January 1950 (Scott, 2005).

A Technical Committee was formed to define technical standards, and a textbook was produced which describes in minute detail, each of the foot, head and arm positions, and the basic movements and steps that combine to create the Highland dances. This textbook has subsequently shaped and regulated Highland dancing. Dancers learn to dance according to the rules and descriptions set out in the textbook and undergo a series of increasingly rigorous practical and theoretical examinations. Each potential Highland dancing teacher undergoes an examination on the contents of the textbook. The Scottish Official Board of Highland Dancing operates as an umbrella organization for each of the member societies with a Highland Dancing section. These societies elect representatives to sit on the Board's technical committee. The committee determines annually which dance steps will be performed in competitions and in the examinations held by member societies in the year ahead. Dancers who intend to compete in the competitions administered by the Board pay an annual fee to the Board.

There have been eight editions of the textbook, *Highland Dancing* since it was first published in 1955. Each edition refines certain movements and steps but there has been little change during this time to the chapter on music theory which appears to owe more to pipe music theory than dance interpretation. The foreword to the sixth edition of 1993 states that as a result of the influence of the textbook 'no longer is it possible to label a [Highland dancing] competitor as Australian, South African, Canadian or American because of the steps used or differences in technical approach.' This is indeed the case. All such differences in approach have disappeared as a result of the availability of the textbook and centralisation of Highland dance teaching around it. This demonstrates how international a sport Highland dancing has become and how a competitor's ethnicity is irrelevant. Full standardisation puts all competitors on an equal footing.

The textbook describes all possible aspects of Highland dancing in as thorough and unambiguous a manner as possible so that all users can perform uniformly. Each part of each position, basic movement and step, is described in as detailed a manner as possible, so that descriptions will be unambiguous and Highland dancing is therefore closely regulated in accordance with the aims of the founders of the SOBHD to create a 'Board of Control' (SOBHD, 2010).

One of the biggest changes to have occurred in Highland dancing since the textbook was first published lies in the speed the dances are now performed at. The tempo of the Highland dances has slowed significantly during the sixty-five years since the textbook was first published. In 1955 the *Highland Fling* had a suggested speed of 152 beats per minute. The latest 2015 edition suggests a speed of 112 beats per minute. The slower speed allows the dancer time to jump as high as possible during each movement and time to execute each movement in as technically precise a manner as possible according to the descriptions laid out in the textbook.

Conclusion

Highland dancing, through regulation and standardization, is now primarily a competition culture, and the dedicated dancer requires to undertake serious training. There is no need for a dancer to ever visit or live for any length of time in Scotland in order to be able to win a world championship competition, nor does that dancer's teacher need to visit Scotland. On the surface, it appears that there is limited room for individual interpretation, for individual or for regional styles to develop on account of the minute detail in which the technical execution of each movement and step has been described by the technical committee and detailed in the textbook. As the *Highland Dancing* foreword suggested, the origin of a dancer is now irrelevant, so it could be argued that through having become globalized, the discipline is no longer closely connected to Scottish Highland culture as Peacock had observed. And this could potentially be considered true of any art discipline anywhere that standardization and regulation, competition and technical expertise are most important, such as in piping, Scottish Country Dancing, and Irish dancing. As we have seen, Highland dancing moved from the Scotch Reel steps described by Peacock in 1805, and away from a lively style of dance where improvisation and musical interpretation were encouraged, and developed, through a series of choreographed dances with a variety of steps and performance styles, to become the highly technical and standardized style of dance that exists today. Professionalisation may have limited unwanted competition by licensing teachers to teach but by so doing it appears to have removed the skills of improvisation. The close attention to music that Peacock insisted on was not retained. Other than metronome speeds and somewhat dense rudiments of the music chapter in the SOBHD textbook, there is no emphasis on improvising dance steps and tailoring them to fit with the music being danced to. Not one of the commentators referred to in this chapter appears to have placed much emphasis on the musical aspect of dance other than suggesting how fast a dance should be performed, nor did any commentator suggest any possibilities for improvisation. Highland dancing is now very much a globalized and standardized practice. The process of the standardization that broke the links with improvisation was started at least partly, if not wholly for business reasons, as the formation of the early dance societies was driven by a demand from professional dancing masters to limit the number of teaching practitioners and therefore to limit business competition. It could be argued that the single regulatory body that oversees all aspects of the contemporary dance form performs the same function today.

Notes

1 The notebook was copied and published by the Hill Manuscript Group in 2009.
2 Mitchell bequeathed his entire collection of dance books and journals and scrapbooks of newspaper cuttings and other dance–related ephemera to Aberdeen Public Library in 1932. His scrapbooks document his professional career and that of many of his predecessors and competitors.
3 There is a complete run of *Dancing* in the Mitchell Collection, MM184.
4 At this time, women were relatively prolific Highland dancers as concert programmes and dance class circulars suggest.
5 Some British Pathé news reels from the early decades of the twentieth century demonstrate different styles of Highland dancing. See www.britishpathe.com.
6 The Imperial Society of Dance Teachers became The Imperial Society of Teachers of Dance in 1925. It is still known by this name. See *100 Years of Dance: A History of the ISTD Dance Examinations Board*, (London: ISTD Dance Examinations Board, 2004), p. 36.
7 This appears to have been the only incidence of a breakaway group. The BATD and UKA continue to operate as national organisations with Highland dancing 'branches'.

Part IV
The past in the present

14 Locating identity in the aural aspects of Thomas Percy's *Reliques of Ancient English Poetry*

A bibliographic perspective

Danni Glover

Thomas Percy (1729–1811) was a clergyman, a writer, and the editor of the finest and most celebrated work of eighteenth-century antiquarian poetry. His most celebrated work is the *Reliques of Ancient English Poetry* (1765), a three-volume collection of antique ballads and contemporary poetry in the ballad style, along with accompanying essays on certain aspects of the ballad tradition. Percy was first inspired to undertake the *Reliques* by the success of James Macpherson's *Ossian* poems, and claimed to have taken as his basis a seventeenth century manuscript he discovered at his friend Humphrey Pitt's house, 'in its present mutilated state . . . unbound and sadly torn, [. . .] lying dirty on the floor, under a bureau, in ye parlour, being used by the maids to light the fire' (Furnival, 1867–1868, lxxiv). An ambitious cleric, Percy was personal chaplain to the Duke and Duchess of Northumberland and, thanks to the influence of his patrons, became Bishop of Dromore in County Down in 1782. Percy's efforts as a man of letters were in part an effort to further his professional ambitions in the church, and the *Reliques* contained a dedication to Elizabeth Percy, Duchess of Northumberland, written by Samuel Johnson. Because of the supplicatory nature of the *Reliques*, and also because of his own moderate, Anglican, Whig agenda, it was necessary to be selective in his editing, and ballads with racy or politically radical themes were omitted or censored. Percy worked in collaboration with celebrated men of letters from all over Great Britain to ensure that his collection represented the finest respectable antiquarian poetry the nation had to offer: a nation which was itself newer than most of the poetry selected to represent it.

The collection had an indisputably positive effect on his career prospects, but Percy also had more ideological reasons for collecting ballads, and in particular Scottish ballads, which have been noted to feature very prominently in the collection (Gilbert, 2009). In 1761, Percy wrote for the first time to the Welsh antiquarian Evan Evans, announcing his wish to restore balance to a book market that he felt was unevenly biased towards an interest in Scots poetry. He believed that the Scots were 'everywhere recommending the antiquities of their country to public notice, vindicating its history, setting off its poetry . . . even our most polite Ladies warble Scottish Airs' (Lewis, 1957, 61). This was not the first time

Percy had envisioned a project with the aim of challenging the vogue for Scottish poetry; in 1760, he outlined his plans for a collection of Norse poetry in a letter to William Shenstone (Brooks, 1977, 70) which, when it first appeared in 1763, was markedly similar in style and layout to James Macpherson's *Fragments of Ancient Poetry* (1760).[1] Percy himself wrote in the preface that 'It would be vain to deny . . . that this attempt is owing to the success of the ERSE fragments' (Percy, 1763: xiv). He also discussed the (at the time unproven) forgery of Macpherson's poetry with the famously Ossian-sceptic Samuel Johnson (Lewis, 1957, 97). It is obvious, then, that Percy had his eye on Macpherson, even if that eye did not always like the look of what it was seeing. If Ossian was an exercise in defining a literary mythology for the Highlands of Scotland, then the *Reliques* aimed to define the literary mythology of Britain, using constituent parts that pre-dated the country itself and in so doing, culturally translating the British ethnicity as being English. I and other scholars of Percy have interpreted this translation as being an effort to alleviate tensions in the country which were rooted in the unpopularity of John Stuart, Earl of Bute, the first Scottish Prime Minister of Great Britain, however it was also an act of Anglo-Patriotism. In defining the British identity as being predominantly English, Scottish identity is absorbed into Englishness, rather than being allowed to carve its own niche in the pantheon of British identities. This fosters an environment of assimilation, a process which is never sensitive to cultural maintenance. This chapter will discuss the effectiveness of this translation of British ethnic identity, considering its efficacy from the perspective of music and sound.

Ballad collections enjoyed a surge of popularity in the eighteenth century. Where previously these materials would have been distributed primarily orally or through broadsides, the enshrinement of the 1710 Statute of Anne into law meant that ballads, being authorless (at least in a legal sense) required no copyright fees to publish. Booksellers filled their lists with hastily compiled anthologies of ballads, and they generally sold well. As with most phenomena in eighteenth-century Britain, however, the Union of 1707 had its part to play. Ballads were popular in part because they were a literature of comfort to a psychology of national unease. In the case of Percy, and many other Anglo-nationalists, this unease was rooted in a perceived loss of English supremacy in the country's newly redefined relationship with Scotland, and the comfort came from reaffirming the roles and histories of both nations. Edward Cowan and Brian Levack have both defined Scotland as having been a 'satellite' of England (Cowan, 1979, 121–140; Levack, 1987, 222), a claim which is somewhat corroborated by the othering of the Scots evident in many eighteenth-century popular publications. Prime Minister John Stuart, the Earl of Bute, was widely disliked because of his unpopular peace treaty with France, seen by many as a betrayal to England in favour of historical Scottish loyalties. Bute's supposed lack of concern with the interests of England were perceived as part of a Caledonian coup, to such an extent that a Scottish style of granite paving was rejected in plans for the civic regeneration of central London lest it appear that Bute was exercising control over the very streets upon which people walked (White, 2010, 83–102). Much of this antagonism was driven by his rivals in government and a hostile press. In response to Bute's newspaper *The Briton*, which he started in an attempt to stabilise relations between the Scots and the English, the politician and journalist John Wilkes spearheaded a campaign of harassment and mockery of the Prime Minister in his lampooningly titled journal *The North Briton*. In the 44th issue of *The North Briton*, Wilkes wrote:

> The restless and turbulent disposition of the Scottish nation before the union, with their constant attachment to France and declared enmity to England, their repeated perfidies and rebellions since that period, with their service behaviour in times of need, and overbearing insolence in power, have justly rendered the very name of Scot hateful to every true Englishman.
> (*The North Britain*, 1763, 17–19)

The North Briton is also notable for its frequent racist caricatures and parodic poetry. Bute was not the only Scottish target of its vitriol: John Wilkes was also a vocal critic of James Macpherson. The paper can be interpreted as an example of the tradition of the press demonising international figures as a reaction to immigration paranoia. Wilkes's insistence on the word 'England' when referring to the whole island, and 'Englishman' when talking about the British people, was carried as a point of principle by supporters who stood against the 'melting [of the] English name . . . down to Briton', indicating a fear of the loss of identity (Stephens, 1813, 61). In Scotland, Anglo-nationalism was felt by those who reacted with it rather than against it in the linguistic low esteem of the country's preeminent thinkers. Enlightenment philosophers such as David Hume and James Beattie compiled lists of 'Scotticisms' (i.e., words and phrases peculiar to Scottish speech) to avoid in speech and writing and published these lists both independently and in magazines. Tobias Smollett observed a division between the north and south of Scotland that matched southern Scots more closely with English people than with Highlanders in his novel *Humphry Clinker*:

> The Highlanders have no other name for the people of the low-country, but *Sassenagh*, or Saxons; a strong presumption, that the Low-land Scots and the English are derived from the same stock.
> (Smollet, 1984, 240)

Percy himself made a similar observation, and defended his preference for the ballad culture of the Lowlands, because 'although [the Lowlands] had [their] own identifiable cultural idiosyncrasies, they were very much in tune with the Gothic myth he was reinventing' (Groom, 2006, 182).

Robert Crawford has argued that English literature did not exist as a distinct and named discipline until Englishness was confronted by Britishness and thus had to be defined in literary (and wider cultural) study (Crawford, 1992). The impact of the Union on literature in Great Britain was to delineate literary works along national borders to align the locale with an intellectual pedigree. Where Chaucer may have been previously read as a poet in the European tradition, for example, he was re-emphasised as an English poet following the Union. The nature of ballads is to both uphold and subvert such national readings. Ballads can be interpreted as being regionally distinct (i.e., every region has its own version of a particular ballad) or as being nationally unifying (i.e., a version of this ballad exists in many regions across the country); thus Allan Ramsay was able to interpret his *Tea-Table Miscellany* as being a collection of Scottish songs, Joseph Ritson was able to say his were English, and Thomas Percy was able to call the *Reliques* British, although all three of these editors published ballads with the same roots and sources. This made ballads a valuable resource in defining the national identities within Great Britain.

Percy's editorial philosophy was to promote the primacy of print above all sources. There was a solidity to print sources that encouraged his Gothic aesthetic. His antiquarian sensibility led him to the conclusion that the material weight of printed and manuscript sources proves the authenticity of a nation, and as the *Reliques* were essentially an exercise in nation-building, printed and manuscript sources added a weight of truth to his argument. Oral sources were nothing more than folk words; too easily lost to be preserved and too difficult to preserve to be considered culturally valuable. In his introductions to each poem, he names its sources. 'The Ancient Ballad of Chevy Chase', for example:

> is printed, from an old manuscript, at the end of Hearne's preface to Gul. Newbrigiensis Hist. 1719, 8vo. Vol. i. To the MS. Copy is subjoined the name of the author, Rychard Sheale; whom Hearne had so little judgement as to suppose to be the same with a R. Sheale, who was living in 1588. But whoever examines the gradation of language and idiom in the following volumes, will be convinced that this is the production of an earlier poet. It is indeed expressly mentioned among some very ancient songs in an old book entitled, The Complaint of Scotland, (fol. 42), under the title of the Huntis of Chevet.
>
> (Percy, 1765: Vol. 1, 1)

Percy argued that the British literary tradition was a component of the Gothic tradition, which was primarily defined by literacy. For the *Reliques*, this narrow definition not only meant that only printed (and, to an extent, manuscript) sources were welcome contributions, it also meant that the printed status of the *Reliques* was emphasised and exaggerated. Every conceivable paratextual element was considered: font, prefaces, illustrations, footnotes, glossaries, commentary, layout, and so on. It is therefore surprising that there is only one leaf of music reproduced in the whole collection. Percy describes the inclusion of 'For the Victory at Agincourt', a fifteenth-century English martial ballad as 'merely a curiosity' (Percy, 1765, Vol. 2, 24). In the mid-eighteenth century, it was not prohibitively expensive to print sheet music. As early as 1501, a Venetian printer named Ottaviano Petrucci used movable type to print polyphonic sheet music in the *Harmonice Musices Odhecaton*. Thomas d'Urfey's *Wit and Mirth, or Pills to Purge Melancholy* (1698–1720) contained more than a thousand songs and poems, most of which were accompanied by musical notation. Indeed, most of the contemporary successes in ballad publication – and in the middle of the eighteenth century there were a good many – contained musical notation. Percy was connected enough to find a printer who would be able to provide that service, yet the *Reliques* exists almost entirely without reference to the musicality of ballads. On the one hand, Percy had an opportunity to present the aural component of ballad literature on his own terms, but on the other, any concession to this component was a tacit acknowledgement that the ballad tradition was neither as strictly antiquarian as he would like to believe, nor as compatible with his Gothic mythology. In the words of Nick Groom, 'The tradition had to be dead before it could be revived, and labouring-class experiences, presences, and performances were not to be permitted to undermine the authority of the written word' (Groom, 2006, 183). Additionally, it was not only the liveliness and untameable orality of the ballad tradition which Percy would find offensive, it was also the producers and consumers of this material. The people who Groom described as 'labouring-class' were predominantly rural, with limited literacy and even more limited access to books, and disproportionately located in Scotland. When Percy ruled out ballads with sexual or political content, not only did he respectfully distance his wealthy patron from these distasteful topics, but he also policed the method of dissent and expression which was most accessible to the labouring classes. As Percy intellectualised the ballads, he excluded the people who composed them on the grounds of 'politeness' (see Langford, 2002; Klein, 1984). In his own words:

> As great care has been taken to admit nothing immoral and indecent, the Editor hopes he need not be ashamed of having bestowed some of his idle hours on the ancient literature of our own country, or in rescuing from oblivion some pieces (though but the amusements of our ancestors) which tend to place in a striking light their taste, genius, sentiments, or manners.
>
> (Percy, 1765: Vol. 1, 15)

Percy's heavy-handed editing in the name of politeness often had the effect of fostering bombastic masculinity at the expense of more delicate medieval poetry, which is never more apparent than in 'The Child of Elle'. In this ballad, the titular hero kills his lover's fiancé and threatens her father into blessing a marriage between them. Percy had an Old English fragment of thirty-nine lines in his Folio Manuscript, which he expanded to over 200 for publication. Francis Child would later consult Percy's extrapolated version along with versions from Scandinavia and Scotland in his production of the ballad (Child, 1882, Vol. 1). Percy substitutes simple, tender, erotic moments between the two lovers for a confused mix of prolonged sentiment, poetic acrobatics, and brusquely masculine martial tropes. An example of his heavy-handed editing can be seen in the following lines from the Folio Manuscript:

> he leaned ore his saddle bow
> to kisse this Lady good
> the teares *that* went them 2 betweene

> were blend water & blood.
> he sett himselfe on one good steed
> this lady of one palfray
> & sett his litle horne to his mouth
> & roundlie he rode away.
>
> (Percy, Folio MS 27, 879: 15–22)

The equivalent lines in the *Reliques* read:

> Fair Emmeline sighed, fair Emmeline wept,
> And aye her heart was woe;
> At length he seized her lilly-white hand,
> And doun the ladder he drewe.
> And thrice he clasped her to his breste,
> And kist her tenderlie;
> The tears that fell from her fair eyes
> Ranne like the fountayne free.
> He mounted himself on a steede so talle,
> And her on a faire palfraye,
> And slung his bugle about his necke,
> And roundlye they rode away.
>
> (Percy, 1765 Vol 2, 99–100)

Percy protracts the description of the lovers parting as if to distract us from a sensual and erotic moment with details, including a description of the horses which is better realised than his description of the kiss. This did not go unnoticed in later criticism of the *Reliques*. Hales and Furnivall, who edited an edition of Percy's manuscript in 1867, wryly noted that Percy was 'unhappily moved to try his hand at [the ballad's] completion. A wax doll-maker might as well try to restore Milo's Venus' (Hales and Furnival, 1867, 132). Grace Trenary also remarked that 'it was generally the primrose path of romance that led Percy astray' (Trenary, 1915, 288). It is also worth commenting, within the context of this particular paper, that Percy removes the horn from the Child's lips and renames it a 'bugle', thus silencing its music and implicitly militarising it. In Percy's version of the ballad, Emmeline (as he christens her; an Old French form of the Germanic name Amelina) is 'come of hye lineage/ And was of a ladye born' (Percy, 1765, Vol 1, 90–98)[2] and her love is revealed to be of 'house and lineage faire:/ My mother she was an earl's daughter,/ And a noble knyght my sire' Percy, 1765, Vol 1, 165–166). Youth and nobility are implied by the word 'childe', but Percy extrapolates the implicit meanings into an explicit narrative for the amusement of his patrons. In 'Child Elle', we see how Percy aligned the ownership of the ballads with his wealthy patrons, brushed away problematic topics which may have interfered with his potential for promotion, and subtly silenced aural elements of the ballads which did not suit his Gothic argument. As is typical with Percy, there can be no inference. Everything is laid out on the page. Thus a ballad fragment that was once subtle, romantic, and vivid becomes bland and obvious.

This chapter has so far discussed music and onomatopoeic background noise in Percy's *Reliques* but there is a further aural component to his work that demands some attention: the phonetic quality of a spoken accent. The sociolinguistic study of accents was beginning to receive some attention in the mid-eighteenth century. Thomas Tyrwhitt's edition of *The Canterbury Tales* (1771–1778) was the first to assert that the terminal <e> in Chaucerian English was to be voiced, an argument that changed readings of Middle English forever. In Scotland, accent became a marker of politeness and integration; in the 1760s, an Irish actor named Thomas Sheridan hosted an extremely popular lecture series at Edinburgh University on purging one's spoken language of Caledonian shibboleths. Meanwhile, the eminent philosopher David Hume bemoaned his Scottish accent privately and held it as a source of shame. Editors in the eighteenth century began to realise that not all Englishes were created equal. Percy's attempts to revive antique words and spellings inadvertently drew attention to accent on the page. His sincere and studious efforts to replicate the accents of, for example, the Borders, or Aberdeenshire, or Somerset, demanded attention to the sound quality of the words he studied. Because these dialects were not standardised, and because his sources were varied, this often meant that his chosen spelling of a word was unusual or out of touch with the other words in a poem. The effect, however, was the same: when one reads a Percy poem from Northumberland, one is reading a recreation of a Northumbrian voice on the page. To return to the words of Nick Groom,

> For a book that at one level asserts the primacy of print over oral culture, it is strange that so much of its language needs to be physically voiced either to be understood or to replicate accents from the North or from Somerset. If the *Reliques* draws attention to the visual quality of outlandish and obsolete spellings that are lost when the word is spoken, the word must still be understood as it is spoken rather than written.
>
> (Groom, 2006, 189)

The academic and social interest in accents were in their infancy at the publication of the *Reliques*, so this aspect of the work may only be of interest in a modern setting, but the contemporary experience of reading it would also have been audible in a musical sense. The English writer John Aikin wrote about the symbiotic relationship between song and poetry in 1772:

> The term *song* may ... be considered in a double sense – if the idea of music prevails, it signifies no more than a set of words calculated for adaptation to a tune; if poetry be the principal object, it is a species of poetical composition regulated by peculiar laws, and susceptible of a certain definition still however retaining so much of the musical idea as to make it an essential circumstance that by a regularly recurring measure it be capable of being set to a tune.
>
> (Aikin, 1772)

It is also worth noting that the lived experience of these ballads meant that anybody who read a copy of Percy's *Reliques* in the years after it was published probably read much of it with a tune – perhaps one of several associated with that ballad – in their heads, akin to if I were to publish a book of Rolling Stones lyrics. Even in spite of Percy's attempt to literate the ballads, the lived experience made its mark.

When literary critics examine aurality and orality in literature, they often turn to the work of Mikhail Bakhtin to give language to their theories. 'Heteroglossia' is the term Bakhtin adopted to describe what he perceived as a hierarchical organisation of language into genre, register, dialect, and what sociolinguists would later refer to as 'sociolect' in novels. He applied his theory to voices which appeared in the text of novels, including social languages within a national language (commonly referred to as dialect) and various national languages within the same culture, but also used it to discuss the interplay of class and language within the printed word. Heteroglossia is represented in both the heteroglot and the writer's control over it, and with the writer's subjective position within the prestige of language:

> When heteroglossia enters the novel it becomes subject to an artistic reworking. The social and historical voices populating language, all its words and all its forms ... are organized into a structured stylistic system that expresses the differentiated socio-ideological position of the author amid the heteroglossia of his epoch.
>
> (Bakhtin, 1981, 300)

While Bakhtin maintained that poetry could not be dialogic, arguing that poetic language was 'authoritarian, dogmatic and conservative, cutting itself off from the influence of extraliterary social dialects' (1981, 287), other writers have made attempts to reconcile poetry with dialogic theory. Robert Crawford, for example, has counter-argued that heteroglossia is 'fruitful' when considering Scottish poetry in particular: 'one may consider writing in Scots as having the effect of what Bakhtin calls "dialogized heteroglossia", that is, utterance or writing in which there is a clear friction of "argument" between different discourses' (Crawford, 1994, 7), while Donald Wesling has shown that the poetry of Tom Leonard and Linton Kwesi Johnson shows a complicated relationship with the theory of heteroglossia that both supports and rejects it (Wesling, 1993, 303–320). For the editor of ballad poetry, a heteroglossic reading can draw illuminating conclusions about the class relationship they have with their composers and their audience. Percy is both wealthier and more literate than the bardic composers of ballads, and the patrons of the *Reliques* were wealthier still. His frequent references to 'polishing' the 'remains of the ancient English Bards and Minstrels' (1765, 5) betrays a reductive appreciation of the aesthetics of the printed form of their language and a complete denial of its oral form. A heteroglossic reading of the language that is present shows a privileging of a prestige English which may be counterintuitive to a project aimed at preserving antique language; a similar reading of the language that is absent – that is, the 'authentic' language of Percy's bards – is trickier. Bakhtin's theory of dialogic discourse depends heavily on printed literature, and would not be compatible with an oral canon. Both Percy and Bakhtin necessarily work exclusively in the printed form, yet they also both ironically depend on living speech for their theories to be valid. In which case, it is clear that new readings of Percy must encapsulate elements of sound theory, and new interpretations of Bakhtin must be more open to the collection, editing, and curation of oral poetry.

If we can understand Scotland through music, then the work of Bishop Percy in its original context shows that we can understand Scotland as British constituent through an *absence* of music. Working within a genre that consciously refers to its own musicality, Percy defies genre conventions in an attempt to stabilise a mode of performance he sees as potentially radicalising. If Britain was to move past the barbaric roots of its constituent nations, then antiquarianism was the only appropriate method of exploring the art of an earlier age, safely historicising it, controlling it on a page or in a museum. The problem with music is that it refuses to be controlled in this way. Song is alive, active, current. In a social and political climate coloured by conflict, both recent and historical, and by a general fear of losing one's national identity, it is easy to see why a moderate conservative such as Percy would not want contemporary representations of a Scotland unfettered by English chauvinism in his thoroughly British collection. Although he very much gave authority to English identities, and although he worked within a medium that was reactionary about Scottish poetry, his vision was one of a unified cultural literature and a unified people. In the sincerest way, he wanted a Britain that appreciated Scottish oral literature as an historical artefact and a linguistic curiosity, which it was not. He recognised that the spoken and sung elements of ballads often represented a cultural marker that separated Scotland from the rest of the Union, and he saw this as a potential threat to the prospect of a harmonious future, so he tried to mute it. Unfortunately for him, his efforts to suppress the musical impulses of the ballads were self-conscious and ineffective, particularly within the context of contemporary ballad and song publications.

Further to the national implications of Percy's unmusical editorial policy, there is also a question of gender. The apocryphal story of Percy 'rescuing' the pages that would become his Folio Manuscript from some maids at a friend's house suggests symbolic confiscation of the ballads from the hands of the labouring-class women who were entrusted with them. The maids' admittedly cavalier attitude to the temporality of oral literature and the sanctity of the manuscript is, to Percy, the greatest act of cultural vandalism. His erasure of women as active participants in ballad culture reaches throughout the *Reliques*. The mythology of minstrelsy within which he works is distinctly masculine, and he largely overlooks the feminine tradition of storytelling and song in many Scottish families and communities. He makes a passing reference to this tradition in his introduction to the ballad 'Edom O' Gordon', in which he credits 'the memory of a lady, that is now dead' (Percy, 1765 Vol. 1, 99): for supplying his collaborator David Dalrymple with the raw materials from which he prepared his version of the ballad. The symbolic silencing, burial, and namelessness of Dalrymple's balladeer lady represents Percy's treatment of the female, Scottish, labouring ballad producers. If they are to be so stuck in the old ways as to entrust their community literature to the ephemerality of the oral tradition, they will be forgotten in history as the modern face of British chauvinistic culture takes their place in the canon. Percy's ignorance of the values of the oral tradition is echoed in the well-known exchange between Sir Walter Scott and Margaret Laidlaw, recounted by her grandson James Hogg. The conservative view of Scottish balladry in the eighteenth century is that it is masculine, English-speaking, and not allowed to sing.

Notes

1 For a facsimile reproduction and comparison of the two title pages, see Margaret Clunies Ross (1998) *The Norse Muse in Britain 1750–1820* (Trieste: Edizioni Parnaso). For a discussion of the similarities in layout, see Gauti Krisstmannsson (2001) *Literary Diplomacy: The Role of Translation in the Construction of National Literatures in Britain and Germany* (Frankfurt: Peter Lang).
2 'Child Elle', *Reliques*, vol. 1, pp. 90–98, l.121–2.

15 Routes, roles and folk on the edge

Scotland's instrumental music through the revival lens

Stuart Eydmann

I came to music scholarship at a time when I had already established a career in architectural conservation, leavened by an engagement in Scottish traditional music that stretched back to my teenage years in the 1960s. In negotiating and taking decisions on preservation and change in buildings and places, the most tangible of our cultural heritage, my work was guided by historical rigour, sensitivity to context, significance and authenticity, the capacity of assets to accommodate change and the Geddesian[1] tradition of survey and analysis before action. In music I shared rehearsal rooms, stages and studios at home and abroad making artistic choices around the old music of Scotland and new material that drew upon the tradition. Knowledge and experience gained in both areas informed and conditioned the attitudes and expectations I brought into the academy.

My doctoral research, concerned with the adoption and use of free-reed instruments in Scotland (Eydmann, 1995a), developed from a programme of field recording I had undertaken in the early 1980s. I commenced this as a collector/preservationist seeking to capture the testimony and music of a fading generation but later began to focus on the role of instruments within music change, including what was happening there and then. In this I was stimulated by the realisation that I was surrounded by, and working within, remarkable musical history as it was being created or had only recently been made. This was, of course, during a particularly dynamic phase of the folk music revival that saw the modern blossoming of instrumental traditional music in Scotland, part of a native cultural renaissance feeding into the wider folk, Celtic and world music phenomena.

As a practising musician I found I could easily locate myself within the trajectory of the revival. I worked to trace and record the pioneers that had come before and from whom I had drawn inspiration, I observed more recent developments at the hands of my contemporaries and sought, with some difficulty, ways of describing and explaining the music of the younger generation taking music in fresh directions. The revival was complex, contradictory, fast moving and exciting and the field was rich in source material and informants for anyone seeking deep analysis and understanding of it.

On entering academic study I was disappointed to find that few others shared my interests. The modern history of, and current developments in, instrumental traditional music in Scotland were clearly poor relations of traditional song scholarship which had its own champions and revival scholars (e.g. Munro, 1984, 1996) and there was little investigation of these on their own terms. Exceptions included my academic supervisor Peter Cooke's work on the fiddle in Shetland (Cooke, 1986) that, unfortunately, stopped short of in-depth consideration of contemporary change, Pam Swing's work on fiddle teaching on those islands (Swing, 1991) and Roderick Cannon's interest in modern developments in piping (Cannon, 1988). Others, such as David Johnson, with whom I enjoyed friendly contact, seemed fixated on the so-called golden age of the Scottish fiddle of the late eighteenth century (Johnson, 1972, 1984; Alburger, 1983), after which Scottish musical traditions were deemed to have become debased. Similarly, the small number of standard texts on Scottish music (Collinson, 1966; Emmerson, 1971; Davie, 1980), were unconcerned with change and development.

At that time, I perceived an anti-scholarship trait within the traditional music community that mistrusted analysis and preferred mythology and stories over interpreted evidence through what I called 'beer tent musicology' (Eydmann, 1988). I found this permeated current Scottish traditional music scholarship too, as did Martin Dowling who, when writing on the situation in Ireland, refers to 'the largely ahistorical discipline of ethnomusicology. . ., a perspective which subtly reinforces the popular understanding that such music is timeless, unchanging, and "ancient"' and of how 'the revisionist debates which have occupied professional histories in recent decades have left prevailing understanding of music largely untouched' (Dowling, 2014, 2). I also found echoes of my frustration in the writing of Fintan Vallely, when he notes that traditional music

> is open to analysis by contemporary cultural criticism which so far has skirted around it, lacking confidence in addressing it. This is possibly on account of a nagging, acculturated bourgeois doubt that because traditional music is by definition 'of the past', is associated with rurality and is essentially passed on orally, it is not 'serious' music.
>
> (Vallely, 2005, 53)

My early ethnomusicology reading offered little theoretical or practical guidance in my chosen area other than a few passing observations and some case studies. Kartomi, for example, talks of 'nativistic musical revival' (Kartomi, 1981, 237) and Nettl includes 'preservation', 'consolidation', 'reintroduction' and 'exaggeration' as potential key elements in music change (Nettl, 1978, 131–134). Some, however, were advocating a move towards a more dynamic and complex picture of music systems in which change is an ever present component that is open to analysis and interpretation (Blacking, 1977, 1986; Rice, 1987) and there was also a growing acknowledgement of revival as a large and complex process, of which the performance of music from earlier periods is only part (Bohlman, 1988, 125–126, 130–131, 134). Nevertheless, I remained uncomfortable studying the music of my own post-industrial, urban environment as most ethnomusicology seemed concerned with Other, normally remote, 'ancient', 'developing' or 'primitive' cultures. Fortunately, published case studies, encounters with like-minded researchers abroad, the 1989 British-Swedish Conference on Ethnomusicology with its concentration on 'doorstep ethnomusicology'[2] and the work of Ruth Finnegan (1989, 1990) on musical processes in a single modern urban community rather than on historical works and texts, brought welcome security and confidence. Also, I took comfort from the fact that much of the work exhibiting these new emphases was focused around instrumental music.

My supervisor Richard Middleton's promotion of the benefit of studying popular music forms within a wide musical-historical framework, his suggested adoption of Raymond Williams's terms 'dominant', 'residual' and 'emergent' in its mapping and interpretation (Middleton, 1990, 11–16), and his caution around some aspects of current folkloristic and ethnomusicological thought and practice (146–171) informed an essay I drafted in 1997 that was published a decade later in Volume 10 of the *Compendium of Scottish Ethnology* (Eydmann, 2007). In this, I promoted the value of a 'music-historical map' as an aid essential to a proper understanding of the music of Scotland in the modern era. I also suggested areas ripe for scholarship and identified gaps that I felt required to be filled, while advocating the need for broad and inclusive definitions of the traditional and the popular.

This has served me as a manifesto and work plan ever since. I continue to believe that the developments in Scotland's instrumental traditional music of the late twentieth century onwards are of cultural significance and revival remains my research focus in a number of areas, particularly around the accordion (Eydmann, 2001, 2015), the clarsach or Celtic harp (Eydmann, 2017), the fiddle (Eydmann, 2013) and the folk music ensemble. That the field offers many opportunities for research is ably demonstrated in recent scholarly and more general writing (Symon, 1997; Duesenberry, 2000; Forsyth, 2005, 2007; Dickson, 2009; MacInnes, 2009; Watson, 2013; Gilchrist, 2012; West, 2012b; Nebel, 2014).

The view through the revival lens does have limitations and it is by no means the only perspective available or appropriate. However, the now substantial body of theoretical and practical work demonstrates that it offers a useful and accessible approach, with potential application beyond traditional music in other cultural spheres. To be effective, however, it requires the herding and deep analysis of a wide range of evidence and the careful selection and application of appropriate techniques and language to accommodate its breadth, complexities and contradictions. I now wish to discuss some of the practical thinking tools that I have come to find useful in this, in the hope that they might assist others in adding to the modern music-historical map and in moving us towards an enhanced understanding of Scotland through traditional music.

As an early means of organising my thoughts around individual musical instruments and specific genres, I found the deceptively simple yet comprehensive organological model of Klaus Wachsmann particularly useful (Wachsmann, 1980, 238). Expressed graphically, this places the instrument at the centre of a range of interlinked determining elements – musical (performance, music and corporeal) and contextual (symbolism, sociology and history/development) – each of which demands consideration. I still find this a useful checklist and recommend it as a starting point for anyone scoping an instrument-based study.

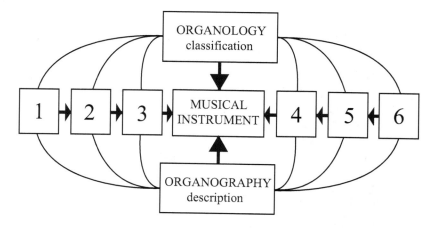

1. Symbolism, folklore, mythologies and intangible associations
2. Sociology of distribution, adoption and use
3. History of invention, development, production and consumption
4. Performance practice and behaviour
5. Technical and corporeal determinants
6. Musical output, sound, aesthetics, style and repertory

Figure 15.1 Wachsmann model adapted by Eydmann

The book *Transforming Tradition. Folk Music Revivals Examined* (Rosenberg, 1993a) marked the acceptance of revival as a legitimate area for study. The first collection of scholarly writings dedicated to traditional music revivals, it remains useful on account of its comprehensiveness and the fact that several of its authors have been active in revivals and offer personal reflection based on their experiences. Feintuch's case study of Northumbrian piping (Feintuch, 1993), which takes us down the route of musical transformation, is highly relevant to Scotland on account of geographical proximity, shared repertory and the folk revival's promotion of this variety of bagpipes as a 'British' (i.e. non-American) instrument, which echoes my own findings on the revived concertina (Eydmann, 1995b). It also invites comparison with the more recent smallpipes revival north of the Border.

We can detect a search for a staged model of revival in an essay by Richard Blaustein that touches briefly on the fiddle in Scotland.[3] In this he proposes Anthony Wallace's theory of cultural revitalisation, 'any deliberate, conscious, organised attempt by members of a society to create a more satisfying culture' (Wallace, 1956, 279), as a tool to help explain revivalist fiddle organisations (Blaustein, 1993, 260, 270–271), including its final phase whereby 'mazeway resynthesis' leads to a 'new steady state' as a means of describing the outcome of the revival process (262).

In common with many others, I find Tamara Livingston's 'Music Revivals: Towards a General Theory' (Livingston, 1999, 2001) an indispensable base-level guide. The practical potential of this 'conceptual framework for thinking about music revivals as a particular musical phenomenon distinguished by a certain set of shared assumptions, activities, and characteristics' (Livingston, 2014, 60) is demonstrated in my concise mapping of aspects of a selection of individual instruments in Scotland against her 'basic recipe' of typical revival ingredients (Tables 15.1–15.4).

Similar tables might be constructed for other traditional genres and instruments including guitar, flute, whistle, cittern, keyboard, percussion and so forth. Some are easier to map than others, especially where the revival usage is self-contained

Table 15.1 The first phase of the clarsach revival in Scotland, 1890–1940

An individual or small group of 'core revivalists'	Patronage of Lord Archibald Campbell in the 1890s. Interest in art and literature of the Celtic Revival. Adoption by Patuffa Kennedy Fraser. Initiatives of Hilda Campbell of Airds and Mrs MacLeod of Skeabost in 1920s. Coming together of a group of enthusiasts in 1931 with the encouragement of An Comunn Gàidhealach to form an association dedicated to the revival of the instrument.
Revival informants and or original sources	Writings of Rev. Neil Ross on the harp in Gaelic bardic literature. Antiquarian interest in early harps in museum collections. Publication of Robert Bruce Armstrong's book on historic harps. The commissioning of prototype modern instruments.
A revivalist ideology or discourse, standards and standardisation	The privileging of the instrument's Gaelic associations, authorised repertory promoted through competitions and teaching, careful selection of adjudicators at Mòd competitions. The founders of the Clarsach Society openly describe their aims as 'revival'. Links to and support from other Scottish cultural and political groupings. Musical standards based on the classical harp tradition.
A group of followers that form the basis of a revivalist community	Establishment of the Clarsach Society in 1931 with a formal constitution, administrative structure and 'propaganda' strategy. Early revivalists were drawn from women of the middle and upper classes and there was strong aristocratic participation and endorsement.
Revivalist activities: (organisations, festivals, competitions)	Newsletters, ceilidhs for members, annual schools, competitions, broadcasts on BBC radio, lecture recitals and 'demonstrations'. Publication of endorsed music and arrangements. Initiatives to establish a learning network. Early aspirations to publish a tutor book. Special competition trophies and much attention paid to the choice of adjudicators and competition set pieces. Royal patronage sought.
Non-profit and/or commercial enterprises catering to the revivalist market	Publication of sheet music. Manufacture of instruments to meet demand. Players become professional teachers.

Table 15.2 The first phase of the revival in Scottish bellows-blown bagpipes, 1975–2000

An individual or small group of 'core revivalists'	Established young players of Highland bagpipes associated with pipe bands and the folk group/session scene explore opportunities for a Scottish response to the prevailing success revival of Irish bellows piping.
Revival informants and or original sources	Francis Collinson's writings on the history of the bellows-blown pipes. Measurements taken from museum collections used for replication of historic instruments. Research by Gordon Mooney into the historical repertory leading to self-published collections. Academic research by Iain MacInnes and others. Much experimentation and trying out in group and informal settings. Parallel revivals in English and French bagpiping.
A revivalist ideology or discourse, standards and standardisation	A search for a distinctly Scottish, especially Lowland, sound and repertory but with debates as to appropriate playing styles and techniques. The shared aim of an intimate, domestic, non-military/marching tradition suited to combining bagpipes with other instruments.
A group of followers that form the basis of a revivalist community	Establishment of the Lowland and Borders Pipers Society in 1983. Promotion and publicity through folk group players and prominent soloists.
Revivalist activities: (organisations, festivals, competitions)	Publication of a dedicated journal including music, articles, historical features and so forth. Competitions, learning events, publication of a tutor book, trophies, 'collogues' and other gatherings.
Non-profit and/or commercial enterprises catering to the revivalist market	Publication of sheet music, gramophone records and so forth. Development and manufacture of instruments including the establishment of several new businesses.

and there is a clear boundary with previous practice. The 'national' instruments of fiddle and Highland bagpipes, for instance, are challenging as there has been considerable porosity between the established and revival contexts with some key actors participating simultaneously in both strands. Of course, Livingston's range of essential ingredients is just a starting point and would require to be extended in more detailed studies.

Claiming it to be neither predictive nor prescriptive, she offers an effective framework for evidence gathering, describing, understanding and explaining revival at an individual instrument/genre level. However, I believe it is less effective when applied to the revival in Scotland as a whole, on account of the varied nature, complexities and contradictions involved. Although the model is not time-based, certain key phases would inevitably proceed in sequence, and the author rightly suggests that each revival follows its own route and timescale and that there may be an end point where the process breaks down or transforms (80–81).

In applying the model to modern Scotland, it could be argued that it simplifies and over stresses the worthiness and cohesiveness of the actors' motivations and ideology, 'to serve as cultural opposition and as an alternative to mainstream

Table 15.3 The revival of the concertina in Scotland, 1950–1980

An individual or small group of 'core revivalists'	The adoption of the largely residual instrument for song accompaniment by a key group within the folk music revival including those of the London Critics Group (AL Lloyd, Peggy Seeger, Ewan MacColl et al.) and artists associated with influential Topic Records.
Revival informants and or original sources	Professional concertinist Alf Edwards adopted as a role model despite having little traditional music experience. Influences from concertina playing in Ireland and England. Several key record releases and BBC broadcasts endorse the instrument as appropriate for folk song accompaniment.
A revivalist ideology or discourse, standards and standardisation	Instrument recognised and promoted for its working class, British, (i.e. non-American) and regional associations. Adoption of the instrument as an alternative to the 'modern' and seemingly less authentic guitar and banjo. Adoption as a more intimate alternative to the larger accordion associated with the dance band tradition in Scotland.
A group of followers that form the basis of a revivalist community	Adoption by Scottish players in folk groups: The Corries, The Clutha, The Whistlebinkies, Battlefield Band, et al.
Revivalist activities: (organisations, festivals, competitions)	Older players are sought out and privileged. Workshops, talks, competitions and gatherings held at folk festivals. Influential articles published in folk revival literature endorses the instrument. Revitalisation of the International Concertina Association by a younger membership. Competitions run by the Traditional Music and Song Association of Scotland.
Non-profit and/ or commercial enterprises catering to the revivalist market	Gramophone records released. A lively market in secondhand instruments and the establishment of several new makers in England.

culture' (68), at the expense of viewing revivals on the ground as a sometimes chaotic, participatory site of social interaction and encounter, of innovation, creativity, competition and fun, especially for the young, reflecting Durkheim's concept of 'collective effervescence' as applied to popular music movements by Nick Crossley (2015, 88). Pub session and festivals have been crucial in the instrumental revivals in the British Isles and have involved quite different experiences and environments from the adult summer camps and folk life festivals of North America.

Also, her concentration on the role of 'core revivalists', while helpful, diverts us away from those highly complex, influential, creative individuals inhabiting the edge of the process (as discussed later) and, on the other hand, from an appreciation of the critical mass of more hidden, often private, musicians and activities upon which a successful revival depends.

Similarly, her, and others scholars' presumptions that revivals always seek authenticity drawn from the past can steer us from cases where revitalisation is achieved through syncretism, as in the 'folk rock' strands of European folk music revivals recognised by Brocken (2003) and by Sweers (2005).

Table 15.4 The revival of the fiddle in Scotland, 1965–1985

An individual or small group of 'core revivalists'	John Junner and Hector McAndrew in Aberdeenshire and Tom Anderson in Shetland. Support of key individuals within the BBC (Arthur Argo, James Hunter). Endorsement by Yehudi Menuhin. A core component of the strategic revival agenda of the Traditional Music and Song Association of Scotland.
Revival informants and or original sources	The 'discovery' of older players suitable for endorsement as role models. The publication of tunes collected in Shetland. Research and publications of musicologists Francis Collinson, David Johnson and Mary Anne Alburger. Old manuscripts and published collections of fiddle music sought out.
A revivalist ideology or discourse, standards and standardisation	Endorsement of the fiddle as one of the 'national instruments' of Scotland. References to fiddle in modern Scottish literature. Privileging of role models/figureheads, for example Aly Bain and Tom Anderson. Promotion of distinct regional styles and repertory.
A group of followers which form the basis of a revivalist community	Traditional Music and Song Association of Scotland, Shetland Folk Society, Fiddler's Rallies, Fiddle and Accordion clubs, competitions, broadcasts and festivals. Use of instrument in folk groups, first for song accompaniment then as a solo instrument. Influences from Irish, English and American fiddle playing.
Revivalist activities: (organisations, festivals, competitions)	The rise of the informal pub session. High profile competitions at popular festivals. Traditional Music and Song Association competitions.
Non-profit and/ or commercial enterprises catering to the revivalist market	Release of a small number of influential gramophone records including re-release of early and archival recordings. Rediscovery and privileging of the Cape Breton Scottish fiddle tradition. Annual schools (e.g. Stirling University). Parallel revivals of Scottish fiddling in North America.

The more recent *Oxford Handbook of Music Revival* (Hill and Bithell, 2014) can be read as a position statement on current revival studies as well as a valuable anthology of cases and useful ideas. Building upon *Transforming Tradition*, much of its content reflects a subsequent growth in both revival scholars and scholar revivalists. The scope and content of its essays exhibit a new collective concern for process and change and offer fresh angles including post-colonial, diaspora and intangible cultural heritage perspectives. It acknowledges a wider range of potential motivations including dissatisfaction, bolstering of identity, innovation, political forces, marketing and post-disaster recovery. The editors note a general acceptance of revival as an everyday, 'recurring and important cultural element across cultures and eras' (4) and 'part of the ebb and flow of culture' (28) with one author offering helpful caution in the suggestion that 'we profit in our understanding of music cultures when we recognise the presence of revivals in them but if we ignore the messy edges and overlaps in the realities of lived musical lives, we may overlook important information' (Rosenberg, 2014, 103–104).

In the collection, Livingston revisits and expands her previous works (Livingston, 2014, 60–72). She now stresses the participatory aspects of music making (including social interaction, communication and creative fulfilment), the vital roles music revivals can play as agents of cultural renewal and social healing and their potential to enable the past to come alive in the present. Acknowledging suggestions that the revival label may have outlived its usefulness, she argues that her earlier work continues to have value 'as a preliminary framework' (62) but now recognises the complexity, contradictory and unpredictable nature of the process. Recognising their dynamic nature she notes how revival trajectories are not always linear but can have counterflows, currents and eddies 'taking the tradition along other paths' and that 'it is incumbent on scholars to trace these paths wherever they may lead' (64). Taking her cue from Turino (2008, 120), she sees a need to unpack 'multiple ideologies' behind motivations and stresses the value of a much more granular approach (64–65).

A number of the writers share a concern for the post-revival phase. This should not be surprising given the facts that the more mature scholars have worked and played through lengthy revivals, have seen the arrival of a fresh generation of academics and now inhabit considerably changed musical worlds. The editors endorse the value of the later stages as a means of bringing a perspective that is 'useful for the way in which it allows us to acknowledge the significance of the original revival impulse and to identify a new musical or social culture as part its legacy' (29). Also, the phase has attracted its own terminology including 'outgrowths and ramifications', 'breakdown', 'absorption', 'normalisation' and 'spinoffs'. Examples of late revival trends in Scottish music include a movement that seeks 'to explore the possibilities of the wire-strung clarsach, acknowledging its historical past and developing different styles of playing which encompass both ancient and modern approaches to technique, repertoire, and the instrument itself,[4] the developing interest in playing eighteenth-century fiddle music on baroque instruments and a reinterpretation of the historical repertory and performance practice of the Highland bagpipe.[5] In addition to these historically informed developments there are others manifest, for example, in the on-stage anarchic antics of the Treacherous Orchestra (McAvoy, this volume) and the tradition-based art music of fiddler Chris Stout and harper Catriona McKay. The last mentioned reflects the stage in Ireland where 'traditional music not only steadily resumed a 'popular' form, but in new conditions of awareness and with fresh sets of values it could explore, develop and assert itself, promoting virtuosity and scholarship in the manner in fact of a "Classical" music' (Vallely, 2005, 53). There are also the 'detached' modern revivals of Scottish fiddle playing in North America and in Australia, including the work of the organisation Scottish F.I.R.E. (Scottish Fiddling Revival Ltd.) (Nebel, 2014) and the recent, strategically planned and officially recognised awakening of interest in Scottish music among the Ulster-Scots community in the north of Ireland. (Vallely, 2003, 2004, 2005, 2008; Dowling, 2007, 2008, 2010; Campbell, Eydmann and Gunn, 2014). Of particular interest to scholars of revival in Scotland, not least for comparative purposes, is a chapter on England that has a useful 'historic context' section on the progress of the folk revival in that country (Keegan-Phipps and Winter, 2014, 489–569). Here the writers adopt the term 'resurgence' to describe the later, ongoing phase and to distinguish it from the earlier revivals on account of its quite different motivations, ideology, behaviours, actors and musical consequences (493–494).

While study of post-revival stages in Scotland is clearly important, I suggest that due attention should also be given to the pre-revival periods in order to properly identify and understand embryonic and gestationary events and forces. This also allows for the identification and acknowledgement of previous, influential but subsequently normalised, revival activity.[6] An understanding of the clarsach in Scotland since 1970, for example, requires an appreciation of developments of the early twentieth century and indeed earlier, as mapped in my testing of Livingston's framework above. Revivals can have lengthy lead-in periods with short-lived false starts and try-outs that founder or lie dormant until circumstances are more conducive. It is therefore important that these early flowerings are recognised. Indeed, it can often be difficult to know exactly when a revival commenced, or one revival ended and another started, supporting suggestions of a continual process of recurring cycles and waves, or even of a state of never-ending transformation and renewal (Hill and Bithell, 2014, 28).[7]

Once more, Blaustein offers Wallace's five-stage movement theory as a 'very powerful and useful starting point for discussion of post revival culture' restating that 'post revival culture is nothing more or less than Wallace's New Steady State' (Blaustein, 2014, 555). Appropriately, his discussion of modern fiddle revivals looks back to Scotland in the eighteenth and nineteenth centuries (559–562). However, although he includes the role of the strathspey and reel societies and recognises a 'new Shetland style', he relies on published texts that are incomplete and outdated and he misses (or ignores) the more recent impact and progress of the less-structured, independent youthful music that flourished outwith the formal constituted fiddle societies. This underlines the need for in-depth historical and ethnographic as well as desk-top research.

In seeking a sequential model that offers a practical framework for understanding and explaining the historical development of individual musical genres in revival and allows mapping of the grain of the change, I have gone outside musicology to adopt Bruce Tuckman's model of group development (Tuckman, 1965) that I first encountered in management training some years ago.

The Tuckman model, developed from behavioural observation, identifies four distinct stages (Forming, Storming, Norming and Performing) that small groups typically pass through before achieving maximum effectiveness. With subsequent modifications, it is widely applied in management as a team building tool at it is easily understood, adaptable to a range of situations and environments and suited to graphic representation in a variety of ways.

Applying it to the music revival process, its stages might be described as follows, although the precise scope, nature and order of events will vary by situation and genre:

Forming

Individuals come together to achieve a collective goal. There may be a long lead in until like-minded individuals make contact, a critical mass is achieved or core revivalists emerge. Similarly, appropriate social, political, economic or technological circumstances may be recognised. Interpersonal relationships and encounters are informal but leadership and directing roles may be important to make progress. Ideas, aspirations, boundaries and viability are tested and discussed. Tradition bearers and role models are sought out. Authenticity and guidance is drawn from historical research. Archives are explored and expert authorities invoked. There may be much excitement and enthusiasm as shared goals begin to emerge.

Storming

A still chaotic stage in which a collective revival ideology is negotiated and lines of action are explored. There might be testing, experimentation, and trying out of ideas, some of which are subsequently abandoned. Leadership roles start to become formalised and formal ground rules and conventions of behaviour emerge. Some actors express their individuality and there may be conflicts leading some to leave the core group as it does not meet their needs and aspirations or match their ideas. A musical canon is established, perhaps through a key published collection or pioneering record release. There is a burst of learning and energy leading to publicity and events. There is some media attention that helps put the revival on the map. Revival spokespersons emerge who speak and write with authority. Commercial opportunities are explored both within and outside the official revival community.

Norming

A formally constituted association with elected office bearers may be established. There is adoption of rules and conventions including 'officially' endorsed musical instrument forms, styles, repertory and behaviour. Gatherings, schools and competitions become regular events. Organisational constitutions are adjusted and promotional and communications systems are put in place. There is a core entity or in-group with relatively fixed and stable roles and a high degree of cohesion and relative harmony. Star performers emerge.

Performing

A degree of equilibrium is reached and the revived music is accepted as part of mainstream culture, with a degree of buy-in or engagement by the media.

> Roles are well-bedded and functional yet flexible. There is an annual calendar of recurring events including schools, festivals, competitions and awards. The roles of figureheads and of senior members are celebrated and as leaders retire, successors are appointed in an orderly manner. Histories of the revivals are written, often by insiders. Branches are formed and there are remote revivals in the diaspora and elsewhere. Young heroes and virtuosi emerge and are celebrated as a measure of the revival's success. State funding is sought and inclusion of the genre in the educational curriculum is pursued. The genre is vigorously defended against any threat. Some boundary breakers are accommodated, others not.

While revival communities and the processes they engage in are much more complex than the short-life, single-function project groups the model was designed for, it is of use as a broad mapping tool. It also has potential applicability in charting the formation and (usually short) lives of musical ensembles that have been a phenomenon of the modern revival. I visualise the model as a vector around which roles, events, processes and outcomes can be positioned. The x-axis represents time while the y-axis broadly indicates progress or levels of engagement. The line represents the core, above, on and below which we can plot the relative influence and centrality of individuals and groups including stylistic, regional or social 'cells', 'groups', 'scenes' and 'schools' (Bastin, 1986, 272, quoted in Rosenberg, 2014, 104).

The graph is not calibrated for precise measurement but does allow broad patterns to be understood, explained and compared. The lines of no two instruments or genres will have the same start and end points, shape or duration. Some waves might be smooth and others highly complex. However, it recognises that the field is continuously in movement and that in revivals 'articulated

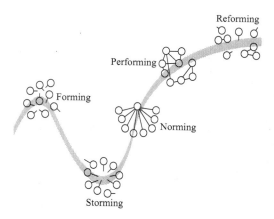

Figure 15.2 Tuckman model adapted by Eydmann

syntheses have vectorial qualities – not only a weight within the field but also a direction'(Middleton, 1990, 12) Also, its diachronic nature allows us to include the pre- and post-revival events before and after the vector.

Tuckman later added a fifth stage *Adjourning* (Tuckman, 1977) to cover the decommissioning of a group after completion of the project it was formed to advance. This equates to the post-revival phase, although music revivals rarely come to a sudden end but rather involve any number of outgrowths and ramifications discussed previously. In its application to music, I suggest the alternative term *Reforming* to cover the later adjustments and new directions.

With the route of the revival expressed in a linear form it is possible to take lateral snapshots through it at any point to explain how individuals and groups might be operating in networks or relating to each other and to the core. This third dimension echoes both Richard Middleton's call for synchronic analysis, 'slicing through the relationships obtaining at any one time in the social-cultural formation' of the continuously moving field (Middleton, 1990, 12) and Richard Blaustein's concept of 'constellations' applied to revivalists' internet-based, common-interest 'affinity groups and networks rotating around and engaging with the musical tradition, changing and shifting over time' (Blaustein, 2014, 554). Much of the foregoing suggests the nodes and links in graphs employed by network theorists to explain complex interacting systems and leads us on into the field of social network analysis with its methods for understanding how social and cultural networks form, function and change. As ably demonstrated by Crossley (2009, 2015) in his relational sociology based exploration of punk and post-punk music scenes in English cities, this approach has considerable potential in helping us weave together essential elements of the revival story.

I recommend the Tuckman model not as a template but as just one tool in the locker of the revival scholar. It facilitates the mapping of a series of separate, though sometimes linked, revival elements all moving at different speeds and with their own agendas and constituencies, to form a broad, layered picture of the revival as a whole. Above the genre/instrument level it is therefore more practically useful than the Wallace theory endorsed by several revival scholars. That, approach, I suggest, is more appropriate for more tightly bound groups such as religious or political movements and cults or for consideration of the innovation of whole cultural systems, its concept of the steady state built on a notion of social and cultural equilibrium that is rarely found in music revivals, certainly at the local or genre levels.

Identifying, plotting and discussing the varied and ever-changing positions of those engaged in revival activity is another useful means of explaining the process and mapping its territory. Much of the key literature on music revivals has seen the authors devising names for the different actor's roles in the process (e.g. 'core revivalist' (Livingston, 1999), 'performance acolyte' (Slobin, 1983; discussed in Rosenberg, 1993b, 195), 'the young blood' (Vallely, 2005, 59) etc.) and I have found it helpful to compile a working list from this, supplemented by some of my own creation and others from folk nomenclature. This is an engaging yet demanding area which I suggest is worthy of further exploration.

Logic would suggest that attempts to understand Scotland musically should focus primarily on those with core roles, including players privileged as 'tradition bearers' and the actors at the heart of revivals. However, I am increasingly fascinated and challenged by those musicians whose activities are located more peripherally, on the messy edges and appearing before and after the main revival trajectories. I term such an actors 'outliers', employing the old Scots meaning of one separate from the burgh or fold, rather than Malcolm Gladwell's recently celebrated application of the term to individuals of extraordinary accomplishments (Gladwell, 2008).[8] Also, I am not concerned here with the 'outsider artist',[9] although some of the people I am interested in might display some or all of the traits associated with such creatives.

While researching the history of the clarsach revival in Scotland I developed an interest in the life and music of the Glasgow-born harpist Heloise Russell Fergusson (1896–1970), and have since worked with her family on compiling her biography and interpreting the papers and recordings she left (Eydmann and Witcher, forthcoming). Here is a musician who preceded, supported, yet consciously stayed apart from the modern revival in the 1930s to follow her own route as a professional musician that led to experimental recordings and audio/visual projects. She also undertook comprehensive research into the harp on a world scale, compiling an important and pioneering study collection. Largely unknown today, her work prefigured many developments within the folk revival including the renaissance of the harp in Brittany where her influence was felt.

I have also been working with recordings made in the 1950s of the poet Norman MacCaig (1910–1996) on which he sings traditional songs and plays fiddle. It is well known that he maintained a lifelong interest in many kinds of music and I was aware that he had played violin, but it is said that he distanced himself from the folk scene as it developed. On the tapes he plays music in manner quite unlike fiddlers of his generation. He clearly understood the bagpipe idiom and developed his own way of interpreting its light music on the violin in a way close to what we might expect from more recent revival Scottish fiddlers. Of particular interest is his performance of pibroch, a unique but otherwise private contribution to Scottish culture and a genre once known in the eighteenth century but only now attracting the attention of post-revival fiddlers.[10]

The singer/songwriter/instrumentalist/storyteller Robin Williamson (born 1943) has been on the edge of the revival since the late 1960s. However, autobiographical notes (Williamson, 1976, 6–7, 60) describe how he discovered the folk scene in Edinburgh as a youth and embarked on learning and absorbing as much as he could including seeking guidance from historian/researcher Francis Collinson. He subsequently embarked on a highly eclectic career most notably with the Incredible String Band but also in other ensembles. There are archive recordings of him playing fiddle and singing as a youth that confirm an early sensitivity to the tradition. He experimented with instruments creating new sounds and soundscapes and was an early adopter of the harp and explorer of its historical repertory.

I distinctly recall the reaction of my fellow folk music enthusiasts in 1975 to *Dreaming of Glenisla*, the debut album of the band Talisker, led by Dundee drummer Ken Hyder (born 1946). This brought a mixing of Scottish musical elements (psalm singing, folk song, pibroch-like variations etc.) with improvisational jazz. Some were angry at the audacity and scope of the project while others questioned his pedigree and credentials in terms of folk authenticity. There was envy of this 'outsider' who had managed to gain a contract with the prestigious Virgin Records. Hyder subsequently worked with singer/guitarist Dick Gaughan and other folk musicians before new collaborations with musicians from across the world including Tibetan and Japanese Buddhist monks, and Siberian shamans[11] (Hyder, 2013). He was subsequently recognised as one who 'provided a blueprint for the increasing number of European musicians who have been incorporating elements of folk music into their jazz' (Larkin, 2006).

It is clear that each of these outlier musicians participated in or influenced the trajectory of Scotland's traditional instrumental music in the modern period and there are many others, some forgotten, who await fuller recognition. Having been viewed as outsiders by those at the core of revivals they rarely have a place in works of the movement historians. When they are present at the forming and storming stages their engagement is typically short after which they choose to leave the herd, moving on to other challenges or working apart although some never come close to the core. However, their experimentation and pioneering contributions, although perhaps not noticed at the time, pave the way and help make subsequent radical action by others possible. Their innovative ideas often come before the availability of the skills, knowledge or technology required to do them justice but they do much to develop the instrumentarium and sound palette for others. Also, they are invariably associated with other musical genres and art forms and engage with foreign cultures.

The collective contribution of such musicians represents a major element of Scottish cultural creativity and expression but is generally overlooked or understated in cultural histories. However, the time is now right to assess them. If it can be said that today's post-revival musicians are able to

> free themselves from the apron strings of 'tradition', laying claim to their right to move forward in the same way that any artist who has never been cast as a spokesperson for a tradition is allowed to move forward, and inviting audiences to judge their work on its own merits.
>
> (Hill and Bithell, 2014, 29–30)

In compiling our histories of the revival, then, we must make room for the early pioneers.

The foregoing is only part of the story. We need to dig deep beneath the descriptions of trends, trajectories and roles to unpack the motivations and experiences of those involved. Ethnomusicology and ethnology have shown us the way and, fortunately, there are many potential informants awaiting attention along with the rich yet untapped resources of institutional and private archive collections of audio, photographs and printed material. The informed insider has an important contribution too in detailing revival stories. The value of such writing has been demonstrated by a number of writers on the music in north of Ireland (Carson, 1996; Dowling, 2010, 2013; Feldman, 2002) and in Scotland by West (2012a).

A fine-grained musical-historical map of the revival should also address many other questions including gender, ethnicity, regional and national identities, international dimensions, the influences and roles of music technology, musical instrument manufacture and distribution, the interface with other popular musics and cultural fields and education and cultural policy. And, of course, the music as made, heard and experienced needs to be analysed, understood and explained. This brings its own challenges in terms of language and technique and in this our work has hardly commenced. Surveying such an expansive landscape clearly calls for a powerful, wide-angle lens.

Notes

1 Sir Patrick Geddes (1854–1932) was a Scottish biologist, sociologist, geographer, philanthropist and pioneering urbanist. His 'conservative surgery' approach to town planning is now central to the theory and practice of urban preservation.
2 It is interesting to note the currency of the expression 'Dig where you stand' within the Scottish traditional arts community. See for instance: http://digwhereyoustand.blogspot.co.uk/2011/12/dig-where-you-what.html.
3 See also Blaustein (2006).
4 www.wirestrungclarsach.org.
5 Including the Alt Pibroch Club that is concerned with 're-extending the idiom by returning to our historical roots, making the tradition available to everyone'. www.altpibroch.com/. See also Dickson (2009).
6 For instance, the Scottish fiddle player/composer James Scott Skinner (1843–1927) was clearly driven by a revivalist and 'improving' ideology (Eydmann, 2006, 37) although we now see his legacy as representing the epitome of tradition. Similarly the resurgence of interest in Piobaireachd commenced in the late nineteenth century and is still being worked through although most of its protagonists would not regard themselves as participants in a revival. The Shetland fiddler/collector Tom Anderson (1910–1991) and the North-East fiddler Hector MacAndrew (1903–1980) can also be viewed as revivalists.
7 Such a condition in Scottish music was suggested by Hamish Henderson (Dickson, 2009, 194).
8 Gladwell: 'I'm interested in people who are outliers – in men and women who, for one reason or another, are so accomplished and so extraordinary and so outside of ordinary experience that they are as puzzling to the rest of us as a cold day in August.' http://gladwell.com/outliers/outliers-q-and-a-with-malcolm/.
9 See http://rawvision.com/about/what-outsider-art.
10 My short paper on MacCaig as fiddler is in draft, awaiting publication.
11 www.allaboutjazz.com/how-to-know-spirit-music-crazy-wisdom-shamanism-and-trips-to-the-black-sky-ken-hyder-by-ken-hyder.php.

16 Links with the past in the present-day performance of Scottish fiddle music; or, the historicity of tradition

Ronnie Gibson

The performance of Scottish fiddle music in the present day is marked by a high degree of diversity and variety unacknowledged in critical studies of the topic heretofore. Previous research has typically emphasised a homogenous national tradition or, since the 1970s, a collective of regional traditions, but even these do not reflect the multiplicity of styles and contexts in which Scottish fiddle music is now performed. Indeed, the range of performance is such, that it is becoming increasingly problematic to define Scottish fiddle music in any detail, with neither performance practice, repertoire, nor the ethnicity of the performer or composer an essential aspect. Ultimately, the performance of Scottish fiddle music in the present day is most convincingly interpreted from a combination of regional, national, and global perspectives, the latter accounting for the greater professionalisation and internationalisation seen in recent decades that has had a wide-ranging impact on performance practices, teaching and learning, and audience expectations. This chapter will determine the relevance and significance of links with the past in the present-day performance of Scottish fiddle music by investigating the creative dialogue between continuity and change.

The dialectic between the past and the future embodied in Henry Glassie's notion of tradition as 'the creation of the future out of the past' (Glassie, 1995, 395) makes the concept relevant to each perspective in different ways, but what it is not is a static, unchanging process of transmission between generations. From the national perspective, tradition connects present-day players with their historical antecedents from as long ago as the 'golden age' of Scottish dance music in the closing decades of the eighteenth century. Regionally, the term 'tradition' signifies a connection between practitioners and their teachers and peers within a local network that extends back as far as living memory; and from the global perspective, tradition often connects players with a distant Celtic past made more ethereal by the dislocation of practice from place. In what follows, the agency and relations of the past in the present-day performance of Scottish fiddle music will be considered before three manifestations of links with the past are evaluated, including musical lineage, old tune collections, and recordings from sound archives.

Continuity, revival, and the invention of a Scottish fiddle tradition

Mary Anne Alburger's claim that 'the music of the fiddle has been played in Scotland for more than half a millennium' (Alburger, 1983, 11), and Katherine Campbell's that 'the fiddle tradition in Scotland has been a continuous one' (Campbell, 2007, xv), highlight the importance of continuity within scholarship on Scottish fiddle music. Crucially, the fiddle tradition is defined in contrast to the many comparatively new or 'reinstated' instrumental traditions of the British folk music revival, such as those of the *clàrsach* and concertina. However, while the case can be made for fiddle music's ancient roots, the implications of this for performers in the present are not immediately clear. Indeed, the privileging of continuity within narratives about Scottish fiddle music potentially obscures present-day practices that have departed from or place less value on the historical narrative of the national tradition. Further, the tacit definition in opposition to revived instrumental traditions downplays the centrality of revival to the music's history, including the substantial revival of interest in the fiddle and its repertoire, which emerged in the 1970s with the growth in participation and number of fiddlers' rallies and competitions. In order to better understand the issue, it is necessary to consider the history of the traditionary mind-set in the performance and reception of Scottish fiddle music.

The received history of Scottish fiddle music presents the notion of a national tradition with roots in the eighteenth century or earlier. While the 'golden age' of Scottish dance music (c. 1780–1820) is privileged (Hunter, 1979, x–xii; Gore, 2008), David Johnson emphasises the compositional achievements of fiddler-composers throughout the eighteenth century (Johnson, 1984), and Alburger has posited the possibility of links with a much earlier pre-violin fiddle tradition (Alburger, 2003). However, it was only in the very closing years of the eighteenth century that the cultural significance of the repertoire and its performance came to be recognised, and practitioners started to conceive of their practice in the context of a tradition.

The first volume of Nathaniel Gow's *Complete Repository of Slow Strathspeys and Dances*, published in 1799, redefined the status of the repertoire from a collection of ephemeral tunes to works of considerable cultural significance. Across the four-volume series (1799–1817), Gow presented what he claimed were definitive texts of many of the most popular dance tunes alongside new compositions by himself, his family, and colleagues, and in so doing laid the foundations of a national fiddle tradition. Significantly, it contrasted with preceding collections by actively historicising the repertoire in a way that collections of mostly new compositions by a named fiddler-composer did not, and in so doing achieved a higher status for Scottish dance music above being only an accompaniment to dancing.

The tradition that Nathaniel Gow invented was a musically literate one defined as much by 'the most fashionable new' as by 'the most approved old', and as such was not static and unchanging. It has been sustained through historically focused collections, the discourse that accompanied it in the popular press, and the public performance of dance music in non-dance contexts. A number of historically focused collections were published in the course of the nineteenth century, including *Davie's Caledonian Repository* (first series: 4 vols, 1829–1835; second series: 2 vols, 1851–1855), *The Athole Collection* (1884), and *The Glen Collection* (2 vols, 1891–1895), and their foregrounding of old tunes from collections published in the 'golden age' is indicative of the strong historicising tendency throughout the century. Indeed, *The Glen Collection* features old tunes exclusively and maintains the original orthography as found in the old collections from which they are sourced (Glen, 1895, iv).

In the nineteenth-century popular press, highly informed critics reviewed concerts and competitions in local and national newspapers, and letters pages regularly featured discussion of repertoire and its performance. At the same time, the publication of the first history of Scottish fiddle music, Alexander Murdoch's *The Fiddle in Scotland* (1888), and David Baptie's many entries on fiddle players in his biographical dictionary, *Musical Scotland, Past and Present* (1894), reinforced the idea of a tradition by discussing both historical and contemporary players and composers.

The earliest documented instance of Scottish dance music being performed on the violin in a concert setting was at a recital at Broughty Ferry on 21 June 1850 (Advertiser, 1850). This event marks a milestone in the process of aestheticisation by which the performance of the repertoire was increasingly valued other than as an accompaniment to dancing. Other concerts followed, and from 1855, Scottish violin competitions were held with regularity. The rise in amateur ensembles also dates from about this time, with institutions such as the Dundee Scottish Musical Society (founded in 1869) and the Edinburgh Highland Reel and Strathspey Society (founded in 1881) affording an opportunity for learners to explore the repertoire of Scottish dance music. There was also a national network of 'Tullochgorum Clubs': social clubs at which amateurs met to perform Scottish dance music together.

The performance of dance music in non-dance contexts had significant implications for performance practice and reception, with performance shaped by the musical expectations of an audience of concentrating listeners. The demands of platform performance encouraged well-rehearsed and highly polished performances that reflected mainstream concert performances, and achieved their apotheosis in the figure of James Scott Skinner (1843–1927), the self-styled 'Scottish Violinist'.

The idea of a homogenous national tradition was challenged in the twentieth century by the identification of a collective of regional traditions, chief among them being those of the Shetland Isles, West Highland, and North East. The shift from a national perspective to a regional perspective was mirrored by the increased use of ethnographic methods in the study of Scottish traditional music (e.g. Henderson, 1964; Porter, 1976). Aided by audio recording technology that facilitates the detailed study of performance practice, fieldworkers from the School of Scottish Studies have been documenting performances by fiddle players from across the country since the 1950s. In the same period, Tom Anderson's advocacy of Shetland fiddle music has had an especially significant impact on perceptions about Scottish fiddle music more generally, posing a challenge to the hegemony of the national tradition. However, while performances by so-called country-fiddlers were being documented more or less across the country, the pervasiveness of literately focused humanistic scholarship continued into the early 1980s, with contributions by Francis Collinson (1966), George Emmerson (1971), Johnson (1972; 1984), and Alburger (1983), retaining a firmly historical perspective delimited primarily by old collections of music.

One of the earliest ethnomusicologically inspired studies of Scottish fiddle music dates from 1976, being Hugh Macdonald's study of fiddle performance in Strathspey, closely followed by Peter Cooke's doctoral study of the fiddle tradition of the Shetland Isles followed in 1982. Similarly, folklorist Alan Bruford was instrumental in the release of the LP, *Angus Grant: Highland Fiddle*, in 1978, one of the first to showcase a non-literate player in the West Highland tradition (Grant, 1978). Macdonald, in particular, is critical of the emphasis given to the literate tradition in studies of Scottish fiddle music, and speaks of a cultural iceberg, the vast, unseen base of which consists of non-literate 'country' players that have been denied a place in the national tradition (Macdonald, 1986, 7).

In the present day, regional traditions have become mostly reified as a series of attributes detached from the players whose performances manifest and perpetuate them, with the eclectic tastes of so-called multi-stylists reflecting the new environment in which Scottish fiddle music is learnt. This is demonstrated by recently published tune collections which 'encompass music from the West Coast, East Coast, Shetland, Orkney, and the Borders of Scotland' (Martin, 2002, front cover), or, more broadly, offer 'a practical introduction to styles from England, Ireland, Scotland, and Wales' (Griffiths, 2015, front cover). Similarly, a vestige of the national tradition remains in the network of competitions, the apex of which is the Glenfiddich Championship, where success by North American competitors in recent years reflects the international arena in which the music in now performed.

Links with the past

In this section, continuous and discontinuous links with the past will be examined. Whilst most emphasis has been placed on the former, especially in the form of 'continuous transmission', the latter is equally ubiquitous in the performance of fiddle music in the present day. At a technical level the links consists of two elements: repertoire, or the tunes and associated tune groupings and tune lore which have formed fiddle players' cultural currency for centuries, and performance practice, including aspects of interpretation and technique. Fundamentally, if a tune continues to be played through successive generations of a tradition it can be said to be in continuous transmission; but it remains possible to 'revive' old tunes as found in historical collections or archive sound recordings.

Macdonald argues that the purely aural transmission of tunes in non-literate rural traditions isolate them from changing tastes and fashions, whereas literate traditions, which tend to be more progressive, mirror changes in mainstream violin performance (Macdonald, 1986, 7). The claim that non-literate traditions represent unchanging performance practices that extend back to the eighteenth century and earlier is appealing for the supposed insight they can give into historical practices, but are also problematic because they cannot be corroborated.

Musical lineage

The idea of musical lineage helpfully situates musicians on a continuum, whether diachronic – the pianist who traces his 'genealogy' back to Chopin, for example – or synchronic, such as the traditional musician who associates each tune in her repertory with the musician from whom it came/was learnt. While most lineages will be of mostly personal significance, others assume greater cultural capital when the individuals involved are more widely recognised and act as markers of authentic practice. For Scottish fiddle music, musical lineage provides an important link with the past for many performers, none more so than Paul Anderson, who traces his musical lineage back to the 'father' of Scottish fiddle music, Niel Gow (1727–1807). As he explains:

> That's quite a cool thing. I mean you've got aa this famous fiddlers, and you've got links to them sort of coming doon the line. So I feel mysel that you're aye getting something passed through . . . every musical generation.
> (Campbell, 2001a)

Anderson resolves the apparent tension between his creative autonomy and his responsibility to the tradition with which he identifies by recognising that the process of transmission is not a static one in which the student becomes a 'clone' of their teacher.

Significantly, audio recordings exist of performances by Anderson, his teacher, Douglas Lawrence, and Lawrence's teacher, Hector MacAndrew (1903–1980), facilitating the study of the impact of musical lineage in the shorter term. Each has recorded 'Lady Charlotte Campbell's Strathspey', a tune composed by Robert Mackintosh (c. 1745–1807) and first published in his *Fourth Book of New Strathspey Reels* (Anderson, 2002; Lawrence, 1977; MacAndrew, 1975; Mackintosh, 1804).[1]

Unsurprisingly, none of the performances replicates the music as notated in Figure 16.1, but while each gives a unique interpretation, it is clear that they share a similar musical aesthetic. The pointed rhythmic articulation and very quick grace notes are particularly prominent in each player's interpretation.

The regional tradition with which they are identified is the North East, defined through its combining of techniques particular to the repertoire with mainstream violin techniques, including extensive use of embellishments such as trills, turns, and double stopping, studiously measured bow control in the execution of highly pointed rhythms, and the pervasiveness of musical literacy among players who make regular use of old collections from the eighteenth and nineteenth centuries. However, it is more helpful to consider this example of musical lineage

Figure 16.1 'Lady Charlotte Campbell's Strathspey'

within the national tradition given the link with Niel Gow (who, from the regional perspective would have been identified with a Perthshire tradition).

Paul Anderson (b. 1970)
|
Douglas Lawrence (b. 1957)
|
Hector MacAndrew (1903–1980)
|
Peter MacAndrew (1867–1951)
|
Peter MacAndrew (c. 1842–1921)
|
Peter MacAndrew (1805–1881)
|
James MacIntosh (1791–1879)
|
Niel Gow (1727–1807)

The above (adapted from Campbell, 2001b) details Anderson's musical lineage, showing the six intermediary teachers between him and Gow. Of course, in practice, each of these fiddle players most likely taught a great many students, making the identification of this particular narrative seemingly arbitrary, but it has gained in eminence as a result of the successes of MacAndrew, Lawrence, and Anderson.

Niel Gow assumed a central place in the tradition that his son, Nathaniel, 'invented'. Even during his lifetime, Niel was somewhat of a national celebrity, with his tunes made popular through the publication of his collections and his portrait painted by Sir Henry Raeburn. However, his status only increased on his death, which was marked by a lengthy biographical note in the *Scots Magazine* (McKnight, 1809). Nathaniel published the three-volume series, *The Beauties of Niel Gow*, in 1819 and Simon Fraser included two tunes dedicated to Niel in *Airs and Melodies Peculiar to the Highlands of Scotland and the Isles*, 'Caledonia's Wail for Niel Gow' and 'Niel Gow's Style' (Fraser, 1816, 70), in addition to including an image of his likeness on the title page. As late as 1862, *The Caledonian Mercury* featured an obituary for William Menzies, 'last of the Niel Gow style of violin players' (Caledonian Mercury, 1862). However, the claim that he was the last of the Niel Gow School is less significant than the identification of the School itself. The obituary refers to 'the "lang bow" and strathspey style of Niel Gow', and it is an aspect of Niel's bowing that his musical descendants claim connects his performance practice with their own.

The aspect in question is what is now called the 'up-driven bow', illustrated in Figure 16.2. It is a bowing pattern or stroke used in the execution of the rhythm of a scotch snap (being a sixteenth note and a dotted eighth note) followed by a dotted eighth note and sixteenth note, especially common in strathspey dance tunes. Alistair Hardie describes its execution thus: 'Take the initial semiquaver near the point of the bow, leaving a whole bow for the following three notes. *Kick* the final semiquaver' (Hardie, 1981, 68). Something potentially like it is described in the biographical note that was published after Niel's death, but it is there referred to as the 'upward or returning stoke' (McKnight, 1809, 3) and described as being particular not to Niel Gow but to the performance of Highland reels in general.

MacAndrew compared what he termed the 'modern' way of playing with the Gow style, with the main difference concerning bowing, and he justified his authority to make such a comparison by citing his musical lineage (MacAndrew, 1960). However, no recordings exist of his teacher or any of the other intermediaries between him and Gow, making an historical analysis problematic. Significantly, he came to prominence during the post-war folk music revival at a time when tradition bearers were sought after and were highly valued by revivalists. As such, he came to be a respected teacher who was largely responsible for reviving interest in the North East style. He communicated a particular musical aesthetic

Figure 16.2 The up-driven bow

founded on bowing patterns, especially the up-driven bow, which is detectable in the aforementioned recordings of him and his musical 'descendants'.

Reconciling present-day and historical performance practices on the strength of musical lineage is made problematic by the complexities of musical transmission and changing tastes, fashions, and technologies. However, whether or not Niel Gow's 'returning stroke' would bear resemblance to the 'up-driven bow' of today is ultimately a moot point. It is ultimately more helpful to recognise the dialectic between continuity and change in the context of musical revival.

Old collections

The history of Scottish fiddle music is constructed around the substantial number of printed collections of dance music that survive among the holdings of national and university libraries throughout the British Isles and North America. Together, they harbour a rich heritage of tunes, many of which continue to be played today, and were indexed in 1994 by Charles Gore and Morag Elder (Gore, 1994). There also exist a significant number of manuscript collections, many of which feature tunes copied from a range of printed sources, and others that feature original content. However, the current lack of an index of manuscript collections makes them considerably less accessible than their printed counterparts.

The publication of more historically focused collections was discussed above in connection with the 'invention' of a Scottish fiddle tradition, but while the editors of such volumes were making tunes from old collections available to a new audience, they also 'updated' or otherwise adapted their texts to reflect current fashions and practices. Indeed, John Glen, in retaining the original orthography, is the exception that proves the rule. Similar volumes were published throughout the twentieth century, with James Hunter's *The Fiddle Music of Scotland* (1979) presenting an authoritative collection of tunes, including notes on performance practice, that has partially defined the canon of fiddle music in recent decades.

There has been renewed interest in making old collections available in their entirety since the 1990s, with the Highland Music Trust publishing a new edition of *The Athole Collection* in 1996 (Stewart-Robertson, 1996), *The Glen Collection* in 2001 (Glen, 2001), and various others since then. As new editions, the notation is reset with minimal editorial input to the melodic line, but only some editions maintain the original bass lines, these being omitted in others on the grounds of their perceived quality and irrelevance to modern performers, and to save space. More recently, libraries have made available online digital facsimile copies of many old collections enabling modern performers minimally mediated access to historical sources. However, while old collections afford a valuable link to the rich heritage of tunes from the eighteenth and nineteenth centuries, the issue of interpreting the notation poses challenges to their performance in the present.

Highland Collections was published by the Highland Music Trust in 2005 and contains the collections of seven fiddler-composers from the nineteenth century (with bass lines omitted). Lauren MacColl makes explicit reference to it in her album, *Strewn with Ribbons* (2009), which juxtaposes old tunes taken from the

Highland Collections with new tunes she composed. Fluency is ensured between the old and new tunes by her performance practice that is consistent throughout the recording. As it states on her website, she 'continues to be inspired by old music from her home area', the Highlands of Scotland (MacColl, 2015). The merging of old and new tunes implicitly reinforces the idea of a living tradition with roots in the past.

The tune, 'Duncan Swine's Wife', is included by MacColl on *Strewn with Ribbons*, and was originally published in William Christie's *A Collection of Strathspeys. Reels, Hornpipes, Waltzes, &c. Arranged as Medleys for the Harp, Piano Forte, Violin, and Violoncello* (Christie, 1821, 27; Highland Collections, 2005, 24).[2] The notation, as seen in Figure 16.3, implies a performance of Western art music, including as it does ornaments such as trills and turns which are not idiomatic in contemporary Scottish fiddle music performance, but her interpretation is only loosely based on the musical notation, with the frequent substitution of rhythms, omission of printed ornaments, and introduction of ornaments at other places in the tune.

It is clear from the title that Christie's intended audience was the domestic amateur music-making market rather than professional dance band musicians, with performance practices inevitably differing considerably between the two

Figure 16.3 'Duncan Swine's Wife'

groups. As such, his settings most likely reflect more of contemporary musical tastes rather than how the music was typically performed for dancing (a step towards the music's aestheticisation achieved in its public performance in non-dance contexts).

In MacColl's case, the inclusion of tunes from the *Highland Collections* on *Strewn with Ribbons* combines a link with the past with the rootedness of performing repertoire from her home area, reflecting aspects of both the national and regional perspectives of tradition. Similar recording projects which foreground old collections include Jonny Hardie's album, *The Captain's Collection*, which includes tunes from Simon Fraser's collection, and Ron Gonella's album, *Scottish Violin Music from the Gow Collections* (Hardie, 1999; Fraser, 1816; Gonella, 1973).

Recordings from the Sound Archive

The links with the past afforded by old collections and musical lineage are limited by the extent to which they can represent historical performance. The imprecision of prescriptive musical notation in representing performance as a sound object and the ethereal nature of long-term musical transmission are such that the links can only ever reflect a feint impression of the past (Seeger, 1958, 184). Old recordings potentially offer a less mediated link with an albeit less distant past, but limitations remain in their representation of performance practice. The often distorted sound quality of very early recordings can mask aspects of performance, and early technology was such that recorded pitch was not absolute; but even a clear recording represents only a single performance, and the lack of an accompanying visual record masks the performer's technical approach (Bradtke, 2010, 41–42). Nonetheless, the link afforded by old recordings remains valuable, and, as with the other links, not only for technical-musical aspects, but geo-cultural reasons, also.

James Scott Skinner, the earliest fiddle music recording artist, cut his first disc in 1899, and the 'Cameron Men' of Kirriemuir recorded for Beltona in 1934 (Dean-Myatt, 2012). The early recordings by Scott Skinner, many of which were re-released most recently on compact disc (Skinner, 2002) bear close and detailed listening; when the limitations of the recording technology and generally poor sound quality are overcome, the audio is found to feature performances of great nuance and subtlety, as seen in Figure 16.4, a transcription of his recorded performance of 'Tullochgorum' from 1910.[3]

Since the advent of recorded sound, fieldworkers have been motivated to capture audio images of practices (musical and otherwise) that they believe to be in danger of being lost to posterity. The results of their efforts are a network of sound archives housed in various institutions around the world that are visited mostly by academics whose aim might be to transcribe and study a particular repertoire or an individual's performance practice. However, a valuable result of many recent digitisation projects to make many holdings in sound archives accessible for free online is that now anyone with an internet connection can explore the archives' contents.

Links with the past 227

Figure 16.4 Author's transcription of James Scott Skinner's 1910 performance of 'Tullochgorum'

Accessibility has long been an issue for archivists and curators keen to facilitate greater engagement with archives. In a Scottish context, the 'Scottish Traditions Series' of recordings was established in the 1980s, in an attempt to bring the recordings held in the School of Scottish Studies sound archive to a wider audience. Complemented by scholarly liner notes, each volume provides an insight into its topic, with the series covering a range of instrumental and vocal traditions. More recently, the School has collaborated with the BBC and NTS on Tobar an Dualchais/Kist o Riches, a website that gives access to many recordings from the respective institutions' sound archives. The recordings of fiddle players on Tobar an Dualchais/Kist o Riches are a rich resource of tunes, performance practices, and factual information, and the ability to search by the location at which a recording was made gives an added regional dimension.

Over 900 individual tracks of fiddle music are currently accessible via Tobar an Dualchais/Kist o Riches, the earliest of which date from 1952. They cover a large if not comprehensive geographical area, but recordings of players from the Shetland Isles predominate, numbering more than 400 of the total. Tom Anderson (1910–1991) is noted as a contributor or reporter on 364 of these tracks, highlighting his central role in the archiving of Shetland fiddle music in the post-war era.

His student, Catriona MacDonald, was described on her website in 2013 as 'embodying the strength and spirit of her heritage with the freshness and diversity of a thoroughly modern performer' (MacDonald, 2011). She demonstrated her engagement with the sound archive in the second track of her debut album, *Bold* (2000). It begins with an old recording of Gibbie Gray (1909–1989), a fiddle player from Shetland, playing the tune, 'Three Drunken Fiddlers'.[4]

Figure 16.5 'Three Drunken Fiddlers'

In the beginning, the archive recording is accompanied by MacDonald's band, before she herself takes up the tune and the archive recording fades out. Differences in recording technology aside, there is an obvious disparity between the performance aesthetics of the two interpretations of the tune: Gray's performance features a strongly inégales treatment of rhythm while MacDonald's features a more equally measured rhythm. Hers is also a more highly 'polished' performance, in comparison to Gray's in which some notes do not sound. Of course, the contrasting functions for which the recordings were made, the former for the sound archive and the latter for a commercial CD, should be taken into account, with the demands of the record industry inevitably shaping MacDonald's performance practice as did playing for dancing shape Gray's. As in the previous examples, the tune has been abstracted to be interpreted within the parameters of the player's own performance practice, but the inclusion of the archive recording on the track foregrounds the centrality of heritage to MacDonald's identity as a Shetland fiddle player.

Conclusion

Glassie defined tradition as the creation of the future out of the past. Looking forward rather than backward avoids the reification of traditional music and the expectation that it should be transmitted in a static form. This chapter examined links with the past in the present-day performance of Scottish fiddle music in order to define the creative dialogue between continuity and revival. As has been demonstrated, a notion of the past is important to many practitioners, whether through their musical lineage or the tunes they play, but each retains their autonomy as a fundamentally creative artist. The identification of Paul Anderson as a leading performer of Scottish fiddle music is certainly enhanced by his musical lineage, but there are many other successful fiddle players who cannot claim such a distinguished pedigree. For Lauren MacColl and Catriona MacDonald, their engagement with the past is manifested in the patrimony of tunes which link them to their heritage and locality. The creative interplay between literacy and aurality which was demonstrated when recordings of tunes were compared with the tunes in their original notation belies the contingency of notation upon performance. The present-day performance of Scottish fiddle music embodies a multiplicity of living traditions that look both backwards and forwards.

Notes

1. Excerpts from each track have been uploaded as 'Example One' to http://scottishfiddlemusic.com/contents/usm.
2. An excerpt from the track has been uploaded as 'Example Two' to http://scottishfiddlemusic.com/contents/usm.
3. An excerpt from the track has been uploaded as 'Example Three' to http://scottishfiddlemusic.com/contents/usm. My aim in transcribing his performance was to achieve a primarily prescriptive notation that could be compared with published prescriptive settings of the tune.
4. An excerpt from the track has been uploaded as 'Example Four' to http://scottishfiddlemusic.com/contents/usm.

17 Wynds, vennels and dual carriageways

The changing nature of Scottish music

Karen E. McAulay

A local historian, handed an old photograph, would try to identify it using distinguishable landmarks and datable details – although sometimes these are hard to find. For example, a run-down Vennel in Greenock on the River Clyde was in the late nineteenth century the home to a bustling community of ship-building labourers, hammer-men and boilermakers. However, the ground today lies buried under tarmac, a municipal car-park sunk into a roundabout, halfway along a dual carriageway. It is the same grid-reference, but a totally different picture. No one would imagine they were standing in the same place.

Furthermore, whilst an old picture is at least hard evidence of a kind (our eyes tell us what we see in front of us), historical published commentary has to be read with an understanding of its context, whilst the handed-down reminiscences that are core to oral history – and indeed, to our own sense of identity – are based on our present-day perceptions of *what was*, and are therefore telling us as much about the present as about the past. This is not said in any sense to privilege print over non-print culture (after all, if the old photograph were shown to a variety of local residents, it would be interpreted in as many different ways, recalling personal memories, not to mention broadcast and other audiovisual media as much as print sources), but to make the point that a landscape can be utterly transformed by subsequent generations.

If it is difficult to pin down actual places over time, then it will be even harder to pin down concepts, and the metaphor of a landscape changed by time is singularly apposite. It is fair to say that attempting to compare our conception of traditional Scottish music today, with what was considered traditional and Scottish in the past, is rather like going back to the home of our forbears, and realising that today's road layout bears no resemblance whatsoever to the historical map that we painstakingly downloaded before we set out.

The present chapter has been written from a musicological rather than an ethnomusicological stance, interrogating published, or at least written evidence gathered during my own research; this has been mainly into printed sources of eighteenth and nineteenth century Scottish songs and dance-tunes, with occasional forays into manuscript collections. Furthermore, although my interest is primarily in the music, I have taken a closer look at the paratext – the title page, prefaces, introductions, annotations, dedications and so on – than has generally been done by musicologists. This approach helps us to determine the aesthetic considerations and editorial approaches of those originally responsible for the historical books, music volumes and manuscripts still available to us today, from the well-known collections of fiddle tunes published by the Gow family, to now generally neglected late Victorian Scottish song anthologies.

When we try to define traditional Scottish music in the broadest possible sense – or even separate out the ideas of 'traditional' and 'Scottish' and address them independently, it soon becomes clear that these are slippery concepts capable of multiple nuances and endless definition. However, I contend that part of the problem can be reconfigured as part of the solution if we recognise the needless difficulty that we cause ourselves by trying to apply today's terminology and concepts to the music of the past.

Despite the apparent disconnect between historical and current conceptions of Scottish music, it is crucial to understand what makes this so, if we are to have an informed appreciation of older Scottish music collections and what they can tell us about the people who compiled and used them. In the latter part of this chapter, I outline some of the practical steps I have taken to share this understanding with today's undergraduates, and I conclude by arguing for a flexible and more accepting approach to what we each consider Scottish music to be.

Trying to define 'folk' and 'traditional'

Throughout at least the first half of the twentieth century, the average layperson would have had little difficulty describing what they thought folk music was. However, after the excitement and upheaval of the folk revival in the middle of the century, there was rather more confusion, and nowadays we have generally deserted the term altogether, preferring to talk about 'traditional music'.

Incalculable hours at numerous conferences have been spent debating the meaning of both 'folk' and 'traditional' as the words appertain to music, and attempting to reach some kind of consensus on who 'the folk' actually were. Cecil Sharp's loving description of mainly rural peasants was sincerely and kindly felt at the time, but today serves merely to indicate what a very different world he inhabited:

> The peasant is the sole survivor of a homogeneous society with few class distinctions. [. . .] This habit of reserve and reticence has often been misinterpreted as proceeding from a low intelligence, a restricted vocabulary, or churlish manners. This is not so [. . .]
>
> This attitude of restraint is illustrated in the songs and dances he invented and performs. His song has no superfluous words; it repeats stock phrases [. . .] and the tune has few ornamental notes. [. . .] He learned both song and dance, as he learned his speech, from his parents.
>
> (Karpeles, 2008, 178)

The International Folk Music Council (now, since 1981, the *International Council for Traditional Music*) struggled to define folk music when it was founded in

1947, but over the next few years, the emphasis was on oral transmission, community selection and group or individual variation. Maud Karpeles was at pains to stress that composed songs could transition into folk songs through a process of 're-creation'; but insisted that the two forms, whilst they could co-exist amid blurred boundaries, were nonetheless distinct. This was made clear in the IFMC's 1954 definition statement:

> Folk music is music that has been submitted to the process of oral transmission. It is the product of evolution and is dependent on the circumstances of continuity, variation and selection.
>
> This definition implies that folk music is the product of an unwritten tradition [...]
>
> The definition rightly leaves out of the account the origin of folk music. The term can therefore be applied to music that has been evolved from rudimentary beginnings by a community uninfluenced by art music; and it can also be applied to music which has originated with an individual composer and has subsequently been absorbed into the unwritten, living tradition of a community. But the term does not cover a song, dance or tune that has been taken over ready-made and remains unchanged.
>
> (Karpeles, 1955)

This binary opposition between 'unwritten tradition' and composed material is fraught with difficulty. Let us agree at the outset that – particularly with music transmitted orally, where far more people may have learned a tune by ear than by reading it in published form – songs and instrumental tunes will in the course of time become moulded and transformed. Tunes will change, and the passage of time will introduce different harmonic and interpretative preferences. Taking this idea beyond the traditional, ethnomusicological field, any group of people learning a new tune may unconsciously introduce modifications (try teaching a new song to a church congregation!); whilst printed, 'classical' music may assume quite different interpretations by subsequent generations – whether in ornamentation, the realisation of a figured bass, or some other aspect of performance practice. Music does not remain in a fixed form. However, logically speaking, any song or tune began somewhere, created – 'composed' – by an individual musician or group of musicians at some stage, whether or not it was written down at the time, and allowing for infinite major or minor variations and changes along the way. The tune we perform today may, consequently, be very different from the earliest known iteration, just as, with poetry, Robert Burns sometimes took the opening lines of a song and wrote a new one onto the end of it. Hamish Henderson's 'carrying stream' (Henderson, 2000) and the nineteenth century poet Allan Cunningham's 'wide sea of oral remembrance' (Cunningham, 1825, 65) are telling metaphors for the process of oral transmission – the very fact that the metaphors have lasted two centuries is confirmation that we find the comparison attractive and feasible. However, the idea that songs literally grew like the flowers and rivers they so often celebrate, in one sense negates the original spark (seed, to continue the analogy) that some 'Anon' initiated in the first place. The tune may become very different, but it surely does have a beginning, a moment between 'not being' and 'being'. There does sometimes seem to be a tendency to privilege the anonymous material as somehow being more genuinely traditional or 'of the folk'. If we know the composer of a song, does that make it less traditional than an anonymous one?

Since the Folk Revival era, additional layers of complexity have been added, with arguments about whether industrial workers and town-dwellers still count as 'folk', and whether modern folk-revival material can even be viewed as traditional folk music at all (Roud and Bishop, 2014: General Introduction, ix–xxv). Moreover, Marxist considerations of folk versus 'fakesong' by Dave Harker and others have, if anything, muddied the water still further, adding to the debates about who the 'folk' are, by questioning the motives and background of folk-music collectors, and how to conserve a purportedly oral tradition (Harker, 1985).

Trying to define 'Scottish'

Throw into the pot all the debates about what makes Scottish music Scottish, and we have a very potent mix. Does it have to be 'traditional' or arising from the oral Scottish folk tradition, to be Scottish? How about art music composed by a Scot, or art music composed in 'traditional Scottish' style?

And do we mean historical or contemporary Scottish music, or both? Today's composers of music in any genre may proudly claim to be Scottish, without there necessarily being anything about their stylistic idiom that would be identified as Scottish, and many of the 'traditional' musicians' recordings defy even the old definitions of traditional or folk music. Historically speaking, presumably an 'imitation traditional' tune composed in nineteenth century Scotland is more Scottish than one produced in London, but is it any more authentic? And is it impossible for a tune composed in the nineteenth century to be as traditional as one found in a source a couple of centuries earlier?

The bottom line, like the Vennel and the dual carriageway, is that it all depends on the era that we are talking about. We can look at eighteenth-century Scottish music through modern eyes, or we can try to interpret what eighteenth-century Scottish music represented to contemporary music-lovers. What cannot be avoided, however, is the inescapable fact that it is as difficult to attempt to compare Scottish music of different eras, as it would be to compare late eighteenth-century ballad opera with Broadway musical theatre. The modern equivalent might be held with the same affection by a similar clientele, but the passage of two centuries makes direct comparison impossible.

Problems with historical 'Scottish' repertoire

Whilst there are admittedly problems with the historical, supposedly Scottish repertoire, some of the conceptual problems associated with the terms 'folk' and 'traditional' are swept away when we accept the eighteenth- and nineteenth-century preference for the word 'national'. Whether songs about simple, unspoiled Scottish peasant girls, brave Scottish soldiers or tragic emigrants, the common factor is that these are perceived primarily as national songs, that is songs of Scotland. Eighteenth- and nineteenth-century Scots did not use the term 'folk music', and 'traditional' was generally used merely as an adjective rather than being immutably attached to the word 'music'. Indeed it took until the later eighteenth century and influential writings such as philosopher James Beattie's essay, 'On Poetry and Music, as they affect the Mind' in 1776, for the idea to gain acceptance that traditional songs might originate from humble farm labourers rather from more highly placed members of society (Beattie, 1996).

We must assume that, at any given period, the people collecting Scottish music were generally in little doubt that at least some of the material they were dealing with was traditionally recognised as Scottish music, in the sense of having long been in the repertoire of songs that Scottish people liked to sing and/or accepted as Scottish. The same songs crop up regularly, although there are certainly substantial shifts in the repertoire over time – compare, for example, George Farquhar Graham's mid-nineteenth-century *Songs of Scotland* with any modern collection – and fiddle tune compilers seemed quite keen to introduce new material alongside the old, because theirs was a repertoire for dancing, and fashion not only dictated what was performed, but also demanded regular injections of new material (Graham, 1848–1849).

Authenticity and inauthenticity

However, if twentieth-century collectors agonised over what was genuine folk music, then their earlier predecessors certainly did have similar if not identical concerns. For purist music collectors of an antiquarian bent in the eighteenth and early nineteenth centuries, the overwhelming preoccupation was that of authenticity. Their definition of 'authenticity' may have had slightly different constructs, but the question as to whether a song is really what it purports to be, has endured to this day.

In eighteenth-century Britain, Scottish melodies were so popular that imitation Scottish tunes sprung up in English collections, too. In the mid- to late-nineteenth century, William Chappell called such songs 'Anglo-Scottish'.[1] This designation met with more or less favour depending on the perceptions and nationality of his readers, because attitudes to this repertoire varied in different eras and amongst different audiences. The Thompson family's famous London publishing firm published their *Thirty Favourite Scots Songs* in 1790 (Thompson S.A. and Thompson P., 1790), but the book's contents were far removed from – and far less Scottish than – the ostensibly more genuine ancestry of Robert Bremner's earlier similarly named collection, *Thirty Scots Songs for a Voice & Harpsichord*, which used Allan Ramsay's even earlier lyrics (Bremner, 1757). Instead, they offered the more 'Anglo-Scottish' repertoire that had found favour in English ballad-operas based on Scottish themes. One might add, incidentally, that Allan Ramsay's own Scottish song lyrics have themselves been described as a one-man attempt to create a Scottish song repertoire, which invites further debate about authenticity! (Johnson, 2003, 134).

Furthermore, fakery abounded from the late eighteenth to the early nineteenth century, with corroborating evidence from the 1820s to be found in the letters between Robert Archibald Smith and William Motherwell about the odd planted 'jewel' in the former's *Scotish Minstrel* compilations. This is but a musical offshoot from the numerous instances of elaborate literary hoaxes (not just in Scotland but in the entire British Isles) such as Allan Cunningham's deception of the unfortunate R. H. Cromek, or indeed Walter Scott's feigned 'discoveries' or disguised authorial identities in his early novels (McAulay, 2013, 105–127). We could also add to these musical examples of fakery, the tunes that do not even claim to be Scottish, but sound as though they might have been, such as the slow movement of Thomas Shaw's Violin Concerto in G, demonstrating the popularity of the Scottish idiom in more strictly 'classical' music.

Really Scottish – but not necessarily of humble origin

Indeed, even where the Scottish origin of published songs was beyond question, their apparently humble origins were often more than questionable, and the oral transmission that was a sine qua non in Sharp's or Karpeles's definition was barely a consideration at all. For example, Joseph Ritson, the Northern English compiler of the two-volume *Scotish Song*, was highly critical of James Macpherson's allegedly Ossianic poems and their Highland Gaelic origins, and took care that his own 'Scotish' songs did, to the best of his knowledge, emanate from Scotland. He was obsessive about accuracy, and carefully classified the songs in his collection, but they were not the kind of folk music that we know today. His view that folk music should be collected from farm labourers was innovative, and was possibly influenced not only by Beattie's writings but also by his own Republican sympathies. However, he was not actually very successful at collecting from farm workers, instead deriving his material from a variety of printed sources, and not hesitating to include material drawn from the printed repertoire of educationally or socially more elevated musicians (see Ritson, 1794).

In his day, Ritson was both admired for his dedicated attention to detail, and loathed for his fussy and pedantic arguments about what was truly authentic. Allan Cunningham derided him for his lack of poetic sensibility, perhaps unfairly, for Ritson's powers of description were lavish when he was so inclined, conjuring pictures and metaphors that rival those in Cunningham's own preface.

Ritson's younger acquaintance, the Highlander Alexander Campbell, who actively collected Scottish tunes in the Hebrides and the Scottish Borders in 1815–1816, and published them as *Albyn's Anthology*, had a somewhat different approach to his repertoire. Unlike Ritson, Campbell certainly did go out into the field (both ethnomusicologically and at times literally), where he transcribed the songs and tunes that his informants played and sang to him. It was a varied repertoire, for the music was not consistently 'ancient'; some may have been composed by the people who played them, whilst others can be traced in somewhat earlier collections. It was also quite progressively egalitarian, for he collected songs from clergy, gentry *and* ordinary working people, such as farm-hands and boatmen.

The Scottish question in the nineteenth century

By the mid-nineteenth century, it appeared that there was more tolerance towards those compilers who had indulged in fakery, and even some appreciation of their artistry. The question of nationality retained its heat, though. The English ballad-collector William Chappell's *Popular Music of the Olden Times*, of 1859, devoted a couple of chapters to Scottish songs. This would have been less problematical had he not ventured the opinion that some of these songs first appeared in English sources. Scottish collectors were concerned or incensed, depending on their dispositions. Some of the arguments can be read in Dundee Central Library, to which Andrew Wighton's Scottish music collection was gifted after his death. Wighton's copy of *Popular Music* contains some of his correspondence with Chappell and Edinburgh librarian David Laing, and there is also further correspondence with his Aberdonian music publisher friend James Davie, which together allow us considerable insight into the passions aroused on this topic (see McAulay, 2013, 201–230).

The subsequent stories of Chappell's *Popular Music*, compared with the contemporary Scotsman George Farquhar Graham's *Songs of Scotland*, published by John Muir Wood, are fascinating. Both went into several editions. Chappell's correspondence records his alternating wishes to write more about Scottish song, and to steer well clear of it, until he eventually decided to leave Scottish music to the Scots, and gave his box of materials to John Muir Wood – a friend of his – to use as he pleased. His friend John Woodfall Ebsworth's copy of *Popular Music* survives in the Bodleian Library, and documents numerous changes that Chappell appears to have planned, carefully copied from Chappell's own copy. However, after Chappell's death, his book was reissued by Wooldridge in 1893, under the title *Old English Popular Music*, with all references to Scottish music excised – certainly one way of closing down the argument!

Muir Wood's book took a totally different direction. First published in 1848–1849, by 1885 the preface conceded that some so-called Scottish songs were actually English; that some were from the Borders; and that some were Scottish only by repute; or by dint of their modern Scottish words. The recognition of blurred or porous boundaries is a progressive note, and we might note that the anonymous *Musical Times* reviewer of the 1885 edition specifically highlighted Muir Wood's contribution in clarifying the difficulty of establishing the nationality of some of the repertoire, noting also that some material is of mixed origin due to its Borders background (McAulay, 2013, 201–230).

Borders and boundaries

Although border ballads as a literary genre received attention from a succession of nineteenth century authorities, there are comparatively few musical collections from this region, and even fewer with meaningful paratext. However, it is hardly surprising that the geographic boundaries will be blurred in terms of musical repertoire. For example, a pipe-tune, 'I saw my love come passing by me', can be found in *Northumbrian Minstrelsy* (Stokoe, 1882). Although claimed as Northumbrian, a very similar tune appeared in the much earlier, eighteenth century collection, *Aria di Camera* – a collection of Scottish, Irish and Welsh tunes published by the Londoner Daniel Wright in the early 1730s, as a 'Hilland [i.e. Highland] lilt' (Wright, 1726). Whilst there is a substantial geographical distance between Northumbria and the Scottish Highlands, a possible explanation reveals itself in the early seventeenth century Skene manuscript, which originates from Hallyards in Lothian (Dauney, 1973[1838], 240 [no. 58]). Here, we find another similar tune entitled, 'Pitt on your shirt on Monday'. Although it is tempting to suggest that the tune perhaps originated in the Scottish Lowlands, travelling both North and South thereafter, it is probably safer simply to accept this single instance as proof that repertoire cannot always be forced into watertight compartments.

Scottish music transformations

Music educationalists go to great lengths to ensure that students understand what 'Scottish music' was like at various stages in the past – whether the folk revival of the '60s and '70s, the Celtic Twilight of Marjory Kennedy Fraser, or eighteenth-century fiddle collections. As with other genres of music – for example, classical Western music or jazz – it is important that students have an appreciation of what went before, in order to understand the context of what is being performed today. That appreciation has to embrace some of the aesthetic considerations of the past, in order to recognise why certain collections have stood the test of time and now stand out from the rest.

For several years, I have taught our second-year Scottish music students about historical song collections, demonstrating their most noteworthy features. Whilst my pedagogical approach has changed from a lecture-style presentation to more student-led seminars, the fundamental aims have remained constant: to highlight the song-compilers' tell-tale comments about the best way to present a Scottish song, their observations about the songs' authenticity, anecdotal remarks about the songs' provenance, and so on; and to set these collections in context by comparison with other contemporary music collections.

It is important to impart an understanding that historical collections – say, Thompson's Scottish song compilations, R.A. Smith's *Scotish Minstrel*, John Muir Wood's *Songs of Scotland*, not to mention Marjory Kennedy-Fraser's misty Hebridean collections – can only really be understood if they are accepted as typical of their day. That means looking both at the musical style of the accompaniments, and the social environment in which the albums would be used. A book of Scottish songs compiled for an antiquarian collector, for parlour use by well-to-do young ladies, or perhaps for didactic use or even on a concert platform, will assuredly be nothing like the mid-twentieth century folk revival collections, or Faber's recent *Language of Folk* books. However, they *will* share some similarities with other art-songs of their era. I have detected some surprise when I introduce the odd Schubert Lied, or play a Debussy chord sequence, but if students have some idea of this contemporary context, they will better understand what was considered artistically effective at the time these collections were compiled.

It is also worth considering the differences in perspective when it came to *selecting* the contents of printed – or manuscript – collections at different points in history. In every collection, be it published or manuscript, we need to establish – if we can – what was behind the ultimate selection of material. Steve Roud, in his General Introduction to *The New Penguin Book of English Folk Songs*, explains that the first edition of the book privileged the rare or unique song 'specimen', whilst the new book sets out to collate the most popular songs in that repertoire. Whatever the nationality or chronology of a tune-book, the same questions can be asked: what exactly did the compilers set out to collect?

There is of course, little point in focusing on historic Scottish collections unless today's undergraduates are enabled to make use of them in the future. Clearly these resources are of little immediate relevance to twenty-first century performers, if you take them at face value, accompaniment and all – whether figured bass, Victorian song or Debussy-esque impressionist chords. Nonetheless, studying these collections gives a sense of continuity – in a sense it is the printed equivalent of Hamish Henderson's 'carrying stream' of tradition – a series of jolting, black and white still images, rather than moving colour ones. These books demonstrate what 'Scottish music' actually meant to past generations. Moreover, who would deny the value of gaining an understanding of the differences in repertoire in different eras? Without exposure to early collections, one would never appreciate how the repertoire changes, reflecting the social conditions of the times in which it was gathered. Pragmatically, learners will also be equipped to assess any old collections that they may come across in their future careers, and to recognise the value of what they encounter.

Most importantly, if the pedagogy facilitates student-led learning, and students are given the opportunity actively to engage with these collections, it means that students will have some idea how they might make use of them in their own practice, for there is always the potential of using the contents of these old anthologies as raw materials for a creative, even innovative modern interpretation.

Porous boundaries

Wood's 1885 *Songs of Scotland* preface acknowledged the difficulty of pinning down what exactly could be considered a Scottish song; and a willingness to leave the definition open is perhaps the most honest approach available to us. The very concept of 'Scottish music' is incredibly difficult to pin down, as was amply demonstrated at the 'Understanding Scotland Musically' conference at which this paper was originally given.

Although we concede that the boundaries are infinitely porous, at the same time, we each have our own invisible 'boundaries' beyond which the definition cannot extend. We are willing to embrace the repertoire of a centuries-old Scottish songbook as 'Scottish' on the grounds that this was what the *compiler* considered Scottish. And yet, if someone whispered the words, *Highland Cathedral* or *Ashokan Farewell*, any self-respecting scholar of Scottish music would shudder, immediately launching into an explanation as to why these late twentieth-century pot-boilers absolutely do not fit under today's Scottish musical umbrella, with their commercialised adoption of a 'Scottish idiom' and no real link to Scottish music at all.

And what are we to make of Peter Maxwell Davies's *Farewell to Stromness*? Maxwell Davies was an English composer, but a long-term resident in the Orkney Islands, and his piece was written as a protest to a proposed uranium mine outside Stromness in 1980. There are many aspects of Scottishness to consider here: a piece composed by someone who made Scotland his adopted domicile; a modern interpretation of the Scottish idiom; and a title and original inspiration that elicits an emotional response to the idea of Scotland. The piece is actually a very good demonstration both of the many ways in which something can be construed as 'Scottish', and of why it does not pay to try to pin things down too precisely.

The arguments about what is authentically Scottish music, truly traditional, or genuinely of the folk, have rumbled on for more than two centuries. Every so often, an authority in the field has endeavoured to pin the concept down; but as soon as their heads were raised above the parapet (or should I say, the hedgerow?), another authority would posit a different interpretation.

In this chapter, I began by drawing a comparison between physical changes on a real landscape – the Vennel supplanted by a roundabout and car-park – with the aesthetic changes that have taken place in Scottish music over the past three centuries. During the course of this discussion, I have metaphorically dug up the roundabout and conducted a full archaeological exploration of the ground underneath the car-park. It is up to the reader whether they share my interest in the historical remains that I have unearthed, or simply restore the roundabout to its present state. I shall still hopefully have increased their understanding about what was there before.

Note

1 William Chappell's letter to Andrew Wighton, 23 December 1857, Dundee CL, Wighton Collection 31669 (Manuscript correspondence at back of *Popular Music of the Olden Time*, Vol. 2, 1859).

18 Understanding Scotland musically
Reflections on place, war and nation

Gary West

My aim in this chapter is to offer some thoughts on the challenge we have set ourselves in the title of this book, and therefore to consider to what extent we actually *can* understand Scotland musically. The implication of the wording is surely that the task before us is to try to achieve an understanding of *Scotland*, and that the road we are being invited to travel in order to attempt this is a *musical* one. Other scholars with differing skillsets, preoccupations and disciplinary backgrounds may well have set about this task by following other paths, attempting to understand Scotland economically, geographically, sociologically, anthropologically, politically. Indeed, many have done exactly that. Our current project, then, has not been to present a holistic deconstruction of Scotland's music, past and present, nor to offer a diachronic analysis of the music Scotland has given to itself and to the world, but rather to shine a light into some of the corners of her music-making to see what may emerge by way of an enhanced understanding of the nation which nurtured it. For my own part, these shinings are largely focused here on song, and in particular on those which deal with that most inhuman of human preoccupations, war.

So what is Scotland? That is a question which has been considered particularly acutely in recent years as we have been invited – several times now – to consider our constitutional future. First, it is a nation. Despite all the forensic examination that has taken place as to what Scotland is, what it is not, what it has been and might yet be, I have seen little or no denial of that fact. It is not a sovereign nation, it does not possess statehood, it is not a body that can confer citizenship, but it is a nation, nonetheless. But what does that mean? How crucial is that fact to our understanding of its character, its essence?

There have been many attempts to define and capture the key qualities of a nation, ranging from the fundamentalist ethnicity-centred assertion that nations are simply 'part of the natural order', developing into the 'perennialist' view that the identity of a nation is a given, and will therefore always remain constant (Smith, 1994, 18). Scholars who see nations in those terms often imbue them with qualities that go well beyond those of an organisational or political unit: Ernest Renan, for example, began a lecture at the Sorbonne in 1882 by claiming that 'A nation is a soul, a spiritual principle' (Renan, 1996, 52). Ernest Gellner's insistence that nations are purely products of modernity, on the other hand, rejects such notions and plays down the importance of a shared past (Gellner, 1983), emphasising instead the practical realities of a political present. To Benedict Anderson (1983), nations are 'imagined communities', constructions which rely on creating and maintaining a perception of commonality and belonging amongst its members within a unit which is quite simply too large to be an *actual* community in any meaningful sense. In one of my favourite recent invocations of this stance in relation to Scotland, the theatre critic, Joyce McMillan, quips that

> Nations are like Tinkerbell from Barrie's Peter Pan: they only exist as long as we believe in them. . . . In that sense nations are fictions, man-made communities conjured up and defined, on the shifting human surface of the earth, within the minds of men and women.
>
> (McMillan in Howard, 2016, 131)

McMillan, in fact, has spent her career helping us to understand Scotland *theatrically*. Theatre is not music, even although in recent decades in Scotland there has been an increasingly strong relationship between the two, yet the parallels are strong and we would do well to reflect on her analysis for our present task.

Having contemplated the issue ethnologically for over three decades now, my own conceptualisation of Scotland as nation also tends towards the modernist Andersonian school, but distilled down to a simple paradigm: a nation is a political and cultural entity comprising its people, their relationships and their creativity. 'People' I view in the civic rather than ethnic sense, denoting residency but also self-elected association or identification. 'Their relationships' I treat holistically, and as such this is a densely packed element of the formula, comprising their relationships with each other, with other peoples, with place and the environment, and with time. Their creativity I see largely as their responses to those relationships manifested in myriad ways; the roots, perhaps, of Renan's soul and Andersons's imaginings. Music belongs there.

Music, then, can help us to understand Scotland as it provides one point of entry to the consideration of the complex interplay which exists between each component of this model of nationhood. I shall not argue that music in Scotland is necessarily *about* Scotland, nor that creators and performers of music have been preoccupied with the idea of nationhood in their work. With some clear exceptions, I do not see much evidence of a conscious tendency amongst music makers to try to define, construct or speak for the nation. Indeed, it seems to me that they are more often concerned with the local and the global than with the national; more motivated by the immediate and the ultimate than with the layers in between. They are, however, acutely concerned with the kinds of relationships I place at the heart of my model, relationships which engage with the universal issues of family, love, work, place, conflict, humanity and inhumanity. In this chapter, I would like to begin to explore a few examples of this engagement through a reflexive consideration of a particular musical show with which I have been involved in recent years as both a piper and singer.

Far Far From Ypres is a narrated musical stage show written and directed by Ian McCalman, and featuring a cast of around thirty singers and instrumentalists. It has been performed widely across Scotland and in France as a contribution to the commemoration of the First World War, and draws on musical material which was performed during the war itself, as well as later songs composed retrospectively about the Scottish soldiers' experiences at the front. Featuring trench songs, marching songs, songs of the popular music hall tradition, and a selection of creative musical responses to the war composed by current and recent songmakers, the show follows the story of one fictitious young soldier who, as the narrator reminds us, was from any and every town and village in Scotland. On a personal level, performing in the show has been a sobering yet extremely inspiring experience. It has captured for me that personal concept of nationhood which I have outlined above, bringing into sharp focus many of the inter-relationships which lie at its heart. It has raised questions as to how we remember, how we forget, the process of personal and collective memorialisation, the ways we relate to and recreate the past, what that means to our present, and indeed how it might shape our future. Can it help us to *understand*, and to do so musically?

The show begins with the pipe march, 'The Battle of the Somme', composed shortly after the event by Pipe Major Willie Lawrie of the Argyll and Sutherland Highlanders. His tune and indeed his pipes made it back from the war, but sadly he did not. It has since become a standard part of any piper's repertoire, a beautifully crafted simple melodic line set in 9/8 time, and versatile enough to handle being played at march tempo, or in more contemplative mood as a lament. There is relatively little said about the bagpipe in this book, perhaps surprisingly, given its iconic yet contested status as a 'national instrument', but in many ways its inclusion in this show captures something of the essence of the complexities inherent in any consideration of the contribution this instrument can make to our understanding of Scotland as nation. As a lifelong piper and the performer of this tune myself within the show, I have been acutely aware of the tension that surrounds such an icon of Scottishness which is loved, hated, revered, dismissed, lauded and joked about in equal measure. It is the music of angels and the music of the devil, both metaphors being well ingrained in the iconography of piping as Hugh Cheape in particular has shown (2008, 30). Words of praise and dis-praise of the bagpipe pepper early Gaelic poetry and that duality has been our constant companion ever since. I have often wondered if it is partly because the whole essence of the bagpipe is to evoke mood, the melody notes against the omnipresent drone giving us both bitter and sweet, consonance and dissonance, triumph and despair.

I was reminded of the power of the instrument to evoke extremes of mood when we took the *Ypres* show to Bordeaux where within a period of twelve hours I was asked to get a party started with a set of good going reels, then invited the next morning to take part in a deeply moving ceremony in the small town of Martignas as part of its commemoration of the Great War. As well as some military pomp and ceremony, a dozen local schoolchildren each read out sections of letters written during that war by soldiers from France, Scotland, Senegal and Germany.

I was asked to play a lament and I have always found playing 'Flowers o the Forest' a deeply moving thing to do; and to do so in front of a French war memorial rather than a Scottish one somehow heightened that. It was an occasion in which nation did come very much into focus: playing the Highland bagpipe in an act of remembrance on foreign soil cannot but bring Scotland into the frame.

Given that they were still 'going over the top' unarmed while playing their comrades into battle, the Great War was very harsh on pipers, some 500 or so losing their lives, with another 600 wounded, and leaving the national instrument temporarily at a low ebb (West, 2012c, 659). Their contribution was lauded, however, by Field Marshal Sir Douglas Haig, here paying tribute to them in 1918:

> The Pipers of Scotland may well be proud of the part they have played in this war. In the heat of battle, by the lonely grave, and during the long hours of waiting, they have called to us to show ourselves worthy of the land to which we belong. Many have fallen in the fight for liberty, but their memories remain.
>
> (Seton and Grant, 1920, 4)

Considering the circumstances of its composing, as a tune 'The Battle of the Somme' might be considered to represent something of a musical oxymoron, given the fact that it commemorates one of the bloodiest campaigns in human history, claiming over one million casualties including over 57,000 British deaths on the first day alone. And yet it is a melodically uplifting piece, the 'scotch snap' in the opening phrase – the cut F sharp followed by the dotted high A – immediately invoking a lightness of mood, almost reminiscent of a strathspey, and very unusual within the retreat march genre. It is what pipers refer to as a 'D' tune, the tonic of the melody sitting on the 4th to the pitch of the drones, less common than 'A' tunes on the pipes, and one considered to evoke a happier frame of mind for

Figure 18.1 The Battle of the Somme (William Lawrie, author's setting)

player and listener alike. We can only speculate as to Willie Lawrie's motivation and inspiration, but the piper's role in battle was clear enough: 'to excite cheerfulness and alacrity in the soldier' (Murray, 1994, 1).

Indeed, while the Great War itself bequeathed us some excellent pipe tunes, very few were laments. Rather, it gifted us the march, that jaunty, cheery, gallus or stately genre: 6/8, 2/4, 4/4 for going forward, 3/4 and 9/8 for coming back again – the retreat air. As well as 'The Battle of the Somme' two more marches feature in the *Ypres* show, both composed by men who saw action on the Western Front, and both of which went on to play a key role in the later folk revival of the 1950s. 'Farewell to the Creeks' was composed by James Robertson of the Gordon Highlanders while a prisoner of war in Germany in 1915, scribbling it down on the back of a piece of yellow blotting paper that he still had forty years later. 'The Bloody Fields of Flanders' came from the pen of John MacLellan, a quiet, shy lad from Dunoon who had fought in the Boer War with the Highland Light Infantry and in the Great War as a piper alongside Willie Lawrie in the 8th Argyll and Sutherland Highlanders. In these tunes, we have two very different flavours of music from two very different war experiences. John MacLellan fought right through the conflict, and knew in intimate detail the horrors of the real bloody fields of Flanders. James Robertson, though, was captured soon after arriving in France, and as a prisoner of war could escape in his mind's ear to the Creeks of Portknockie, a favourite childhood hideaway on the Banffshire coast, and the inspiration for his tune.

In terms of my three keywords – people, relationships, creativity – James Robertson means a lot to me personally for he was the first mentor of my main piping teacher, Ian Duncan, and so I can trace my own piping pedigree directly back to that young man who was incarcerated on foreign soil in 1915. Indeed, these same threads connect to other musicians discussed in the present volume, for Ian Duncan was brother and early mentor to Gordon Duncan, who was in turn the key influence and guru for Ross Ainslie, an influential contributor to the fusion bands, Salsa Celtica and the Treacherous Orchestra (see Alexander and McAvoy, this volume). The timelines from the mud of Flanders to the sweat of the Barrowlands are short indeed. Understanding the lines of connection of which we are a part, respecting them, being inspired by them, but not being bound by them is a central philosophy in successful traditional music. Roots are not tethers, they do not bind us to the past, but they do connect us to it, and nurture our present.

Both of those tunes do have something very much in common, for they were each given a new pathway after the Second World War when they were borrowed by Hamish Henderson and used for two of his best known songs – 'The Highland Division's Farewell to Sicily' and 'Freedom Come All Ye'. There we have the communal recreation process at work, and it was beautifully captured on tape when Henderson visited James Robertson in 1953, by that time working as a janitor in Banff Academy, and Hamish first sang James the words he had put to 'Farewell to the Creeks'. To me it is a seminal moment of the meeting of two highly creative minds, a symbolic synthesis flowering out of the combined experiences of two world wars. I listen to that, and I understand just a little more (see West, 2012a, 111–113).

A fairly recent song by Jim Malcolm, sung in the *Ypres* show by Siobhan Miller, in my opinion sits comfortably alongside the best work of the celebrated soldier poets themselves: of Owen, Sassoon, Brooke, Graves, Rosenberg, Gurney, Thomas – and the Scottish voices: Charles Sorley, Roderick Watson Kerr, Violet Jacob, E.A. Mackintosh, John Buchan, W. D Cocker, Joseph Lee (see Goldie and Watson, 2014) – 'Jimmy's Gone Tae Flanders'. Both title and refrain, that is a straightforward, unembellished, stark fact; Jimmy has gone to Flanders. The speaker is his mother, perhaps talking to a neighbour, perhaps just to herself, or simply to the walls of her modest Perthshire cottage on the banks of the River Earn. Jimmy and his pals have volunteered with the local regiment, The Black Watch, and they have found themselves in the thick of action on the Western front. Jimmy's gone tae Flanders: the fear of that fact, the pain of that fact, is left unsaid, but it is there in the song, an unavoidable subtext simmering under the surface. But she has to stay *on* the surface, she cannot let herself imagine, cannot allow her mind to wander and wonder what he is doing, what his life in the trenches is like. And so she does what mothers do, and she talks like mothers talk. She complains that he's a messy brat, he's taken himself away to war but has left his fiddle lying about (and it was his late father's fiddle – has he no respect?). And look at his football boots, discarded and thick with mud. As for his fishing gear, it's lying twisted and tangled from the last time he and his mate were out on the river, and he and Willie should never have been out that night anyway, there was no moonlight, for goodness sake. How can you fish at night without moonlight? She cannot bring herself to contemplate his part in the war, but she can allow herself a cheering glimpse into the future, when Jimmy comes home to his fiddle and his mucky boots and to *good* fishing.

It is a love song which nods to that most unbendable, unshakable, unspeakable form of love: the love of a mother for her son. And here it is indeed left unspoken, the sentiment understated, its power dressed in the mundane concerns of daily life, and for me, a song that is all the more powerful for that:

Jimmy's gone tae Flanders, his fiddle lies upon his bed.
It was his faither's fiddle, though he's aye been shy tae practise it.
Jimmy's gone tae Flanders, his fishing gear's a tangle
Frae the nicht he and Willie fished the Earn though there was nae moon.

Jimmy's gone tae Flanders, he's spoilt the old dog rotten
Wi scraps below the table, though I tellt him time and time again.
Jimmy's gone tae Flanders, his fitba boots are sodden
For they've no been near dubbin since he bocht them new fae Sandy Broon.

When Jimmy's hame fae Flanders he'll be shamed tae clean they fitba boots
And sort oot a yon tangle, for the Earn I hear is fishin good.
When Jimmy's hame fae Flanders we'll be sat doon by the table
And we'll coax him tae his fiddle, 'Jimmy – gie's the Bonawe Highlanders'.

Jimmy's gone tae Flanders, though he has a job at Logie's yard
But a' the lads were joining – it'll all be o'er by Christmas time.

> Jimmy's gone tae Flanders, though he's no the strength his faither wis
> I'm sure he'll be worthy, and that Jocky would hae burst wi pride.
>
> Jimmy's gone tae Flanders, I ken he has a lassie
> Her faither saw them walking by themselves below the Falls of May.
> Jimmy's gone tae Flanders, he's as secret as his faither was
> But I saw her weepin as the sergeant marched them to the train.
>
> When Jimmy's hame fae Flanders he'll be shamed tae clean they fitba boots
> And sort oot a yon tangle, for the Earn I hear is fishin good.
> When Jimmy's hame fae Flanders we'll be sat doon by the table
> And we'll coax him tae his fiddle, 'Jimmy – gie's the Bonawe Highlanders.'
>
> (Malcolm, *Resonance*, 2000)

You will notice that Jim Malcolm has left us in full control of Jimmy's fate, which may well change with each performance. I am reminded here of the theory concerning the ability of traditional ballad singers to recreate the story on each telling, based on a framework of the plot, a firm knowledge and deep understanding of ballad structure and metre, and a lively imagination. Referred to as the oral formulaic theory, it was initiated by Milman Parry (1930), developed by Albert Lord (1960), taken to new levels by the late John Miles Foley (1985) and championed as far as Scotland was concerned by the folklorist, David Buchan (1972). In the case of this song, however, it is not the singer who can recreate the tale, for the text remains the same on each telling: rather it is we who must recreate the after-story on each *listening*. Does Jimmy come home, sit in by the table and play them the Bonawe Highlanders? Or are his boots left uncleaned, his gear tangled, his fiddle silent, his girl bereft and his mother broken? I have a boy just about the age Jimmy must have been, and he too leaves his boots uncleaned and his fiddle discarded on his bed. So for me, Jimmy has to have come home: I cannot contemplate it any other way. And in Jimmy's mother well, she is *my* mother, but no doubt many of us recognise her and claim her as our own. Her vernacular Perthshire tongue, the fishing of the Earn, the imagined playing of the pipe march, 'The Bonawe Highlanders', place this song's narrator firmly in the heart of Scotland. And yet she is surely also the universal mother, sharing that tragically timeless heartache of helplessness as her son goes to war. Performing this maternal sentiment goes well beyond national boundaries, but the melodic flavour and the dialect of delivery render this particular manifestation distinctly Scottish. She is local, national, global: in hearing, learning and singing her song, I have come to understand her world and ours just a little more deeply.

In Angus, just over the county march from Jimmy's mother lived another mother, a very real mother, whose boy, sadly, did not come home. This was a mother who also happened to be one of the most creative Scottish voices of the first half of the twentieth century: a mother called Violet Jacob. To listen to her poetry – some of it later set to music by Jim Reid – one might think of her as a kind of Chris Guthrie figure from Lewis Grassic Gibbon's *Sunset Song*, a lass of the fields, a living example of that confused duality of land and books, of soil and learning. In fact she belonged to a very different social class to Chris, born Violet

Augusta Mary Frederica Kennedy-Erskine, of Angus landed gentry and granddaughter of the illegitimate child of King William IV. Yet she is nonetheless in every sense a folk poet, and one who time and time again catches the essence of locality, of community, of people and their inter-relations, of the seasonal cycles of work and belief and celebration and time, and in the case of her war poems, of deep personal grief. Her poem, 'Halloween', set to music by Jim Reid and sung *a cappella* in *Far Far From Ypres* by Anne Murray, sketches out a bucolic autumn scene of post-harvest relief, the ploughmen relaxing after their day's work, while the young folk begin their ritual celebrations marking entry into the liminal space between two quarters of the year. The narrator this time is one of the ploughmen, quietly looking on at all the Halloween fun and frolics, but thinking of Lachlan, his friend, lying in his grave in France. The names may have changed, but this is certainly Violet herself speaking. Her only son, Harry, died in the final weeks of the Battle of the Somme, on 31 October 1916. As with her fictional counterpart created by Jim Malcolm, this real mother was giving voice to a very Scottish sense of loss. The emotion is powerful and universal, but we need these 'national' voices to provide its vehicle for our understanding to be that bit more acute. In 'Halloween', it is certainly that:

> The tattie-liftin's nearly through,
> They're plooin whaur the barley grew.
> And efter dark roond ilka stack
> You'll see the horsemen stand and crack –
> O Lachlan, but I mind on you.
>
> I mind fu aften we hae seen
> Ten thoosand stars keek doon atween
> The naked branches, and below
> Baith fairm and bothy hae their show
> Aglow wi lichts o Hallowe'en.
>
> There's bairns wi guisards at their tail
> Cloorin the doors wi runts o' kail.
> And fine you'll hear the screechs an skirls
> O lassies wi their drookit curls
> Bobbin for aipples i the pail.
>
> The bothy fire is loupin het,
> A new heid-horseman's kist is set.
> Richt's o'er the lamp whaur by the blaze
> The auld yin stood that kept yer claes.
> I cannae thole tae see it yet.
>
> But gin the auld folks' tales are richt
> An ghaists cam hame on Hallow nicht,
> Oh freend, oh freends, what would I gie
> Tae feel ye rax yer hand tae me
> Atween the dark an caun'l licht!

> Awa in France across the wave,
> The wee lichts burn on ilka grave.
> An you an me their lowes hae seen.
> Ye'll maybe hae yer Hallowe'en
> Yont, whaur you're lyin wi the lave.
>
> There's drink an daffin, sang an dance,
> An ploys an kisses get their chance,
> But Lachlan, man, the place I see
> Is whaur the auld kist used tae be,
> An the lichts o Hallowe'en in France.
>
> (As performed in *Far From Ypres*: see also Gordon, 2006, 252)

Violet Jacob belonged to that strident cultural movement which emerged in the wake of the Great War which we tend to label the Scottish Literary Renaissance. It was a time of deep intellectual fervour, of fresh thinking and of outright rejection of what many considered to be the shameful legacy of mediocrity inherited from nineteenth century romanticism gone wild. Leading from the front was Christopher Murray Grieve, who was later to recast himself as Scotland's greatest modernist poet, Hugh MacDiarmid. Grieve's collection of essays published as *Contemporary Scottish Studies* in 1925 was a clarion call for something much better. Almost comical in its intensity of polemics, very few of the period's leading cultural figures escaped his vitriolic pen. A few examples will make the point:

> There are quite a large number of solemn 'well-read' Scots even today . . . who swear by Neil Munro and regard him as a great writer. There is no need to be hard on them for this misconception: . . . Neil Munro is not a great writer, he is not even a good writer.
>
> (Grieve, 1925, 29)

> There are a large number of people in Scotland, and Scots abroad . . . who regard Charles Murray as a great poet as, indeed, the greatest contemporary Scottish poet and one of the very few of his successors who have inherited aught of the 'magic of Burns'. I am not one of them. On the contrary, I say that Charles Murray has not only never written a line of poetry in his life, but that he is constitutionally incapable of doing so.
>
> (Grieve, 1925, 35)

Musicians fared little better:

> The position of Scottish literature compared with that of any other European country is deplorable enough: but that of Scottish music is infinitely worse. In music, as in drama, we have failed to develop any worth considering at all.
>
> (Grieve, 1925, 120)

Violet Jacob, however, emerges from Grieve's critical gaze relatively unscathed, although his conclusion that her work was 'conservative rather than creative' is hardly a ringing endorsement (Grieve, 1925, 40). Perhaps Grieve saw her as being just too close for comfort to the style of the Kailyard writers he loathed, although he was careful to point out that she rose well above them in quality and achievement. As McKerrell has argued (2016, 104–105), Grieve himself maintained a life-long obsession with his own childhood home of Langholm in the Scottish Borders, converting the agency of the rural place into his radical nationalism later in life: perhaps he saw something of himself in the Angus poet.

Nonetheless, as a 'folk poet' Jacob was much closer in outlook and spirit to another of the intellectual giants of the period in Scotland than she was to Grieve. Given my emphasis in this chapter on 'folk music', I shall take a detour at this point into the world of the man who had so much to say to us about 'the folk', Patrick Geddes. Geddes had a very interesting take on the folk – it was he, for instance, who picked up and adapted Frederic Le Play's ideas and moulded them to his own experience in Scotland. Le Play was a French polymath and protagonist of several of the Great Exhibitions of the second half of the nineteenth century, and he was fascinated by the interactions of the constituent parts of society, insisting that a true understanding of how it all works requires the close study of the basic components: of the parts rather than the whole. And the parts he held in highest regard were place, work, family, a triumvirate which was later to be re-framed in Edinburgh by Geddes who preferred to think in terms of place, work, *folk*. Folk rather than family, then – a widening out, perhaps? A recognition that there had to be a bridge between the parts and the whole and that it was the people, the folk, which provided it. But which folk? Who are the folk? Why folk, particularly, and not just the rather more neutral 'people'?

The answer for Geddes lay partly in one issue which fascinated him which was the nature of relationships *between* people. He had been a student of Thomas Henry Huxley, a biologist of great note and one of the key disciples of Charles Darwin, but who took his mentor's point about the competition of species to extremes that Darwin himself had not done, Huxley believing that the survival of the fittest was the central rule of any species' success. Geddes preferred the ideas of another line of Darwinian thought, which asserted that cooperation was just as important as competition. One of the key thinkers on that side was the Russian anarchist, Peter Kropotkin, who wrote a very influential book called *Mutual Aid* in which he attempted to prove the point that cooperation was crucial to the development and success of *anything*, and cited all manner of examples which ranged from reciprocity amongst crustaceans to the continued existence of the Royal National Life Boat Institution (Kropotkin, 1908). Kropotkin travelled to Edinburgh in 1886 to visit Geddes and several other like-minded people – or like-minded folk perhaps (although there is no evidence that she met him, Marjory Kennedy Fraser, whose contribution to the celebration of Scottish music was significant though highly contested, was part of Geddes' Edinburgh social circle too at the time). Lying at the heart of Geddes's conceptualisation of folk, then, was the desire and need for mutual understanding, for working with, rather than working against. The folk, for Geddes, were people who cooperate. Place, work and folk lie at the heart of Violet Jacob's poetry, given a second life much later in the century as song in the hands of Jim Reid.

Both Jim Malcolm and Violet Jacob approach their song-poem commentaries on war through subtle, understated language, immersing their lyrics in the mundane realities of daily household and community life. Dick Gaughan, on the other hand, tends to take a more direct route in his creative responses to war, as indeed he does with his creative responses to all things. 'Childhood's End' which features in the *Ypres* show, is Gaughan's utopian imagining of a future in which the last soldier has been buried, putting an end to humanity's immature squabblings, and marking the beginning of a world without war. The soldier – a 'lingering relic of the older way' – is laid to rest with no pomp and ceremony, no crashing rifles, no roaring drums, no bagpipe lament. It is instead a moment of quiet reflection, of prayer (for those who had something to pray to), of the joining of hands. It is a moment of mass apology from the living to the dead, a final reckoning for man's inhumanity to man, 'for we know now where the blame lay'. But where does it lie? Is it the politicians who deserve our disdain? Or incompetent generals? Or do we all have to reflect on our own silence and inaction in the face of conflict? The song is indeed a musical question mark, a command to self-interrogation at every level. It may feature in a show 'about Scotland' but the answers must surely come from humanity at large.

As the narrator of *Ypres* reminds us from the start, the First World War was very much a marching war, and so there is a subtle but regular pulse to the show. It is the same pulse that was literally drummed into the recruits from the first days of their training, and which was their constant companion as they marched between the various theatres of war on the Western front. By the dawn of the twentieth century, standard British army marching pace had settled at 120 steps per minute, and to evoke the constancy of that rhythmic mantra, *Ypres* is liberally sprinkled with marching songs throughout. 'The Last Long Mile', 'It's a Long Way to Tipperary', 'Mademoiselle from Armentieres', 'Keep Your Head Down Fritzy Boy', 'Whiter than the Whitewash on the Wall' and 'Goodbyee' provide light relief from the heavy emotional challenges of the songs discussed above, yet their inclusion also speaks to an important subtext of Scottish cultural debate in particular. They are songs of the music hall, that much maligned yet wildly popular genre which served as the bête noire of the dominant Scottish cultural commentators of the entire twentieth century. For the likes of Hugh MacDiarmid in the 1920s, Hamish Henderson in the 1950s and Tom Nairn in the 1970s, this Scottish contribution to UK-wide popular mass entertainment was an embarrassing joke, a nauseating parody of cultural self-loathing, the epitome of the Scottish cringe (West, 2012a, 160–162). The most reviled exponent was also the most famous, Sir Harry Lauder's kilted kitsch jocularity keeping MacDiarmid's vitriolic pen busy for years (Goldie, 2006), and serving as the prime whipping boy of the folk revivalists ever since.

The inclusion at the climax of the *Ypres* show of Lauder's most famous marching song, 'Keep Right on to the End of the Road' may therefore seem like something of an odd choice for writer and director Ian McCalman, who has spent his career championing the spirit of radical folksong. What it does in fact do is offer one final challenge to performers and audience alike to pause and think, to perhaps revisit our assumptions, for the script explains the circumstances of its composing. The song was Harry Lauder's response to the fact that like Violet Jacob, his boy did not come home. It is a stiff upper lip response, religiously resolute (for 'all you've loved and are dreaming of/will be there, at the end of the road'), and very different to the quiet mourning of 'Halloween'. Yet his pain was intense and it was real:

> 'Captain John Lauder killed in action, December 28. Official War Office'. That was all it said. I knew nothing of how my boy had died, or where – save that it was for his country. The black despair that had been hovering over me for hours closed down now and enveloped all my sense. Everything was unreal. For a time I was quite numb. But then, as I began to realise, and to visualize what it was to mean in my life that my boy was dead, there came great pain. The iron of realisation slowly seared every word of that curt telegram upon my heart. I said it to myself over and over again. And as I whispered to myself as my thoughts took form, over and over, the one terrible word: Dead!
> (Lauder, 1918, 70–71, adapted by McCalman, 2008)

These brief reflections on *Far Far From Ypres* represent a personal glimpse at Scotland through a little of her music and song as I have experienced it directly as performer and audience of one particular show (I had witnessed it from the stalls before later being invited to join the cast). As an autoethnographic contribution, it is of course limited in scope and narrow in focus, yet it does represent my views on some of the ways in which we might try to understand Scotland musically.

'The nation' may not necessarily be at the centre of musical conceptions or preoccupations – indeed, as I argue above, it very often is not. But it does seem to me that 'Scotland' has for long served as a form of relational agency for the construction of traditional music and song, and that this agency relies upon the deeply local and place-bound concepts of family, love, work and landscape for its inspiration and impetus. These lie at the heart of the relationships which I consider to be the essence of a nation, and remain as pertinent today as at any period considered within this volume. Clearly, there is a tendency when representing these relationships in music and song to lean towards the rural and indeed the nostalgic, even although (or perhaps because) the engine room of both the mid-twentieth century folk revival and the late twentieth century Scottish Musical Renaissance has been largely urban in setting. But the agency of the Scottish landscape remains foundational and is mobilised by many musicians and composers to construct their views of the world, be that in times of war or peace.

I still do not pretend to understand Scotland. Yet I do firmly believe that we can edge closer to some kind of reasoned understanding by listening intently to its music.

19 Afterword

Simon Frith

1

The first time I had to think seriously about what it meant to understand Scotland musically was in 2009, the year of Homecoming Scotland. The culminating event of that year of events was Homecoming Live, a weekend series of concerts in Glasgow. The promoter of this mini-festival, DF Concerts, commissioned me to write an essay on Scottish music for the programme. The concerts didn't develop as originally planned, in terms of either line-ups or ticket sales, and as far as I know my piece was never published (I certainly never saw a programme), but I was paid well anyway and liked the challenge of describing concisely the Scottishness of Scottish music in a pop context (there were no traditional or folk musicians booked for these events). Here are some extracts of what I then wrote.

****

In the autumn of 2003 the *Scotsman* published the results of a readers' poll designed to produce a people's list of the 100 best Scottish albums. The top two places were occupied by Primal Scream's 1989 *Screamadelica* and the Proclaimers' 1987 *This Is the Story*. The Proclaimers are obviously a Scottish band, perhaps nowadays the best loved music makers in the land. Their ballads of dashed dreams are ideal for tearful, tipsy sing-a-longs. Their accent, exaggerated by close sibling harmonies, is so obviously Scottish that an early reviewer in a London newspaper thought they sang in Gaelic. Their account of the historical Scottish experience – the longing to get away, the longing to return – is at once angry, rueful and engaging. Their look, the big specs and gawky charm gives them the air of a music hall or variety act. One could imagine them treading the boards of Scottish theatres a hundred years ago. All this is brilliantly captured in the Proclaimers musical, *Sunshine on Leith*, which looks set to become a ritual Scottish theatre event, a new kind of pantomime.[1]

Screamadelica is another sort of record entirely. Its Scottishness is much less obvious and works in quite a different way. The record won the first ever Mercury Music Prize and at the time I didn't think of it as a Scottish record at all. It was an album that gave triumphant musical shape to a new alliance of indie rock and dance culture, that redefined psychedelia, and only in retrospect did I realise how

Scottish Bobby Gillespie's sources and intentions were. This is Scottish music made under the influence of black America, over-amplified guitars, the Rolling Stones, sonic impatience, substances and a defiance of boundaries, not least the boundaries of Scottishness. It's as if Bobby Gillespie (and Alan McGee, by whose Creation label the record was released) had taken the trips that the Proclaimers just sang about. Primal Scream (and McGee), after all, became successful only when they left Scotland. And this is a recurring theme in the history of Scottish music too.

Ask a visitor to Scotland to describe Scottish (as against other forms of British or European) music and they are likely to come up with a number of characteristics, the invented tradition of the last 200 years or so: the ballad; specific instruments (bagpipes, fiddle, accordion); a distinctive rhythmic feel (the Scottish snap); a special kind of social dance (the *ceilidh*). These are the musical elements of tartanry mass mediated to foreigners, tourists and the Scots themselves, starting with Burns's ballads and Haydn's and Beethoven's orchestrations of Scots tunes, evolving through the music hall (Harry Lauder), dance hall (Jimmy Shand) and concert hall (Kenneth McKellar), through postwar TV programmes like *The Hootenanny Show* and the *White Heather Club* (with Andy Stewart and Moira Anderson) to today's transatlantic popularity of pipe band versions of 'Amazing Grace' and the obligatory *ceilidhs* for international conference delegates.

Ask a musician to define Scottish music and they're more likely to scratch their heads and wonder if it's possible to describe any musical style or approach that Scottish musicians might have in common or that might distinguish them from non-Scottish music makers. To musicians some things seem self-evident. Scottish music travels and changes on its travels. The Scottish ballad found its way to the southern states of the USA and fed into old time music, country and western, bluegrass; Scottish folk songs and singers went to England and Ireland and fed into what became English and Irish folk music. Music and musicians from elsewhere came into Scotland and fed into Scottish music making, not just in person but also through the airwaves, in the cinema, on record. The influence of the sounds of the USA (jazz, folk, rock) on Scottish music has been just as significant as the contribution of Scottish balladry to American musical traditions. In the end, for all musicians, 'Scottishness' is just one thing among many that make up a musical identity.

And ask me about Scottish music – an English sociologist who's lived in Scotland for over twenty years – and I'd say that what makes Scottish music culture distinctive is the remarkable importance here of playing and listening and dancing to music *live*. Analyse music in straight market terms and Scotland is obviously too small to sustain a record industry and has too marginal a media sector to provide career opportunities for musicians in film or television or advertising. But music – live music – is at the heart of everyday culture and hence the great Scottish musical contradiction: a full-time career of music making in Scotland is both vital and impossible. On the one hand, then, Scottish musicians are of necessity always on the move, out of Scotland and back again, on tour or in residence in North America and Europe and further afield; this has an immensely enriching effect on their music. On the other hand, in Scotland itself, the distinction between professional and amateur music makers is often blurred. People move in and out of full time music making, at different times of the year, at different stages of their careers; in many musical genres performance means amateurs and professionals working together. This has had a number of effects: players' restless movements from band to band; the importance of local scenes; the lack of clear distinctions between different musical genres; the constant reappearance of unexpected stylistic traces.

In the 1960s a new generation of Scottish acoustic musicians, Bert Jansch, John Martyn, the Incredible String Band, and others, learnt their craft in new kinds of pub based folk clubs in Edinburgh and Glasgow. These musicians had absorbed the Scottish folk music revived in the 1950s but unlike the singers who were now getting TV slots, these performers were developing their own material and performing styles. Their repertoire (following the example of Archie Fisher and Hamish Imlach) was as likely to include North American as Scottish songs – blues, the new urban folk – as well as, soon, their own contemporary songs. Their guitar playing (following the example of Davey Graham) had an experimental, modal virtuosity with influences from the hippy trail. They attracted a new kind of bohemian audience and when they left Scotland for London they were to have a major formative influence on British rock.

The legacy of these 1960s musicians fifty years on is apparent: a respect for traditional music was combined with a need to experiment; musicianship meant serving a craft apprenticeship and adopting new technology. To be a singer was to be a singer-songwriter; personality mattered but so did a clear-eyed and often polemical sense of what was going on culturally and politically. Above all these musicians refused to fit into market or commercially defined genres or always to give their audiences what they thought they wanted.

If Bert Jansch took one route from local live circuit to mythical status in British musical history, Alex Harvey took another. I doubt if there's another musician anywhere who has embodied so enthusiastically in one career the history of classic rock from its origins in the 1950s to its demise (with punk) at the end of the 1970s. Harvey led bands that successively played trad jazz, rock'n'roll, R&B, soul and rock. What was consistent was Harvey's commitment to giving live audiences a *spectacularly* good time, leaving them exhausted. He had a long musical career (he was in his late forties when he died in 1982) without ever making it really big. He'd played the German beat scene in the early 1960s, the UK rock touring circuit in the late 1970s, but his music remained rooted in the Scottish working class weekend, in local dance halls and clubs, and the affinity his music always suggested between a Scottish and a black American musical sensibility is another recurring theme in Scotland's musical history.[2]

Since the development of the mass musical media – publishing, records, radio, cinema – people have had two musical histories, a live musical history that is by its nature local, the experience of homes and clubs and concerts and pubs and dancehalls, and a mediated musical history that knows no geographical borders. Scottish musicians like everyone else may hear and be inspired by music from anywhere but they necessarily start out as music makers in Scotland itself. And it's this double sense of music – a fantasy community of players and listeners in the ether, the real community of players and listeners in this place now – that has driven Scottish music history. However far the musicians travel – in their heads, in their sounds, in their careers – there's something hardwired into what they do, something they'll always come home to: the buzz and rush and discovery of a Scottish Saturday night.

****

2

The second time I had to think seriously about what it meant to understand Scotland musically was in 2014, at the conference that was the source of this book. Listening to the papers then, reading them now, I had contradictory feelings. On the one hand, I was an outsider, a popular music scholar among traditional music scholars who rarely referenced either popular musicians or popular music studies; on the other hand, much of what was said about Scotland musically didn't seem to be so very different from what I'd argued in that Homecoming programme essay. This is to raise two issues that I want to discuss here, one concerning methodology, one concerning language, both reflecting the shift in the scholarly approach to Scottish traditional music that was described recurrently at the conference: the shift from defining traditional music as an object to defining it as a process, a methodological shift, that is, from musicology and textual analysis to ethnography and historical analysis. Or, from my perspective, from studying music to studying music making.

To understand why musicians make the music they make we have to understand the historical, cultural and technological conditions in which they live and work. All the chapters in this book make this point one way or another and all of them share, more or less explicitly, the following assumptions. Music making is a *social* activity: it is made for and with other people – in the family, as friends, in local and more extended communities, above all with other musicians; M. J. Grant's term, 'singsong', is a wonderfully simple description of what is actually a complex cultural process. Music making is a *learned* activity, learned formally and informally, orally and through study, by imitation and technical practice. It involves accredited teachers in schools, workshops, conservatories and the *feis* movement; it involves mentors, models, recordings and manuals, parents, siblings and neighbours and, of course, again, other musicians. Music making is a *functional* activity, music is made for a variety of purposes and audiences. And it is an *ideological* activity, music is made with a particular (if ever changing) set of beliefs about how music should sound, what works, what doesn't, and why.

In this book these points are made about traditional musicians working in different historical and cultural contexts; my point is that they can be made about all musicians and that certain things follow from this, of which the most important is that music makers have to be understood by reference not just to the sounds they make but also by reference to the socio-musical worlds in which these sounds are legitimated, are heard as music. And such worlds include not just the music makers themselves but other cultural actors too, and the institutions that they sustain – teachers, instrument makers, publishers and promoters, employers and audiences, dancers, listeners, fans and scholars.

What is also clear from this book is that the boundaries between different music worlds are always porous. The histories of all music worlds are overlapping and complex. Like electrical circuits, musical networks may sparkle and illuminate or fizzle and die as a result of unexpected connections.[3] Either way, in dealing with the changing circumstances in which they work, musicians have to be pragmatic, experimental and opportunistic; this is the nature of what they do. To put this another way, musicians have to develop strategies for dealing with the resources that are (or that become) available: their own skills, repertoires, and training; the changing technologies of musical instruments, recording, amplification and means of communication; spatial constraints and possibilities – dance floors, living rooms, halls and pubs, fields and festivals; institutional offers and demands, from conservatories and preservation societies, from publishers, broadcasters and record companies, from socio-political events like competitions, rallies and jubilees; and, not least, the resources of history. Traditional musicians have a distinctive concern for historical resources to which I will return. First, a comment on language.

To focus traditional music studies on process means to rethink the terms by which the music has been defined and differentiated from other sorts of music. Take, for example, the concept of 'authenticity', which in Scotland, as Simon McKerrell explains:

> has been collapsing in the last decade or more into the sonic aspects of performance, and is far less contingent today on the provenance or 'oldness' of a source. Indeed my own research in this area . . . suggests that that oral transmission and the internal musical structures of musical material are more important today than any fixed notions of oldness, ethnicity, place, nationalism or race, which have traditionally been the key concepts in any discussion of authenticity in traditional (or folk) music.
>
> (McKerrell, forthcoming)

Josh Dickson points out the implications of this for the traditional music degree at the Royal Conservatory of Scotland. Since the programme started there has been a subtle change in students' own account of the authenticity of their practice, from 'the musician whose outlook, musical identity, style and repertoire are rooted in the notion of place and provenance (specifically their own)' to 'the musician who approaches folk and traditional music as a vehicle for their personal, eclectic and contemporary aspirations for professional performance' (see Dickson, this volume). Authenticity now means individual integrity, displayed in a performing practice that must be somehow original and creative. This is still expressive of Romantic ideology but by reference not to the 'the folk' but to the individual artist.

In my book, *Performing Rites* (Frith, 1996), I suggested that the three dominant ways of thinking about musical value – in terms of art, folk or entertainment – were not homologous to different sorts of music (classical, folk and pop) but were, rather, ideological terms deployed in all musical worlds, if in different ways, to address the shared problems of making music in the historical context of the rise and development of industrial capitalism. All music makers since the late eighteenth century, to put this another way, have made music in settings of changing class relations, new technologies, mass mediation, industrialisation and globalisation, and so forth (digitisation is a new stage in this process but not, in itself, revolutionary). This is the reason, for example, why 'authenticity' and 'commerce' are issues in all music worlds and why the suggestion (of which there are still traces in this book) that, say, rock music is always made for 'purely' commercial reasons is no more sensible than the suggestion that traditional music is always made for 'purely' folk reasons (whatever they might be) and as problematic as the assumption that we can clearly distinguish between active musical participation and passive musical consumption. Folk discourse was as essential as art college ideology to the way rock distinguished itself from 'pop' (itself an ideological term – 'mainstream' seems to be the equivalent in this collection) just as recording and publishing technology and commerce were always imbricated with the processes of song collecting and the construction of traditional music archives (see Frith, 1981; Western, 2015).

Equally, the past is the context for learning in all music worlds, as can be seen in the general importance of teachers, their credibility resting on provenance as well as skill, and in the common processes of canon formation and shared use of the term 'classic' (there are, for example, 'classic' avant-garde works as well as 'classic' pop songs). In all music worlds the past is continuously being rethought in line with present concerns (as in the effect of feminism on our understanding of the history of all sorts of Scottish music), and from my sociological perspective it is not immediately apparent why to understand Scotland musically is necessarily to do so through the lens of arguments in traditional music studies. The creation of the future out of the past is an aspect of all music making.

3

On reflection, though, I realise that the claim here is not that traditional musicians are concerned with history and that other musicians are not, but that traditional music is made with a particular kind of historical ideology. This is perhaps more obvious immediately in traditional music scholarship than in the music itself. The writers in this book are thus transparent about their interest in issues of nationalism, preservation and sustainability, issues with policy as well as analytical effects. My first response to the conference title, 'Understanding Scotland Musically', was to wonder why we would want to do this and how we would know when we'd done it! The answer turned out to be practical rather than theoretical: 'Scotland' is, in this context, a political construction. And so, to put it over simply, the underlying assumption in this book is that traditional and folk musicians in

Scotland (unlike pop, rock, jazz or classical musicians) look to musical history as a particular *way* of understanding Scotland musically.

This lies behind Gary West's and Simon McKerrell's contention (of which I was initially sceptical) that it is

> because of the authenticity lent to it by the process of oral development and historical transmission that the 'traditional music' of Scotland lies at the core of almost all claims to 'Scottishness' or nationalist constructions of Scotland across musical genres. We contend that the process of re-imagining and mythologizing Scotland is, and has been, always overwhelmingly constructed via the traditional music of Scotland. Such that when the notion of 'Scottishness' or a 'Scottish' voice has been explored within classical, or popular traditions, it almost always relies at source upon the orally developed and transmitted traditional music for the sonic signification of Scotland.
>
> (see McKerrell and West, this volume)

'Tradition', in other words, is a way of dealing with history (just as autobiography is a way of dealing with memory) in which a narrative is constructed by reference to cultural indicators ('the process of oral development and historical transmission') which are primarily symbolic, indicating processes that are valued, imagined and invented as ideals rather than as empirically documented practices. This is why the change of scholarly attention from musical text to musical process can retain, nevertheless, a clear sense of tradition. For Josh Dickson's students authenticity may now be defined by personal integrity rather than being rooted in place and provenance but an understanding of the latter (indicated in how the music is made) is how such integrity is realised and understood.

This is a persuasive argument but rests, as I've suggested, on a particular account of Scottishness and a particular approach to musical politics. There are other ways of thinking about Scotland musically, involving different aesthetics and alternative ways of reading Scottish experience historically. In my 2009 essay I was thus thinking more about how music expressed what Scotland felt like than about what it meant. To experience music is not necessarily to interpret it.

I draw two conclusions from this. First, this book is essential reading for popular as well as traditional music scholars. It offers a new perspective on issues that have long concerned us and shows clearly the importance of comparative musical studies. The focus here on musical processes, on music making, is particularly helpful for comparative analysis. I'm not advocating relativism here or suggesting that all musical practices are of equal value. The point of comparison is, rather, as a way of better understanding the differences between musical ideologies. After all, one of the things shared by all music makers (and listeners) is the ongoing work of defining what they do as different from what other musicians do; in all socio-musical worlds it is constantly necessary to point out that other music is not 'really' jazz or folk or grime or metal or, in the case of this book, Scottish. In all music worlds, it seems, it is necessary to draw as well as to challenge boundaries, to position musical sounds in dialogue with each other within an ideological soundscape (see Slobin, 1987).

This brings me to my final point: music making is an argumentative affair. I mean by this both that musicians (and audiences) argue a lot and that to make music – and to write about it – is, among other things, to make an argument. This is obvious enough in these pages: all the authors here are arguing *about* Scottish music and all of them are arguing *against* other people's positions. This is what it means to be engaged in music. One of my goals in *Performing Rites* was to show that arguing about good and bad music is essential to music as a social activity; a good topic for sociological study is thus how musicians *fall out*. What is meant in everyday practice by 'musical differences' or the assertion that one's fellow players are 'moving in the wrong musical direction'?

Understanding Scotland musically means showing how musical arguments articulate alternative accounts of what Scotland means. While I was writing this, the film, *Where You Are Meant To Be*, went on general release. This is a documentary (made by Paul Fegan) about Aidan Moffat's 2014 tour of Scotland performing 'reinvented' Scottish folk songs. Before the tour starts, Moffat (from the band Arab Strap) meets Sheila Stewart, some of whose songs he sings. As the film's publicity puts it, 'Moffat believes Scotland's oldest songs are ripe for re-working against a contemporary urban back drop. Stewart does not.' Their differences – about traditional music, about popular music, about Scotland, what it was, is and should be, are what this book is about too.

Notes

1 I note, for example, that it is programmed for the duration of the 2016 Edinburgh Fringe Festival.
2 An even longer history than I then realised. These are the opening words of Vic Gammon's sleeve notes to the CD, *Early Scottish Ragtime*: 'Since the eighteenth century, tunes which originated in North America, and many of which are probably African-American in origin, have appeared in British tune books. Many of these tunes were published in Scotland' (Gammon, 2016).
3 An interesting term from this perspective is 'fusion', used mostly positively in this book, but an anathema to jazz buffs. See, for example, Washburne (2004).

References

Adams, D. 1999. How to Stop Worrying and Learn to Love the Internet. *The Sunday Times*, 28 August 1999. www.douglasadams.com/dna/19990901-00-a.html [Accessed 11 November 2015].

Advertiser. 1850. [Author unknown], Broughty Ferry. *Dundee, Perth, and Cupar Advertiser*, 25 June 1850, 3.

Ahlander, P. 2008. *Marjory Kennedy-Fraser (1857–1930) and Her Time: A Contextual Study*. Unpublished PhD Thesis, University of Edinburgh.

Aikin, J. 1772. *Essays on Song-Writing: With a Collection of Such English Songs as Are Most Eminent for Poetical Merit*. London: R. H. Evans.

Alburger, M. 1983. *Scottish Fiddlers and Their Music*. London: V. Gollancz.

Alburger, M. 2003. *Thistle, Rose and Fleur-de-Lys: Musical Connections between Scotland, England and France*, [conference presentation], University of Aberdeen, 15–16 November 2003.

Alexander, V. D. 2007. State Support of Artists: The Case of the United Kingdom in a New Labour Environment and Beyond. *The Journal of Arts Management, Law, and Society*, 37, 185–200. https://doi.org/10.3200/JAML.37.3.185-200

Amin, A., and Thrift, N.. 2002. *Cities: Reimagining the Urban*. Cambridge: Polity Press.

Anderson, B. 2006 [1983]. *Imagined Communities*. New York and London: Verso.

Anderson, P. 2002. *Traditional Scottish Fiddling*. Skye: Taigh na Teud TNTCD009.

Anonymous. 2013. *Music Sector Review: Final Report for Creative Scotland*. Glasgow: EKOS Consultants.

Anonymous. 2014. Scottish Independence: Yes Protest at BBC "bias". *The Scotsman*, 14 September 2014, online edition. http://www.scotsman.com/news/politics/top-stories/scottish-independence-yes-protest-at-bbc-bias-1-3541445.

Appadurai, A. 1991. Afterword. In A. Appadurai, F. J. Korom and M. A. Mills (eds.), *Gender, Genre, and Power in South Asian Expressive Traditions*. Philadelphia: University of Pennsylvania Press, pp. 465–476.

Appadurai, A. 1996. *Modernity at Large: Cultural Dimensions of Globalization*. Minneapolis: University of Minnesota Press.

Atkins, G. H. 2010. *German Literature Through Nazi Eyes* (RLE Responding to Fascism). Hoboken: Taylor & Francis.

Atkinson, D. 2014. *The Anglo-Scottish Ballad and its Imaginary Contexts*. Cambridge: Open Book.

Bakhtin, M. 1968. *Rabelais and His World*, trans. Hélène Iswolsky. Cambridge, MA: MIT Press.

Bakhtin, M. 1981 [1934]. Discourse in the Novel. In C. Emerson and M. Holquist (trans. and eds), *The Dialogic Imagination: Four Essays*. Austin: University of Texas.

Ballantyne, P. H. 2003. Fashionable Dancing – the Dance Manuals of James Scott Skinner. *Northern Scotland*, 23 (First Series), 107–116. http://doi.org/10.3366/nor.2003.0006

Ballantyne, P. H. 2016. *Regulation and Reaction: The Development of Scottish Traditional Dance With Particular Reference to Aberdeenshire, From 1805 to the Present Day*. Unpublished doctoral thesis, University of Aberdeen.

Balloch, E. F. 1939. But They Make The World Scottish – Conscious. *Aberdeen Weekly Journal*, 29 June, 2a, b.

Banet-Weiser, S. 2012. *AuthenticTM: The Politics of Ambivalence in a Brand Culture*. New York: New York University Press.

Baptie, D. 1894. *Musical Scotland, Past and Present*. Paisley: Parlane.

Bastin, B. 1986. *Red River Blues: The Blues Tradition in the Southeast*. Urbana: University of Illinois Press.

Battlefield Band. 1988. *Forward With Scotland's Past: A Collection of Their Songs and Music*. Shillinghill, Midlothian: Kinmor Music.

Beattie, J. 1996. *Essays on Poetry and Music*, ed. R. J. Robinson. London: Routledge.

Beech, J., Hand, O., MacDonald, F., Mulhern, M. A., and Jeremy, W. (eds). 2007. *Scottish Life and Society: A Compendium of Scottish Ethnology, Vol. 10: Oral Literature and Performance Culture*. Edinburgh: John Donald.

Bella Caledonia. 2007. *Bella Caledonia: It's Time to Get Above Ourselves*. [Online] http://bellacaledonia.org.uk/ [Accessed 31 March 2017].

Bella Caledonia. 2014. *Songs for Scotland at Oran Mor*. [Online] http://bellacaledonia.org.uk/2014/09/04/songs-for-scotland-a-night-at-oran-mor/ [Accessed 31 March 2017].

Bella Caledonia. 2015. *Songs for Scotland*. [Online] http://bellacaledonia.org.uk/2015/07/24/songs-for-scotland-4 [Accessed 30 March 2017].

Bennett, M. 1998. Traditions of the Taigh Ceilidh. In *Oatmeal and the Catechism: Scottish Gaelic Settlers in Quebec*. Eastern Townships, Quebec: J. Donald Publishers.

Biddle, I. D., and Knights, V. 2007. *Music, National Identity and the Politics of Location: Between the Global and the Local*. Ashgate Popular and Folk Music Series. Aldershot: Ashgate.

Bishop, C. 2004. Antagonism and Relational Aesthetics. *October*, 110, 51–79.

Bishop Percy's Folio Manuscript, British Library Additional MS. 27,879, "A Fragment of the Ballad of the Child of Ell", l.15–22.

Bissell, L. & Overend, D. 2015. Early Days: Reflections on the Performance of a Referendum, Contemporary Theatre Review, 25(2), 242–250.

Blacking, J. 1977. Some Problems of Theory and Method in the Study of Musical Change. *Yearbook of the International Folk Music Council*, 9, 1–26.

Blacking, J. 1986. Identifying Processes of Musical Change. *World of Music*, 28, 3–15.

Blake, A. 1997. *The Land Without Music: Music, Culture and Society in Twentieth-Century Britain*. Manchester: Manchester University Press.

Blaustein, R. 1993. Rethinking Folk Revivalism: Grass-Roots Preservationism and Folk Romaticism. In N. V. Rosenberg (ed.), *Transforming Tradition: Folk Music Revivals Examined*. Urbana: University of Illinois, pp. 258–274.

Blaustein, R. 2006. Folk Music Revivals in Comparative Perspective. In I. Russell and M. A. Alburger (eds), *Play It Like It Is: Fiddle and Dance Studies From Around the North Atlantic*. Aberdeen: University of Aberdeen, pp. 50–60.

Blaustein, R. 2014. Grassroots Revitalization of North American and Western European Instrumental Music Traditions From Fiddlers Associations to Cyberspace. In J. Hill and

C. Bithell (eds), *The Oxford Handbook of Music Revival*. London: Oxford University Press, pp. 551–569.

Bohlman, P. 1988. *The Study of Folk Music in the Modern World*. Bloomington: Indiana University Press.

Bohlman, P. 2002. *Focus: Music, Nationalism and the Making of New Europe*. New York: Routledge.

Bohlman, P. 2004. *The Music of European Nationalism: Cultural Identity and Modern History*. Santa Barbara, CA: ABC-CLIO.

Bohlman, P. 2011. *Music, Nationalism and the Making of the New Europe*, 2nd edn. New York: Routledge.

Bold, V. 2003. Border Raids and Spoilt Songs: Collection as Colonization. In T.A. McKean (ed.), *The Flowering Thorn: International Ballad Studies*. Logan: Utah State University Press, pp. 353–362.

Bonnar, A. *Indicators of the Scottish Government's Firm Commitment to Culture: 2011 Roundup*. https://annebonnar.wordpress.com/2012/01/02/indicators-of-the-scottish-governments-firm-commitment-to-culture-2011-roundup [Accessed 28 October 2015].

Born, G. 2011. Music and the Materialisation of Identities. *Journal of Material Cultures*, 16(4), 376–388.

Born, G. and Hesmondhalgh, D. 2000. *Western Music and Its Others: Difference, Representation and Appropriation in Music*. Berkeley: University of California Press.

Bort, E. (ed.). 2012. *Tis Sixty Years Since: The First People's Festival Ceilidh and the Scottish Folk Revival*. Ochtertyre: Grace Notes.

Bourriaud, N. 2002 [1998]. *Relational Aesthetics*, trans. S. Pleasance and F. Woods. Dijon: Les Presses du Réel.

Boyes, G. 1993. *The Imagined Village: Culture, Ideology, and the English Folk Revival*. Manchester: Manchester University Press.

Boyes, G. 2010. *The Imagined Village : Culture, Ideology, and the English Folk Revival*. Leeds: No Masters Co-operative.

Bradtke, E. 2010. Fiddle Tunes From Under the Bed: Extracting Music From Carpenter's Recordings. In I. Russell and A. Kearney Guigne (eds), *Crossing Over: Fiddle and Dance Studies From Around the North Atlantic 3*. Aberdeen: The Elphinstone Institute, University of Aberdeen, in association with the Department of Folklore, MMap and the School of Music, Memorial University of Newfoundland, pp. 35–48. http://aura.abdn.ac.uk/bitstream/2164/4986/1/Crossing_Over_2010_ed._Russell_and_Kearney_Guign_.pdf?_ga=1.251357391.834974470.1436435012 [Accessed 23 July 2016].

Bremner, R. 1757. *Thirty Scots Songs for a Voice & Harpsichord, the Music Taken From the Most Genuine Sets Extant; the Words From Allan Ramsay*. Edinburgh: Privately Published.

Broad, S. and France, J. 2006. *25 Years of the Fèisean. The participants' story: research on the Fèis movement in Scotland*. Glasgow: RSAMD: National Centre for Research in the Performing Arts.

Brocken, M. 2003. *The British Folk Revival: 1944–2002*. Aldershot: Ashgate.

Brook, P. 1990 [1968]. *The Empty Space*. London: Penguin.

Brooks, C. (ed.). 1977. *The Percy Letters: Correspondence of Thomas Percy and William Shenstone*. New Haven, CT and London: Yale University Press.

Brooks, L. 2014. Scotland: Activists Re-Energise With a Shot of Independence Spirit. *The Guardian*, 15 September. www.theguardian.com/politics/2014/sep/15/night-for-scotland-concert-mogwai-franz-ferdinant

Brown, K. 2014. *The Songs for Scotland Festival*. Crowdfunding website. Indiegogo.com. 2014. https://www.indiegogo.com/projects/the-songs-for-scotland-festival#/story

References

Buchan, D. 1972. *The Ballad and the Folk*. London and New York: Routledge and Keegan Paul.

Buchan, P. 1828. *Ancient Ballads and Songs of the North of Scotland*, vol. II. Edinburgh: Laing.

Buchanan, D. A. 2002. Soccer, Popular Music and National Consciousness in Post-State-Socialist Bulgaria, 1994–96. *British Journal of Ethnomusicology*, 11, 1–27.

Buckland, T. J. 2006. Edward Scott: The Last of the English Dancing Masters. *Dance Research*, 21(2), 3–35.

Buckland, T. J. 2007. Crompton's Campaign. *Dance Research*, 22(1), 1–34.

Buckland, T. J. 2011. *Society Dancing: Fashionable Bodies in England, 1870–1920*. London: Palgrave Macmillan.

Caledonian Mercury. 1862. Death of William Menzies, Last of the Niel Gow School of Violin Players. *The Caledonian Mercury*, 24 November.

Cameron, J. 1977 [1934]. William Cameron, and George Cameron. *The Cameron Men*, Topic Records 12T321.

Campbell, J. L. 1984. *Canna, the Story of a Hebridean Island*. Edinburgh: Birlinn.

Campbell, K. 2001a. Paul Anderson: Fiddle Teachers. *The Fiddle Tradition of North-East Scotland*. University of Edinburgh. https://web.archive.org/web/20070921034306/www.celtscot.ed.ac.uk/fiddle/paulteach.htm [Accessed 1 November 2015].

Campbell, K. 2001b. Teacher Tree Relating to Paul Anderson. *The Fiddle Tradition of North-East Scotland*. University of Edinburgh. https://web.archive.org/web/20060925054403/www.celtscot.ed.ac.uk/fiddle/teachertree.htm [Accessed 1 November 2015].

Campbell, K. 2007. *The Fiddle in Scottish Culture: Aspects of the Tradition*. Edinburgh: John Donald.

Campbell, K., Eydmann, S., and Gunn, L. 2014. *Research Scoping Study: Ulster-Scots Music Traditions: A Report for MAGUS and DCAL*. Belfast: DCAL.

Campsie, A. 2013. James MacMillan Likens Indy Group National Collective to 'Mussolini's Cheerleaders. [Online] www.heraldscotland.com/news/13119861.James_Mac Millan_likens_indy_group_National_Collective_to__Mussolini_s_cheerleaders_/ [Accessed 30 March 2017].

Cannon, R. 1988. *The Highland Bagpipe and Its Music*. Edinburgh: John Donald.

Carson, C. 1996. *Last Night's Fun*. London: Jonathan Cape.

Ceribašić, N. 2014. Revivalist Articulations of Traditional Music in War and Postwar Croatia. In *The Oxford Handbook of Music Revival*, edited by C. Bithell and J. Hill. Oxford & New York: Oxford University Press, pp. 325–349.

Chaimbeul, A. P. 2002. Unpublished Poem.

Chapman, M. 1997. Thoughts on Celtic Music. In M. Stokes (ed.), *Ethnicity, Identity and Music: The Musical Construction of Place*. Oxford and New York: Berg.

Cheape, H. 2008. *Bagpipes: A National Collection of a National Treasure*. Edinburgh: NMS Publishing.

Child, F. J. 1882–1894. *The English and Scottish Popular Ballads*, vol. 1, 'Earl Brand'. London: Houghton, Mifflin and Co.

Christie, W. 1821. *A Collection of Strathspeys. Reels, Hornpipes, Waltzes, &c. Arranged as Medleys for the Harp, Piano Forte, Violin, and Violoncello*. Edinburgh: Christie.

Clarke, J. 1976. Style. In S. Hall and T. Jefferson (eds), *Resistance Through Rituals: Youth Subcultures in Post-War Britain*. Routledge: Oxon.

Collinson, F. 1966. *The Traditional and National Music of Scotland*. London: Routledge and Kegan Paul.

Common Weal. 2012. *Common Weal.* [Online] www.allofusfirst.org/ [Accessed 31 March 2017].

Cook, N. 2001. Theorizing Musical Meaning. *Music Theory Spectrum*, 23, 170–195. www.jstor.org/stable/10.1525/mts.2001.23.2.170 [Accessed 9 August 2013].

Cook, N. 2012. Anatomy of the Encounter: Intercultural Analysis as Relational Musicology. In S. Hawkins (ed.), *Critical Musicological Reflections: Essays in Honour of Derek B. Scott.* London: Routledge.

Cooke, P. 1982. *The Fiddle Tradition of the Shetland Isles.* PhD thesis, University of Edinburgh.

Cooke, P. 1986. *The Fiddle Tradition of the Shetland Isles.* Cambridge: Cambridge University Press.

Costello, E. 2015. *Sean-nós singing and Oireachtas na Gaeilge: Identity, Romantic Nationalism and the Agency of the Gaeltacht Community Nexus.* Unpublished PhD thesis, University of Limerick.

Cowan, E. J. 1979. The Union of the Crowns and the Crisis of the Constitution on 17th-Century Scotland. In S. Dyrvik et al. (ed.), *The Satellite State in the 17th and 18th Centuries.* Bergen: University of Bergen Press.

Craig, C. 1982. Myths Against History: Tartanry and Kailyard in 19th-Century Scottish Literature. In C. McArthur (ed.), *Scotch Reels: Scotland in Cinema and Television.* London: British Film Institute.

Craig, C. 1989. Series Preface. In C. Beveridge and R. Turnbull (eds), *The Eclipse of Scottish Culture.* Edinburgh: Polygon. n.p.

Crawford, R. 1992. *Devolving English Literature.* London: Clarendon Press.

Crawford, R. 1994. *Identifying Poets: Self and Territory in Twentieth-Century Poetry.* Edinburgh: Edinburgh University Press.

Creech, A. et al. 2008. Investigating Musical Performance: Commonality and Diversity Among Classical and Non-classical Musicians. *Music Education Research*, 10(2), 215–235.

Crompton, R. M. 1891. Editorial. *Dancing*, 1(1), 2.

Crossley, N. 2009. The Man Whose Web Expanded: Network Dynamics in Manchester's Post/Punk Music Scene 1976–1980. *Poetics*, 37(1), 24–49.

Crossley, N. 2015. *Networks of Sound, Style and Subversion: The Punk and Post-Punk Worlds of Manchester, London, Liverpool and Sheffield, 1975–80.* Manchester: Manchester University Press.

Cudmore, P. 1995. *Does Scotland Need a Traditional Music Development Agency?* Edinburgh: Scottish Arts Council.

Cunningham, A. 1825. *The Songs of Scotland, Ancient and Modern*, vol. 1. London: Printed for John Taylor.

Dauney, W. 1973 [1838]. *Ancient Scotish Melodies, from a Manuscript of the Reign of King James.* New York: AMS Press.

Davie, C. T. 1980. *Scotland's Music.* Edinburgh: William Blackwood.

Davie, J. 1829–1835. *Davie's Caledonian Repository*, First Series, I–IV. Aberdeen: Davie.

Davie, J. 1851–1855. *Davie's Caledonian Repository*, Second Series, I–II. Aberdeen: Davie.

De Nora, T. 2000. *Music in Everyday Life.* Cambridge: Cambridge University Press.

De Witt, M. 2009. Louisiana bals de maison in California and the accumulation of social capital, *The World of Music*, 51(1), 17–34.

Dean-Myatt, B. 2012. *Scottish Vernacular Discography.* NLS. www.nls.uk/catalogues/scottish-discography [Accessed 1 November 2015].

Dentith, S. 2006. *Epic and Empire in Nineteenth-Century Britain*. Cambridge: Cambridge University Press.

Devine, T. M. 2006. *The Scottish Nation: 1700–2007*, 2nd edn. London: Penguin.

Dick, J. 1903. *The Songs of Robert Burns*. London: H. Frowde.

Dickson, J. (ed.). 2009. *The Highland Bagpipe: Music, History, Tradition*. Farnham: Ashgate.

Dickson, J. 2009. "Tullochgorum Transformed": A Case Study in Revivalism and the Highland Pipe. In J. Dickson (ed.), *The Highland Bagpipe: Music, History, Tradition*. Farnham: Ashgate, pp. 191–220.

Dickson, J. 2013. *Hamish MacCunn (1868–1916): a Musical Life* by Jennifer L. Oates. Review, www.scottishjournalofperformance.org

Dickson, J. 2015. BA with Honours (Scottish Music) and (Scottish Music – Piping) Reflective Analysis, March 2015. Unpublished report, Royal Conservatoire of Scotland.

Documenting Yes. 2013. *Documenting Yes*. [Online] http://documentingyes.com/ [Accessed 31 March 2017].

Documenting Yes. 2014. *Documenting Yes – Yestival*. [Online] http://documentingyes.com/yestival [Accessed 31 March 2017].

Dolan, J. 2005. *Utopia in Performance: Finding Hope at the Theatre*. Ann Arbor: University of Michigan Press.

Donaldson, W. 2008. *The Highland Pipe and Scottish Society, 1750–1950*. Edinburgh: John Donald.

Dowling, M. 2007. Confusing Culture and Politics: Ulster Scots Culture and Music. *New Hibernia Review*, 11(3), 51–80.

Dowling, M. 2008. Fiddling for Outcomes: Traditional Music, Social Capital, and Arts Policy in Northern Ireland. *International Journal of Cultural Policy*, 14(2), 179–194.

Dowling, M. 2010. *Folk and Traditional Music and the Conflict in Northern Ireland: A Troubles Archive Essay*. Belfast: Arts Council of Northern Ireland.

Dowling, M. 2013. Reflecting on Tradition: Four Ulster Musical Lives. *Ulster Folklife*, 56.

Dowling, M. 2014. Traditional Music and Irish Society: Historical Perspectives. Aldershot: Ashgate, 3.

Duesenberry, M. P. 2000. *Fiddle Tunes on Air: A Study of Gatekeeping and Traditional Music at the BBC in Scotland, 1923–1957*. PhD Thesis, Berkeley, UCLA.

Duffy, C. and Duesenberry, P. 2014. Wha's like us? A new Scottish Conservatoire tradition. In I. Papageorgi and G. Welch (eds), *Advanced Musical Performance: Investigations in Higher Education Learning*. Aldershot: Ashgate, pp. 49–63.

Dundes, A. 1965. *The Study of Folklore*. Englewood Cliffs, NJ: Wiley.

Dunphy, K. 2015. A holistic framework of evaluation for arts engagement. In L. MacDowall, M. Badham, E. Blomkamp & K. Dunphy (eds), *Making Culture Count: the politics of cultural measurement*. London: Palgrave, pp. 243–263.

EKOS. 2013 (revised 2014). *Music Sector Review: Final Report for Creative Scotland*. Glasgow.

Emmerson, G. 1971. *Rantin Pipe and Tremblin String: A History of Scottish Dance Music*. London: Dent.

Everist, M. 1990. From Paris to St Andrews: The Origins of W_1. *Journal of the American Musicological Society*, 43(1), Spring, 1–42.

Eydmann, S. 1988. Beer Tent Musicology. *Cencrastus*, Summer, 24–25.

Eydmann, S. 1995a. *The Life and Times of the Concertina*. PhD Thesis, Open University.

Eydmann, S. 1995b. The Concertina as an Emblem of the Folk Music Revival in the British Isles. *British Journal of Ethnomusicology*, 4, 41–48.

Eydmann, S. 2001. From the "Wee Melodeon" to the "Big Box": The Accordion in Scotland Since 1945. *Musical Performance*, 3, 107–125.

Eydmann, S. 2006. Unravelling the Birl: Using Basic Computer Technology to Understand Traditional Fiddle Decorations. In Ian Russell and Mary Anne Alburger (eds), *Play It Like It Is: Fiddle and Dance Studies from Around the North Atlantic*. Aberdeen: University of Aberdeen, pp. 33–41.

Eydmann, S. 2007. Diversity and Diversification in Scottish Music. In J. Beech, O. Hand, F. MacDonald, M. A. Mulhern, and Weston Jeremy (eds), *Scottish Life and Society: A Compendium of Scottish Ethnology, Vol. 10: Oral Literature and Performance Culture*. Edinburgh: John Donald pp. 193–212.

Eydmann, S. 2013. *The Fiddle in the Scottish Folk Music Revival*. Blog www.blogs.hss.ed.ac.uk/revival-fiddle/

Eydmann, S. 2015. *Twenty Years a-Blowing: Recent Developments in the Free Reeds in Scotland*. Paper read at Button Boxes and Moothies Study Day, University of Aberdeen, 6 November.

Eydmann, S. 2017. *In Good Hands. The Clarsach Society and the Renaissance of the Scottish Harp*. Edinburgh: The Clarsach Society.

Eydmann, S. and Witcher, H. Forthcoming. Heloise Russell Fergusson. *Musica Scotica: Conference Proceedings 2015*. Glasgow: Musica Scotica.

Facebook. 2013. *Trad YES 2014*. [Online] www.facebook.com/TradYes2014/ [Accessed 31 March 2017].

Faux, T. 2009. Don Roy, Fiddle Music, and Social Sustenance in Franco New England, *The World of Music*, 51(1), 35–54.

Feintuch, B. 1993. Musical Revival as Musical Transformation. In N. V. Rosenberg (ed.), *Transforming Tradition: Folk Music Revivals Examined*. Urbana: University of Illinois Press, pp. 183–193.

Feld, S. 1988. Aesthetics as Iconicity of Style, or "Lift-up-over Sounding": Getting into the Kaluli Groove. *Yearbook for Traditional Music*, 20, 74–113.

Feldman, A. 2002. Music of the Border: The Northern Fiddler Project, Media Provenance and the Nationalisation of Irish Music. *Radharc*, 3, 97–122.

Ferguson, B. 2014. *Celtic Connections Celebrates Record Ticket Sales* [Online] www.scotsman.com/lifestyle/culture/music/celtic-connections-celebrates-record-tickets-sales-1-3291720 [Accessed 1 April 2017].

Finlay, A. (ed.). 1996. *The Armstrong Nose: Selected Letters of Hamish Henderson*. Edinburgh: Polygon.

Finnegan, R. 1989. *The Hidden Musicians. Music-Making in an English Town*. Cambridge: Cambridge University Press.

Finnegan, R. 1990. Studying Musical Practice in an English Town: A "Doorstep" Ethnographic Study and Its Implications. Paper presented to British-Swedish Conference of Ethnomusicology (Cambridge 5–10 August, 1989). *Journal of the Royal Musical Association*, 115(2), 279.

Fisher, T. 2011. Radical Democratic Theatre. *Performance Research*, 16(4), 15–26.

Fleming, R. C. 2004. Resisting Cultural Standardization: Comhaltas Coltoiri Eireann and the Revitalization of Traditional Music in Ireland, *Journal of Folklore Research*, 41(2/3), 227–257.

Foley, J. M. (ed.). 1985. *The Oral Formulaic Theory and Research: an Introduction and Annotated Bibliography*. New York: Garland Publishing.

Foley, J.M. 1990. *Immanent Art: From Structure to Meaning in Traditional Oral Epic*. Bloomington: Indiana University Press.

Folkestad, G. 2006. Formal and Informal Learning Situations or Practices vs Formal and Informal Ways of Learning. *British Journal of Music Education*, 23(2), 135–145.

Ford, E. 2016. *The Flute in Musical Life in Eighteenth-Century Scotland*. PhD, University of Glasgow.

Forsyth, M. 2005. *Shetland Isles Traditional Music, Composition, Performance, and Identity*. M.Phil Dissertation, University of Cambridge.

Forsyth, M. 2007. Reinventing "Springs": Constructing Identity in the Fiddle Tradition of the Shetland Isles. *Shima: The International Journal of Research into Island Cultures*, 1(2), 49–58.

Foster, J. 2013. *The Value of TradYES*. [Online] http://nationalcollective.com/2013/09/23/the-value-of-tradyes [Accessed 30 March 2017].

Francis, D. 1999. *Traditional Music in Scotland: Education, Information, Advocacy*. Edinburgh: Scottish Arts Council.

Francis, D. 2010. *Traditional Arts Working Group Report – January 2010*. Edinburgh: The Scottish Government.

Francis, D. 2015. An Emerging Policy Context for the Traditional Arts in Scotland. Unpublished conference paper, *Ethnomusicology and Policy (British Forum for Ethnomusicology One-Day Conference)*, Newcastle University.

Fraser, S. 1816. *Airs and Melodies Peculiar to the Highlands of Scotland and the Isles*. Edinburgh: Printed and Sold for the Editor.

Frith, S. 1981. "The Magic That Can Set You Free": The Ideology of Folk and the Myth of the Rock Community. *Popular Music*, 1, 159–168.

Frith, S. 1996a. *Performing Rites*. Cambridge, MA: Harvard University Press.

Frith, S. 1996b. Music and Identity. In S. Hall and P. du Gay (eds), *Questions of Cultural Identity*. Sage: London.

Frith, S. 2000. The Discourse of World Music. In G. Born and D. Hesmondhalgh (eds), *Western Music and Its Others*. Berkeley and London: University of California Press.

Frith, S. 2007. *Taking Popular Music Seriously: Selected Essays*. Aldershot: Ashgate.

Fumerton, P. Guerrini, A. and McAbee, K. (eds). 2010. *Ballads and Broadsides in Britain, 1500–1800*. Farnham: Ashgate.

Gammon, V. 2016. *Early Scottish Rags*. Workington: Fellside Records.

Gammon, V. n.d. The Blaydon Races. Folk Articles | Tynefolk | Folk Music. n.d. http://www.tynefolk.co.uk/folk-articles-blaydon-races-scandal.php

Garner, R. 2014. Exclusive: Exam Reforms Give "Dead White Germans" Lead on the Classical Music Syllabus. *The Independent*, 14 September 2014, online edition. http://www.independent.co.uk/news/education/education-news/exclusive-exam-reforms-give-dead-white-germans-lead-on-the-classical-music-syllabus-9732478.html.

Gaughan, D. 1981. *Handful of Earth*. [Vinyl] Topic.

Gaughan, D. 2006. *Lucky for Some*. [CD] Greentrax.

Gaughan, D. n.d. Song Notes. *Dick Gaughan's Song Archive*. [online] www.dickgaughan.co.uk/songs/texts/tweed.html [Accessed August 2016].

Gelbart, M. 2007. *The Invention of "Folk Music" and "Art Music": Emerging Categories from Ossian to Wagner*. Cambridge: Cambridge University Press.

Gellner, E. 1983. *Nations and Nationalism*. Ithaca, NY: Cornell University Press.

Gellner, E., and Breuilly, J. 2008. *Nations and Nationalism*. New York: Cornell University Press.

GFW. 2013. *Annual Report 2012–13*. Glasgow Fiddle Workshop.

Gibson, C. 2009. Tomorrow, Songs/Will Flow Free Again, and New Voices/Be Born on the Carrying Stream: Hamish Henderson's Conception of the Scottish Folk-Song Revival and Its Place in Literary Scotland. *The Drouth*, 32, 48–59.

Gibson, C. 2013. The Politics of the Modern Scottish Folk Revival. In S. Dunnigan and S. Gilbert (ed.), *The Edinburgh Companion to Scottish Traditional Literatures*. Edinburgh: Edinburgh University Press, pp. 134–144.

Gibson, C. 2015. *Voice of the People: Hamish Henderson and Scottish Cultural Politics*. Edinburgh: Edinburgh University Press.

Gilbert, S. Scottish Ballads and Popular Culture. *The Bottle Imp*, no. 5, May 2009, online edition www.arts.gla.ac.uk/ScotLit/ASLS/SWE/TBI/TBIIssue5/Ballads.pdf [Accessed 12 March 2015].

Gilchrist, J. 2012. Landscape with Fiddles. In E. Bort (ed.), *Tis Sixty Years Since: The First People's Festival Ceilidh and the Scottish Folk Revival*. Ochtertyre: Grace Notes.

Gillies, A. L. 2005. *Songs of Gaelic Scotland*. Edinburgh: Birlinn.

Gillies, A. L. 2007. Review of *A Life of Song, the Autobiography of Marjory Kennedy-Fraser (1857–1930)*. Islands Book Trust, 2007. Grian Press. [Online] www.northwordsnow.co.uk/docs/Life-of-song-reviewrev.pdf.

Gladwell, M. 2008. *Outliers: The Story of Success*. Boston: Little, Brown and Company.

Glasgow Song Guild. 1962. *Ding Dong Dollar: Anti-Polaris and Scottish Republican Songs*. [Vinyl] Folkways. Lyrics and Sleevenotes reproduced at The Balladeers Scotland. [online] www.theballadeersscotland.com/scots/ge_d02_Ding_Dong.htm [Accessed August 2016].

Glassie, H. 1995. Tradition. *Journal of American Folklore*, 108(430), 395–412.

Glen, J. 1891–1895. *The Glen Collection of Scottish Dance Music*, I–II. Edinburgh: Glen.

Glen, J. 2001. *The Glen Collection of Scottish Dance Music*. Inverness: Highland Music Trust.

Goldie, D. 2006. Hugh MacDiarmid, Harry Lauder and Scottish Popular Culture. *International Journal of Scottish Literature*, 1. [online] www.ijsl.stir.ac.uk/issue1/goldie.htm [Accessed August 2016].

Goldie, D. and Watson, R. (eds). 2014. *From the Line: Scottish War Poetry 1914–1945*. Glasgow: The Association for Scottish Literary Studies.

Gonella, R. 1973. *Scottish Violin Music From the Gow Collections*. Scottish Records 33SR135.

Gordon, K. (ed.). 2006. *Voices From Their Ain Countrie: The Poems of Marion Angus and Violet Jacob*. Glasgow: The Association for Scottish Literary Studies.

Gore, C. 1994. *The Scottish Fiddle Music Index*. Musselburgh: Amaising.

Gore, C. 2008. *Echoes of a Golden Age: Rediscovering Scotland's Original Fiddle Music*. Inverness: Highland Music Trust.

Gore, C. *The Scottish Music Index*. www.scottishmusicindex.org [Accessed 20 February 2012].

Gow, N. 1799–1817. *A Complete Repository of Slow Strathspeys and Dances*, I–IV. Edinburgh: Gow and Shepherd. [the title of volume 2 is *A Complete Repository of Scots Tunes, Strathspeys, Jigs, and Dances*].

Gow, N. 1800. *Callar Herring [. . .] (from the Original Cry of the Newheavn Fish Wives, Selling their fresh Herrings in the Streets of Edinr.) To Which Is Added Three Favorite Tunes*. Edinburgh: Gow & Shepherd.

Gow, N. 1817. *First Set of the Favorite French Quadrilles as Performed by Mr. Gow and His Band, at the Queens Assembly in George Street Rooms. The 20th. January 1817. With Their Proper Figures as Danced at Mr. Smarts Academy 95 Princes Street*. Edinburgh: Robert Purdie.

Gow, N. 1819. *The Beauties of Niel Gow*, I–III. Edinburgh: Nathaniel Gow and Son.

Gow, Niel & Sons. 1805. *Part Second of the Complete Repository of Original Scots Tunes, Strathspeys, Jigs and Dances*, 2nd ed. Edinburgh: Gow & Shepherd.

Gow, Niel & Sons. 1817. *Part Fourth of the Complete Repository, of Original Scots Slow Strathspeys and Dances*. Edinburgh: Gow & Sons.

Graham, G. F. (ed.). 1848–1849. *The Songs of Scotland Adapted to Their Appropriate Melodies*. Edinburgh: Wood.

Grant, A. 1978. *Angus Grant: Highland Fiddle*. Topic Records, 12TS347.

Grant, C. 2013. Music Sustainability, *Oxford Bibliographies in Music*, Available: Oxford University Press.

Grant, M. J. 2008. Myth and Reality in the Songs of Robert Burns. In K. Elliott, H. Kelsall, G.-M. Hair and G. Hair (eds), *Musica Scotica: 800 Years of Scottish Music. Proceedings from the 2005 and 2006 Conference*. Glasgow: Musica Scotica Trust, pp. 29–35.

Green, L. 2008. *Music, Informal Learning and the School: A New Classroom Pedagogy*. Ashgate Popular and Folk Music Series. Aldershot: Ashgate.

Greig, D. 2007. Rough Theatre. In R. d'Monté and G. Saunders (eds), *Cool Britannia? British Political Drama in the 1990s*. Basingstoke: Palgrave, pp. 208–221.

Greig, D. 2011. *The Strange Undoing of Prudencia Hart*. London: Faber.

Greig, D. 2013. Why the Debate on Scottish Independence Might Be More Interesting Than You Think? Bella Caledonia [Online] Available at http://bellacaledonia.org.uk/2013/08/04/why-the-debate-on-scottish-independence-might-be-more-interesting-than-you-think/ [Accessed 12 November 2013].

Grieve, C. M. 1925. *Contemporary Scottish Studies*. London: Leonard Parsons.

Griffiths, J. 2015. *Traditional Fiddle*. New York and London: Oxford University Press.

Groom, N. 2006 "The Purest English": Ballads and the English Literary Dialect. *The Eighteenth Century*, 47(2/3), 179–202.

Grosjean, A., and Murdoch, S. (eds). 2005. *Scottish Communities Abroad in the Early Modern Period*. Leiden: Brill.

Guilbault, J. 2010. Music, Politics, and Pleasure: Live Soca in Trinidad. *Small Axe*, 14(1): 16–29.

Gunn, N. 1989[1956]. *The Atom of Delight*. Edinburgh: Polygon.

Haggerty, A. 2015. Loki vs National Collective: A Timeline of the Debate Over Democracy and Artistic Dissent. [online] *Common Space*, 12 March 2015. www.commonspace.scot/articles/681/loki-vs-national-collective-timeline-debate-over-democracy-and-artistic-dissent [Accessed August 2016].

Haines, J. 2014. Antiquarian Nostalgia and the Institutionalization of Early Music. In C. Bithell and J. Hill (eds), *The Oxford Handbook of Music Revival*. New York: Oxford University Press, pp. 73–90.

Hales, J. W., and Furnival, F. J. (eds). 1867–1868. *Bishop Percy's Folio Manuscript: Ballads and Romances*, 3 vols. London: N. Trübner and Co.

Hames, S. 2013. On Vernacular Scottishness and its Limits: Devolution and the Spectacle of 'Voice'. *Studies in Scottish Literature*, 39(1), 201–222.

Hands Up for Trad. 2017. *Distil*. [Online] https://projects.handsupfortrad.scot/handsupfortrad/distil/ [Accessed 1 April 2017].

Hardie, A. 1981. *The Caledonian Companion*. London: EMI.

Hardie, J. et al. 1999. *The Captain's Collection*. Greentrax, CDTRAX 187.

Harding, F. 1982. *Report on the Arts of the Ethnic Minorities of Scotland: A Survey of the Arts of the Minority Ethnic Groups Which Have Settled in Scotland*. Edinburgh: Scottish Arts Council/Commission for Racial Equality.

Harker, D. 1985. *Fakesong: The Manufacture of British "Folksong" 1700 to the Present Day*. Milton Keynes: Open University Press.

Harvey, H. 2005. *Franz Ferdinand and the Pop Renaissance*. London: Reynolds and Hearn.

Henderson, G. 1905. *Lady Nairne and Her Songs*. Paisley: Gardiner.
Henderson, H. 1992. *Alias MacAlias: Writings on Songs, Folk and Literature*. Edinburgh: Polygon.
Henderson, H. 2000a. *Collected Poems and Songs*. Edinburgh: Curly Snake.
Henderson, H. 2000b. Under the Earth I Go. In R. Ross (ed.), *Collected Poems and Songs*. Edinburgh: Curly Snake Publishing, pp. 154–155.
Henderson, H. 2004. *Alias MacAlias, Writings on Song, Folk and Literature*. Edinburgh: Birlinn.
Henderson, H. 1964. Scots Folk-Song Today. *Folklore*, 75(1), 48–58.
Hesmondhalgh, D. 2012. *The Cultural Industries*, 3rd edn. Thousand Oaks, CA: Sage.
Hesmondhalgh, D. 2013. *Why Music Matters*. Chichester: Wiley Blackwell.
Hield, F. 2013. Negotiating Participation in an English Folk Singing Session. In I. Russell and C. Ingram (eds), *Taking Part in Music: Case Studies in Ethnomusicology*. Aberdeen: Aberdeen University Press, pp. 99–120.
Highland Collections. 2005. *Highland Collections*. Inverness: Highland Music Trust.
Hill, J. 2009. The Influence of Conservatory Folk Music Programmes: The Sibelius Academy in Comparative Context. *Ethnomusicology Forum*, 18(2), 205–239.
Hill, J. 2016. *Becoming Creative: Insights from Musicians in a Diverse World*. New York: Oxford University Press.
Hill, J., and Bithell, C. 2014. An Introduction to Music Revival as Concept, Cultural Process, and Medium of Change. In *The Oxford Handbook of Music Revival*. Oxford: Oxford University Press, pp. 3–43.
Hillier, P. 1997. *Arvo Pärt*. Oxford Studies of Composers. Oxford: Oxford University Press.
Hobsbawm, E. J., and Ranger, T. O. 1983. *The Invention of Tradition*. Cambridge and New York: Cambridge University Press.
Hobsbawm, E. J. 2012. *Nations and Nationalism Since 1780: Programme, Myth, Reality*. Cambridge: Cambridge University Press
Howard, P. (ed.). 2016. *Theatre in Scotland: A Field of Dreams. Reviews by Joyce McMillan*. London: Nick Hearn Books.
Hunter, J. 1979. *The Fiddle Music of Scotland*. Edinburgh: Chalmers.
Hyder, K. 2013. *How to Know*. Amazon Digital Services.
Ignatieff, M. 1993. *Blood and Belonging: Journeys into the New Nationalism*. Farrar, Straus, Giroux.
Irvine, R. P. (ed.). 2013. *Robert Burns, Selected Poems and Songs*. Oxford: Oxford University Press.
ISDT. 1911. *Dance Journal*, 4(22), 12.
Johnson, D. 1972 [2003]. *Music and Society in Lowland Scotland in the 18th Century*. Cambridge: Cambridge University Press, with 2nd edition 2003, Edinburgh: Mercat Press.
Johnson, D. 1984a. *The Fiddle Music of Eighteenth-Century Scotland*. Edinburgh: John Donald.
Johnson, D. 1984b. *Scottish Fiddle Music in the 18th Century*. Edinburgh: John Donald.
Jones, P. M. 2010. Developing Social Capital: A Role for Music Education and Community Music in Fostering Civic Engagement and Intercultural Understanding. *International Journal of Community Music*, 3(2), 291–302.
Karpeles, M. 1955. Definition of Folk Music. *Journal of the International Folk Music Council*, no. 7, 6–7.
Karpeles, M. 2008. *Cecil Sharp: His Life and Work*. London: Faber.

Kartomi, M. 1981. The Processes and Results of Culture Contact: A Discussion of Terminology and Concepts. *Ethnomusicology*, 23, 227–250.

Keegan-Phipps, S. 2007. Déjà Vu? Folk Music, Education and Institutionalization in Contemporary England. *Yearbook for Traditional Music*, 39, 84–107.

Keegan-Phipps, S. 2016. *Digital Folk*. www.digitalfolk.org. [Accessed 16 January 2016].

Keegan-Phipps, S., and Winter, T. 2014. Contemporary English Folk Music and the Folk Industry. In *The Oxford Handbook of Music Revival*. Oxford: Oxford University Press, pp. 489–519.

Kelman, J. 1987 [1985]. *A Chancer*. London: Picador.

Kenny, A. 2016. *Communities of Musical Practice*. Sempre Studies in the Psychology of Music. Abingdon: Routledge.

Kershaw, B. 1983. The Barn Dance. In C. Tony and B. Kershaw (ed.), *Engineers of the Imagination: The Welfare State Handbook*. London: Methuen.

Khomami, N. 2015. Student Demands Female Composers on A-Level Music Syllabus. *The Guardian* [Online] www.theguardian.com/education/2015/aug/18/female-composers-a-level-music-syllabus-petition [Accessed 19 August 2015].

Klein, L. 1984 *Shaftesbury and the Culture of Politeness: Moral Discourse and Cultural Politics in Early Eighteenth Century England*. Cambridge: Cambridge University Press.

KMH Royal College of Music Stockholm. About the Folk Music Department. www.kmh.se/about-the-folk-music-department

Korb, M., and Roever, U. n.d. *Highland Cathedral – Das Original*. www.highlandcathedral.de/inde.html [Accessed 19 August 2015].

Koskoff, E. (ed.). 2001. *The Garland Encyclopaedia of World Music, Vol. 3, United States and Canada*. New York: Routledge, pp. 55–59.

Kropotkin, P. 1908. *Mutual Aid: A Factor of Evolution*. London: Heimemann.

Labadi, S. 2012. *UNESCO, Cultural Heritage, and Outstanding Universal Value: Value-Based Analyses of the World Heritage and Intangible Cultural Heritage Conventions*. Lanham: AltaMira Press.

Langford, P. 2002. The Uses of Eighteenth-Century Politeness in *Transactions of the Royal Historical Society*, Vol. 12, pp. 311–331.

Larkin, C. (ed.). 2006. Ken Hyder. In *Encyclopaedia of Popular Music*. Oxford: Oxford University Press. Published online (2009) at: www.oxfordreference.com

Lauder, H. 1918. *A Minstrel in France*. New York: Hearst's International Library Company.

Lave, J., and Wenger, E. 1991. *Situated Learning: Legitimate Peripheral Participation*. Cambridge: Cambridge University Press.

Lawrence, D. 1977. *The National Fiddle Championship*. EMI Records NTS 130.

Lee, D., Hesmondhalgh, D., Oakley, K., and Nisbett, M.. 2014. Regional Creative Industries Policy-Making Under New Labour. *Cultural Trends*, 23, 217–231. https://doi.org/10.1080/09548963.2014.912044

Leonard, P., and McLaren, P. 1993. *Paulo Freire: A Critical Encounter*. Abingdon and New York: Routledge.

Lesure, F. n.d. France. In *Grove Music Online, Oxford Music Online*. Oxford: Oxford University Press. www.oxfordmusiconline.com/subscriber/article/grove/music/40051 [Accessed 15 August 2015].

Levack, B. P. 1987. *The Formation of the British State: England, Scotland, and the Union 1603–1707*. London: Clarendon Press.

Levi-Strauss, C. (trans. Weightman and Weightman). 1968. *The Savage Mind*. Chicago and London: University of Chicago Press.

Lewis, A. (ed.). 1957. *The Percy Letters: Correspondence of Thomas Percy and Evan Evans*. Baton Rouge: Louisiana State University Press.

Livingston, T. 2001. Musical Revivals. In E. Koskoff (ed.), *The Garland Encyclopaedia of World Music, Vol. 3, United States and Canada*. New York: Routledge, pp. 55–59.

Livingston, T. 2014. An Expanded Theory for Revivals as Cosmopolitan Participatory Music Making. In J. Hill and C. Bithell (eds), *The Oxford Handbook of Music Revival*. Oxford: Oxford University Press, pp. 60–72.

Livingston, T. E. 1999. Music Revivals: Towards a General Theory. *Ethnomusicology*, 43(1), 66–85.

Lockhart, G. W. 1998. *Fiddles and Folk*. Edinburgh: Luath Press.

Lord, Albert B. 1960. *The Singer of Tales*. Cambridge, MA: Harvard University Press.

MacAndrew, H. 1960. Lady Mary Ramsay/Fairy Dance. Tobar an Dualchais/Kist o Riches. http://tobarandualchais.co.uk/en/fullrecord/87390/41 [Accessed 23 July 2016].

MacAndrew, H. 1975. *Scots Fiddle*. Scottish Records SR138.

MacColl, L. 2009. *Strewn with Ribbons*. Make Believe Records MBR2CD.

MacColl, L. 2015. *Lauren MacColl Scottish Fiddler*. www.laurenmaccoll.co.uk/lauren/ [Accessed 1 November 2015].

MacDiarmid, H. 1962. *The Ugly Birds Without Wings*. Edinburgh: A Donaldson.

MacDiarmid, H. 1984. *The Letters of Hugh MacDiarmid*. London: Hamilton.

MacDonald, C. 2000. *Bold*. Compass Records, B00004TE25.

MacDonald, C. 2011. Biography. *Catriona MacDonald Shetland Fiddler*. https://web.archive.org/web/20130821070910/http://catrionamacdonald.co.uk/page.php?2 [Accessed 1 November 2015].

MacDonald, F. 2013. *National Collective's TradYES*. [Online] www.frasermacdonald.com/national-collectives-tradyes/ [Accessed 30 March 2017].

Macdonald, H. 1976. Traditional Fiddling in Strathspey: The Unschooled Scots Fiddler and His Style. MLitt dissertation, University of Edinburgh. www.era.lib.ed.ac.uk/bitstream/handle/1842/7669/Macdonald1976_FULL.pdf?sequence=1&isAllowed=y [Accessed 23 July 2016].

Macdonald, H. 1986. Scotch Myths and a Theory of Icebergs: Some Thoughts on Our National Music. *Stretto: Journal of the Scottish Music Information Centre*, 6–10.

MacFadyen, A., and Macpherson, A. (eds). 2009. *Frederick Hill's Book of Quadrilles & Country Dances Etc. Etc. March 22nd, 1841*. Stirling: The Hill Manuscript Group.

Machell, T. 1888. The Dulcitone: A New and Portable Musical Instrument, Having Forks of Steel for Its Sound-Producers. *Proceedings of the Philosophical Society of Glasgow*, 19, 360–362.

Machin, D., and Richardson, J. E. 2012. Discourses of Unity and Purpose in the Sounds of Fascist Music: A Multimodal Approach. *Critical Discourse Studies*, 9, 329–345. http://doi.org/10.1080/17405904.2012.713203

MacInnes, I. 2009. Taking Stock: Lowland and Border Piping in a Highland World. In J. Dickson (ed.), *The Highland Bagpipe: Music, History, Tradition*. Farnham: Ashgate, pp. 169–190.

Mackay, D. 2016. The Spirit of the Ceilidh. *Blethers*, 32, 7.

Mackenzie, D. R. 1910. *Illustrated Guide to the National Dances of Scotland*. Stirling: s.n.

MacKenzie, E. 2014. Eilidh MacKenzie: Scotland – the Welcome Table. http://nationalcollective.com/2014/06/05/eilidh-mackenzie-scotland-the-welcome-table/ [Accessed 16 June 2014].

MacKinnon, N. 1994. *The British Folk Scene: Musical Performance and Social Identity*. Milton Keynes: Open University Press.

Mackintosh, R. 1804. *Fourth Book of New Strathspey Reels*. London: Printed for the Author by Lavenu & Mitchell.

Malcolm, J. 2000. *Resonance*, Beltane CD 101.

Mantie, R. 2012. Learners or Participants? The Pros and Cons of "Lifelong Learning". *International Journal of Community Music*, 5(3), 217–235.

Martin, C. 2002. *Traditional Scottish Fiddling*. Isle of Skye: Taigh na Teud.

Martin, K. 2006. *The First Twenty-Five Years of the fèis Movement*. Isle of Skye: Fèisean nan Gàidheal.

Massie, A. 2015. Where's the Art, National Collective? *The Scotsman* [online] Saturday 14 March 2015. www.scotsman.com/lifestyle/alex-massie-where-s-the-art-national-collective-1-3718728 [Accessed August 2016].

Matarasso, F. 1996. *Northern Lights: The Social Impact of the Fèisean*. Stroud: Comedia.

McArthur, C. 1982. Scotland and Cinema: The Iniquity of the Fathers. In C. McArthur (ed.), *Scotch Reels: Scotland in Cinema and Television*. London: British Film Institute.

McAulay, K.E. 2013. *Our Ancient National Airs: Scottish Song Collecting From the Enlightenment to the Romantic Era*. Farnham, Surrey: Ashgate.

McCalman, I. 2008. *Far Far From Ypres*. Unpublished Theatre Script and Live Show.

McCue, K. 1996. Burns, Women, and Song. In R. Crawford (ed.), *Robert Burns and Cultural Authority*. Edinburgh: Edinburgh University Press, pp. 40–57.

McCue, K, and Rycroft, M. 2014. The Reception of Robert Burns in Music. In M. Pittock (ed.), *The Reception of Robert Burns in Europe*. London: Bloomsbury, pp. 267–289.

McFadyen, M. 2012. "Presencing" Imagined Worlds – Understanding the Maysie : A Contemporary Ethnomusicological Enquiry into the Embodied Ballad Singing Experience. [Online] www.era.lib.ed.ac.uk/handle/1842/7948 [Accessed 30 October 2014].

McFadyen, M. 2013a. *National Collective Launches #TradYES*. [Online] http://nationalcollective.com/2013/07/10/national-collective-launches-tradyes/ [Accessed 30 March 2017].

McFadyen, M. 2013b. *Open Fields: The Future of Trads*. Edinburgh: TRACS.

McFadyen, M. 2013c. Together in *Sang*: The Embodied "Ballad Experience" as Singularly Plural. In I. Russell and C. Ingram (eds), *Taking Part in Music: Case Studies in Ethnomusicology*. Aberdeen: Aberdeen University Press, pp. 154–165.

McFadyen, M., 2014. *Think Global, Act Local: Think Global; Act Local: A Post-National Cultural-Ecological Perspective*. [Online] http://nationalcollective.com/2014/02/03/think-global-act-local-a-post-national-cultural-ecological-perspective/[Accessed 31 March 2017].

McFadyen, M. 2014b. *TradYES: Looking Back, Looking Forward*. [Online] http://nationalcollective.com/2014/01/02/tradyes-looking-back-looking-forward/[Accessed 30 March 2017].

McFadyen, M. 2016. *GRIT: It Was a Marvellous in Our Eyes*. [Online] www.mairimcfadyen.scot/blog/2016/8/27/grit-eif [Accessed 1 April 2017].

McGrath, J. 1974. *The Cheviot The Stag and The Black Black Oil*. Kyleakin: West Highland Publishing Co.

McGrattan, A. 1997. The Solo Trumpet in Scotland, 1695–1800. In S. Carter (ed.), *Perspectives in Brass Scholarship: Proceedings of the International Historic Brass Symposium, Amherst, 1995*. Stuyvesant, NY: Pendragon Press, pp. 79–90.

McGuinness, D. 2012. Folk Music: A Very Short Introduction. By Slobin. Oxford and New York: Oxford University Press, 2011. ISBN 978-0-19-539502-0. *Popular Music* 31.03.2012, pp. 504–506.

McGuirk, C. 2014. *Reading Robert Burns: Texts, Contexts, Transformations*. London and Vermont: Pickering and Chatto.

McKean, T. 1996. *Hebridean Song-Maker: Iain MacNeacail of the Isle of Skye*. Edinburgh: Polygon.

McKerrell, S. 2011. Modern Scottish Bands 1970–1990: Cash as Authenticity. *Scottish Music Review*, 2(1). www.scottishmusicreview.org/index.php/SMR/article/view/22

McKerrell, S. 2014a. Traditional Arts and the State: The Scottish Case. *Cultural Trends*, 23(3), 159–168.

McKerrell, S. 2014b. 'Folk' and 'Traditional', Understanding Scotland Musically project blogpost (www.musicalmeaning.com), posted 2 June 2014.

McKerrell, S. 2016. *Focus: Scottish Traditional Music*. New York and London: Routledge.

McKerrell, S. Forthcoming. Repositioning the Value of Traditional Music as Intangible Cultural Heritage, Commodity, Commerce and Tacit Heritage. *Unpublished draft research paper*.

[Dr McKnight]. 1809. A Brief Biographical Account of Neil [sic] Gow. *Scots Magazine*, January, 3–5.

McLaughlin, B. (ed.). 1990. *A Spiel Amang Us: Glasgow People Writing*. Edinburgh: Mainstream.

McMillan, Joyce. 1993. *The Charter for the Arts in Scotland*. Edinburgh: HMSO.

McNeill, B. 1991. *The Back o' the North Wind: the Songs and Music of Brian McNeill*. Newbiggin-by-the-Sea, Northumberland: Dragonfly Music.

McVicar, E. 2010. *The Eskimo Republic: Scots Political Song in Action, 1951–1999*. Linlithgow: Gallus.

Middleton, R. 1981. Folk or Popular? Distinctions, Influences, Continuities. *Popular Music*, 1.

Middleton, R. 1990. *Studying Popular Music*. Milton Keynes: Open University Press.

Milhous, J. 2003. The Economics of Theatrical Dance in Eighteenth-Century London, *Theatre Journal*, 55(3), 496–497. www.jstor.org/stable/25069282 [Accessed 10 July 2013].

Miller, J. 2007. Learning and Teaching Traditional Music. In Beech, J. et al. (eds), *Scottish Life and Society: A Compendium of Scottish Ethnology, Vol. 10: Oral Literature and Performance Culture*. Edinburgh: John Donald, pp. 288–304.

Miller, J. and Duesenberry, P. 2007. *Where Are They Now? The First Graduates of the BA (Scottish Music) Degree*. Paper delivered at 'True North' Palatine Conference, Perth College/UHI, June. https://www.heacademy.ac.uk/knowledge-hub/where-are-they-now-first-graduates-ba-scottish-music-degree

Miller, J.L. 2016. *An Ethnographic Analysis of Participation, Learning and Agency in a Scottish Traditional Music Organisation*. PhD, University of Sheffield, unpublished.

Mitchell, A.C. 1932a. Dance Class Prospectuses and Related Ephemera, MM 194. Aberdeen: Central Library.

Mitchell, A.C. 1932b. Dance Class Prospectuses and Related Ephemera, MM195. Aberdeen: Central Library.

Mitchell, A.C. 1932c. Dancing 1891–1893, MM184. Aberdeen: Central Library.

Mitchell, A.C. 1932d. Dance Class Prospectuses and Related Ephemera, W. Scott, MM196. Aberdeen: Central Library.

Mitchell, A.C. 1932e. School Assembly and Exhibition programmes, MM203. Aberdeen: Central Library.

Mitchell, A.C. 1932f. School Assembly and Exhibition programmes, MM204. Aberdeen: Central Library.

Mitchell, A.C. 1932g. Newspaper Cuttings, MM161. Aberdeen: Central Library.

Morra, I. 2013. *Britishness, Popular Music, and National Identity: The Making of Modern Britain*. Hoboken: Taylor and Francis.

Morrison, A. 2014. Review: A Night For Scotland. *The Herald*, 15 September. www.heraldscotland.com/arts_ents/13179959.Review__A_Night_For_Scotland/.

Morton, F. 2014. Spaces of Learning and the Place of the Conservatoire in Scottish Music. In Ioulia Papageorgi and Graham Welch (eds), *Advanced Musical Performance: Investigations in Higher Education Learning*. Aldershot: Ashgate, pp. 187–199.

Munro, A. 1984. *The Folk Music Revival in Scotland*. London: Kahn and Averill.

Munro, A. 1996. *The Democratic Muse: Folk Music Revival in Scotland*. Aberdeen: Scottish Cultural Press.

Munro, M. 1990. A Song for Glasgow. In McLaughlin (ed.), *A Spiel Amang Us: Glasgow People Writing*. Edinburgh: Mainstream, pp. 159–164.

Murdoch, A. G. 1888. *The Fiddle in Scotland, Being Sketches of "Scotch Fiddlers" and "Fiddle Makers"* London: Simpkin, Marshall, and Co.; Glasgow and Edinburgh: Menzies and Co.

Murphy, J. Personal Communication. 26 October, 2015.

Murray, D. 1994. *Music of the Scottish Regiments: Cogadh no Sith (War or Peace)*. Edinburgh: Mainstream Publishing.

Murray, I. 1910. *The Complete Text-Book of Physical Exercises*. Aberdeen: Alexander Murray; London: Simpkin; Edinburgh: Marshall and Co., John Menzies and Co.

Nairn, T. 1979. *The Break-Up of Britain: Crisis and Neo-Nationalism*, London: Verso.

National Theatre of Scotland. 2014. The National Theatre of Scotland presents The Great Yes, No, Don't Know, Five Minute Theatre Show Created by Anyone, for an Audience of Everyone, [online] http://fiveminutetheatre.com/great_yes_no_dont_know_launch/ [Accessed 2 July 2014].

Nebel, D. 2014. Reviving Scottish Fiddling: An Ethnographic Study of Scottish Fiddling Competitions in the United States. *Excellence in Performing Arts Research*, 1, Article 3. http://digitalcommons.kent.edu/epar/vol1/iss1/3

Nercessian, A. 2000. A Look at the Emergence of the Concept of National Culture in Armenia: The Former Soviet Folk Ensemble. *International Review of the Aesthetics and Sociology of Music*, 79–94.

Nettl, B. 1978. Some Aspects of the History of World Music in the Twentieth Century: Questions, Problems, Concepts. *Ethnomusicology*, 22, 123–136.

Oates, J. L. 2013. *Hamish MacCunn (1868–1916): A Musical Life*. Aldershot: Ashgate.

O'Brien, D. 2013. *Cultural Policy: Management, Value and Modernity in the Creative Industries*. Hoboken: Taylor and Francis.

Oki, T. 2015. Irish Music in Japan: From Nostalgia and Tradition to a New Cosmopolitanism. Presented at the *North Atlantic Fiddle Convention*, Sydney, NS, Canada, 13 October. www.abdn.ac.uk/nafco/previous-conventions/

O Laoire, L. 2005. *On a Rock in the Middle of the Ocean: Songs and Singers in Tory Island*. Ireland: Clo Iar-Chonnachta.

Oliver, S. 2005. *Scott, Byron and the Poetics of Cultural Encounter*. Basingstoke: Palgrave Macmillan.

Olson, I. A. 2007. Scottish Contemporary Traditional Music and Song. In John Beech et al. (eds), *Oral Literature and Performance Culture*, 9, Scottish Life and Society: A Compendium of Scottish Ethnology, Alexander Fenton, general editor. Edinburgh: John Donald in association with the European Ethnological Research Centre and the National Museums of Scotland.

Parry, M. 1930. Studies in the Epic Technique of Oral Verse-Making: Homer and Homeric Style. *Harvard Studies in Classical Philology*, 41, 80.

Pattie, D. 2013. "Who's Scotland?": David Greig, Identity and Scottish Nationhood. In C. Wallace (ed.), *The Theatre of David Greig*. London: Methuen, pp. 194–210.

Pattie, D. 2016. Dissolving into Scotland: National Identity in *Dunsinane* and *The Strange Undoing of Prudencia Hart*. *Contemporary Theatre Review*, 26(1), 19–30.

Peacock, F. 1805. *Sketches Relative to the History and Theory, But More Especially to the Practice of Dancing; as a Necessary Accomplishment to the Youth of Both Sexes; Together with Remarks on the Defects and Bad Habits They Are Liable to in Early Life; and the Best Means of Correcting or Preventing Them. Intended as Hints to the Young Teachers of the Art of Dancing*. Aberdeen: s.n.

Percy, T. 1763. *Five Pieces of Runic Poetry Translated from the Islandic Language*. London: R. and J. Dodsley.

Percy, T. (ed.). 1765. *Reliques of Ancient English Poetry*, 3 vols. London: J. Dodsley.

Peterkin, T. 2016. 'Fewer than a Quarter of Scot Schools Offering Bagpipe Lessons to Pupils – The Scotsman'. *The Scotsman*, 2 May 2016, online edition. http://www.scotsman.com/news/politics/fewer-than-a-quarter-of-scot-schools-offering-bagpipe-lessons-to-pupils-1-4022681.

Porter, J. 1976. Jeannie Robertson's My Son David: A Conceptual Performance Model. *Journal of American Folklore*, 89(351), 7–26.

Porter, J. 2009. *Genre, Conflict, Presence: Traditional Ballads in a Modernizing World*. Trier: WVT.

Pound, E. with Schafer, R. M. (ed.). 1978. *Ezra Pound and Music: The Complete Criticism*. London: Faber.

Purser, J. 2007. *Scotland's Music: A History of the Traditional and Classical Music of Scotland From Early Times to the Present Day*. Mainstream: Edinburgh.

Radical Independence Campaign (RIC). 2012. *Radical Independence Campaign (RIC)*. [Online] https://radical.scot/ [Accessed 31 March 2017].

Ramsay, D. C. 1871. *"Caller Herrin'" Versus the "Herald's" Musical Critic*. For the author, Glasgow.

Ramsden, H., et al. 2011. *The Role of Grassroots Arts Activities in Communities: A Scoping Study*. Birmingham: Third Sector Research Centre, University of Birmingham, Working Paper 68. www.birmingham.ac.uk/generic/tsrc/documents/tsrc/working-papers/working-paper-68.pdf

Rastagno, E., Brauneis, L., Kareda, S., and Pärt, A. 2010. *Arvo Pärt im Gespräch*. Vienna: Universal Edition.

Rebellato, D. 2002. Introduction. In *David Greig: Plays 1*. London: Bloomsbury, pp. ix–xxiii.

Reid, T. 2013. *Theatre & Scotland*. Basingstoke: Palgrave Macmillan.

Renan, E. 1996. What Is a Nation? In G. Eley and R. Suny (eds) *Becoming National: a Reader*. Oxford and New York: Oxford University Press, pp. 42–56.

Rice, T. 1987. Towards a Remodelling of Ethnomusicology. *Ethnomusicology*, 31, 473.

Rice, T. 2002. Bulgaria or Chalgaria: The Attenuation of Bulgarian Nationalism in a Mass-Mediated Popular Music. *Yearbook for Traditional Music*, 34, 25–46.

Riddoch, L. 2014. *Blossom: What Scotland Needs to Flourish*, Revised edn. Edinburgh: Luath Press.

Ritson, J. 1794. *Scottish Song: In Two Volumes*. London: Privately printed for J. Johnson.

Ronström, O. 2010. Fiddling with Pasts: From Tradition to Heritage. In I. Russell and A. Kearney Guigné, Elphinstone Institute (eds), *Crossing Over*. Aberdeen: Elphinstone Institute, pp. 265–282.

Ronström, O. 2014. Traditional Music, Heritage Music. In C. Bithell and J. Hill (eds), *The Oxford Handbook of Music Revival*. New York: Oxford University Press, pp. 43–56.

Rosenberg, N. V. 1986. Big Fish, Small Pond: Country Musicians and Their Markets. In P. Narváez and M. Laba (eds), *Media Sense: The Folklore-Popular Culture Continuum.* Bowling Green, OH: Bowling Green State University Popular Press, pp. 148–166.

Rosenberg, N. V. (ed.). 1993a. *Transforming Tradition: Folk Music Revivals Examined.* Urbana: University of Illinois Press.

Rosenberg, N. V. 1993b. Starvation, Serendipity and the Ambivalence of Bluegrass Revivalism. In N. V. Rosenberg (ed.), *Transforming Tradition: Folk Music Revivals Examined.* Urbana: University of Illinois Press, pp. 194–202.

Rosenberg, N. V. 2014. A Folklorist's Exploration of the Revival Metaphor. In J. Hill and C. Bithell (eds), *The Oxford Handbook of Music Revival.* London: Oxford University Press, pp. 94–115.

Rosenberg, S. 2014. Personal correspondence with the author.

Roud, S., and Bishop, J. (eds). 2014. *The New Penguin Book of English Folk Songs.* London: Penguin Classics.

Runrig. 1987. *The Cutter and the Clan.* [Vinyl] Chrysalis.

Russell, I., and Alburger, M. (eds). 2006. *Play It Like It Is: Fiddle and Dance Studies from around the North Atlantic.* Aberdeen: University of Aberdeen Press.

SAC. 1993. *A Charter for the Arts in Scotland.* Edinburgh: Scottish Arts Council.

Saïd, E. 1991. *Musical Elaborations.* s.l.: Columbia University Press.

Sanderson, D. 2015. Ballet and Bagpipes – £250k Government Ad Campaign Sparks Mixed Response. *The Herald*, [online] www.heraldscotland.com/news/13199221. Ballet_and_bagpipes____250k_government_ad_campaign_sparks_mixed_response/ [Accessed 30 January 2015].

Sanger, K., and Kinnaird, A. 1992. *Tree of Strings: Crann Nan Teud: A History of the Harp in Scotland.* Kinmor Music, Temple, Midlothian, Scotland.

Scahill, A. 2004. *The Knotted Chord: Harmonic Accompaniment in Printed and Recorded Sources of Irish Traditional Music.* PhD, University College, Dublin.

Schechner, R. 2006. *Performance Studies.* Oxon: Routledge.

Scotland Yet. 2014. [Film] Directed by Jack Foster. Produced by Christopher Silver.

Scott, C. M. 2005. *The Scottish Highland Dancing Tradition.* Unpublished doctoral thesis, University of Edinburgh.

Scott Skinner, J. 1910. Tullochgorum. Regal Gramophone Records, G. 6619.

Scott Skinner, J. 2002. *James Scott Skinner: The Strathspey King.* Temple Records COMD 2084.

Scott, W. 1849, 1855. Dance Assembly Programmes [ephemera] A. C. Mitchell Collection. MM196. Aberdeen: Central Library.

Scott, W. 1902 [1802–1803]. *Minstrely of the Scottish Border*, 4 vols. Edinburgh: Blackwood.

Scottish Arts Council. 1984. *The Traditional Arts of Scotland: Report of the Traditional and Folk Arts of Scotland Working Party.* Edinburgh: SAC.

Scottish Executive. 2000. *Creating Our Future . . . Minding Our Past: Scotland's National Cultural Strategy.* Edinburgh: Scottish Executive.

Scottish Government. 2010. *Traditional Arts Working Group Report*, January. www.gov.scot/Publications/2010/01/28100441/14 [Accessed 29 October 2015].

Scottish Government (ed.). 2013. *Scotland's Future: Your Guide to an Independent Scotland.* Edinburgh: Scottish Government.

Scottish Government. 2013a. 'Scotland's People Annual Report: Results from 2012 Scottish Household Survey'. Edinburgh: The Scottish Government, National Statistics. http://www.scotland.gov.uk/Publications/2013/08/6973/downloads

References 279

Scottish Government. 2014. 'Scotland's People Annual Report: Results from 2013 Scottish Household Survey'. Edinburgh: The Scottish Government, National Statistics. http://www.scotland.gov.uk/Publications/2014/08/7973/downloads#res-1

Scottish Government. 2015. *Response to the Traditional Arts Working Group Report.* www.gov.scot/Publications/2010/12/03105348/1 [Accessed 29 October 2015].

Scruton, R. 1997. *The Aesthetics of Music.* Oxford: Clarendon Press.

SDTA [Scottish Dance Teachers' Alliance]. 2015. *History.* [online] http://sdta.co.uk/about/ [Accessed 8 April 2015].

Seattle, M. 2014. Facebook Group - Theme for the Early Days of a Better Nation. https://www.facebook.com/ThemeForTheEarlyDays/ [accessed 25 June 2014].

Seeger, C. 1958. Prescriptive and Descriptive Music-Writing. *The Musical Quarterly,* 44(2), 184–195.

Service, J. 1891. Suggested Association of British Dancing Preceptors. *Dancing,* 1(1), 6.

Seton, B., and Grant, J. 1920. *Pipes of War.* Glasgow: Maclehose, Jackson and Co.

Sharp, C. 1907. *English Folk-Song: Some Conclusions.* London: Simpkin and Co. Ltd.

Shaw, M.F. 1955. *Folksongs and Folklore of South Uist.* London: Rutland and Keegan Paul.

Shaw, M.F. 1993. *From the Alleghenies to the Hebrides.* Edinburgh: Canongate Books Ltd.

Shelton, R. 2011. *No Direction Home: The Life and Music of Bob Dylan.* Omnibus, London, pp. 305–314.

Shepherd, F. 2012. The Treacherous Orchestra Stay Faithful to Their Reputation for Loudness Without Betraying Folk Roots. *The Scotsman* [online] 15 January 2012. www.scotsman.com/what-s-on/music/the-treacherous-orchestra-stay-faithful-to-their-reputation-for-loudness-without-betraying-folk-roots-1-2058041 [Accessed August 2016].

Sheridan, M., and Byrne, C. 2008. Ceilidh Culture and Higher Education. *International Journal of Music Education,* 26, 147–159.

Shoolbraid, M. (ed.). 2010. *The High-Kilted Muse: Peter Buchan and his Secret Songs of Silence.* Jackson: University of Mississippi Press in association with the Elphinstone Institute, University of Aberdeen.

Skinner, J.S. 1881. *The Miller o' Hirn.* Elgin: s.n.

Skinner, J.S. 1884. *The Elgin Collection.* Elgin: s.n.

Skinner, J.S. (ed.). 1905. *The People's Ball Room Guide.* Dundee and London: John Leng and Co. Ltd.

Skinner, J.S. 1994. *My Life and Adventures.* Aberdeen: Arts and Recreation Division, Central Library in association with Wallace Music, Pathhead, Midlothian.

Slobin, M. 1983. Rethinking "Revival" of American Ethnic Music. *New York Folklore,* 9(3–4), 37–44.

Slobin, M. 1987. *Subcultural Sounds: Micromusic of the West.* Middletown, CT: Wesleyan University Press.

Slobin, M. 2011. *Folk Music: A Very Short Introduction.* Oxford and New York: Oxford University Press.

Small, C. 1998. *Musicking: The Meaning of Performance and Listening.* Hanover, NH: University Press of New England.

Smith, A.D. 1994. Gastronomy or Geology? The Role of Nationalism in the Reconstruction of Nations. *Nations and Nationalism,* 1(1), 3–23.

Smollett, T. 1771; this edition 1984. *The Expedition of Humphry Clinker.* Oxford: Oxford University Press.

SOBHD. 2010. [Scottish Official Board of Highland Dancing] 2010. *Assemble and Leap.* Edinburgh: SOBHD, p. 102.

SOBHD. 2015. *Highland Dancing: The Official Textbook of the Scottish Official Board of Highland Dancing*. Edinburgh: Thomas Nelson 1955 1st ed.; Glasgow: Lindsay Publications 1993 6th ed., 2015 8th ed.

Sorensen, J. 2007. The Debatable Borders of English and Scottish Song and Ballad Collections. In C. Lamont and M. Rossington (eds), *Romanticism's Debatable Lands*. Basingstoke: Palgrave Macmillan, pp. 80–91.

Spracklen, K. 2013. Nazi Punks Folk off: Leisure, Nationalism, Cultural Identity and the Consumption of Metal and Folk Music. *Leisure Studies*, 32, 415–428. http://doi.org/10.1080/02614367.2012.674152

Stafford, F. 2007. Writing on the Borders. In C. Lamont and M. Rossington (eds), *Romanticism's Debatable Lands*. Basingstoke: Palgrave Macmillan, pp. 13–26.

Steele, D. 1998. *Chasing Shadows*. [CD] Temple.

Stenhouse, W. 1853. *Illustrations of the Lyric Poetry and Music of Scotland*. Edinburgh: William Blackwood and Sons.

Stephens, A. 1813. *Memoirs of John Horne Tooke*, 2 vols. London: J. Johnson and Co.

Stewart, C. 2015. Packed, Positive and Proud... on the Road with Yestival. [Online] www.heraldscotland.com/news/13168735.Packed__positive_and_proud____on_the_road_with_Yestival/ [Accessed 30 March 2017].

Stewart-Robertson, J. 1884 [1996]. *The Athole Collection of the Dance Music of Scotland*. Edinburgh and London: MacLachlan and Stewart; Cramer, 1884, re-published 1996 by The Highland Music Trust.

Stock, J. 2008. New Directions in Ethnomusicology: Seven Themes Towards Disciplinary Renewal. In H. Stobart (ed.), *The New (Ethno)musicologies. Europea: Ethnomusicologies and Modernities, No. 8*. Lanham, Toronto and Plymouth: Scarecrow Press.

Stokes, Martin. 1997. Introduction: Ethnicity, Identity and Music. In Stokes (ed.), *Ethnicity, Identity and Music: The Musical Construction of Place*. Oxford and New York: Berg.

Stokoe, J. (ed.). 1882. *Northumbrian Minstrelsy: A Collection of Bag-Pipe Tunes, Chiefly of the Olden Time, Adapted to the Northumberland Small-Pipes*. Newcastle upon Tyne: Society of Antiquaries of Newcastle upon Tyne.

Sunday Post. 2014. *Meet the Face Behind Lady Alba Dr Zara Gladman*. [Online] www.sundaypost.com/in10/health/meet-the-face-behind-lady-alba-dr-zara-gladman/ [Accessed 30 March 2017].

Sweers, B. 2005. *Electric Folk: The Changing Face of English Traditional Music*. Oxford: Oxford University Press.

Swing, P. S. 1991. *Fiddle Teaching in Shetland Isles Schools, 1973–1985*. PhD Thesis, University of Texas, Austin.

Symon, P. 1997. Music and National Identity in Scotland: A Study of Jock Tamson's Bairns. *Popular Music*, 16(2), 203–216.

Tagg, P. 2000. "The Work": An Evaluative Charge. In M. Talbot (ed.), *The Musical Work: Reality or Invention? Liverpool Music Symposium*. Liverpool: Liverpool University Press, pp. 153–167.

Tajbakhsh, K. 2001. *The Promise of the City: Space, Identity and Politics in Contemporary Social Thought*. Berkeley, Los Angeles and London: University of California Press.

Taudevin, J. 2014. *Julia Taudevin: My Yes*. [Online] http://nationalcollective.com/2014/06/20/julia-taudevin-my-yes/ [Accessed 30 March 2017].

Taylor, G. D. 1929. *Some Traditional Scottish Dances*. London: C. W. Beaumont, Imperial Society Dance Monograph.

Taylor, T. D. 2012. *The Sounds of Capitalism: Advertising, Music, and the Conquest of Culture*. Chicago: University of Chicago Press.

Taylor, T. D. 2014. Fields, Genres, Brands, Culture. *Theory and Critique*, 55(2), 159–174.
Thompson, S. A., and Thompson, P. 1790. *Thirty Favourite Scots Songs*. London: Privately Published.
Thomson, D. S. 1983. *The Companion to Gaelic Scotland*. Oxford: Blackwell, p. 179.
Titon, J. T. 2009. Music and Sustainability: An Ecological Viewpoint. *The World of Music*, 51, 119–137. https://doi.org/10.2307/41699866
Tomlinson, J. 2003. Globalization and Cultural Identity. In D. Held and A. McGrew (eds), *The Global Transformations Reader: An Introduction to the Globalization Debate*. Oxford: Polity Press, pp. 269–277.
Traditional Music Forum. 2017. *Census of Traditional Music Learning in the Community 2015–16*. Edinburgh: Traditional Music Forum.
Treacherous Orchestra. 2012. *Origins*. [CD] Navigator.
Treacherous Orchestra. 2013. *Blueprint*. [score] Self-published by band members.
Treacherous Orchestra. 2015a. *Grind*. [CD] Reveal.
Treacherous Orchestra. 2015b. *Press Release/Biography* [pdf]. www.treacherousorchestra.com/wp-content/uploads/2014/10/TreacherousOrchGRIND-PR.pdf [Accessed August 2016].
Trenary, G. 1915. Ballad Collections of the Eighteenth Century. *The Modern Language Review*, 10(3), 283–303.
Trevor-Roper, H. 2008. *The Invention of Scotland*. Ithaca, NY: Yale University Press.
Tuckman, B. W. 1965. Developmental Sequence in small Groups. *Psychological Bulletin*, 63(6), 384–399.
Tuckman, B. W., and Jensen, M. A. 1977. Stages of Small-Group Development Revisited. *Group Organization Management*, 2, 419–427.
Turino, T. 2008. *Music as Social Life. The Politics of Participation*. Chicago: University of Chicago Press.
Turner, V. 1969. *The Ritual Process: Structure and Anti-Structure*. Chicago: Aldine.
Tyson, R. 1988. The Economy of Aberdeen. In J. Smith and D. Stevenson (eds), *Aberdeen in the Nineteenth Century*. Aberdeen: Centre for Scottish Studies, University of Aberdeen, pp. 19–36.
UNESCO. 2003. *International Convention for the Safeguarding of the Intangible Cultural Heritage*. Paris: UNESCO. http://unesdoc.unesco.org/images/0013/001325/132540e.pdf
Vallely, F. 2003. Invention of Tradition, Imagined Community and the Ulster-Scots Quest for Identity Through Music. *Proceedings of Society for Musicology in Ireland Conference 2003* (published online, 2004).
Vallely, F. 2004. Singing the Boundaries: Music and Identity Politics in Northern Ireland. In U. Kockel and M. Nic Craith (eds), *Communicating Cultures*, vol. 1. Münster/London: LIT Verlag, pp. 129–148.
Vallely, F. 2005. Authenticity to Classicisation: The Course of Revival in Irish Traditional Music. *Irish Review*, 33, 51–69.
Vallely, F. 2008. *Tuned Out: Traditional Music and Identity in Northern Ireland*. Cork: Cork University Press.
Veblen, K. 2005. Community Music and Praxialism. In D. Elliot (ed.), *Praxial Music Education*. Oxford: Oxford University Press, pp. 308–328.
Wachsmann, K. 1980. Musical Instruments: Classification. In *New Grove Dictionary of Music and Musicians*, vol. 9. London: Palgrave Macmillan, p. 238.
Wallace, A. 1956. Revitalization Movements. *American Anthropologist*, 58, 264–281.
Wallace, C. 2013. *The Theatre of David Greig*. London: Methuen.

Washburne, C. J. 2004. Does Kenny G Play Bad Jazz? A Case Study. In C. J. Washburne and M. Derno (eds), *Bad Music: The Music We Love To Hate*. Abingdon: Routledge, pp. 123–147.

Watson, L. 2012. The New Traditional School in Scotland: Innovation, Beyond-Tune Composition and a Traditional Musician's Creative Practice. Unpublished PhD thesis, Royal Conservatoire of Scotland.

Watson, L. 2013. *The New Traditional School in Scotland: Innovation, Beyond-Tune Composition and a Traditional Musician's Creative Practice*. PhD Thesis, University of St Andrews.

Weinberger, E. 2006. Introduction. In Alan Riach and Michael Grieve (eds), *Hugh MacDiarmid: Selected Poetry*. New York: New Directions.

Wenger, E. 1998. *Communities of Practice: Learning, Meaning and Doing*. Cambridge: Cambridge University Press.

Wesling, D. 1993. Mikhail Bakhtin and the Social Poetics of Dialect. *Papers in Language and Literature*, 29(3), 303–220.

West, G. 2004. Land and Lyrics: The Dynamics of Music and Song in Rural Society. *Review of Scottish Culture*, 15, 57–66.

West, G. 2012a. *Voicing Scotland. Folk, Culture, Nation*. Edinburgh: Luath Press.

West, G. 2012b. Piping and the Folk Revival. In E. Bort (ed.), *Tis Sixty Years Since: The First People's Festival Ceilidh and the Scottish Folk Revival*. Ochtertyre: Grace Note.

West, G. 2012c. Scottish Military Music. In E. Spiers, J. Crang and M. Strickland (eds), *A Military History of Scotland*. Edinburgh: Edinburgh University Press, pp. 648–668.

Westbrook, S., Anderson, S., Brownlee, S., and Gregson-MacLeod, L. 2010. *The Economic and Social Impacts of the Fèisean: Final Report for Highlands and Islands Enterprise*. Nairn: S. Westbrook.

Western, T. 2015. *National Phonography: Field Recording and Sound Archiving in Postwar Britain*. Ph.D Thesis, Reid School of Music, University of Edinburgh.

White, J. 2010. City Rivalries and the Modernisation of Eighteenth-Century London, 1720–1770. *Literatur in Wissenschaft und Unterricht*, 43(2/3), 83–102.

Wilkes, J. 1763. *The North Briton*. No. 44. 2 April. National Library of Scotland [Ac].7.17–19.

Williamson, R. 1976. *English, Welsh, Scottish & Irish Fiddle Tunes*. New York: Oak Publications.

Wilson, T. 1808. *An Analysis of Country Dancing*. London: s.n.

Wood, N. 2012. Playing with "Scottishness": Musical Performance, Non-Representational Thinking and the "doings" of National Identity. *Cultural Geographies*, 19, 195–215. http://doi.org/10.1177/1474474011420543

Wright, D. 1726. *Aria di Camera: Being a Choice Collection of Scotch, Irish & Welsh air's for the Violin and German Flute, by the Following Masters. Mr. Alex: Urquahart, of Edinburgh. Mr. Dermt. O'connor, of Limrick. Mr. Hugh Edwards, of Carmarthen*. London: Privately printed.

Zaroulia, M. 2013. "Sharing the Moment"; Europe, Affect, and Utopian Performatives in the Eurovision Song Contest. In K. Fricker and M. Gluhovic (eds), *Performing the 'New' Europe: Identities, Feelings, and Politics in the Eurovision Song Contest*. Basingstoke: Palgrave Macmillan, pp. 31–52.

Index

accents 197–198
AC/DC 8
Aikin, John 197
Ainslie, Ross 244
Airs and Melodies Peculiar to the Highlands of Scotland and the Isles (Fraser) 223
Alburger, Mary Anne 218
Anderson, Benedict 241
Anderson, Paul 221–222
Anderson, Tom 219
Anglo-Scottish Ballad and its Imaginary Context, The (Atkinson) 117
Angus Grant: Highland Fiddle (Grant) 220
anti-Polaris singers 61, 71, 93, 95, 98–101, 106
Arab Strap 259
art music 6–7
Athole Collection of the Dance Music of Scotland, The (Stewart-Robertson) 219, 224
Atkinson, David 117
Atom of Delight, The (Gunn) 163
Auld Lang Syne 170
authenticity 19–21, 81–82, 89, 234–235, 256–259

Baby Please Don't Go (blues song) 164
Badcock, Jack 67
bagpipes 8, 23–25, 63, 84, 97, 106–107, 127, 134, 141–147, 168, 175, 184, 204–206, 209, 214, 242–246, 253
  see also pipes
Bakhtin, Mikhail 68, 198
'Ballad of Co Lin' (Greig) 112, 115, 119
ballads 109–120, 192, 236–237
Baptie, David 219
Barrie, J. M. 44
Battlefield Band 47, 102

'Battle of the Somme, The' (Lawrie) 242–244
Beattie, James 193
Beaumont, Cyril 185
Beauties of Niel Gow, The (Gow) 223
'Bedroom Tax Song: Ye Cannae Have A Spare Room in a Pokey Cooncil Flat' (McNaughtan) 72
Bennett, Martyn 68, 75
Bishop, Henry 164
Blake, Andrew 7
Blaustein, Richard 204, 210
Blaydon Races, The (folk song) 5
Blazing Fiddles 141
'Bloody Fields of Flanders, The' (pipe march) 100
Blues Poets, The 164
Blythman, Morris (alias 'Thurso Berwick') 98
Bohlman, Philip 102, 108
'Bonny Portmore' (folk song) 161
Born, Georgina 69
'Both Sides the Tweed' (Gaughan) 101–102
'Both Sides the Tweed' (Hogg) 72
Bourriaud, Nicholas 69
Brexit 4, 18
British Association of Teachers of Dance (BATD) 183
British Library 28
'British traditional music' 7–8
Britten, Benjamin 7, 165
Brown, Kevin 73
Bruford, Alan 220
Buchan, John 245
Buchan, Peter 160
Burn, Ali 73
Burns, Robert 2, 20, 65, 72, 159–162, 170, 253
Byrne, Steve 64, 67

Caledonia (Maclean) 72, 170
Callar Herring (Gow) 126
Cambridge Folk Festival 139
Cameron, Donald 161
Campaign for Nuclear Disarmament (CND) 98
Campbell, Angus Peter 54, 55
Campbell, John Lorne 51
Campbell, Katherine 218
Canna Collection 55, 59
Canna House 59
Canterbury Tales, The (Chaucer) 197
Capercaillie 9, 74, 141
Captain's Collection, The (Hardie) 226
Carlyle, Alison 67
Carthy, Eliza 153
Celtic Colours festival 83
Celtic Connections festival 75, 82, 83, 139, 153
Chappell, William 236
Charter for the Arts, The 47–48
Chaucer, Geoffrey 193–194, 197
Cheviot the Stag and the Black, Black Oil, The (ceilidh play) 67
Child, Francis 103
Chisholm, Jori 23
Chorolistha (Scott) 181
Christie, William 225
'civic' nationalism 63
Clarsach Society, The 20
Cocker, W. D. 245
Collection of New Strathspey Reels, A (Morison) 135
Collection of Strathspeys (Christie) 225
Collinson, Francis 220
Commonwealth Games 100
community-based traditional music 23, 30–42, 132–133
Compendium of Scottish Ethnology (Eydmann) 203
Complete Repository of Original Scots Tunes, Strathspeys, Jigs and Dances, The (Gow) 129–130, 218
Connolly, Billy 163–164
conservatoires 83–92
Contemporary Scottish Studies (Grieve) 248
Convention for the Safeguarding of the Intangible Cultural Heritage 17–18, 26, 28
Cooke, Peter 220
'Coronation Coronach' (Glasgow Song Guild) 98
Cowan, Edward 192

Craig, Cairns 47, 93
Craig, David 94
Craigie Dhu (Maclean) 170
Crawford, Robert 193, 198
Creative Scotland 22, 23, 27, 28, 31, 35, 49, 50, 132
Crochallan (Burns) 160
Crockett, S. R. 44
Crompton, Robert Morris 181–182, 183

Dalrymple, David 199
dancing *see* Highland Dancing
Dancing (Crompton) 181
Darwin, Charles 249
Davie's Caledonian Repository (Davie) 219
Davies, Terence 165
Deans, Effie 164
Debussy, Claude 7
DeNora, Tia 69
Dewar, Donald 48
Dickson, Josh 256
Dietz, Karen 73
Ding Dong Dollar: Anti-Polaris and Scottish Republican Songs (record) 98, 100
Discourse of World Music, The (Frith) 145
'Dissolving into Scotland' (Pattie) 117
Distant Voices, Still Lives (Davies) 165, 166
DJ Dolphin Boy 74
Dolan, Jill 109, 115–116
Dreaming of Glenisla (Talisker) 214–215
Dublin Institute of Technology Conservatory 89
Duncan, Gordon 106, 244
Duncan, Ian 244
Dundee Scottish Musical Society 219
d'Urfey, Thomas 194
Dylan, Bob 164

Easy Club 47
Ebsworth, John Woodfall 236
Edinburgh Festival 163
Edinburgh Highland Reel and Strathspey Society 219
education: Bachelor of Arts in Scottish Music 81, 82; Glasgow Fiddle Workshop 30–42
'El Agua de la Vida' (Salsa Celtica) 139, 151
'El Camino' (Salsa Celtica) 152
Elder, Morag 224
Elgar, Edward 7

Elgin Collection, The (Skinner) 179
Elliot, Jean 103
Emmerson, George 220
'ethnic' nationalism 63
'Eun Bheag Chanaidh' ('The Little Bird of Canna') 55–56
European classical tradition 7
Evans, Evan 191

Fält, Marit 68
Farewell to Stromness (Maxwell Davies) 239
Far Far From Ypres (McCalman) 242–251
Fegan, Paul 259
Fèisean nan Gàidheal 48
Fergusson, Heloise Russell 214
Festival Interceltique de Lorient 83
Fiddle in Scotland, The (Murdoch) 219
Fiddle Music of Scotland, The (Hunter) 224
Fiddler's Bid 141
fiddles 206, 209, 226
Fifield, Fraser 152
Finnie, David 67, 72–73
Fisher, Tony 120
'Flowers of the Forest' (Elliot) 103
Foley, John Miles 246
folk 'fusion' music 103–108
folk music 9, 94–98, 122–125, 129, 134–135, 231–233, 254, 259
folk music revival 23, 45–47, 66, 82–83, 95–98, 103–108, 201–216
Folksongs and Folklore of South Uist (Shaw) 51, 55
Fourth Book of New Strathspey Reels (Mackintosh) 221
Fowlis, Julie 153
France 7
Fraser, Alasdair 33
Fraser, Iain 32
Fraser, Simon 223, 226
'Freedom Come Aa Ye' (Henderson) 64–65, 72, 244
Frith, Simon 120, 143, 145

Gaelic folklore 52–59
Gallacher, George 164
Gallini, Giovanni 180
Gaughan, Dick 47, 67, 71, 72, 93, 101–102, 171–172, 215, 250
Geddes, Amy 67
Geddes, Patrick 249
Gelbart, Matthew 123
Gellner, Ernest 240
Germany 7
Ghillie Callum (Peacock) 177

Gibbon, Lewis Grassic 246
Gibson, Corey 95, 101, 104
Gille-Goillidh, Will MC 74
Gillespie, Bobby 253
Gillies, Anne Lorne 67
Glasgow Fiddle Workshop (GFW): aims of 31–32; case study 30–42; challenges facing 35–40; cultural capital generated at 38–41; 'informal education' setting 37; members 32; public funding 35; roots and development of 32–34; tutors 35–37
Glastonbury festival 139
Glen, John 224
Glen Collection, The (Glen) 218, 224
Glenfiddich Championship 220
globalisation 6
Gonella, Ron 226
Gore, Charles 223
Gow, Nathaniel 125–127, 129–130, 131, 218, 223
Gow, Niel 20, 221–224
Graham, George Farquhar 236
Gramsci, Antonio 62
Grant, Aonghas 67
Gray, Gibbie 227–228
'Great Scottish Latin Adventure, The' (Salsa Celtica) 151
Great War 242–251
Green, Mairearad 68
Greig, David 109–110
Greig, Robbie 67
Grieve, Christopher Murray 248–249
Groom, Nick 197
Guilbault, Jocelyne 70
Gunn, George 68
Gunn, Neil 163
Guthrie, Chris 246
Guthrie, Woody 72

Haig, Douglas 243
Haines, John 134
Hames, Scott 107
Hamish the Movie (film) 75
Handful of Earth (Gaughan) 101
Hardie, Jony 226
Harker, Dave 95, 233
Harmonice Musices Odhecaton (Petrucci) 194
Harvey, Alex 254
Helsinki University of the Arts 90
Henderson, Hamish 2, 62, 64, 75, 93, 94, 98, 100–101, 103, 104, 128, 244, 250
Henderson, Ingrid 67
Herder, Johannes Gottfried 5–6, 81

heritage 134
Heritage Lottery Fund 27
Highland Cathedral (tune) 5
Highland Collections (Highland Music Trust) 224–226
Highland dancing: eighteenth-century background 176–177; globalisation of 175–188; nineteenth-century developments 177–183; twentieth-century developments 183–187
Highland Dancing (SOBHD and Scott) 186–187
'Highland Division's Farewell to Sicily, The' (Henderson) 244
Highland Fling (Wilson) 176, 179, 184, 185
Highland Music Trust 224
Hill, Frederick 178–179
historically informed performance (HIP) 133–134
Hogg, James 72, 101–102, 200
home 169–170
Home, Sweet Home (Bishop) 164
Hue and Cry 8
Hume, David 193, 197
Humphry Clinker (Smollett) 193
Hunter, James 224
Hurley, Kieran 67
Hutton, Ali 104
Huxley, Thomas Henry 249
Hyder, Ken 215
Hyslop, Fiona 49

'Iain Duncan Smith's a Ratbag' (song) 72
identity myths 44–47, 82
Illustrated Guide to the National Dances of Scotland (Mackenzie) 184
Imperial Society of Dance Teachers (ISDT) 180, 183, 184–186
inauthenticity 234–235
Incredible String Band 254
independence referendum: alternative performative response 66–68; 'relational aesthetic' 68–71; role of traditional music 3–4, 67–76, 96–98, 133; role of TradYES 63–66; songs for Scotland 71–74
Intangible Cultural Heritage (ICH) 17–21, 26–29
'invented tradition' 127–129
Irish dancing 187

Jackson, Billy 47
Jacob, Violet 245–251
Jacobite Relics (Hoggs) 101

Jansch, Bert 254
jazz 130–131
'Jazz at Lincoln Center' programme 130–131
'Jeely Piece' (McNaughtan) 72
Jenkins, George 176
Johnson, David 218
Johnson, Linton Kwesi 198

Kailyard 44–45, 46–47, 93, 249
Karpeles, Maud 124, 135
'Keep Right on to the End of the Road' (Lauder) 250
Kelman, James 164
Kennedy Fraser, Marjorie 52–53, 237
Kennedy, Mary-Ann 68, 74
Kerr, Roderick Watson 245
Kershaw, Baz 70
Kloss, Jürgen 165
Kropotkin, Peter 249

'Lads O' the Fair' (McNeill) 103
Lady Alba (Zara Gladman) 67, 74
'Lady Charlotte Campbell's Strathspey' (Mackintosh) 221
Laidlaw, Margaret 199
Lauder, Harry 93, 253
Lauder, John 251
Lawrence, Douglas 221–222
Lawrie, Willie 242–244
Lawson, Greg 82
Lee, Joseph 245
Leonard, Tom 198
Levack, Brian 192
Livingston, Tamara 205–206, 209
Livingston, Thomas 104
Lomax, Alan 103
Louie (hip-hop artist) 74

MacAndrew, Hector 221–222
MacAndrew, Peter 222–223
MacCaig, Norman 45, 214
MacColl, Ewan 127
MacColl, Lauren 224–226, 228
MacCunn, Hamish 6, 82
MacDiarmid, Hugh 2, 45, 93, 94, 100–101, 250
MacDonald, Allan 74
MacDonald, Catriona 227–228
MacDonald, Fraser 64
Macdonald, Hugh 220
MacFarlane, Iain 67
MacGibbon, William 6
Machell, Thomas 124

MacInnes, Kathleen 67, 153
MacIntosh, James 222
MacKenzie, Alexander 6
Mackenzie, Donald R. 184–185
MacKenzie, Eilidh 71, 74
Mackenzie, Fiona 67
MacKinnon, Dòl Eoin 67
MacKinnon, Niall 93, 95
Mackintosh, E. A. 245
Mackintosh, Robert 221
MacLachlan, Ewan 176
Maclean, Dougie 72, 170
MacLean, John 100
MacLennan, Dolina 67
MacMillan, James 6
McNaughton, Adam 72
Macpherson, James 6, 193
MacRae, Peggy 53
Malcolm, Jim 245–250
Malinky 67
'Man's a Man, A' (Burns) 65, 72
Mantie, Roger 40
March, Strathspey and Reel (MSR) 134
Marquis of Huntly's Highland Fling, The (Jenkins) 176, 177, 179, 184
Marsden, Stuart 135
Marshall, William 129
Martyn, John 254
Massie, Alex 97
Matheson, Karen 9
Maxwell Davies, Peter 6, 239
McCalman, Ian 242, 250
McConnell, Jack 48
McFadyen, Mairi 115, 117–118
McGarvey, Darren 'Loki' 97
McGinn, Matt 98
McGuire, Eddie 6
McGuirk, Carol 160, 162
McInnes, Kathleen 74
McKay, Catriona 82, 209
McKellar, Kenneth 253
McKerrell, Simon 93, 97, 102, 105, 133, 249, 258
McLennan, Ewan 74
McMaster, Natalie 32
McMillan, Joyce 47, 241
McNeill, Brian 72, 93, 102–103, 105
McVicar, Ewan 98, 101
Middleton, Richard 203
migration 159–172
Miller, Siobhan 74
Miller of Hirn (Skinner) 179
Mitchell, A. Cosmo 180–181, 183
Moffat, Aidan 259

'Monstruos y Demonios, Angels and Lovers' (Salsa Celtica) 150
Moore, Hamish 67
Morison, John 135
Mr McFall's Chamber 141
Muir Wood, John 236
Munro, Ailie 98
Munro, Michael 167
Murdoch, Alexander 219
Murphy, John 46
Murray, Anne 247
Musgrave, Theo 6
musical lineage 221–224
musical nationalism: deterritorialisation of 2–3; genre and 5–10; Scottish song and 98–103, 167–169; traditional music and 9, 63–64
Musical Scotland, Past and Present (Baptie) 219
'Music and Identity' (Frith) 120
'Music Revivals: Towards a General Theory' (Livingston) 205
Musica Nova festival 163
musicians 21–23, 83–87, 254–256
Musicking (Small) 114
Mutual Aid (Kropotkin) 249
My Heart's in the Highlands (or *Farewell to the Highlands*) (Burns) 159–162

Nairn, Tom 93, 101, 250
Napier, Findlay 74
National Piping Centre 25–26, 83
National Theatre of Scotland (NTS) 51, 109–120
National Trust for Scotland 56–58, 59
National Youth Pipe Band of Scotland 83
New Penguin Book of English Folk Songs, The (Bishop and Roud) 238
'No Gods (and Precious Few Heroes)' (McNeil) 72, 102
North Briton (journal) 193
North Country Fair (Dylan) 164
'Notebook of Dances' (Hill) 178

Oban High School's School of Traditional Music 83
Odd, Stanley 74
O Headhra, Brian 67
Olson, Ian A. 49
Olumide, Eunice 68
'O Mo Dhùthaich' ('Oh My Land') (folksong) 51
One, Two, Hey (Kelman) 164
online teaching 23–25

oral transmission 129–130
origin myths 143–145
Oswald, James 6
Oxford Handbook of Music Revival (Hill and Bithell) 208

Parry, Milman 246
Pärt, Arvo 159
Peacock, Francis 176–177, 180, 181–182, 187
Peatbog Faeries 141
Percy, Elizabeth 191
Percy, Thomas: background 191–194; editorial philosophy 194–197; erasure of women as active participants in ballad culture 199–200; *Reliques of Ancient English Poetry* 191–200; study of accents 197–198
Performing Rites (Frith) 257
Petrucci, Ottaviano 194
pipes 68, 106, 124, 134, 141–142, 147–148, 242–243 *see also* bagpipes
Piping Live festival 83
Plockton High School Centre of Excellence in Traditional Music 83
policy: emergence of framework for traditional music 44–50; ICH support for traditional music 17–21, 26–29; inequity in current cultural 26–29
popular music 8–9, 133
Popular Music of the Olden Times (Chappell) 236
Porter, James 114–115
Primal Scream 252
Proclaimers, The 74, 168, 252
Proms in the Park 139

'Radical Democratic Theatre' (Fisher) 120
Raeburn, Henry 223
Ramsay, Allan 164, 194
Randolph's Leap 74
Rantin (ceilidh play) 67
Ravel, Maurice 7
Redwood Cathedral (Gaughan) 171
Reid, Charlie 168
Reid, Craig 168
Reid, Trish 118–119
'relational aesthetic' 68–71
Reliques of Ancient English Poetry (Percy) 191–200
Renan, Ernest 240
Riddoch, Leslie 172
Ring, Brendan 106
Roberts, Alasdair 9

Robertson, James 244
Rocha, Lino 148
Ronström, Owe 134
Ross, Adam 74
Roud, Steve 238
Rousseau, Jean-Jacques 5
Roussel, Albert 7
Rowan, Kaela 74
Roy, Don 38
Royal College of Music in Stockholm 90, 91
Royal Conservatoire of Scotland 25, 81, 124, 256
Royal Scottish Academy of Music and Drama 81, 82
Royal Scottish National Orchestra (RSNO) 44

Sagarzazu, Magda 55
Salsa Celtica: background 139–140; bricolage approach 146–150; 'El Agua de la Vida' 151; 'El Camino' 152; 'The Great Scottish Latin Adventure' 151; influential contributor to 244; lineup 140–141; look and feel 150–154; 'Monstruos y Demonios, Angels and Lovers' 150; origin myths 143–145; sound of 141–142, 146–150; traditional music and 145–146
'Sash My Father Wore, The' (Orange anthem) 98
'Say Yes' (Burns) 73
Schmitz, Oskar 7
School of Scottish Studies sound archive 226–228
Scotish Minstrel (Smith) 237
Scotland's Sounds 28
Scotland's Story (The Proclaimers) 168
'Scotland Yet' (Steele) 98
Scots Music Group 48
Scott, Edward 181
Scottish Arts Council 45–48
Scottish Association of Teachers of Dancing 182
Scottish Ballet 44
Scottish Chamber Orchestra 44
Scottish Country Dancing 187
Scottish Dance Teachers Alliance (SDTA) 186
Scottish Dance Teachers Association (SDTA) 183
Scottish fiddle music: continuity/revival/invention of 218–220; modern revivals of 209; musical lineage 221–224; old collections 224–226; present-day

performance of 217–228; recordings from sound archive 226–228
Scottish National Jazz Orchestra 141
Scottish National Orchestra 163
Scottish Official Board of Highland Dancing (SOBHD) 183
Scottish Opera 44
Scottish Storytelling Forum 50
Scottish Violin Music from the Gow Collections (Gonella) 226
Scott, Walter 2, 103, 117, 164–165, 199
Scott, William 178
Screamadelica (Primal Scream) 252
Seattle, Matt 67, 72–73
'Se Diuram' (song) 53
Service, John 182–183
'Se t-churam' (song) 53
Shand, Jimmy 253
Shantruse (Wilson) 176
Sharp, Cecil 165
Shaw, Margaret Fay 51–58
Sheridan, Thomas 197
Shippey, Toby 140, 143–145
Shooglenifty 74, 106, 141
Shotts and Dykehead Caledonia Pipe Band 20
Sibelius Academy 90
Silly Wizard 93
Simple Minds 8
sing-songs 165–166
Sketches (Peacock) 176, 182
Skinner, James Scott 129, 179, 219, 226
Skinner, Sandy 179
Slobin, Mark 124
Small, Christopher 114
Smith, Elaine C. 67
Smith, Emily 74
Smith, R. A. 237
Smollett, Tobias 193
Social Contract, The (Rousseau) 5
social media 3
Some Traditional Scottish Dances (Taylor) 185
Songs of Scotland (Graham) 236
Songs of Scotland (Muir Wood) 237
Sorley, Charles 245
sound preservation 28
Statute of Anne 192
Steele, Davy 68, 98
Stephenson, Sophie 65
Stevenson, Ronald 6
Stewart, Shelia 9, 259
Stock, Jonathan 144
Stout, Chris 152, 209

Strange Undoing of Prudencia Hart, The (NTS) 109–120
strathspeys 135–136, 184
Stravinsky, Igor 7
Strewn with Ribbons (MacColl) 224
Strong Walls of Derry, The (Burns) 160–161
Stuart, John, Earl of Bute 192–193
Sunset Song (Gibbon) 246
sustainability 19–21, 26
Sweeney, Bill 6
Sword Dance (Mackenzie) 184

taigh-ceilidh 70
Talisker 214–215
Tannahill, Robert 129
'Tartan Monster' (Nairn) 93, 101, 107
Tartanry 44–45, 46–47, 253
Taudevin, Julia 67
Taylor, G. Douglas 183, 185–186
Tea-Table Miscellany (Ramsay) 194
Telemark University College 90
Texas 8
'Theme for the Early Days of a Better Nation' (Seattle and Finnie) 67, 72–73
This Is the Story (The Proclaimers) 252
'This Land is a Song' (Burns) 73
'This Land is Your Land' (Guthrie) 72
Thomson, George 129
Thomson, William 164
Tippett, Michael 7
Titon, Jeff Todd 19
Tobar an Dualchais/Kist o Riches website 28, 227
Tønder festival 139
Traditional and National Music of Scotland, The (Collinson) 82
Traditional Arts and Cultures Scotland (TRACS) 18, 23, 27, 50, 61
Traditional Dance Forum 50
traditional music: authenticity of 19–21, 81–82, 89, 234–235, 256–259; becoming tradition-conscious 136–137; border ballads 236–237; characteristics of 253; community-based 23, 30–42, 132–133; conceptual frameworks for thinking about revivals 206–214; conceptualisation of 89; in conservatoire context 83–87; in content/genre 125–127; cultural sustainability in Scotland 17–29; cultural value of community-based 30–42; current established commercial models in 21; defining 122–125, 133, 134–136,

231–233; education landscape in 81–92; emergence of cultural policy framework for 44–50; experimental 254; five-stage movement theory 210–215; future in Scottish policy and practice 26–28; geographic boundaries 236–239; historically informed performance and 133–134; ICH policy and 17–18, 23, 26–29; identity myths and 44–47; inauthenticity of 234–235; independence referendum and 3–4, 67–76, 96–98, 133; institutional context 25–26; 'invented tradition' and 127–129; links with past 220–221; mainstreaming of 87–91, 103–108; musicians 21–23; nationalism and 9, 63–64; new aestheticism in 103–108; online teaching 23–25; oral transmission and 129–130; politics of 95–98; popular music and 8–9; problems with historical 'Scottish' repertoire 233–234; professionalisation of 22–23; Salsa Celtica and 145–146; scholarship view through revival lens 201–216; Scottish fiddle music 209, 217–228; Scottish music transformations 237–238; Scottish origin of published songs 235–236; socially constituted tradition as canon 130–132; sonic markers of Scottish 6–9; sustainability of 19–21, 26
Traditional Music and Song Association of Scotland (TMSA) 48
Traditional Music Forum 49–50
TradYES 63–66
Trainspotting (Welsh) 107
Transforming Tradition. Folk Music Revivals Examined (Rosenberg) 204
Treacherous Orchestra 82, 93, 103, 106–108, 141, 209
Trenary, Grace 196
Triubhas (Wilson) 176
'True Thomas Lay on Huntly Bank' (ballad) 83
Tyrwhitt, Thomas 197

UNESCO 17–18, 26–29
United Kingdom Alliance (UKA) 183
University of Limerick 89
University of Newcastle 90
University of the Highlands and Islands 90
'up-driven bow' 223
Utopia in Performance (Dolan) 115
'utopian performatives' 115–116

Vass, Mike 67
Veblen, Ken 38

Wachsmann, Klaus 203
'Walk in Strathnaver, A'(Gunn) 68
Wallace, Anthony 204, 210, 213
Wallace, Loki 74
Wallace, Rebecca 74
Washburne, Christopher 131
Water Is Wide, The (folk song) 165–167
'Welcome Table: A song for all the people of Scotland, The' (MacKenzie) 72
Wellington, Sheena 65
Welsh, Irvine 107
Wesling, Donald 198
West, Gary 61–62, 258
Where You Are Meant To Be (Fegan) 259
Why Old Men Cry (Gaughan) 171
Wighton, Andrew 236
Wilkes, John 193
Wilkie, Rona 68
Williams, Raymond 203
Williams, Vaughan 7
Williamson, Robin 214
Wilson, Thomas 176
Wit and Mirth, or Pills to Purge Melancholy (d'Urfey) 194
Wolfstone 93, 106
Womad festival 139
Womex Seville festival 139
World Pipe Band Championships 20, 83

'Ye Unionists By Name' (Burns) 72
'Yew Tree, The' McNeill 103
Young, Angus 7
Young, George 7
Young, Malcolm 7